A
PARADISE
BUILT
IN
HELL

ALSO BY REBECCA SOLNIT

Secret Exhibition: Six California Artists of the Cold War Era

*Savage Dreams: A Journey into the Landscape Wars
of the American West*

A Book of Migrations: Some Passages in Ireland

Wanderlust: A History of Walking

*Hollow City: The Siege of San Francisco and the Crisis
of American Urbanism*

As Eve Said to the Serpent: On Landscape, Gender, and Art

*River of Shadows: Eadweard Muybridge and
the Technological Wild West*

Hope in the Dark: Untold Histories, Wild Possibilities

A Field Guide to Getting Lost

Storming the Gates of Paradise: Landscapes for Politics

A
PARADISE
BUILT
IN
HELL

The Extraordinary

Communities That Arise

in Disaster

REBECCA SOLNIT

VIKING

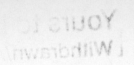

VIKING
Published by the Penguin Group
Penguin Group (USA) Inc., 375 Hudson Street, New York, New York 10014, U.S.A.
Penguin Group (Canada), 90 Eglinton Avenue East, Suite 700, Toronto, Ontario,
Canada M4P 2Y3 (a division of Pearson Penguin Canada Inc.)
Penguin Books Ltd, 80 Strand, London WC2R 0RL, England
Penguin Ireland, 25 St. Stephen's Green, Dublin 2, Ireland (a division of Penguin Books Ltd)
Penguin Books Australia Ltd, 250 Camberwell Road, Camberwell, Victoria 3124, Australia
(a division of Pearson Australia Group Pty Ltd)
Penguin Books India Pvt Ltd, 11 Community Centre, Panchsheel Park,
New Delhi – 110 017, India
Penguin Group (NZ), 67 Apollo Drive, Rosedale, North Shore 0632, New Zealand
(a division of Pearson New Zealand Ltd)
Penguin Books (South Africa) (Pty) Ltd, 24 Sturdee Avenue, Rosebank,
Johannesburg 2196, South Africa

Penguin Books Ltd, Registered Offices: 80 Strand, London WC2R 0RL, England

First published in 2009 by Viking Penguin, a member of Penguin Group (USA) Inc.

1   3   5   7   9   10   8   6   4   2

LIBRARY OF CONGRESS CATALOGING IN PUBLICATION DATA
Solnit, Rebecca.
A paradise built in hell : the extraordinary communities that arise in disaster / Rebecca Solnit.
p.   cm
Includes bibliographical references and index.
ISBN 978-0-670-02107-9
1. Disasters—Social aspects.   2. Disasters—Psychological aspects.   I. Title.
HV553.S59 2009
303.48'5—dc22   2009004101

Printed in the United States of America

CONTENTS

Prelude: Falling Together   1

I. A MILLENNIAL GOOD FELLOWSHIP: THE SAN FRANCISCO EARTHQUAKE

The Mizpah Café   13
Pauline Jacobson's Joy   23
General Funston's Fear   34
William James's Moral Equivalents   49
Dorothy Day's Other Loves   58

II. HALIFAX TO HOLLYWOOD: THE GREAT DEBATE

A Tale of Two Princes: The Halifax Explosion and After   73
From the Blitz and the Bomb to Vietnam   98
Hobbes in Hollywood, or the Few Versus the Many   120

III. CARNIVAL AND REVOLUTION: MEXICO CITY'S EARTHQUAKE

Power from Below   135
Losing the Mandate of Heaven   151
Standing on Top of Golden Hours   165

IV. THE CITY TRANSFIGURED: NEW YORK
IN GRIEF AND GLORY

Mutual Aid in the Marketplace   183
The Need to Help   195
Nine Hundred and Eleven Questions   211

V. NEW ORLEANS:
COMMON GROUNDS AND KILLERS

What Difference Would It Make?   231
Murderers   247
Love and Lifeboats   267
Beloved Community   282

Epilogue: The Doorway in the Ruins   305

Gratitude   315
Notes   321
Index   347

A
PARADISE
BUILT
IN
HELL

PRELUDE: FALLING TOGETHER

Who are you? Who are we? In times of crisis, these are life-and-death questions. Thousands of people survived Hurricane Katrina because grandsons or aunts or neighbors or complete strangers reached out to those in need all through the Gulf Coast and because an armada of boat owners from the surrounding communities and as far away as Texas went into New Orleans to pull stranded people to safety. Hundreds of people died in the aftermath of Katrina because others, including police, vigilantes, high government officials, and the media, decided that the people of New Orleans were too dangerous to allow them to evacuate the septic, drowned city or to rescue them, even from hospitals. Some who attempted to flee were turned back at gunpoint or shot down. Rumors proliferated about mass rapes, mass murders, and mayhem that turned out later to be untrue, though the national media and New Orleans's police chief believed and perpetuated those rumors during the crucial days when people were dying on rooftops and elevated highways and in crowded shelters and hospitals in the unbearable heat, without adequate water, without food, without medicine and medical attention. Those rumors led soldiers and others dispatched as rescuers to regard victims as enemies. Beliefs matter—though as many people act generously despite their beliefs as the reverse.

Katrina was an extreme version of what goes on in many disasters, wherein how you behave depends on whether you think your neighbors or fellow citizens are a greater threat than the havoc wrought by a disaster or a greater good than the property in houses and stores around you.

(*Citizen,* in this book, means members of a city or community, not people in possession of legal citizenship in a nation.) What you believe shapes how you act. How you act results in life or death, for yourself or others, as in everyday life, only more so. Katrina was, like most disasters, also marked by altruism: of young men who took it upon themselves to supply water, food, diapers, and protection to the strangers stranded with them; of people who rescued or sheltered neighbors; of the uncounted hundreds or thousands who set out in boats—armed, often, but also armed with compassion—to find those who were stranded in the stagnant waters and bring them to safety; of the two hundred thousand or more who (via the Internet site HurricaneHousing.org in the weeks after) volunteered to house complete strangers, mostly in their own homes, persuaded more by the pictures of suffering than the rumors of monstrosity; of the uncounted tens of thousands of volunteers who came to the Gulf Coast to rebuild and restore.

In the wake of an earthquake, a bombing, or a major storm, most people are altruistic, urgently engaged in caring for themselves and those around them, strangers and neighbors as well as friends and loved ones. The image of the selfish, panicky, or regressively savage human being in times of disaster has little truth to it. Decades of meticulous sociological research on behavior in disasters, from the bombings of World War II to floods, tornadoes, earthquakes, and storms across the continent and around the world, have demonstrated this. But belief lags behind, and often the worst behavior in the wake of a calamity is on the part of those who believe that others will behave savagely and that they themselves are taking defensive measures against barbarism. From earthquake-shattered San Francisco in 1906 to flooded New Orleans in 2005, innocents have been killed by people who believed or asserted that their victims were the criminals and they themselves were the protectors of the shaken order. Beliefs matter.

"Today Cain is still killing his brother" proclaims a faded church mural in the Lower Ninth Ward of New Orleans, which was so devastated by the failure of the government levees. In quick succession, the Book of Genesis gives us the creation of the universe, the illicit acquisition of knowledge, the expulsion from Paradise, and the slaying of Abel by Cain, a second fall from grace into jealousy, competition, alienation, and violence. When God asks Cain where his brother is, Cain asks back,

"Am I my brother's keeper?" He is refusing to say what God already knows: that the spilled blood of Abel cries out from the ground that has absorbed it. He is also raising one of the perennial social questions: are we beholden to each other, must we take care of each other, or is it every man for himself?

Most traditional societies have deeply entrenched commitments and connections between individuals, families, and groups. The very concept of society rests on the idea of networks of affinity and affection, and the freestanding individual exists largely as an outcast or exile. Mobile and individualistic modern societies shed some of these old ties and vacillate about taking on others, especially those expressed through economic arrangements—including provisions for the aged and vulnerable, the mitigation of poverty and desperation—the keeping of one's brothers and sisters. The argument against such keeping is often framed as an argument about human nature: we are essentially selfish, and because you will not care for me, I cannot care for you. I will not feed you because I must hoard against starvation, since I too cannot count on others. Better yet, I will take your wealth and add it to mine—if I believe that my well-being is independent of yours or pitted against yours—and justify my conduct as natural law. If I am not my brother's keeper, then we have been expelled from paradise, a paradise of unbroken solidarities.

Thus does everyday life become a social disaster. Sometimes disaster intensifies this; sometimes it provides a remarkable reprieve from it, a view into another world for our other selves. When all the ordinary divides and patterns are shattered, people step up—not all, but the great preponderance—to become their brothers' keepers. And that purposefulness and connectedness bring joy even amid death, chaos, fear, and loss. Were we to know and believe this, our sense of what is possible at any time might change. We speak of self-fulfilling prophesies, but any belief that is acted on makes the world in its image. Beliefs matter. And so do the facts behind them. The astonishing gap between common beliefs and actualities about disaster behavior limits the possibilities, and changing beliefs could fundamentally change much more. Horrible in itself, disaster is sometimes a door back into paradise, the paradise at least in which we are who we hope to be, do the work we desire, and are each our sister's and brother's keeper.

I landed in Halifax, Nova Scotia, shortly after a big hurricane tore up the city in October of 2003. The man in charge of taking me around told me about the hurricane—not about the winds that roared at more than a hundred miles an hour and tore up trees, roofs, and telephone poles or about the seas that rose nearly ten feet, but about the neighbors. He spoke of the few days when everything was disrupted, and he lit up with happiness as he did so. In his neighborhood all the people had come out of their houses to speak with each other, aid each other, improvise a community kitchen, make sure the elders were okay, and spend time together, no longer strangers. "Everybody woke up the next morning and everything was different," he mused. "There was no electricity, all the stores were closed, no one had access to media. The consequence was that everyone poured out into the street to bear witness. Not quite a street party, but everyone out at once—it was a sense of happiness to see everybody even though we didn't know each other." His joy struck me powerfully.

A friend told me of being trapped in a terrible fog, one of the dense tule fogs that overtakes California's Central Valley periodically. On this occasion the fog mixed with dust from the cotton fields created a shroud so perilous that the highway patrol stopped all traffic on the highway. For two days she was stranded with many others in a small diner. She and her husband slept upright, shoulder to shoulder with strangers, in the banquettes of the diner's booths. Although food and water began to run short, they had a marvelous time. The people gathered there had little in common, but they all opened up, began to tell each other the stories of their lives, and by the time the road was safe, my friend and her husband were reluctant to leave. But they went onward, home to New Mexico for the holidays, where everyone looked at them perplexedly as they told the story of their stranding with such ebullience. That time in the diner was the first time ever her partner, a Native American, had felt a sense of belonging in society at large. Such redemption amid disruption is common.

It reminded me of how many of us in the San Francisco Bay Area had loved the Loma Prieta earthquake that took place three weeks before the Berlin Wall fell in 1989. Or loved not the earthquake but the way communities had responded to it. It was alarming for most of us as well, devastating for some, and fatal for sixty people (a very low death count for a major earthquake in an area inhabited by millions). When the subject of the quake came up with a new acquaintance, she too glowed with recollection about how her San Francisco neighborhood had, during the days the power was off, cooked up all its thawing frozen food and held barbecues on the street; how gregarious everyone had been, how people from all walks of life had mixed in candlelit bars that became community centers. Another friend recently remembered with unextinguished amazement that when he traveled the several miles from the World Series baseball game at Candlestick Park in the city's southeast to his home in the central city, someone was at every blacked-out intersection, directing traffic. Without orders or centralized organization, people had stepped up to meet the needs of the moment, suddenly in charge of their communities and streets.

When that earthquake shook the central California coast on October 17, 1989, I was surprised to find that the person I was angry at no longer mattered. The anger had evaporated along with everything else abstract and remote, and I was thrown into an intensely absorbing present. I was more surprised to realize that most of the people I knew and met in the Bay Area were also enjoying immensely the disaster that shut down much of the region for several days, the Bay Bridge for months, and certain unloved elevated freeways forever—if *enjoyment* is the right word for that sense of immersion in the moment and solidarity with others caused by the rupture in everyday life, an emotion graver than happiness but deeply positive. We don't even have a language for this emotion, in which the wonderful comes wrapped in the terrible, joy in sorrow, courage in fear. We cannot welcome disaster, but we can value the responses, both practical and psychological.

For weeks after the big earthquake of 1989, friendship and love counted for a lot, long-term plans and old anxieties for very little. Life was situated in the here and now, and many inessentials had been pared away. The earthquake was unnerving, as were the aftershocks that continued for months. Most of us were at least a little on edge, but many of us were enriched rather than impoverished, overall, at least emotionally. A more somber version of that strange pleasure in disaster emerged after September 11, 2001, when many Americans seemed stirred, moved, and motivated by the newfound sense of urgency, purpose, solidarity, and danger they had encountered. They abhorred what had happened, but they clearly relished who they briefly became.

What is this feeling that crops up during so many disasters? After the Loma Prieta quake, I began to wonder about it. After 9/11, I began to see how strange a phenomenon it was and how deeply it mattered. After I met the man in Halifax who lit up with joy when he talked about the great hurricane there, I began to study it. After I began to write about the 1906 earthquake as its centennial approached, I started to see how often this peculiar feeling arose and how much it remade the world of disaster. After Hurricane Katrina tore up the Gulf Coast, I began to understand the limits and possibilities of disasters. This book is about that emotion, as important as it is surprising, and the circumstances that arouse it and those that it generates. These things count as we enter an era of increasing and intensifying disaster. And more than that, they matter as we enter an era when questions about everyday social possibilities and human nature arise again, as they often have in turbulent times.

When I ask people about the disasters they have lived through, I find on many faces that retrospective basking as they recount tales of Canadian ice storms, midwestern snow days, New York City blackouts, oppressive heat in southern India, fire in New Mexico, the great earthquake in Mexico City, earlier hurricanes in Louisiana, the economic collapse in Argentina, earthquakes in California and Mexico, and a strange pleasure overall. It was the joy on their faces that surprised me. And with those whom I read rather than spoke to, it was the joy in their words that surprised me. It should not be so, is not so, in the familiar version of what disaster brings, and yet it is there, arising from rubble, from ice, from fire, from storms and floods. The joy matters as a measure of otherwise neglected desires, desires for public life and civil society, for inclusion, purpose, and power.

Disasters are, most basically, terrible, tragic, grievous, and no matter what positive side effects and possibilities they produce, they are not to be desired. But by the same measure, those side effects should not be ignored because they arise amid devastation. The desires and possibilities awakened are so powerful they shine even from wreckage, carnage, and ashes. What happens here is relevant elsewhere. And the point is not to welcome disasters. They do not create these gifts, but they are one avenue through which the gifts arrive. Disasters provide an extraordinary window into social desire and possibility, and what manifests there matters elsewhere, in ordinary times and in other extraordinary times.

Most social change is chosen—you want to belong to a co-op, you believe in social safety nets or community-supported agriculture. But disaster doesn't sort us out by preferences; it drags us into emergencies that require we act, and act altruistically, bravely, and with initiative in order to survive or save the neighbors, no matter how we vote or what we do for a living. The positive emotions that arise in those unpromising circumstances demonstrate that social ties and meaningful work are deeply desired, readily improvised, and intensely rewarding. The very structure of our economy and society prevents these goals from being achieved. The structure is also ideological, a philosophy that best serves the wealthy and powerful but shapes all of our lives, reinforced as the conventional wisdom disseminated by the media, from news hours to disaster movies. The facets of that ideology have been called individualism, capitalism, and Social Darwinism and have appeared in the political philosophies of Thomas Hobbes and Thomas Malthus, as well as the work of most conventional contemporary economists, who presume we seek personal gain for rational reasons and refrain from looking at the ways a system skewed to that end damages much else we need for our survival and desire for our well-being. Disaster demonstrates this, since among the factors determining whether you will live or die are the health of your immediate community and the justness of your society. We need ties, but they along with purposefulness, immediacy, and agency also give us joy—the startling, sharp joy I found in accounts of disaster survivors. These accounts demonstrate that the citizens any paradise would need—the people who are brave enough, resourceful enough, and generous enough—already exist. The possibility of paradise hovers on the cusp of coming into being, so much so that it takes powerful forces to keep such a paradise at bay. If paradise now arises in hell, it's because in the suspension of the usual order and the failure of most systems, we are free to live and act another way.

This book investigates five disasters in depth, from the 1906 earthquake in San Francisco to the hurricane and flood in New Orleans ninety-nine years later. In between come the Halifax explosion of 1917, the extraordinary Mexico City earthquake that killed so many and changed so much, and the neglected tales of how ordinary New Yorkers responded to the calamity that struck their city on September 11, 2001. In and around these principal examples come stories of the London Blitz; of earthquakes in China and Argentina; of the Chernobyl nuclear accident; the Chicago heat wave of 1995; the Managua, Nicaragua, earthquake that helped topple a regime; a smallpox epidemic in New York; and a volcanic eruption in Iceland. Though the worst natural disasters in recent years have been in Asia—the 2004 tsunami in the Indian Ocean, the 2005 earthquake in Pakistan, the 2008 earthquake in China and typhoon in Burma—I have not written about them. They matter immensely, but language and distance as well as culture kept these disasters out of reach for me.

Since postmodernism reshaped the intellectual landscape, it has been problematic to even use the term *human nature*, with its implication of a stable and universal human essence. The study of disasters makes it clear that there are plural and contingent natures—but the prevalent human nature in disaster is resilient, resourceful, generous, empathic, and brave. The language of therapy speaks almost exclusively of the consequence of disaster as trauma, suggesting a humanity that is unbearably fragile, a self that does not act but is acted upon, the most basic recipe of the victim. Disaster movies and the media continue to portray ordinary people as hysterical or vicious in the face of calamity. We believe these sources telling us we are victims or brutes more than we trust our own experience. Most people know this other human nature from experience, though almost nothing official or mainstream confirms it. This book is an account of that rising from the ruins that is the ordinary human response to disaster and of what that rising can mean in other arenas—a subject that slips between the languages we have been given to talk about who we are when everything goes wrong.

But to understand both that rising and what hinders and hides it, there are two other important subjects to consider. One is the behavior of the minority in power, who often act savagely in a disaster. The other is the beliefs and representations of the media, the people who hold up a distorting mirror to us in which it is almost impossible to recognize these paradises and our possibilities. Beliefs matter, and the overlapping beliefs of the media and the elites can become a second wave of disaster—as they did most dramatically in the aftermath of Hurricane Katrina. These three subjects are woven together in almost every disaster, and finding the one that matters most—this glimpse of paradise—means understanding the forces that obscure, oppose, and sometimes rub out that possibility.

This social desire and social possibility go against the grain of the dominant stories of recent decades. You can read recent history as a history of privatization not just of the economy but also of society, as marketing and media shove imagination more and more toward private life and private satisfaction, as citizens are redefined as consumers, as public participation falters and with it any sense of collective or individual political power, as even the language for public emotions and satisfactions withers. There is no money in what is aptly called free association: we are instead encouraged by media and advertising to fear each other and regard public life as a danger and a nuisance, to live in secured spaces, communicate by electronic means, and acquire our information from media rather than each other. But in disaster people come together, and though some fear this gathering as a mob, many cherish it as an experience of a civil society that is close enough to paradise. In contemporary terms, *privatization* is largely an economic term, for the consignment of jurisdictions, goods, services, and powers—railways, water rights, policing, education—to the private sector and the vagaries of the marketplace. But this economic privatization is impossible without the privatization of desire and imagination that tells us we are not each other's keeper. Disasters, in returning their sufferers to public and collective life, undo some of this privatization, which is a slower, subtler disaster all its own. In a society in which participation, agency, purposefulness, and freedom are all adequately present, a disaster would be only a disaster.

Few speak of paradise now, except as something remote enough to be impossible. The ideal societies we hear of are mostly far away or long ago or both, situated in some primordial society before the Fall or a spiritual kingdom in a remote Himalayan vastness. The implication is that we here and now are far from capable of living such ideals. But what if paradise flashed up among us from time to time—at the worst of times? What if we glimpsed it in the jaws of hell? These flashes give us, as the long ago and far away do not, a glimpse of who else we ourselves may be and what else our society could become. This is a paradise of rising to the occasion that points out by contrast how the rest of the time most of us fall down from the heights of possibility, down into diminished selves and dismal societies. Many now do not even hope for a better society, but they recognize it when they encounter it, and that discovery shines out even through the namelessness of their experience. Others recognize it, grasp it, and make something of it, and long-term social and political transformations, both good and bad, arise from the wreckage. The door to this era's potential paradises is in hell.

The word *emergency* comes from *emerge*, to rise out of, the opposite of merge, which comes from *mergere*, to be within or under a liquid, immersed, submerged. An emergency is a separation from the familiar, a sudden emergence into a new atmosphere, one that often demands we ourselves rise to the occasion. *Catastrophe* comes from the Greek *kata*, or down, and *streiphen*, or turning over. It means an upset of what is expected and was originally used to mean a plot twist. To emerge into the unexpected is not always terrible, though these words have evolved to imply ill fortune. The word *disaster* comes from the Latin compound of *dis-*, or away, without, and *astro*, star or planet; literally, without a star. It originally suggested misfortune due to astrologically generated trouble, as in the blues musician Albert King's classic "Born Under a Bad Sign."

In some of the disasters of the twentieth century—the big northeastern blackouts in 1965 and 2003, the 1989 Loma Prieta earthquake in the San Francisco Bay Area, 2005's Hurricane Katrina on the Gulf Coast—the loss of electrical power meant that the light pollution blotting out the night sky vanished. In these disaster-struck cities, people suddenly found themselves under the canopy of stars still visible in small and remote places. On the warm night of August 15, 2003, the Milky Way could be seen in New York City, a heavenly realm long lost to view until the blackout that hit the Northeast late that afternoon. You can think of the current social order as something akin to this artificial light: another kind of power that fails in disaster. In its place appears a reversion to improvised, collaborative, cooperative, and local society. However beautiful the stars of a suddenly visible night sky, few nowadays could find their way by them. But the constellations of solidarity, altruism, and improvisation are within most of us and reappear at these times. People know what to do in a disaster. The loss of power, the disaster in the modern sense, is an affliction, but the reappearance of these old heavens is its opposite. This is the paradise entered through hell.

I

A MILLENNIAL GOOD FELLOWSHIP: THE SAN FRANCISCO EARTHQUAKE

THE MIZPAH CAFÉ

The Gathering Place

The outlines of this particular disaster are familiar. At 5:12 in the morning on April 18, 1906, about a minute of seismic shaking tore up San Francisco, toppling buildings, particularly those on landfill and swampy ground, cracking and shifting others, collapsing chimneys, breaking water mains and gas lines, twisting streetcar tracks, even tipping headstones in the cemeteries. It was a major earthquake, centered right off the coast of the peninsular city, and the damage it did was considerable. Afterward came the fires, both those caused by broken gas mains and chimneys and those caused and augmented by the misguided policy of trying to blast firebreaks ahead of the flames and preventing citizens from firefighting in their own homes and neighborhoods. The way the authorities handled the fires was a major reason why so much of the city—nearly five square miles, more than twenty-eight thousand structures—was incinerated in one of history's biggest urban infernos before aerial warfare. Nearly every municipal building was destroyed, and so were many of the downtown businesses, along with mansions, slums, middle-class neighborhoods, the dense residential-commercial district of Chinatown, newspaper offices, and warehouses.

The response of the citizens is less familiar. Here is one. Mrs. Anna Amelia Holshouser, whom a local newspaper described as a "woman of middle age, buxom and comely," woke up on the floor of her bedroom on Sacramento Street, where the earthquake had thrown her. She took time to dress herself while the ground and her home were still shaking, in that era when getting dressed was no simple matter of throwing on clothes. "Powder, paint, jewelry, hair switch, all were on when I started my flight down one hundred twenty stairs to the street," she recalled. The house in western San Francisco was slightly damaged, her downtown place of business—she was a beautician and masseuse—was "a total wreck," and so she salvaged what she could and moved on with a friend, Mr. Paulson. They camped out in Union Square downtown until the fires came close and soldiers drove them onward. Like thousands of others, they ended up trudging with their bundles to Golden Gate Park, the thousand-acre park that runs all the way west to the Pacific Ocean. There they spread an old quilt "and lay down . . . not to sleep, but to shiver with cold from fog and mist and watch the flames of the burning city, whose blaze shone far above the trees." On their third day in the park, she stitched together blankets, carpets, and sheets to make a tent that sheltered twenty-two people, including thirteen children. And Holshouser started a tiny soup kitchen with one tin can to drink from and one pie plate to eat from. All over the city stoves were hauled out of damaged buildings—fire was forbidden indoors, since many standing homes had gas leaks or damaged flues or chimneys—or primitive stoves were built out of rubble, and people commenced to cook for each other, for strangers, for anyone in need. Her generosity was typical, even if her initiative was exceptional.

Holshouser got funds to buy eating utensils across the bay in Oakland. The kitchen began to grow, and she was soon feeding two to three hundred people a day, not a victim of the disaster but a victor over it and the hostess of a popular social center—her brothers' and sisters' keeper. Some visitors from Oakland liked her makeshift dining camp so well they put up a sign—"Palace Hotel"—naming it after the burned-out downtown luxury establishment that was reputedly once the largest hotel in the world. Humorous signs were common around the camps and street-side shelters. Nearby on Oak Street a few women ran "The Oyster Loaf" and the "Chat Noir"—two little shacks with their names in fancy cursive. A shack in Jefferson Square was titled "The House of Mirth," with additional signs jokingly offering rooms for rent with steam heat and elevators. The inscription on the side of "Hoffman's Café," another little street-side shack, read "Cheer up, have one on me . . . come in and spend a quiet evening." A menu chalked on the door of "Camp Necessity," a tiny shack, included the items "fleas eyes raw, 98¢, pickled eels, nails fried, 13¢, flies legs on toast, .09¢, crab's tongues, stewed," ending with "rain water fritters with umbrella sauce, $9.10." "The Appetite Killery" may be the most ironic name, but the most famous inscription read, "Eat, drink, and be merry, for tomorrow we may have to go to Oakland." Many had already gone there or to hospitable Berkeley, and the railroads carried many much farther away for free.

About three thousand people had died, at least half the city was homeless, families were shattered, the commercial district was smoldering ashes, and the army from the military base at the city's north end was terrorizing many citizens. As soon as the newspapers resumed printing, they began to publish long lists of missing people and of the new locations at which displaced citizens and sundered families could be found. Despite or perhaps because of this, the people were for the most part calm and cheerful, and many survived the earthquake with gratitude and generosity. Edwin Emerson recalled that after the quake, "when the tents of the refugees, and the funny street kitchens, improvised from doors and shutters and pieces of roofing, overspread all the city, such merriment became an accepted thing. Everywhere, during those long moonlit evenings, one could hear the tinkle of guitars and mandolins, from among the tents. Or, passing by the grotesque rows of curbstone kitchens, one became dimly aware of the low murmurings of couples who had sought refuge in those dark recesses as in bowers of love. It was at this time that the droll signs and inscriptions began to appear on walls and tent flaps, which soon became one of the familiar sights of reconstructing San Francisco. The overworked marriage license clerk has deposed that the fees collected by him for issuing such licenses during April and May 1906 far exceeded the totals for the same months of any preceding years in San Francisco." Emerson had rushed to the scene of disaster from New York, pausing to telegraph a marriage proposal of his own to a young woman in San Francisco, who wrote a letter of rejection that was still in the mail when she met her suitor in person amid the wreckage and accepted. They were married a few weeks later.

Disaster requires an ability to embrace contradiction in both the minds of those undergoing it and those trying to understand it from afar. In each disaster, there is suffering, there are psychic scars that will be felt most when the emergency is over, there are deaths and losses. Satisfactions, newborn social bonds, and liberations are often also profound. Of course one factor in the gap between the usual accounts of disaster and actual experience is that those accounts focus on the small percentage of people who are wounded, killed, orphaned, and otherwise devastated, often at the epicenter of the disaster, along with the officials involved. Surrounding them, often in the same city or even neighborhood, is a periphery of many more who are largely undamaged but profoundly disrupted—and it is the disruptive power of disaster that matters here, the ability of disasters to topple old orders and open new possibilities. This broader effect is what disaster does to society. In the moment of disaster, the old order no longer exists and people improvise rescues, shelters, and communities. Thereafter, a struggle takes place over whether the old order with all its shortcomings and injustices will be reimposed or a new one, perhaps more oppressive or perhaps more just and free, like the disaster utopia, will arise.

Of course people who are deeply and devastatingly affected may yet find something redemptive in their experience, while those who are largely unaffected may be so rattled they are immune to the other possibilities (curiously, people farther from the epicenter of a disaster are often more frightened, but this seems to be because what you imagine as overwhelming or terrifying while at leisure becomes something you can cope with when you must—there is no time for fear). There are no simple rules for the emotions. We speak mostly of happy and sad emotions, a divide that suggests a certain comic lightness to the one side and pure negativity to the other, but perhaps we would navigate our experiences better by thinking in terms of deep and shallow, rich and poor. The very depth of emotion, the connecting to the core of one's being, the calling into play one's strongest feelings and abilities, can be rich, even on deathbeds, in wars and emergencies, while what is often assumed to be the circumstance of happiness sometimes is only insulation from the depths, or so the plagues of ennui and angst among the comfortable suggest.

Next door to Holshouser's kitchen, an aid team from the mining boomtown of Tonopah, Nevada, set up and began to deliver wagonloads of supplies to the back of Holshouser's tent. The Nevadans got on so well with the impromptu cook and hostess they gave her a guest register whose inscription read in part: "in cordial appreciation of her prompt, philanthropic, and efficient service to the people in general, and particularly to the Tonopah Board of Trade Relief Committee. . . . May her good deeds never be forgotten." Thinking that the place's "Palace Hotel" sign might cause confusion, they rebaptized it the Mizpah Café after the Mizpah Saloon in Tonopah, and a new sign was installed. The ornamental letters spelled out above the name "One Touch of Nature Makes the Whole World Kin" and those below "Established April 23, 1906." The Hebrew word *mizpah*, says one encyclopedia, "is an emotional bond between those who are separated (either physically or by death)." Another says it was the Old Testament watchtower "where the people were accustomed to meet in great national emergencies." Another source describes it as "symbolizing a sanctuary and place of hopeful anticipation." The ramshackle material reality of Holshouser's improvised kitchen seemed to matter not at all in comparison with its shining social role. It ran through June of 1906, when Holshouser wrote her memoir of the earthquake. Her piece is as remarkable for what it doesn't say: it doesn't speak of fear, enemies, conflict, chaos, crime, despondency, or trauma.

Just as her kitchen was one of many spontaneously launched community centers and relief projects, so her resilient resourcefulness represents the ordinary response in many disasters. In them, strangers become friends and collaborators, goods are shared freely, people improvise new roles for themselves. Imagine a society where money plays little or no role, where people rescue each other and then care for each other, where food is given away, where life is mostly out of doors in public, where the old divides between people seem to have fallen away, and the fate that faces them, no matter how grim, is far less so for being shared, where much once considered impossible, both good and bad, is now possible or present, and where the moment is so pressing that old complaints and worries fall away, where people feel important, purposeful, at the center of the world. It is by its very nature unsustainable and evanescent, but like a lightning flash it illuminates ordinary life, and like lightning it sometimes shatters the old forms. It is utopia itself for many people, though it is only a brief moment during terrible times. And at the time they manage to hold both irreconcilable experiences, the joy and the grief.

A Map of Utopia

This utopia matters, because almost everyone has experienced some version of it and because it is not the result of a partisan agenda but rather a broad, unplanned effort to salvage society and take care of the neighbors amid the wreckage. "A map of the world that does not include Utopia is not worth even glancing at, for it leaves out the one country at which humanity is always heading," wrote Oscar Wilde fifteen years before San Francisco's great quake. The utopias built by citizens like Anna Holshouser are not yet on that map. But they should be. They could change the map of our own beliefs, our sense of what is possible and who we are. Utopia is in trouble these days. Many no longer believe that a better world, as opposed to a better life, is possible, and the rhetoric of private well-being trumps public good, at least in the English-speaking world. And yet the yearning remains—all the riches piled up, the security gates and stock options, are only defenses against a world of insecurity and animosity, piecemeal solutions to a pervasive problem. Sometimes it seems as though home improvement has trumped the idealistic notion of a better world. Sometimes. But utopia flares up in other parts of the world, where hope is fiercer and dreams are larger.

"There is no alternative," the conservative British prime minister Margaret Thatcher liked to say, but there is, and it appears where it is least expected, as well as where it is most diligently cultivated. Changing the world is the other way to imagine salvaging the self—and others, for the utopian impulse is generous even when it's wrongheaded. And utopias of sorts arise in the present, in Argentina, in Mexico, in countless social, economic, and agricultural experiments in Europe, in India, and in the United States; among other places. The map of utopias is cluttered nowadays with experiments by other names, and the very idea is expanding. It needs to open up a little more to contain disaster communities. These remarkable societies suggest that, just as many machines reset themselves to their original settings after a power outage, so human beings reset themselves to something altruistic, communitarian, resourceful, and imaginative after a disaster, that we revert to something we already know how to do. The possibility of paradise is already within us as a default setting.

The two most basic goals of social utopias are to eliminate deprivation—hunger, ignorance, homelessness—and to forge a society in which no one is an outsider, no one is alienated. By this standard, Holshouser's free food and warm social atmosphere achieved both, on however tiny a scale, and versions of the Mizpah Café sprung up all over the ruined city.

Some religious attempts at utopia are authoritarian, led by a charismatic leader, by elders, by rigid rules that create outcasts, but the secular utopias have mostly been committed to liberty, democracy, and shared power. The widespread disdain for revolution and utopia takes as its object lesson the Soviet-style attempts at coercive utopias, in which the original ideals of leveling and sharing go deeply awry, the achievement critiqued in George Orwell's *Animal Farm* and *1984* and other dystopian novels. Many fail to notice that it is not the ideals, the ends, but the coercive and authoritarian means that poison paradise. There are utopias whose ideals pointedly include freedom from coercion and dispersal of power to the many. Most utopian visions nowadays include many worlds, many versions, rather than a coercive one true way. The anthropologist David Graeber writes, "Stalinists and their ilk did not kill because they dreamed great dreams—actually, Stalinists were famous for being rather short on imagination—but because they mistook their dreams for scientific certainties. This led them to feel they had a right to impose their visions through a machinery of violence." There are plenty of failed revolutions and revolutions such as the French Revolution that lapse into bloodbaths—and yet when that revolution was over, France would never be dominated by an absolutist monarchy again; ordinary French people had more rights, and people around the world had an enlarged sense of the possible. All revolutions fail because they set their sights heaven-high, but none of them fail to do something, and many increase the amount of liberty, justice, and hope for their heirs.

Unpoliced utopian experiments have arisen often in the United States. The ascetic rural Shakers have lasted from 1775, when they arrived in New York from England, into—by the tenuous thread of a few older survivors—the present. Less stable experiments proliferated in the nineteenth century. There was, for example, Brook Farm in Massachusetts in the 1840s, in which a lot of bookish idealists tried, not very effectively, to till the earth to realize an ideal union of mental and physical labor and collective life. There was also the socialist Kaweah Colony in the mountains of California in the 1880s and 1890s (the land they homesteaded is now part of Sequoia National Park, and the giant tree they named the Karl Marx Tree is now the General Sherman sequoia). Many argue that the United States was founded on utopian dreams, from the conquistador fantasies of a gold-drenched El Dorado to the pioneer reading of the American West as an unfallen Eden the woodsman entered as an ax-swinging Adam. Some even include the seventeenth-century New England Puritans among the Utopians, though their regime of sober piety, stern patriarchs, and enforced conformity resembles a lot of other peoples' gulags. And the Puritans were not social experimentalists; the pervasive utopian preoccupation with sharing wealth and finding a communal mode of dealing with practical needs and social goals had little to do with them, though it surfaced in other conservative religious movements, such as Mormonism.

I often argue with my friend Sam about what has become of the dream of Utopia. He believes it has faded with the end of communist and universalist fantasies; I believe it has evolved into more viable, modest versions. A certain kind of twentieth-century utopian idealism has died, the kind that believed we could and should erase everything and start over: new language, new society, new ways of organizing power, work, even family, home, and more. Projects for abandoning the past wholesale and inventing a whole new human being seem, like the idea of one-size-fits-all universalism, more ominous than utopian to us now. It may be because *we* now includes people who forcibly lost their language, whether it was Yiddish in Poland or Cree in Canada, that as we lose the past, we cherish it more and look at the devouring mouth of the future with more apprehension. But we have also learned that you can reinvent the government but not human nature in one fell stroke, and the process of reinventing human nature is a much more subtle, personal, incremental process. Mostly nowadays we draw our hopes from fragments and traditions from a richly varied past rather than an imagined future. But disaster throws us into the temporary utopia of a transformed human nature and society, one that is bolder, freer, less attached and divided than in ordinary times, not blank, but not tied down.

Utopianism was a driving force in the nineteenth century. Union activists sought to improve working conditions and wages for the vast majority of laborers, and many were radicals who also hoped for or worked for a socialist or anarchist revolution that would change the whole society and eliminate the causes of suffering, poverty, and powerlessness rather than merely mitigate some of the effects (how viable and desirable their versions of the ideal were is another story). The socialist-anarchist Kaweah commune included many union members, while the French commune

Icaria-Speranza, eighty miles north of San Francisco, included refugees from the 1848 revolution in France and the Paris Commune, the populist takeover of that city for two months in 1871.

This list of utopian possibilities leaves off the underground utopias, the odd ways in which people improvise their hopes or just improve their lives in the most adverse circumstances. I once met a young Polish émi-gré who told me that many Poles were nostalgic, not for the Communist regime that fell in 1989 but for the close-knit communities that developed to survive that malevolent era, circulating black-market goods and ideas, helping each other with the long food lines and other tasks of survival, banding together to survive. In the democratic-capitalist regime that replaced Poland's communism, such alliances were no longer necessary, and people drifted apart, free at last but no longer a community. Finding the balance between independence and fellowship is one of the ongoing utopian struggles. And under the false brotherhood of Soviet-style com-munism, a true communal solidarity of resistance was born (as well as an independent Polish labor union, Solidarity, that eventually brought down that system). This nostalgia for a time that was in many ways much harder but is remembered as better, morally and socially, is common. And it brings us to the ubiquitous fleeting utopias that are neither coerced nor countercultural but universal, albeit overlooked: disaster utopias, the subject of this book.

You don't have to subscribe to a political ideology, move to a com-mune, or join the guerrillas in the mountains; you wake up in a society suddenly transformed, and chances are good you will be part of that transformation in what you do, in whom you connect to, in how you feel. Something changes. Elites and authorities often fear the changes of disas-ter or anticipate that the change means chaos and destruction, or at least the undermining of the foundations of their power. So a power struggle often takes place in disaster—and real political and social change can result, from that struggle or from the new sense of self and society that emerges. Too, the elite often believe that if they themselves are not in control, the situation is out of control, and in their fear take repressive measures that become secondary disasters. But many others who don't hold radical ideas, don't believe in revolution, don't consciously desire profound social change find themselves in a transformed world leading a life they could not have imagined and rejoice in it.

The future holds many more disasters because of such factors as climate change and the likelihood of large earthquakes on long-dormant or semidormant faults, as well as increases in the vulnerability of populations who have moved to coasts, to cities, to areas at risk, to flimsy housing, to deeper poverty, shallower roots, and frailer support networks. The relief organization Oxfam reported in 2007, "The number of weather-related disasters has quadrupled over the past twenty years and the world should do more to prepare for them. The report argues that climate change is responsible for the growing number of weather-related disasters—more intense rain, combined with frequent droughts, make damaging floods much more likely." Disaster is never terribly far away. Knowing how people behave in disasters is fundamental to knowing how to prepare for them. And what can be learned about resilience, social and psychological response, and possibility from sudden disasters is relevant as well for the slower disasters of poverty, economic upheaval, and incremental environmental degradation as well as the abiding questions about social possibilities.

The Mizpah Café was at once nothing special and a miracle, chaos and deprivation turned into order and abundance by will, empathy, and one woman's resourcefulness. It is a miniature of the communities that often arise out of disasters. In the 1906 earthquake, a Jewish newspaperwoman would find a social paradise, a Chinese boy would find a new life, the country's leading philosopher would find confirmation of his deepest beliefs about human nature, and an eight-year-old girl would find herself in a community so generous it served as a model for the radical social experiments she initiated that continue across the United States today. Disasters are extraordinarily generative, and though disaster utopias recur again and again, there is no simple formula for what arises: it has everything to do with who or what individuals or communities were before the disaster and the circumstances they find themselves in. But those circumstances are far richer and stranger than has ever been accounted for.

PAULINE JACOBSON'S JOY

Countless Acts

For ninety-nine years, the worst disaster in U.S. history was at least arguably the 1906 earthquake centered in San Francisco that killed an estimated three thousand people, annihilated the center of that city, and shattered structures along a hundred-mile stretch from San Jose in the south to Santa Rosa in the north. What happened after the quake has been told over and over as a story about geology, about firefighting, about politics, and about people in power. It has never really been told as a story of ordinary citizens' responses, except as the long series of first-person accounts that the San Francisco–based weekly *Argonaut* ran during the disaster's twentieth anniversary. In those accounts and the letters and essays of the survivors, a remarkable picture emerges of improvisation, heroism, and solidarity, similar to what can be seen in most disasters but is seldom recorded.

San Francisco has been called "the city that destroyed itself," but a king is not his country, and a government is not the people. Neither the city nor its citizens destroyed San Francisco. A handful of men in power and a swarm of soldiers, National Guardsmen, and militiamen did. Or they destroyed much of the city made of architecture and property, even as they claimed to defend it from fire and from the public that was portrayed, over and over, as a potential or actual mob or bunch of thieves. The citizens responded differently to the occasion as they took care of each other and reinforced the society that each city is first and foremost.

The writer Mary Austin, who was there for the earthquake and its aftermath, said that the people of San Francisco became houseless, but not homeless, "for it comes to this with the bulk of San Franciscans, that they discovered the place and the spirit to be home rather than the walls and the furnishings. No matter how the insurance totals foot up, what landmarks, what treasures of art are evanished, San Francisco, *our* San Francisco is all there yet. Fast as the tall banners of smoke rose up and the flames reddened them, rose up with it something impalpable, like an exhalation." Mary Austin's San Francisco didn't burn down, it rose up.

The morning of the quake, policeman H. C. Schmitt was on patrol in the city's produce district, near the downtown and the bay. The fires had begun downtown, and to stay cool near the blazes he periodically dunked himself in the fountain surrounding the Mechanics Monument—a bronze group of muscular near-naked men operating a huge press. On his rounds, Schmitt obliged some petty thieves to put back the boxes of cigars they had taken (and regretted it when the cigars went up in smoke soon after), shut some saloons, shot wounded horses, brought a dead Italian grocer out of the rubble, and finally got permission to go home and check on his family. A passerby had told him, wrongly, that all the houses in his part of the Mission District had been destroyed, and he feared for his family but found the house damaged but standing. His wife and daughters came down to greet him from a friend's house, glad to see him after hearing exaggerated reports that made them fear he had been killed. Rumor is the first rat to infest a disaster.

The military had already placed a guard around his section of the neighborhood, but with his police badge, Schmitt was able to get through to his home and, with the help of some young volunteers, take his new stove out and set it up nearby at one corner of the four square blocks just then being converted from a Jewish cemetery into Dolores Park, which still exists near the old Spanish mission church that gave the neighborhood its name. The area filled with refugees, mostly working people from damaged buildings in the immediate vicinity and from the crumpled and burning rooming houses nearer downtown. Schmitt recalled afterward that they had also salvaged two of the huge pots used for boiling laundry. "Mrs. Schmitt and the two girls soon set to work cooking in them, and making tea and stew for all that could not help themselves. The girls would go out moseying around the graveyard, and come back and tell of some poor old woman with nobody to look after her, or some poor old sick man, or some children with the mother helpless. And they would fill up a can with coffee or tea and milk and another can with meat stew, and off they would go with them. Empty fruit and vegetable cans were our soup tureens, cups, saucers, plates, and side dishes. They were very handy.

"The grocer on the corner put out all his supplies the first day; so we had plenty of tea and coffee and sugar and butter and everything; as well as canned goods, while they lasted, and then the Red Cross people began supplying things. The wholesale butchers used to send out meat for the refugee camps from the Potrero; and when a wagon was passing our place, the man would dump out a few fine slabs of meat on the corner, and that kept the stew-boiler going. It was the same with the dairymen from down the Peninsula. They always dumped down one or two big ten-gallon cans of milk at our corner as they drove by. So that all Mrs. Schmitt and the girls had to do was to keep awake and keep the boilers full and the fire going." Like the Mizpah Café, Schmitt's family kitchen became a community center, a site in which strangers and neighbors took care of each other. Billy Delaney, a local entertainer with considerable charm, took on the task of foraging for firewood and water to keep the kitchen going.

Schmitt's reminiscences continue, "Then when the dynamite explosions were making the night noisy and keeping everybody awake and anxious, the girls or some of the refugees would start playing the piano, and Billy Delaney and other folks would start singing; so that the place became quite homey and sociable, considering it was on the sidewalk, outside the high school, and the town all around it was on fire."

Thomas A. Burns, who was a partner in one of those produce firms Schmitt routinely patrolled, also took care of his neighbors. He lived on Lyon Street next to the Panhandle—the long strip of greensward east of Golden Gate Park—and he owned a wagon and team of horses. That first day, he took fifty boxes of oranges to the Panhandle and gave them away, then went to his house, which had been shaken from its foundation but was otherwise fine. Into it he moved dozens of guests, "some that we knew before and some that we did not know from Adam. All were refugees from the fire. And, for some reason that I cannot explain, the house still had its supply of running water. Therefore, it was the great central rendezvous of all the refugees in that neighborhood. They came with buckets, and pails, and bottles, and everything else in the way of a container, to draw water from our faucets. Thus the place was crowded from about four o'clock each morning to about twelve o'clock each night. When we found out that the water was still flowing, and that hundreds of persons were suffering from lack of it, we passed the word around." With the help of a borrowed police badge, he was able to keep his team and wagon from being commandeered by the army or National Guard and continued hauling food out to the neighborhood to give away for the next three weeks. He said of the people he gave food to, "No questions were asked, no investigations were attempted. Whatever the applicant required was given to him or her, if I had it; and the plan seemed to work excellently."

Another policeman downtown that first morning, Sergeant Maurice Behan, helped rescue a woman with a baby and commented, "Men were taking all sorts of risks to help other people who were in danger." A pawnbroker he saw bought a whole load of bread from a baker's wagon and began giving loaves away to people fleeing the flames. Nearby an agent for a mineral water company set up a primitive bar out of a plank and a couple of trestles and gave water away all day and all night to the thirsty crowd. Later Behan and some citizens helped firemen rescue five people from a damaged building. They were taken to the hospital in a fish cart, a laundry wagon, and an automobile—still a relatively rare piece of machinery in those days. Behan commented, "What impressed me particularly was the lighthearted way in which everybody seemed to be taking the calamity. All seemed to be merry, many of them were cracking jokes as they pushed along. . . . Of course it was heartrending to see some of the mothers with their babies in their arms and other tiny children hanging on to their skirts or trotting behind. But the spirit of them all was a wonderful thing to see. No matter where you went or who you spoke to, in the thick of that ruin with the fire blazing all around you, somebody found something to joke about."

There were tragedies nonetheless. A man from the business department of one of the city's many newspapers found a baby about four months old abandoned, orphaned, or lost the day of the quake, carried it with him, joined up with a stray company of opera singers whose female members helped care for the child and found it some milk, and took it to sleep with him in Golden Gate Park that night, embraced it to keep

it warm, but found it cold and dead when he awoke. Tragedies and gen-
erosities: the plumbers union decided, five days after the earthquake, to
volunteer their services without pay for a week, "and in pursuance of this
action about five hundred plumbers worked day and night for over a week
repairing all broken pipes and stopping waste of water in the unburned
district."

Charles Reddy, the manager of Miller & Lux, one of the big slaugh-
terhouses on the city's southeast shore, also tells of the openhandedness
that sprang up in the hours and days of the disaster. Reddy says that the
proprietor's "first thought that morning was that homeless people would
soon be wanting meat, and my straight orders were to give every applicant all he needed and take money from nobody. Black, white, and yellow were to be treated just the same; and they were treated just the same,
even if we had all Chinatown camped down quite near us. Thousands of
the excited Chinese from Chinatown proper trekked down to our end
of the Potrero to be near their cousins, the shrimp catchers on the bay
below us. At the time of the earthquake we had on hand, slaughtered and
ready for delivery, about three hundred head of cattle, five or six hundred
sheep, thirty or forty calves, and about a hundred and fifty hogs. None
of this meat was lost or destroyed; every bit of it was distributed to the
people, and the supply lasted seven days. We started distributing at five
o'clock the afternoon of the earthquake. . . . All the firms, except two,
were giving away their meat or allowing the people to take it. . . . The
two firms that did not open up their warehouses had all their meat rot on
their hands."

Giving away the meat rather than letting it rot made sense. But going
to the lengths that Miller & Lux did, of hiring more men and coming
up with distribution plans to meet the needs of as many refugees as possible, was not a business decision but an altruistic gesture. So was driving
injured people to the hospital in your laundry wagon, or buying a whole
load of bread to give away, or hauling oranges across town to distribute.
You can argue that sustaining the city through a crisis served the interests of businesses that depended on a local customer base, but few seem to
have been making such long-term calculations. Just as Mrs. Holshouser
and Mrs. Schmitt seemed to need no explanation for why they set up public kitchens and began feeding their neighbors, so Reddy needed none for
giving away a fortune in food. It was what you did.

It's not as though hunger did not exist in San Francisco before April 18, though it was less visible and less widespread; the city was in 1906 a many-tiered society with enormous opulence at the top and grim destitution at the bottom. It's tempting to ask why if you fed your neighbors during the time of the earthquake and fire, you didn't do so before or after. One reason was that you were not focused on long-term plans—giving away thousands of pounds of meat was, of course, not profitable for Miller & Lux, but in the days after the disaster there were no long-term plans, just the immediate demands of survival. Another is social: people at that moment felt a solidarity and an empathy for each other that they did not at other times. They were literally in proximity to each other, the walls literally fallen away from around them as they clustered in squares and parks, moved stoves out onto the street to cook, lined up for supplies. They had all survived the same ordeal. They were members of the same society, and it had been threatened by the calamity.

Though disasters are not necessarily great levelers, some of the formerly wealthy in this one no longer owned more than the poor, and many of the poor were receiving relief for the first time. Nearly all shared an uncertain future—though because they were all in it together, few seemed to worry about that future. (Many left town to start again elsewhere in the state or the country, but the city's population rebounded in a few years.) That lack of concern made it easier to be generous in the present, since much self-interest is more often about amassing future benefit than protecting present comfort. More than a hundred thousand people were camped out in San Francisco in the days and weeks after the earthquake. In the first few days, people took care of each other, and the methods and networks they developed continued to matter even after the Red Cross and other relief organizations moved in.

And the rules were clear. William G. Harvey, who managed an automobile dealership, wrote, "All the big hotels, such as the St. Francis, the Palace, and others, were filled with eastern and other tourists who seem to have lost their heads entirely. Indeed, the only really scared people that I can remember having seen through the first three days of the fire were people of this class. In many cases these would come to the garage offering to pay any price for the use of an automobile that would take them out of the city. However, we absolutely refused to accept money from any such applicant, and as long as we saw that the petitioner was able to walk, we refused to furnish a machine. All our machines were kept busy carrying the sick and wounded." There were extortionists who charged people huge sums to transport goods, but there was also this giveaway, this refusal of profit, that brought those with resources into community with those who needed them. The hotel dwellers seem to have been scared because, as outsiders, they did not feel part of this community or know how to navigate the city, but many of the affluent responded with fear in part because they feared their fellow citizens would deprive them of their advantages. (In many cases the disaster had already done so, albeit temporarily.)

Most San Franciscans seem to have been at home in the city even when they had no homes. But a series of groups felt ill at ease: the occupying armed forces, who had been instructed to see chaos and impose order; the wealthy who feared an uprising; the city's governors who knew only that they were not in power and believed their task was to take it back; the outsiders who did not navigate the city with ease.

States of Mind

Generosity was one highlight of the postquake citizenry, equanimity was another. Everyone would say then that it was the spirit of San Francisco, as they would talk about British composure during the bombing of London or New Yorkers' resilience after the attacks of September 11, 2001. Eric Temple Bell, who was a teacher in 1906 San Francisco but would later become known as a mathematician and science-fiction writer, recalled, "The best thing about the earthquake and fire was the way the people took them. There was no running around the streets, or shrieking, or anything of that sort. Any garbled accounts to the contrary are simply lies. They walked calmly from place to place and watched the fire with almost indifference, and then with jokes that were not forced either, but wholly spontaneous. In the whole of these two awful days and nights I did not see a single woman crying, and did not hear a whine or a whimper from anybody. The rich and poor alike just watched and waited, it being useless to try to save anything but a few immediate necessities, and when the intense heat made it necessary to move, they get up with a laugh."

The socialist novelist Jack London, whose birthplace in the poor district south of Market Street burned in the quake aftermath, agreed:

"Remarkable as it may seem, Wednesday night while the whole city crashed and roared into ruin, was a quiet night. There were no crowds. There was no shouting and yelling. There was no hysteria, no disorder. I passed Wednesday night in the path of the advancing flames, and in all those terrible hours I saw not one woman who wept, not one man who was excited, not one person who was in the slightest degree panic-stricken. The most perfect courtesy obtained. Never in all San Francisco's history, were her people so kind and courteous as on this night of terror." Though almost no one seemed terrified either once the shaking stopped. People watched the firestorms with detachment.

Charles B. Sedgewick's earthquake was so ennobling it begins to test the limits of belief, though more moderate accounts of the same phenomenon are widespread. He wrote, "The strong helped the weak with their burdens, and when pause was made for refreshment, food was voluntarily divided; the milk was given to the children, and any little delicacies that could be found were pressed upon the aged and the ailing." And then he says, "Would that it could always be so!" And here you get to the remarkable fact that people wish some aspects of disasters would last. He continues, "No one richer, none poorer than his fellow; no coveting the other's goods; no envy; no greedy grasping for more than one's fair share of that given for all. True it is, I reflected, that money is the root of all evil, the curse of our civilization, seeing that it is the instrument which frail mortals use to take unjust advantages. What a difference those few days when there was no money, or when money had no value!"

Money was irrelevent for many of the transactions: food was given away, and the public kitchens ran into the summertime. And cash was in short supply, so people made their own. One newspaper reported, "Owing to the fact that every bank in the Bay Counties has been more or less injured, to the fact that every reserve bank has been destroyed in San Francisco, that the coin and currency in the vaults will not be recoverable for several weeks, the citizens of San Francisco and Northern California are quietly using bills of exchange, private checks, and ordinary notes as currency. This . . . is a sign of the faith of Californians in the stability of their communities." Other forms of relief included donated clothing and free medical care. The U.S. Post Office at San Francisco forwarded unstamped mail, often written on scraps and oddments, from the survivors to destinations around the country. There were thieves, opportunists, and people who refused to help the needy, but the citizens for the most part seem to have entered a phase of solidarity that crossed many social divides and to have felt for each other deeply. There were callous and fearful authorities who lashed out, but also institutions such as the post office that just quietly broke the rules to make life a little less disastrous. For Sedgewick, the disaster was a corrective to a society poisoned by money.

No one had a better time of it than the journalist who published a piece in her San Francisco newspaper, the *Bulletin*, eleven days after the quake, titled "How It Feels to Be a Refugee and Have Nothing in the World, by Pauline Jacobson, Who Is One of Them." Jacobson, an observant Jew and playful writer who had studied philosophy at the University of California, plunges straight into the reasons for that joy that hovers around the other accounts. She had lost everything in the earthquake (except, unlike the majority of her fellow citizens, her job), gone over to Oakland to buy "a stock of face creams and soap and dresses," and then decided against the purchases. Had she bought the goods, she explained, she would have had to buy a trunk to put them in, to buy a trunk would entail hiring someone to carry it, and that "meant a return to at least a partial degree of the old permanency." That permanency for her included class divides, becoming an employer, owning something while others owned nothing. "And I slipped my money back in my purse. All too soon would return the halo encircling exclusiveness. All too short would be this reign of inclusiveness. There was plenty of time for petty possessions, plenty of time for the supercilious snubbing of the man or woman not clad according to the canons of the fashionable dressmaker or tailor. In the meantime how nice to feel that no one would take it sadly amiss were you to embrace the scavenger man in an excess of joy at seeing him among the living, or to walk the main street with the Chinese cook. Have you noticed with your merest acquaintance of ten days back how you wring his hand when you encounter him these days, how you hang onto it like grim death as if he were some dearly beloved relative you are afraid the bowels of the earth will swallow up again? It is like a glad gay good holiday—all this reunioning."

For those who had been maimed or lost family members, the earthquake was not so positive—though Jacobson describes being shaken and disturbed, as well as feeling fond of even the merest acquaintance. The

truly destitute had no such ready opportunity to choose or reject expanding their possessions or hiring an expressman to carry them. It's also hard
to say how happy the scavenger man was to be embraced or the Chinese
cook to promenade with a white newspaperwoman. The joys of disaster are not ubiquitous. But they are often widespread, and they are profound, and they may well have been embraced by these working men.
And Jacobson gets at something essential when she talks about walking
through the ruins at dusk when a man asked, "May I walk with you? It's
lonesome walking alone." She says, "We smiled and nodded and took him
in as if we had known him all our lives," a bold welcome in those days of
strict boundaries for women. When a soldier said that "ladies" could walk
on the sidewalk but men must stick to the street, Jacobson and her friends
chose to walk through the burned bricks and fallen telegraph wires in
the middle of the street with their newfound acquaintance. "Everybody
talks to everybody else," a young woman wrote a friend. "I've added
hundreds to my acquaintance without introductions." Women who had
been bound by Victorian conventions about whom they might speak to
or know felt liberated by the lifting of all those rules, as do people in most
disasters when the boundaries fall away, and every stranger can be spoken to and all share the experience. This was behind the joy that shone
out of my guide's face in Halifax, of many of the tales of San Francisco in
1989 and of other disasters I heard directly from glowing people.

Jacobson believed that something in that joy was lasting. She concludes, "Most of us since then have run the whole gamut of human emotions from glad to sad and back again, but underneath it all a new note is
struck, a quiet bubbling joy is felt. It is that note that makes all our loss
worth the while. It is the note of a millennial good fellowship. . . . In all
the grand exodus . . . everybody was your friend and you in turn everybody's friend. The individual, the isolated self was dead. The social self
was regnant. Never even when the four walls of one's own room in a new
city shall close around us again shall we sense the old lonesomeness shutting us off from our neighbors. Never again shall we feel singled out by
fate for the hardships and ill luck that's going. And that is the sweetness
and the gladness of the earthquake and the fire. Not of bravery, nor of
strength, nor of a new city, but of a new inclusiveness.

"The joy in the other fellow."

The same page of the *Bulletin* (which showed sketches of embracing the scavenger man and walking with the Chinese cook) has an update on Paris fashions below Jacobson's big spread and a few small items typical for the postdisaster phase: a request to return milk cans to dairymen so they can keep supplying milk, and a note on the Women's Relief Corps of Oakland and the charitable programs of the Improved Order of Red Men, a fraternal organization. Tens of thousands of warehoused army boots from the Spanish-American War were issued to the citizens of San Francisco, some of whom had fled the earthquake and fire in little more than their nightshirts and nightgowns, so it is hard to say who was the beneficiary of the fashion advice about hats and the news that "sleeves are shorter than in winter." A day later, the *Bulletin* revised this fashion advice: "Modish young women whose plain shirtwaists never cost less than twenty dollars in the ancient time that ended on the morning of April 18, have discovered that the blue army shirt, distributed free at the supply stations, when pleated to reduce the girth and improve the lines, makes a warm and not unbecoming waist [blouse]. It can be worn a week and any child can wash it." An article below this one was titled, "San Francisco Greater in Poverty Than Prosperity," and a brief report below that mentioned the arrest of two men for trying to break into a safe.

The day before the quake, the *Bulletin's* lead stories had been about chasms between races and classes. The biggest headlines were for the sixteen-year-old boy who had been kidnapped by a ship's crew, part of the semislave labor of the seas that persisted into the twentieth century. A race war seemed near in Missouri after a grand jury investigated a white mob of lynchers. Two thousand Japanese immigrants were denounced for violating labor law to work in the Alaska canneries. Other stories from around the nation in the weeks after the earthquake were about union power, about the reformist impact of Upton Sinclair's novel *The Jungle*, exposing the foul Chicago meatpacking industry, and the case for breaking up Standard Oil's monopoly. The society was made of schisms at that moment. It's this pervasive atmosphere of conflict that made Jacobson's "millennial good fellowship" so remarkable.

GENERAL FUNSTON'S FEAR

Shoot to Kill

B rigadier General Frederick Funston, the commanding officer at the Presidio military base on San Francisco's northern edge, perceived his job as saving the city from the people, rather than saving the people from the material city of cracked and crumbling buildings, fallen power lines, and towering flames. And so what Pauline Jacobson saw as a "millennial good fellowship," Funston and others in power saw as a mob to be repressed and a flock to be herded. "Without warrant of law and without being requested to do so," Funston wrote in his own defense a few months later, "I marched the troops into the city, merely to aid the municipal authorities and not to supercede them." It is true that he had the cooperation of the mayor at the outset, though conflicts over authority arose during the three days of the conflagration and the weeks of military occupation. Most citizens and many soldiers believed that martial law had been declared and the army was legitimately in command of the city, though only Congress could then authorize martial law, and it had done no such thing. (In 2007, federal law was changed to allow the president to send in army troops to occupy American cities, a huge setback for domestic liberty.) The belief that martial law was in effect was later used as a defense by soldiers and militiamen who acted as though it was by shooting down citizens and forcing them at gunpoint out of their homes and into conscripted labor. General Sheridan, the Civil War hero, had ordered his troops into Chicago after the Great Fire there in 1871, but was immediately rebuked by the governor and forced to withdraw them.

No disaster is truly natural. In earthquakes, trees fall, rarely, the earth fissures in the great ones, but barring tsunamis, the natural world survives well. The earthquake could be called nature's contribution to the destruction of San Francisco's structures and infrastructure, if you left aside the question of why after the big earthquake of 1868 the city didn't develop better building codes and the fact that architecture itself, and anyone trapped within, is the principal victim of earthquakes. In the hours after the quake came man's contribution. The city would be taken over by a hostile army, its citizens treated as enemies, and much of what had survived would be burned down, wantonly if inadvertently, by soldiers who in the course of thinking they must take control sent things spiraling out of control and up in flames. In treating the citizens as enemies, the occupying armies drove residents and volunteers away from scenes where fire could be prevented. In many parts of the city only those who eluded the authorities by diplomacy, stealth, or countering invocation of authority were able to fight the blaze. Those who did saved many homes and work sites. There are no reliable figures on mortality in the earthquake, but the best estimates are that about three thousand died, mostly from the earthquake itself. One historian suspects that as many as five hundred citizens were killed by the occupying forces; another estimates fifty to seventy-five.

The fires and booming explosions raged for three days. It sounded like war. When they were done, half the city was ash and rubble, more than twenty-eight thousand buildings had been destroyed, and more than half the population of four hundred thousand was homeless. Mansions burned down atop Nob Hill; the slum district south of Market Street was nearly erased. The disaster provoked, as most do, a mixed reaction: generosity and solidarity among most of the citizens, and hostility from those who feared that public and sought to control it, in the belief that an unsubjugated citizenry was—in the words of Funston—"an unlicked mob." For all the picturesqueness of men in bowler hats and women in long skirts fleeing a disaster more than a century ago, the San Francisco earthquake has, in all its essentials, the same ingredients as most contemporary disasters, the same social solidarities and schisms, the same generous and destructive characters. It certainly prefigures the clashes of Hurricane Katrina in New Orleans. What makes the small utopias like the Mizpah Café all the more remarkable is that they took place in the context of devastation and of conflict—the response of one social sector, just as those welcoming kitchens were the response of another.

Funston was only the second-in-command at the Presidio. Even the absent commanding officer, General Greeley, would be disturbed by how Funston had handled the crisis. Short, hard-drinking, belligerent, sandy-haired, apparently full of boundless confidence, Funston was a man of decisive action who often decided unwisely. A brave soldier, he had been decorated and promoted for actions in the Philippines during the Spanish-American War, a few years before the earthquake. He had also been reviled and investigated for shooting prisoners without trials and using underhanded methods to capture an enemy leader's camp. Upon his return from the war, he was dressed down by President Theodore Roosevelt himself for too aggressive a public attack on an antiwar senator. Shortly after the 1906 earthquake, Funston was sent to quell the labor unrest in Goldfield, Nevada, led by the anarchist union the International Workers of the World. He was a hothead who served power and privilege unquestioningly, and he may have served his country best by dropping dead on the eve of his appointment as commander of the U.S. forces in the First World War. The extreme measures he took in the 1906 earthquake are partly signs of his own disposition and worldview, but they were widely supported by the businessmen and politicians in the crisis, and similar reactions have been taken in other disasters into the present.

San Francisco's mayor, Eugene Schmitz, was a handsome populist who had risen from a working-class background to become first an orchestra conductor and then a surprise successful candidate for mayor in 1901 on the Union Labor ticket. But he responded similarly to Funston, infamously issuing a proclamation that day which read: "The Federal Troops, the members of the Regular Police Force, and all Special Police Officers have been authorized by me to KILL any and all persons found engaged in Looting or in the Commission of Any Other Crime." Copies were quickly printed up and plastered around the city. Like Funston, Schmitz was protecting the city from the people that day and in the days afterward (though he was more sympathetic in other respects: the morning of the quake, he freed all the prisoners from the city jail, except those charged with serious felonies, and sent them off with a scolding). The death penalty is an extreme measure for theft, to say the least, and that theft was the primary crime the poster addressed is indicative. Many would not consider property crimes significant when lives are at stake— and the term *looting* conflates the emergency requisitioning of supplies in a crisis without a cash economy with opportunistic stealing. Disaster scholars now call this fear-driven overreaction elite panic.

In the hours and days after the earthquake, more than seventeen thousand army troops were joined by members of the U.S. Navy, the U.S. Marines, the California National Guard, and military cadets from the University of California, Berkeley. In his magisterial history of the quake, Philip Fradkin comments, "What Funston unwittingly set into motion was the gathering on the city streets of the largest peacetime military presence in this country's history." One of the cadets from the University of California, sophomore Stuart Ingram, remembered long afterward, "About noon the university announced that college work for the rest of the term was abandoned, all students graduated or promoted without the usual examinations. With the announcement the whole town took on a kind of holiday air of gaiety. As news continued to get worse the air of gaiety faded. San Francisco was hard hit, more fires started, and uneasiness began to arise that total demoralization was close and the danger of riots would require National Guard troops."

Total demoralization doesn't describe the mood of the city, and there was no evidence that riots were likely, but the city got the National Guard troops anyway (and the governor kept them there even after the mayor requested their removal). The military and National Guard were deployed to prevent things that often existed largely in their imagination. Funston wrote, "I have no doubt, and have heard the same opinion expressed by scores of citizens, that had it not been for the prompt arrival of the large force of Regular Troops, who are acting under orders to shoot all looters, the saloons would have been broken into, and then the crowd, becoming turbulent, would have begun sacking the banks and jewelry stores." The same claim has been made in many other situations—that the reason there was no malicious or mob behavior was police or military action. Logically, the argument is akin to the one that the amulet you wear wards off the evil eye; that something has not happened is not always evidence that it was prevented by the measures taken. Major William Stephenson of the U.S. Army wrote to his college classmates in Maine, "The prompt appearance of our troops was all that saved the city from the terror of a mob, plundering first the saloons, of which there were thirty-four hundred, and then the stores and mansions."

Colonel Charles Morris, who was in command of the western side of the city, said, "I was waited upon at my headquarters on Broadway by a committee of highly respected citizens of the district, who stated they had learned on good authority that the poor who had been burned out, felt that the rich had not suffered losses as had the poor, and were therefore determined to invade the Western Addition and lay it waste by incendiarism and attendant acts of spoil, looting, and violence. I completely reassured this committee by informing them of the precautionary measures, particularly as regarded the destruction of liquor, adopted to safeguard the lives and property of the people residing in my district." Morris, like much of the occupying army, may not have known the city very well. The fires had ravaged many mansions, luxury hotels, and the central business district almost as soon as it burned the poor neighborhoods nearby. Other working-class districts—Telegraph Hill, Potrero Hill, and the Mission District—came through with earthquake damage but little fire damage.

The authorities' fear was not precipitated by anything the public did in those days, but by earlier anxieties in that era of upheaval. They believed uncontrolled crowds routinely degenerated into mobs, and they doubted the legitimacy of the system they dominated, since they expected mobs to tear it apart given the least opportunity. San Francisco had a lively working class, a strong labor movement, and a history of dramatic public actions, from parades to real mob activities such as the anti-Chinese riots of 1877. But there is no evidence of civil unrest in the period of the 1906 earthquake. The mayor had ordered all saloons closed to preserve the public peace, but soldiers and marines took the orders too literally, and with an order given by Colonel Morris to justify them, began breaking into closed saloons and grocery stores on the west side of town and destroying the whole stock of alcohol. The rampage frightened the citizens. You could argue that the army sent to prevent mobs became a mob.

Opportunistic theft began with the cigar stealers Officer Schmitt thwarted early in the morning on April 18. There isn't evidence that it constituted a major problem. Far, far more property, including homes, warehouses, and workplaces and all their contents, was lost in the fires for which those in command bore partial responsibility. And some of the thieves were soldiers. A banker who stayed in the old Montgomery Building downtown, which survived the flames, witnessed the soldiers who were supposed to be guarding it "going in and out at all times except when the officers were coming to pass the word along to post the guard— then they would skip out like rats from a trap—I don't think that the officers ever saw them. . . . I saw the soldiers carrying out cigar boxes loaded under their arms, ten or twenty boxes, as much as they could carry." A navy man saw two drunken sailors trying to rob a jewelry store and was nearly shot by one of them when he intervened.

Others were engaged in what might better be called "requisitioning"— the obtaining of necessary goods by taking them where they could be found. One improvised emergency hospital was supplied with mattresses and bedding that volunteers took out of abandoned hotels. Volunteers, including some from the Salvation Army, broke the windows of drug-stores on Market Street to get medical supplies. Among those participating in such ethical pillaging were cable car company president James B. Stetson and his son Harry, an attorney. Another man was seen picking over the rubble of a ruin, and the discoverer fired a warning shot. The man ran, and a soldier shot him dead. He had been trying to free someone trapped in that rubble.

The police invited Mormon elders to take supplies from a grocery store about to be destroyed by fire. On their second trip to bring food to their camp in Jefferson Square, a soldier ordered everyone out and then shot and killed the man standing behind them. They had returned to the wrong store, and the penalty for the mistake was death. A woman told a cadet that a grocer invited the crowd to help themselves before the fire got his store, and a soldier bayonetted one of the invitees who was leaving laden with groceries. A grocer who charged extortionate prices had his goods expropriated by soldiers and "a dozen rifle barrels were leveled at the grocer's head"—perhaps slightly more just, but not much less violent a response. A National Guardsman yelled at an African American man stooping over something on the ground to "get out but he paid no attention to me, so I up and fired at him. I missed of course, but the shot must have scared him and he started to run. I was just getting ready to shoot again, when a shot was fired from across the street and the fellow toppled over. . . . An officer came along and ordered us to throw the body into the still burning ruins, so in it went." On April 21, the *Bulletin* reported that soldiers shot four men breaking into a safe; another story on the same page stated that twenty men on the waterfront were executed for refusing to help with the firefighting effort. The cashier of a bank was shot as a looter while he was trying to open his company's vault two days after the quake. Many of the executed were incinerated in the fires or dumped in the bay. Their numbers will never be known.

General Funston later wrote, "Market Street was full of excited, anxious people watching the progress of the various fires now being merged into one great conflagration. A few moments before seven o'clock there arrived the first detachment of regular troops, the men of the Engineer Corps at Fort Mason. Their presence had an instantly reassuring effect on all awe-inspired persons." And the non-awe-inspired? In a long letter about life in one of San Francisco's refugee camps, an upper-class woman wrote, "A drunken soldier had pushed his way into a tent full of sleeping women and threatened to shoot them. Hardly a day passed that all camping there were not roughly ordered to leave the ground by some uniformed person who strode shouting over the sands. On the first of these occasions after our arrival, there being only two or three women of us present, we were much distressed." Mary Doyle wrote a cousin on a scrap of brown-paper bag, "A large number of men and even women have been shot down for disobeying orders of soldiers." An officer's daughter wrote a friend, "A good many awful men are loose in the city, but the soldiers shoot everyone disobeying in the slightest, no explanations asked or given." Henry Fitchner, a nurse, reported, "I saw one soldier on O'Farrell Street, between Van Ness Avenue and Franklin Street, beat with the butt of his gun a woman—apparently a servant girl—who wanted to get a bundle of clothing that she had left on the sidewalk in that block."

"The terrible days of the earthquake and fire," General Greeley reported on May 17, "were neither accompanied nor followed by rioting, disorder, drunkenness (save in a very few cases), nor by crime. The orderly and law-abiding conduct of the people rendered the maintenance of order a comparatively easy task." Not all authorities were terrified of the people they were supposed to serve—but Greeley had been away during the earthquake, and it is impossible to know what his first response would have been.

The Great Fire

Early historians chose to emphasize the fire over the earthquake, and in the decades afterward, 1906 was remembered for "the Great Fire." Some recent historians charge that this was a cover-up, geared toward reassuring investors that San Francisco was not a peculiarly disaster-prone place, since fires, unlike earthquakes, can happen anywhere. It may also be that the public remembered the three days and nights of fiery inferno better than the one minute of earthquake at dawn, and while there is no struggle against a quake once it has begun, the fire was fought fiercely—if ineptly on many counts. Flames destroyed much of the evidence of earthquake damage too. San Francisco's fire chief, Dennis Sullivan, was fatally injured in the earthquake, and so the city lost at the inception of the disaster the person who might have directed subsequent efforts wisely. The earthquake broke many water mains, so fighting the fires became far harder than it could have been. Sullivan had long worried about a major fire and thought about how to fight it. In his absence, the firefighters were joined by the army, and the latter tried reckless experiments in using explosives to make firebreaks. Their mistakes were many.

One was the use of black powder, or gunpowder, in place of dynamite. The latter simply blows things up; the former tends to also ignite them. Thus many buildings were turning into burning, flying brands that spread the fire farther or started new conflagrations entirely. Another was setting the firebreaks too close to the existing flames, thereby simply breaking buildings up into more flammable debris. A third was setting explosives to buildings that contained chemicals, alcohol, and other highly flammable substances. A fourth was setting explosions that restarted or started fires in areas that were previously secure. And a fifth was keeping away from the flames the public who might have supplied the power to fight the fire by hand.

Many of the most successful firefighting efforts were by groups of citizens armed with buckets of water, with shovels, with wet gunnysacks, with whatever came to hand—and often by smothering sparks on roofs, fires could be prevented from becoming overwhelming conflagrations, when people were allowed onto those roofs. Another important firefighting tactic was summoning the political clout to turn back the dynamiters and break through the military lines. It was a struggle between the reckless technological tactics of the occupying forces, convinced that their strategy of destruction could save structures and neighborhoods elsewhere, and the citizens committed to saving as much as possible through hands-on methods. Former fireman Dennis Smith reports in his *San Francisco Is Burning* that by the second day the National Guard allowed citizens to fight fires, but the army persisted in evacuating, or evicting, them. Historian Frank Hittell writes of fighting fire himself with professional firemen who asked where the rest of the volunteers were. They were being kept back by soldiers, so the two uniformed groups were in open conflict. Hittell was struck by soldiers when he volunteered again.

Jerome Barker Landfield lived at the north end of the city, and he wrote afterward, "Water was lacking, but the proprietress of a little grocery at Larkin and Greenwich Streets gave me two barrels of vinegar. This proved to be a godsend. A score of volunteers armed with blankets soaked in vinegar, extinguished flaming cinders on neighboring roofs, and we held Greenwich Street safe from Larkin to Van Ness. Two agile schoolboys with pails and cups climbed to the roof of the Robert Louis Stevenson house at Chestnut and Hyde and saved the mansion by putting out sparks as they fell. By eleven o'clock Friday morning we believed that the rest of our district was out of danger." Then the military blew up a nearby patent-medicine company, whose thousands of gallons of alcohol went up in flames, threatening to destroy what they had just saved. Landfield saw the mayor but was unable to convince him to stop the dynamiting. Fortunately Abe Ruef, the political boss who had put Schmitz in power and organized the network of bribes that enriched both men, came by in his automobile, listened to Landfield, and put an end to it.

The big post office still standing today at Seventh and Mission streets was saved because ten employees refused direct orders to evacuate and put out the flames with wet mail sacks. The U.S. Mint downtown was also saved by its own employees. Blazes started by dynamite raced ahead of the fire into the district southeast of downtown, but huge crowds fought them. A hundred men at a time pulled houses down by ropes and removed the dismantled structures from reach of the flames. A miller reported that ten of the Globe Grain and Milling Company's employees were prepared to save the mill, and could have, in his opinion, but were driven away at gunpoint. Losses totaled $220,000. The Mission District was saved by sheer manpower, and the crucial battle was near the kitchen operated by Officer Schmitt's family at Dolores Park. A volunteer named Edwards worked for twenty-four hours without stopping, and when the fire was out, his shoes had burned through and the soles of his feet had been so badly scorched he could no longer walk. A mail carrier named Roland M. Roche credited the men and boys of the neighborhood with saving it, fighting fire by hand, carrying milk cans of water from a laundry to the fire: "This improvised bucket brigade, working in the face of almost insufferable heat, saved their own valley from imminent destruction, and thus probably saved the greater part of San Francisco that survived the fire."

Another angry citizen summed up the fire history of 1906 San Francisco: "The stories have but one beginning and one end. They begin with the criminal idiocy of the military; they end with the surmounting heroism of the citizen." He was the writer Henry Anderson Lafler, and his long attack on Funston and the military attack on San Francisco was never published. In it he summed up the aftermath of the earthquake thus: "During those unforgettable days the city of San Francisco was even as, a city captured in war, the possession of an alien foe. We were strangers on our own streets; driven from our own houses; gray-haired men, our foremost citizens, the sport of the whims of young boys, whose knowledge of the city was confined to its dance halls, its brothels, and saloons. Were we children—we, the citizens of San Francisco—that we should have thus been suddenly gripped by the throat by a stupid soldiery, and held fast till all our city burned?"

Utopia Besieged

Lafler calls it a war, and two worldviews and two responses were at war in the earthquake. It is true that most of the citizenry had little responsibility beyond their own survival and their own property. But they reached out to each other, improvising public kitchens and large camps and fighting fires by hand. The city government and military were responsible for preserving a larger-scale version of the city, for fighting the fire, and for preserving the peace. And they accomplished much, from the navy's successful efforts to fight the fire on the waterfront to the city's Committee for Housing the Homeless's building of temporary shelter for seventy-five hundred people in the parks. There's no question about why these powers succeeded in doing what they were supposed to do. The question is about why they chose, for the most part, to regard the public as an enemy and to presume that they needed to control them. The fires undermine the case that the people in power were working in the city's best interest, and so does the apparent murder of dozens to hundreds of citizens by soldiers, National Guardsmen, and vigilantes. But the evidence is much more extensive than that.

Take, for example, the Committee of Fifty that Mayor Schmitz appointed. Its name was drawn from the old Committee of Thirteen, or Committee of Vigilance, that had in the 1850s taken over San Francisco and run it to serve the members' business interests. The Committee of Fifty served for months afterward as an unelected government. It included many commonsensical appointments—a subcommittee on Restoration of Light and Telephone, and another on Roofing the Homeless. But before the quake was a week old, Schmitz had also appointed his backer, Abe Ruef, his enemy, James Phelan, and others to the subcommittee on the Permanent Relocation of Chinatown. The plan was nothing more than a real-estate grab fueled by racism. The Chinese occupied one of the most desirable sections of the city, and pushing them to the city's southern border or beyond would free up the land for real-estate interests.

Modern histories of the earthquake tend to broaden this particular group's self-interested animosity to a blanket racism. The actual record on non-Chinese reactions to the Chinese population of San Francisco is more complicated. There were racists, and there were allies. Hugh Kwong Liang was fourteen or fifteen when the earthquake struck, and he was already leading a difficult, isolated life. His mother and younger siblings had returned to China to escape the anti-Chinese sentiment in the city, and he had stayed behind to help his father, who died before the quake. He was entrusted to the care of a cousin, who after the quake took all the money from Liang's father's store and left him to his own devices. The boy dragged his father's trunk to safety, joined the crowd in the Presidio, met another abandoned Chinese boy of sixteen, and concentrated on keeping sparks from setting their army tent on fire. The other boy left him that night to find his own family, and the trunk was stolen.

Alone again, the despondent Liang headed for the waterfront to drown himself. When he arrived, he decided instead to stow away on a ship and leave the burning city behind. "To my surprise," he recounted to his nieces and grandnieces many decades later, "the captain and men were all very sympathetic and told me that everything would be all right." They fed him, took up a collection, gave him the proceeds, and set him down in Napa, where he soon found his way to another branch of the Liang family that embraced him warmly. He began a new life, better off than he had been before the earthquake. Disaster's upsetting of the status quo causes some to plummet, others to rise or find new niches and allies. Liang passed through all phases on his journey.

The other accounts are mixed too. Many Chinese men worked as live-in cooks and household servants, and their lives remained intertwined with their employers' after the earthquake, at least through the evacuation. One policeman told of helping an elderly Chinese woman, giving her looted food and drink and leading her to the safety of other Chinese Americans in flight. One of the photographs of refugees in Golden Gate Park shows two Asian men standing among the white throng, part of the crowd waiting for food. On the other hand, many white people were seen picking through the ashes of Chinatown for loot or "souvenirs"—but soon afterward indignant citizens broke the Chinese porcelain one looter offered for sale on a ferryboat to Oakland. When it came to relocating Chinatown, some businessmen pointed out the economic role Chinatown played in the city, and the government of China weighed in, and with that Chinatown was saved. In the aftermath of the earthquake, the city fathers obsessed so much about excluding the Japanese from the public school system that they provoked an international incident with Japan. Racism was a potent force, but not ubiquitous, as this relief committee report makes clear: "The Japanese asked for very little relief, in part because many had difficulty in speaking English, but more generally because all were aware of the anti-Japanese feeling of a small but aggressive part of the community; this in spite of the fact that Japan contributed directly to the local [relief] committee and through the American National Red Cross nearly a quarter of a million dollars."

The self-interest of the business community played out elsewhere as well. Phelan and Adolph Spreckels were competing to take over the streetcar lines in San Francisco, and the latter man—one of the wealthiest in San Francisco—tried to shut down a rival who was running streetcars for free immediately after the quake. Safety precautions were cited, but the assistant director of the United Railroads recalled, "Prior to the earthquake, Mr. Spreckels was directing a fight against the United Railroads, and on the day before the earthquake, Tuesday, April 17, a rival system of his own had been incorporated." The mayor gave the company the go-ahead, Spreckels stopped them again, and finally General Greeley—who had been away during the quake—intervened, and the cars resumed running on April 27. There are worse stories, like that of a waterfront man pressured by his banker to obtain dynamite—so the embezzling banker could blow up the bank and its crooked books. Ruef attempted to reduce wages by arguing that in the crisis "there is pressing need for mutual concession," so unskilled workmen should accept $2.50 for a nine-hour day rather than $8.00, as it had been before. What made the concession mutual was not specified. By summer, the unions were striking for better wages and the newspapers were deploring them. The United Railroads strike was particularly long and bitter.

Employer-employee relations were turbulent all through this period. A story by the *Argonaut*, which served the elite of San Francisco, complained in July of "the extreme scarcity of house servants, although there are many thousands of people out of employment. The Relief Committee frequently receives communications asking where all the female servants have gone. According to General Greeley, it seems the relief camps are full of idle domestics." The general remarked, "The sooner this feeding of able-bodied men and women is stopped, the better it will be for the city." The *Argonaut* admitted the following week that there were few "drones" in the camps, though only six of one thousand women accepted employment when it was offered to them. The *Bulletin* had run a more sympathetic piece, "The Dignity of Labor," in late May, which itemized some of the callous treatment meted out to women servants during the earthquake and reported that with the dearth of servants "mistresses who have been the severest of taskmasters . . . have been forced into the position of the scorned menials, and a strange world opens before their startled eyes." The journalist Jane Carr saw the disaster as a great leveler and liberator, though not everyone was eager to be leveled or happy others had been freed from drudgery.

The immediate aftermath of the disaster, in which everything was topsy-turvy, money was scarce to irrelevant, citizens improvised their own care, and much was given away rapidly, yielded to more institutional management of the disaster, which was often effective but seldom joyous. The informal citizen-run kitchens were replaced in many parts of the city by soup kitchens, which required people to show tickets. The authorities had a great fear that people would eat twice or collect extra supplies, and the system was meant to prevent people from getting too much. "Pauperization," the transformation of independent citizens into dependents, was another great concern of the time and an argument against all but the most unattractive forms of relief and assistance. The *Argonaut* reported, "The great majority of refugees who had established their own cooking arrangements, and preferred cooking in their own way the meat and other supplies that they drew from the relief stations, greatly resented the new regime. Nevertheless, it was put in force, and the immediate result of its adoption was an extraordinary decline in the number of refugees applying for relief. The method was so unattractive—many people called it revolting—and the system so extraordinarily unpopular that people preferred the hardships of hunger."

Only in the Mission District did citizens successfully resist the institutionalization of their eating sites and systems. The *Argonaut* reports that about two-thirds of the remaining population of San Francisco got their meals in that neighborhood, so the resistance mattered. The difference between citizens feeding themselves and each other and being given food according to a system involving tickets and outside administrators is the difference between independence and dependence, between mutual aid and charity. The providers and the needy had become two different groups, and there was no joy or solidarity in being handed food by people who required you to prove your right to it first.

After Hurricane Katrina devastated the Gulf Coast, I heard the infamous former Federal Emergency Management Agency (FEMA) director Michael Brown tell a group of disaster experts that business was the best leader of recovery because business had the best interests of the community at heart—a curious statement, to say the least. What all these stories add up to is a picture of men in power who provided some relief and got the city going again but also reinstated the old injustices and discriminations. They acted in their own self-interest as often or more often than in the public interest and sometimes viewed the public as an enemy to be conquered, controlled, and contained. The brief solidarity and harmony ended in part because the business community pitted its interests against those of the majority.

The destruction of the city by the soldiers' unskilled use of explosives and prevention of hands-on firefighting is equally serious, and the murders are more serious, far more so than the looting they were supposed to prevent (or the looting that the soldiers also carried out). And the attempt to grab Chinatown was opportunistic plunder on a grand scale. It would be a mistake to portray these men in power as wholly bad. The army supplied tents and worked to make the camps sanitary, during a time of real threat of typhus and cholera—the old diseases of dense population and bad sewage systems. The city fathers worked tirelessly to bring back the city of ordinary institutions as it had existed before the earthquake. But they served themselves first. There's a philosophical problem at the root of this foul behavior by those in power, particularly when contrasted with that of so many of the ordinary people. The best person to address it is the philosopher who wandered inquiringly through the ruins the day of the earthquake.

WILLIAM JAMES'S MORAL EQUIVALENTS

"What difference would it practically make to anyone if this notion rather than that notion were true?" asked William James in his second lecture on pragmatism, the philosophical approach he and a few other American philosophers developed at the turn of the twentieth century. The question is an important one to bring to bear on disaster response. If the military notion that San Franciscans were a mob on the brink of mayhem were true, the right response to disaster was authoritarian, armed, and aggressive. If the main psychosocial consequence of disaster was a "millennial good fellowship," then a very different and much milder response was appropriate, the response that Officer Schmitt, Mrs. Holshouser, and others offer. At stake in disaster is the question of human nature.

The term itself has fallen out of fashion. It implies a fixed essence, a universal and stable inner self, but if you concede that there are many human natures, shaped by culture and circumstance, that each of us contains multitudes, then the majority of human natures on display in disaster may not suggest who we are ordinarily or always, but they do suggest who we could be and tend to be in these circumstances. There are at least two tendencies on display in disasters, Funston's fear that bred conflict and Jacobson's solidarity that generated joy. The response to disaster depends in part on who you are—a journalist has different duties than a general—but who you become is also an outgrowth of what you believe. Funston believed in authority, power, and an underlying tide of human savagery. Jacobson believed in her fellow man. William James believed many things, and thought more, and the earthquake fed his thoughts, or rather touched on much of what he had been thinking.

"What difference would it make" is at the core of his philosophy, which was practical, or pragmatic, in its concern for what the consequences of a belief are rather than what its truth is. That is to say, most philosophy is geared toward finding out the existing condition of things. James focused instead on how beliefs shape the world. Rather than ask whether or not God existed, James might try to ascertain what difference belief in God would make to how you live your life or how a society conducts itself. What is the consequence of the belief, rather than the truth of it? It is a deeply American approach, directed toward the malleability rather than the immutability of the world, toward what we make of it, rather than what it is made of. This aspect of James's philosophy is sometimes misinterpreted as a kind of easy solipsism akin to the contemporary New Age notion that we each create our reality (a crass way of overlooking culture, politics, and economics—that is, realities are made, but by groups, movements, ideologies, religions, societies, economics, and more, as well as natural forces, over long stretches of time, not by individuals alone).

But if we do not wholly create our worlds, they do not arise without us; we shape them, from the most intimate relationships to the most public and enduring institutions, and these conditions arise out of acts guided by beliefs. Thus it is, for example, that the founding political document of the United States opens with a belief that "all men are created equal." The American Revolution is an outcome, in part, of that belief; subsequent revolutions have attempted to broaden who is sheltered under that umbrella of equality. The struggles of our times have been as much to change beliefs—about gender, about race—as to change policy, for the policy changes are largely an outcome of changed belief. Ideas matter. In disaster, they matter urgently, and the disaster James found himself in the middle of in April of 1906 gave him a great crucible to test his own.

In 1905, James had delivered the lectures that became his 1907 book *Pragmatism: A New Name for Some Old Ways of Thinking,* the book in which he asks the question quoted at the beginning of this chapter. He was intermittently ill in the first decade of the twentieth century, his last decade of life, but he was also at the height of his intellectual powers and fame, writing prolifically, lecturing in the United States and Europe, collecting honorary degrees and membership in various national academies, a revered public intellectual who weighed in on war, religion, spiritualism, psychology, and almost everything else. He had been born in 1842 in New York City to a wealthy Irish American family, the oldest of five children—the next oldest was his brother Henry, who became as renowned as a novelist. Their father was an enthusiastic dabbler in spiritual ideas, an occasional writer of books on ethics and religion, a friend of the Transcendentalist Ralph Waldo Emerson, and heir to a considerable fortune.

William James wavered a great deal as a young man, avoiding service in the Civil War, studying art and hoping to become a painter, then studying medicine. Medicine led him to a position in anatomy at Harvard College that eventually evolved into his long professorship in philosophy and the new discipline of psychology, in which he did pioneering work. He suffered one severe depression in his early adulthood, and the rest of his life can be seen as a struggle for sufficient meaning and purpose to keep from being pulled under again, a struggle perhaps made more intense by his relief from the necessity of struggling for economic survival. (And like his brother Henry, he suffered regularly from various ailments and was, if not a hypochondriac, at least exceedingly preoccupied with his symptoms.) He was a tenderhearted friend, husband, and father, and even his writings convey warmth, informality, open-mindedness, an interest in the most subtle minutiae of experience, and hope. He sometimes thought the breezy informality of his writing and talking style undermined his intellectual standing, but it made him widely accessible and popular.

He had been ready to retire from teaching when Stanford University pursued him and paid him lavishly to come and teach in the spring of 1906 at the shining new country campus some thirty miles south of San Francisco. Delighted by the situation, he wrote to friends again and again some version of "the University is absolutely Utopian. It realizes all those simplifications and freedoms from corruption, of which seers have dreamed. Classic landscape, climate perfect, no one rich, sexes equal, manual labor practiced to some degree by all, especially by students, noble harmonious architecture, fine laboratories and collections, admirable music, all these latter things belonging to the community as such, while individuals live in the simplest conceivable way." He added in another letter of praise, "It is verily the simple life, and democracy at its best." James was skeptical about the possibility of Utopia but admired the efforts toward it. In an aside in *The Varieties of Religious Experience*, he remarked, "The Utopian dreams of social justice in which many contemporary socialists and anarchists indulge are, in spite of their impracticality and nonadaptation to present environmental conditions, analogous to the saint's belief in an existent kingdom of heaven. They help to break the general reign of hardness, and are slow leavens of a better order." It's a pragmatic response: a comprehensive Utopia may be out of reach, but the effort to realize it shapes the world for the better all the same. The belief may not be true, but it is useful. Belief makes the world.

At Stanford, James lectured to a class of 300 students with as many as 150 others in attendance at times. As his public address, he delivered an early version of his great manifesto, "The Moral Equivalent of War," in late February, about six weeks before the earthquake. The issues he addressed there would be answered another way in the earthquake, and so his "Moral Equivalent" manifesto makes, with his earthquake essay, a pair examining purpose, meaning, heroism, and satisfaction in life. In its 1910 published version, it begins "The war against war is going to be no holiday excursion or camping party." He had joined the Anti-Imperialist League founded in 1898 to oppose the United States' war against Spain and its annexation of Spain's former colony of the Philippines. The public appetite for war had been whipped up by the newspapers during the era of sensationalistic "yellow journalism," though James tended to believe that there was an inherent appetite for war. Many prominent intellectuals and public figures, including writer Mark Twain (who was vice president of the Anti-Imperialist League from 1901 to 1910), were ferociously opposed to the explicit amorality of that war and feared the transformation of their country into an imperial power. James moved from the question of shaping—or checking—American foreign policy to the larger question of whether war could be eliminated.

He admitted that war was itself a sort of utopia for some, because "all the qualities of a man acquire dignity when he knows that the service of the collectivity that owns him needs him. If proud of the collectivity, his own pride rises in proportion. No collectivity is like an army for nourishing such pride. . . . Having said thus much in preparation, I will now confess my own utopia. I devoutly believe in the reign of peace and in the gradual advent of some sort of socialistic equilibrium. The fatalistic view of the war function is to me nonsense, for I know that war-making is due to definite motives and subject to prudential checks and reasonable criticisms, just like any other form of enterprise." That is, war is not inevitable; it arises for particular reasons—but ending war requires coming to terms with what human ideals and desires it feeds. James, of course, was living in a time when Civil War monuments proliferated, heroism on the battlefield was a major subject for poetry, and the abstracted, mechanized wars against unseen armies and civilians hardly yet existed (though massacres of nonwhite peoples were exceedingly common, if seldom reported as such).

He argued that a permanent peacetime was only viable in a society devoted to something more than pleasure, that there must be causes, hardships, demands, common struggles. He had been born into pleasure and had to struggle for meaning himself. He proposed something akin to the Peace Corps or the War on Poverty—if "there were, instead of military conscription, a conscription of the whole youthful population to form for a certain number of years a part of the army enlisted against *Nature*," then even privileged youths would understand "man's relations to the globe he lives on, and to the permanently sour and hard foundations of his higher life. To coal and iron mines, to freight trains, to fishing fleets in December, to dishwashing, clotheswashing, and windowwashing, to road-building and tunnel-making, to foundries and stoke-holes, and to the frames of skyscrapers, would our gilded youths be drafted off, according to their choice, to get the childishness knocked out of them and to come back into society with healthier sympathies and soberer ideas." The essential argument that human beings are at their best when much is demanded of them doesn't depend on the particulars of his proposals. "The martial type of character can be bred without war," James continued. "The only thing needed henceforward is to inflame the civic temper as past history has inflamed the military temper."

James's ideas about what the moral equivalents, the great struggles to which humanity might dedicate itself, might be, didn't take a more practical form than this universal enlistment in community works—until the earthquake. He was already awake when the earthquake struck: his instant response "consisted wholly of glee and admiration . . . I felt no trace whatsoever of fear; it was pure delight and welcome. . . . I ran into my wife's room and found that she, although awakened from sound sleep, had felt no fear, either." In the essay he wrote that June, "On Some Mental Effects of the Earthquake," he added, "A good instance of the way in which the tremendousness of a catastrophe may banish fear was given me by a Stanford student." The student was on the fourth floor of a stone dormitory that collapsed; he felt no pain and no fear, though he expected to die as he plummeted through the three stories below, crawled through daylight, realized he was in his nightshirt, walked back for clothing, and only later realized that his feet had been seriously injured. On the campus, James reported, "Everybody was excited, but the excitement at first, at any rate, seemed to be almost joyous. . . . Most people slept outdoors for several subsequent nights, partly to be safer in case of a recurrence, but also to work off their emotion and get the full unusualness out of the experience." Much of the heavy architecture of the Stanford campus was devastated, spectacularly, though casualties were almost nil.

That morning, James's colleague, the psychologist Lillien Jane Martin, was worried about her sister in San Francisco—news of the city's devastation had already come—so they set out together on the lone train for the city that day. Eight days later he returned for another view of the city, and throughout the rest of his stay—which was shortened by the disaster and Stanford's cancellation of the rest of the semester—he quizzed everyone as to their psychological responses. "My business," he wrote afterward, "is with 'subjective' phenomena exclusively; so I will say nothing of the material ruin that greeted us on every hand—the daily papers and the weekly journals have done full justice to that topic. By midday . . . everyone [was] at work who *could* work. There was no appearance of general dismay, and little of chatter or of inco-ordinated excitement. . . . Physical fatigue and seriousness were the only inner states that one could read on countenances. Every one looked cheerful, in spite of the awful discontinuity of past and future, with every familiar association with material things dissevered; and the discipline and order were practically perfect." (Later he wrote to the president of Stanford University, "The crop of nervous wrecks may yet have to be reaped.") One of his biographers charges that James "simply could not bring himself to empathise with the sufferers in San Francisco, but insisted that work and a sense of community were prescriptions for overcoming the disaster." But he saw conduct that called for a more complex response than pity.

His earthquake essay continued: "Two things in retrospect strike me especially, and are the most emphatic of all my impressions. Both are reassuring as to human nature. The first was the rapidity of the improvisation of order out of chaos." He described how people took initiative, without leadership or coordination, for much of what needed to be done, giving as an example the way two admirers of the painter William Keith went to the centrally located homes doomed to burn and saved his paintings from the flames. (They brought the salvaged roll of canvases to him in his studio, where he had given up his work for lost and was already painting more.) An echo of "The Moral Equivalent of War" is evident in his statement that this purposeful energy, "like soldiering . . . always lies latent in human nature." The second thing that struck him was "the universal equanimity. We soon got letters from the East, ringing with anxiety and pathos; but I now know fully what I have always believed, that the pathetic way of feeling great disasters belongs rather to the point of view of people at a distance than to the immediate victims. I heard not a single really pathetic or sentimental word in California expressed by anyone."

One of the most pathetic came from his brother Henry James, reading sensational newspaper accounts and imagining the worst while he waited to hear from his family. The novelist effused, "I feel that I have collapsed, simply, with the tension of all these dismal days . . . I should have told you that I have shared every pulse of your nightmare with you if I didn't hold you quite capable of telling me that it hasn't *been* a nightmare." The older brother did just that in breezy reply: "We never reckoned on this extremity of anxiety on your part," with Henry's concern for "our mangled forms, hollow eyes, starving bodies, minds insane with fear, haunting you so." He added that such agony is felt most at a distance. In the essay he went on to say, "Surely the cutting edge of all our usual misfortunes comes from their character of loneliness." That is, a major loss usually isolates us from the community, where no one else has suffered thus, and we are alone in being bereft of beloved, or home, or security, or health. When the loss is general, one is not cast out by suffering but finds fellowship in it.

A friend tells me, as I write, of someone we know who has joined a support group for his grim disease; these groups create communities of

sufferers so that one feels neither alone nor marked out uniquely for suffering. The religious contemplation of suffering and work with the sick,
the poor, and the dying likewise serve to develop compassion and sub-
vert tendencies to self-pity and its twin, self-aggrandizement. Or as Pauline Jacobson had put it, "Never again shall we feel singled out by fate for
the hardships and ill luck that's going." James continued, "The cheerfulness, or, at any rate, the steadfastness of tone, was universal. Not a single
whine or plaintive word did I hear from the hundred losers whom I spoke
to. Instead of that there was a temper of helpfulness beyond the counting. It is easy to glorify this as something characteristically American,
or especially Californian. . . . In an exhausted country, with no marginal
resources, the outlook on the future would be much darker. But I like
to think that what I write of is a normal and universal trait of human
nature."

James took up the subject of the earthquake again in his keynote
address to the American Philosophical Association that December. His
talk was called "The Energies of Men" and its subject was the "energies
slumbering" in most people that only extreme situations and extreme
individuals awaken and put to use. He spoke of a friend of his, a Western
student of yoga, "breaking through the barriers which life's routine had
concreted around the deeper strata of the will, and gradually bringing
its unused energies into action." And he spoke of the "stores of bottled
up energy and endurance" that people in the earthquake had discovered within themselves. One of his ongoing inquiries was about human
nature's extremes, about the mental and emotional states of saints, mys-
tics, visionaries, the mentally ill, people under duress, about the forces that
produced selflessness, heroism, transcendence, sacrifice—the sources of
the extraordinary rather than the ordinary. In disaster, the state of mind
he describes is neither sought nor exceptional: these remarkable qualities
become widespread.

His is in many ways the first good empirical investigation of human
nature in the crucible of disaster, and its conclusions are in line with those
the disaster sociologists would reach through methodical study of many
more calamities. James's investigation concluded that human beings
respond with initiative, orderliness, and helpfulness; they remain calm;
and suffering and loss are transformed when they are shared experiences. In the earthquake he found what he had been looking for: a moral

equivalent of war, a situation that would "inflame the civic temper as past history has inflamed the military temper." The *civic temper*—the phrase suggests social engagement not just as a duty but also as an appetite and an orientation. The earthquake awoke something of that temperament in one child, and though William James had only four years left to live when the quake struck, she had seventy-four in which to make her mark and exercise that appetite, and she did so with vigor.

DOROTHY DAY'S OTHER LOVES

The Rattled Child

What are the consequences of a major event? The usual measure takes stock of changes in what is already visible: the prominent players and large-scale institutions. The 1906 earthquake, for example, helped prompt what is sometimes described as reform of the corrupt Schmitz-Ruef administration in San Francisco but could be equally described as the replacement of one coalition by another that was more patrician but no less self-serving. Ruef and Schmitz were indicted for graft and bribery, and the former was given a long prison sentence, a witness's house was bombed, an editor was sued for libel, a prosecutor was shot in the courtroom. Though the corruption put on trial was real, the relentless pursuit of the pair was equally due to anti-Semitism and rage against Schmitz's alignment with labor. The *New York Times* reported that the Progressive coalition headed by Spreckels and Phelan was engaged in the "formation of a political machine . . . to carry out their plans of revenge and the ruination of certain corporations which stood in the way of their plans." Or as Fradkin puts it, "The California Progressives, with President Theodre Roosevelt quietly cheering them on from the sidelines, were guilty of unleashing a violent, divisive drama in a city that badly needed an intermission from chaos in order to heal."

The city administrators made only minor changes in its safety infrastructure and rebuilt without improvements to the building standards and codes. The forests of the Pacific Coast were logged for lumber as far north as Washington State, and thousands of horses were worked to death to speedily rebuild the city. San Francisco arose again, a city with the same general institutions, injustices, and divisions, extraordinary still in some ways, ordinary in others. The political fracas was part of business as usual—self-interest, corruption, and the plays of power.

What became of that moment when everything was different? What are the unseen, far-reaching consequences of an event? With what scale can you weigh an event that affects a million people or more? What of the differences that are immeasurable, a sense of possibility or a sense of grief that redirects a life? What if one minor figure who will come to have a major impact is shaped by that event? What if the consequences of an event begin so quietly they are imperceptible for decades even if they come to affect millions? Many events plant seeds, imperceptible at the time, that bear fruit long afterward.

Dorothy Day was eight and a half when the earthquake struck. She was then the odd, thoughtful third child of a racetrack journalist; she is now, nearly three decades after her death, the revered founder of a radical movement with more than a hundred centers still active in the United States alone and a candidate for sainthood in the Catholic Church. She was already looking for something beyond the usual pleasures and woes of childhood, a hungry reader, a voyager into the neighbors' churches and religions, a strong-willed child full of longing. At eight, her apprehensions of God as "a great noise that became louder and louder, and approached nearer and nearer to me until I woke up sweating with fear and shrieking for my mother" got mixed up with her remembrance of the earthquake—"the noise which kept getting louder and louder, and the keen fear of death makes me think now that it might have been due only to the earthquake."

The quake itself "started with a deep rumbling and the convulsions of the earth started afterward, so that the earth became a sea which rocked our house in a most tumultuous manner." Her father pulled her older brothers from their beds, her mother grabbed her younger sister, and Day was left in a big brass bed that rolled around the floor of the family's house in Oakland. She was equally struck by the social aftermath. In the 1930s, she wrote, "What I remember most plainly about the earthquake was the human warmth and kindliness of everyone afterward. For days refugees poured out of burning San Francisco and camped in Idora Park and the race track in Oakland. People came in their night clothes; there were new-born babies. Mother and all our neighbors were busy from morning to night cooking hot meals. They gave away every extra garment they possessed. They stripped themselves to the bone in giving, forgetful of the morrow. While the crisis lasted, people loved each other."

Love in Practice

"While the crisis lasted, people loved each other." Day remembered this all her life, and she dedicated that long life to trying to realize and stabilize that love as a practical force in meeting the needs of the poor and making a more just and generous society. Because of that moment of the earthquake and moments of social engagement afterward, she was able to see this as a reality she had already tasted rather than as an abstract possibility. But the road toward it was a long one. After the earthquake, her family—which had lived in Oakland only a few years—sold the furniture for cash and got on a train to Chicago. They had been middle class, but in Chicago they moved into a flat over a tavern and underwent a long period of comparative poverty, eating overripe bananas and toast for dinner and getting to know the poor people around them. She writes of her high-school self, "I did not want just the few, the missionary-minded people like the Salvation Army, to be kind to the poor, as the poor. I wanted everyone to be kind. I wanted every home to be open to the lame, the halt, and the blind, the way it had been after the San Francisco earthquake. Only then did people really live, really love their brothers. In such love was the abundant life and I did not have the slightest idea how to find it."

Day grew up with a yearning for God and an empathic love for those at the bottom, neither of them a legacy from her parents, who were uninvolved in either religion or politics. Reconciling the two would be her great challenge. She wanted to mitigate the suffering of the poor, but she saw something holy about poverty too. In her autobiography she writes, "One afternoon as I sat on the beach, I read a book of essays by William James and came on these lines: . . . *one wonders whether the revival of the belief that poverty is a worthy religious vocation may not be the transformation of military courage, and the spiritual reform which our time stands most in need of. Among us English-speaking peoples especially do the praises of poverty need once more to be boldly sung. . . . We have lost the power even of imagining what the ancient realization of poverty could have meant; the liberation from material attachments, the unbribed soul, the manlier indifference, the paying our way by who we are and not by what we have, the right to fling away our life at any moment."* Upton Sinclair's novel *The Jungle* made the invisible lives of the poor living nearby in Chicago real to her, and this "made me feel that from then on my life was to be linked to theirs, their interests were to be mine; I had received a call, a vocation, a direction to my life."

She used the language of religion intentionally. All her life before her conversion to Catholicism just before she turned thirty, she longed for prayer, for the shelter of the church and the larger meanings religion provided, for something grander and more mystical than everyday life or revolutionary politics could offer. But religion didn't seem compatible with the other part of her life in the radical America of the early twentieth century, and only the radicals seemed to address the needs of the poor. And Day was radical. She was a tall, striking woman with a strong jaw, pale skin, black hair, usually cut in a bob, a decisive stride, strong opinions, and like many young people, a lot of pieces she could not quite put together. She fell in with anarchists, Communists, feminists, and other revolutionaries, worked with them on newspapers, marched with them on Washington, drank and danced with them at balls and bars, went to prison with them, talked with them about what the world could be and should be.

She fell in love with many things, and she uses the term intentionally to describe objects of enthusiasm and devotion entirely unlike romantic, erotic love. In *The Long Loneliness*, her autobiography published when she was in her fifties, she recalls, "There was a new baby that year, born in May. I fell in love that year too—I was fourteen years old—and first love is sweet." The love was for a band conductor down the street to whom she never spoke. And she goes on to say, "The love for my baby brother was as profound and never-to-be-forgotten as that first love. The two seemed to go together." The Russian Revolution came in 1917, when she was nearly twenty, and she joined the thousands singing and celebrating in Madison Square Garden. "I was in love now with the masses. I do not remember that I was articulate or reasoned about this love, but it warmed and filled my heart." One love led to another; of Forster, the man she was deeply in love with ten years later, she wrote: "I have always felt that it was life with him that brought me natural happiness, that brought me to God. His ardent love of creation brought me to the Creator of all things." And in coming to God, she destroyed her common-law marriage with the antireligious Forster.

Mapping the Landscape of Love

There are other loves. But we have little language for them. In an era whose sense of the human psyche is dominated by entertainment and consumerism and by therapy culture—that amalgamation of ideas drawn from pop psychology and counseling—the personal and private are most often emphasized to the exclusion of almost everything else. Even the scope of psychotherapy generally leaves out the soul, the creator, and the citizen, those aspects of being human that extend into realms beyond private life. Conventional therapy, necessary and valuable at times to resolve personal crises and suffering, presents a very incomplete sense of self. As a guide to the range of human possibility it is grimly reductive. It will help you deal with your private shames and pains, but it won't generally have much to say about your society and your purpose on earth. It won't even suggest, most of the time, that you provide yourself with relief from and perspective on the purely personal by living in the larger world. Nor will it ordinarily diagnose people as suffering from social alienation, meaninglessness, or other anomies that arise from something other than familial and erotic life. It more often leads to personal adjustment than social change (during the 1950s, for example, psychology went to work bullying women into accepting their status as housewives, the language of Freudianism was deployed to condemn their desires for more power, more independence, more dignity, and more of a role in public life). Such a confinement of desire and possibility to the private serves the status quo as well: it describes no role for citizenship and no need for social change or engagement.

Popular culture feeds on this privatized sense of self. A recent movie about political activists proposed that they opposed the government because they had issues with their fathers. The implication was that the proper sphere of human activity is personal, that there is no legitimate reason to engage with public life, that the very act of engaging is juvenile, blindly emotional, a transference of the real sources of passion. What if that government is destroying other human lives, or your own, and is leading to a devastating future? What if a vision of a better world or just, say, a better transit system is a legitimate passion? What if your sense of self is so vast that your well-being includes these broad and idealistic engagements? Oscar Wilde asked for maps of the world with Utopia on them. Where are the maps of the human psyche with altruism, idealism, and even ideas on them, the utopian part of the psyche, or just the soul at its most expansive? In his book *Arctic Dreams*, Barry Lopez writes of whalers in the far north in 1823: "They felt exhilaration in the constant light; and a sense of satisfaction and worth, which came partly from their arduous work." The sentence stands out for measuring human purpose and pleasure by different standards than the familiar ones. Work gives worth, light gives exhilaration, and the world becomes larger and richer, even for men toiling in cold and dangerous seas far from home.

I don't have a television. For many years the devices seemed like forbidden fruit when I encountered them in hotels and motels, and I would eagerly turn on the TV and look for something to watch. Situation comedies would catch my attention, for several always seemed to be in rerun on the cable channels. In them, the world often seemed reduced to a realm almost without the serious suffering of poverty, illness, and death that puts minor emotional trials in perspective, but without ideals, without larger possibilities beyond pursuing almost always deeply selfish needs (the characters were constantly pitted against each other, and the laugh tracks chimed in most reliably at these moments). If someone aspired to something more, their folly was shown up immediately; even romantic love was always risibly self-serving, delusional, or lecherous. Along with therapy culture, the sitcoms seemed to define down what it means to be human. It wasn't that I condemned them morally; it's just that they made me feel lousy. (Fortunately, in those hotels I could usually find an old movie, or the Weather Channel, with its inexhaustible supply of spectacular disasters, or *The Simpsons*.) Even best-selling semiliterary novels I picked up seemed to shrink away from the full scope of being human. It was as though the rooms in which the characters lived had no windows, or more terrifyingly yet, there was nothing outside those windows. We were consigned to the purely personal—it was not the warm home to which we might return from the politics of Day or the seascapes of Lopez. It was not the shelter at the center of the world, but all that was left: a prison.

The world is much larger, and these other loves lead you to its vastness. We are often told of public and political life merely as a force, a duty, and occasionally a terror. But it is sometimes also a joy. The human being you recognize in reading, for example, Tom Paine's *Rights of Man* or Nelson Mandela's autobiography is far larger than this creature of family and erotic life. That being has a soul, ethics, ideals, a chance at heroism, at shaping history, a set of motivations based on principles. Paine writes that nature "has not only forced man into society by a diversity of wants that the reciprocal aid of each other can supply, but she has implanted in him a system of social affections, which, though not necessary to his existence, are essential to his happiness. There is no period in life when this love for society ceases to act. It begins and ends with our being." But that love and that happiness have no place in the conventional configuration of who we are and what we should want. We lack the language for that aspect of our existence, the language we need to describe what happens during disaster.

And yet the experience happens anyway. Again and again I have seen people slip into this realm and light up with joy. The lack of a language doesn't prevent them from experiencing it, only from grasping and making something of it. During the buildup to the beginning of the war on Iraq in 2003, huge crowds assembled to march in opposition to it. I joined—and though this was about a particular political stance, the expression on people's faces wasn't partisan. The crowd—one march I joined had two hundred thousand participants, on a weekend when people marched and demonstrated on all seven continents of the earth (if you counted the protesting scientists in Antarctica)—radiated ebullience and exhilaration. They seemed to have found something they had long craved, a chance to speak out, to participate, to have voices and feel in their numbers a sense of power, to feel that they mattered, that they could step into history rather than merely watch it.

It was moving to see this idealistic joy on so many thousands of faces, disconcerting to realize how uncommon the experience seemed to be— this experience, which was essentially that of citizenship itself, of playing a role in public life, of being connected to strangers around you and thereby to that abstraction we call society. An even more powerful and pervasive form of it came during the election of Barack Obama, when people around the nation and the world wept, suddenly able to feel the pain of centuries as it was in some way lifted and a hope that seemed out of reach before. The global wave of emotion was about a deep and too often dormant passion for justice, for meaning, for the well-being of others, and the fate of nations. We should feel like that regularly, routinely, in a democracy, but the experience is rare in too many societies and nations. Some part of this joy is sometimes found in disaster, and its effect is so profound that some people remember disasters, from the London Blitz to the collapse of the World Trade Center towers, with strange ardor.

We have, most of us, a deep desire for this democratic public life, for a voice, for membership, for purpose and meaning that cannot be only personal. We want larger selves and a larger world. It is part of the seduction of war William James warned against—for life during wartime often serves to bring people into this sense of common cause, sacrifice, absorption in something larger. Chris Hedges inveighed against it too, in his book *War Is a Force That Gives Us Meaning*: "The enduring attraction of war is this: Even with its destruction and carnage it can give us what we long for in life. It can give us purpose, meaning, a reason for living. Only when we are in the midst of conflict does the shallowness and vapidity of our lives become apparent. Trivia dominates our conversations and increasingly our airwaves. And war is an enticing elixir. It gives us resolve, a cause. It allows us to be noble." Which only brings us back to James's question: What is the moral equivalent of war—not the equivalent of its carnage, its xenophobias, its savagery—but its urgency, its meaning, its solidarity? What else generates what he called the "civic temperament"? Many aspects of public life open up room for such emotion, some quietly, as anyone long devoted to a cause or a community understands, some dramatically, as those who have lived through the warlike suspension of everyday life and solidarity of a major disaster or upheaval know. The extremes of joy are limited to extreme situations—to great public events and historic moments. Yet something of their satisfaction tides over into everyday life, when that life is deep and broad.

There are many other loves than the personal. The largeness of the world is one of the balms to personal woe, and each of us enlarges the world by idealistic passion and engagement. Meaning must be sought out; it is not built into most people's lives. The tasks that arise in disaster often restore this meaning. The writer Stephen Doheny-Farina says of the great ice storm that paralyzed and rendered powerless much of the northeastern United States and Canada in 1998: "Although all disasters have their unique dangers, in many ways the impact of the ice storm was less a sudden catastrophe than an unforeseen change in the way we had to live. . . . And during that process a fascinating phenomenon evolved: as the power grid failed, in its place arose a vibrant grid of social ties—formal and informal, organized and serendipitous, public and private, official and ad hoc." He loved it so much that when the power went on and he returned to preparing his college classes, he found, "The job seemed so distant to me. It was almost as if I had changed careers over the course of two weeks from teacher to home handyman—klutzy, semi-clueless, but coachable, very willing to learn new skills like how to run and maintain a two-cycle generator engine. Suddenly the power went out again. I got up quickly and looked out the window to see if there was evidence of power anywhere in sight. I got on the phone and started calling people. Power seemed to be out across the village. I was alive—it was as if the power left the grid and poured into me."

Day's Impact

Principles and ideas are among the other loves, and Dorothy Day describes even her feeling for the books of Dostoyevsky, DeQuincy, and Dickens as a great passion and an important part of her life. Day believed that "people have so great a need to reverence, to worship, to adore; it is a psychological necessity of human nature that must be taken into account. We do not like to admit how people fail us." And thus we need something more. In her view, this includes love of God and religious practice. And so, after long anguish and indecision, she left her lover and partner so that she could baptize her daughter and become a member of the Catholic Church. Afterward, her long loneliness left her, but another dilemma arose, since she had left her life among radicals behind as well. "How little, how puny my work had been since becoming a Catholic, I thought. How self-centered, how ingrown, how lacking in sense of community!" She moved back to New York City and worked again as a journalist, covering a march of the poor on Washington—the Great Depression had spread desperation over the land a year after her conversion—but she felt isolated and disengaged, until 1932, when she met Peter Maurin, the French peasant who was as radical as he was devout. He changed her life.

He was waiting for her in her own apartment, and the two of them together founded a mission neither of them could have carried out independently. Day called him a "genius, a saint, an agitator, a writer, a lecturer, a poor man, and a shabby tramp, all in one." Not everyone was so enthused about Maurin, an autodidact who happily lectured anyone under any circumstances, but his unshakable self-confidence in their vision made it possible for her to throw her considerable energies into realizing it. On May Day, 1933, they began. They had launched a penny newspaper—twenty-five hundred copies of the first issue were already printed—that would preach their mix of pacifism, solidarity with the poor, social reform, and works of kindness as acts of faith. It was called the *Catholic Worker,* a name that was a riposte to the popular Communist *Daily Worker* but also an insistence on work and workers as central to its vision. Day and Maurin were regular contributors, and a motley crew of writers, illustrators, and newspaper sellers began to gather round. Some of them were homeless, many of them were otherwise unemployed, and it was a logical next step to turn the *Catholic Worker* from a newspaper into a movement by opening "houses of hospitality" to lodge these and other destitute and displaced people. After attempting to locate in several parts of New York City, they settled in the Bowery, famed for its skid-row atmosphere and tough citizens.

By 1939, the *Catholic Worker* was no longer entirely under their direction; they had formed a template that begat twenty-three sister Houses of Hospitality, two farms, and study groups around the country. The newspaper's circulation exploded; two years after its founding it had reached 110,000; by 1939 it would reach nearly 200,000. Day and Maurin were not enthusiasts for the New Deal that arose from the radical politics and radical needs of Depression America; they believed that "the works of mercy could be practiced to combat the taking over by the state of all those services which could be built up by mutual aid." They wanted the needs of the poor to be met personally and the poor to become participants in their own care and thereby members of the community. The state removed that obligation—Day never really ceased to be an anarchist, a person who believed in as much autonomy for the individual and as little role for the state as possible. She and Maurin were much influenced by the French philosopher Emmanuel Mounier's idea of "personalism"—of addressing people as individuals rather than members of a class and of taking personal responsibility for social problems. She was also a pacifist who saw the grand gestures of war as only myriad unjustifiable acts of killing individuals. During the Second World War, this led to a decline in support for the movement, but the same position led to a resurgence of support and interest during the Vietnam War.

Day deplored Catholics who claimed to love God but did not love him in the form of the poor and the needy, and she saw her two loves as one. She spoke of the "sense of solidarity which made me gradually understand the doctrine of the Mystical Body of Christ, whereby we are the members one of another." The Catholic Church preaches the "Corporal Works of Mercy" that include feeding the hungry, clothing the naked, harboring the homeless, visiting the sick, and burying the dead, and the Catholic Worker, both radical and devout, attempted to practice all these, along with the Spiritual Works of Mercy, which include instructing the ignorant, counseling the doubtful, admonishing sinners, comforting the afflicted, and praying for all. These works of mercy had been much more integral parts of medieval society, when huge religious orders ran hospitals and charity was considered a part of everyone's religious duty. There is something medieval about Day, with her stark face, fierce will, and simplifying approach to complex problems. Her devoutness often appeased the church officials who looked askance at the radical rhetoric and practice of the Catholic Worker.

The idea of community was central to Day's work. And the houses of hospitality were communes of a sort, in which the poor were taken in and the core workers ministered to the residents and others in need. The phrase *the poor* sounds far more pleasant than the actuality of people in crisis, alcoholics, drug addicts, and the mentally ill, then and now—though one Catholic Worker house near San Francisco now ministers largely to immigrant farmworkers. Maurin had been raised on a farm and dreamed that the poor could be returned to the countryside, where they could produce their food communally, outside the cash economy. Though the Catholic Worker maintained two farms, the farming activities were often comic—the characters they sent out to the farms were not always enthused about the simple diet or motivated to undertake hard work without bosses. Day and Maurin were trying to avoid what had happened to the food relief in the 1906 earthquake—the institutionalization that reduced the hungry to passive consumers rather than participants in their own survival. With this empowerment, of course, came a degree of chaos and uncertainty—but they were always clear that what the poor needed was much more than food, and power and possibility were also shared.

Even disasters that don't beget broad social change often beget transformed individuals who impact their society. The Great Depression triggered vast economic and social reforms, from changes in the banking system and the economy to the social services of the New Deal. It also served as the long disaster to which Dorothy Day was able to work out a lasting equivalent to the brief moment of disaster solidarity and generosity she had experienced at age eight. The Catholic Worker was her answer to how to extend that engagement, a wedding of her radical commitments and her spiritual desires. More than a century after the earthquake moved a little girl in Oakland, it is still going, still benefiting the bereft, the marginal, the incapacitated. Few would choose a life lived so exclusively and intensively for the other loves. And yet, Dorothy Day's life is only an extreme and enduring version of the altruism that arises in disasters.

When I was a child we used to play a game in any big open space on summer evenings. One of us would stand at the far end of an expanse and shout out "green light," and everyone else would surge forward from the starting line, then freeze when "red light" was heard. A disaster is a little like a game of red light/green light in which everyone is suddenly freed to rush in their own direction, faster and harder than in ordinary times. The people in San Francisco in 1906 did not become something other than what they always were. General Funston loosed his fears and his belief in the legitimacy of violence and dispatched an army to act on them. The city fathers rushed forward with their schemes for improving their own situations as regards money and power, and sometimes also carried out their duties to serve the public interest as they saw it. The wealthy were sometimes cowed by the idea of an unregulated public and sometimes a part of that public. Ordinary citizens had less impact individually but collectively did much to shape the disaster's aftermath. Pauline Jacobson dashed forward with her gregariousness and her reinforced positivity about human nature, as did Jack London, Mary Austin, and William James. Anna Amelia Holshouser, like Thomas Burns, Officer Schmitt and his wife and daughters, and countless others, showed up with generosity and resourcefulness. Some people sprinted toward opportunities to help themselvs to unsecured goods, but what theft took place was dwarfed by the gifts and gestures of altruism in the aftermath of the ruin of the city. Many fear that in disaster we become something other than we normally are—helpless or bestial and savage in the most common myths—or that is who we really are when the superstructure of society crumbles. We remain ourselves for the most part, but freed to act on, most often, not the worst but the best within. The ruts and routines of ordinary life hide more beauty than brutality.

II

HALIFAX TO
HOLLYWOOD:
THE GREAT DEBATE

A TALE OF TWO PRINCES:
THE HALIFAX EXPLOSION AND AFTER

The Explosion

A little after 9:00 a.m. on December 6, 1917, Gertrude Pettipas was leaning out an open window watching the cargo ship on fire in the Halifax, Nova Scotia, harbor below. Then it exploded. "A great black ball of smoke rose up to about four or five hundred feet and out of this came lurid cardinal colored flames. It was a magnificent though terrifying sight. . . . I saw a blinding sheet of fire shoot a mile high in the air. It seemed to me to cover the whole sky. It blinded me, and immediately the concussion struck me in the face throwing me with terrific force across the room. I struck the wall and fell. The house swayed and rocked, and the doors and windows were blown to pieces." The First World War had come home to this quiet Canadian port town already bustling with soldiers and supplies for the front in Europe. Many thought the Germans had invaded, but it was a harbor accident involving a tremendous quantity of explosives bound for the European front. It created the largest man-made explosion in history before nuclear weapons.

That morning, a Norwegian ship, the *Imo*, draped with a "Belgian Relief" banner, had taken an unorthodox course, as if to pass the munitions ship the *Mont Blanc* on the wrong side in the long narrow channel of the sheltered Halifax harbor. The *Mont Blanc* signaled frantically, but the two ships were unable to agree upon a safe passage past each other. The *Imo* steamed on fast and plowed into the side of the *Mont Blanc*, tearing into the side of the ship. The latter ship was loaded with nearly three thousand tons of explosive powder, along with highly flammable oil, gun cotton, benzol, and picric acid. It was intended to join a convoy headed for France. The impact ignited some of the cargo, and the fire spread to the most volatile material. Some precautions had been taken when the ship was loaded in New York; the iron hull was lined with wood nailed in with copper nails to prevent sparks, and the crew was forbidden to smoke almost anywhere on the ship, including the deck laden with barrels of fuel. But the load was still a reckless one. The collision started a fire that began to spread, but only the crew on board knew how deadly it would be. Unable to warn anyone, they evacuated. The ship drifted toward the shore, hundred-foot flames clawing the sky, and then the nearly three thousand tons of explosives detonated.

The explosion lifted the entire six million pounds of the *Mont Blanc* a thousand feet into the air, vaporized much of it, and dropped a shower of white-hot shrapnel over Halifax and Dartmouth, the city across the strait. The ship's anchor shank, weighing half a ton, was thrown two miles, and the barrel of a large ship-mounted gun nearly three and a half. Water was sucked up into a column and then dropped again into the torrential wave that overswept the surroundings, rising nearly sixty feet beyond the high-water level. A cloud of white smoke rose twenty thousand feet into the sky. What remained of the benzol mixed with a cloud of water to form a sticky black rain that fell on both sides of the harbor for several minutes. A sound wave shot out, and the sound was audible more than two hundred miles away. An air blast rolled over the city, knocking down buildings, tearing through doors, windows, and walls, crushing the bodies of those who were hit head-on nearby, exploding eardrums and lungs, lifting people and hurling them into whatever was nearby or carrying them away, snapping trees and telegraph poles like twigs, reducing whole neighborhoods to splinters and rubble. A fireball followed, igniting much of what was within a mile or so surrounding what had been the *Mont Blanc*. Every building within a mile was destroyed, and many farther away were shattered or ignited. Then the fire began to spread: 325 acres were totally destroyed, 1,630 buildings annihilated, and 12,000 damaged. More than 1,500 people were killed, leaving behind widows, widowers, orphans, and bereaved parents. Nearly 9,000 people were injured, families torn apart, and ultimately 41 adults and children were blinded and 249 lost one eye or the sight in it.

After they despaired of doing anything about the conflagration, the crew of the *Mont Blanc* rushed to the lifeboats, rowed frantically ashore, and then ran. They landed near the Mi'kmaq village of Turtle Grove on the Dartmouth coast opposite Halifax. A native woman, Aggie March, stood with a baby in her arms, watching the spectacular, oddly colored flames. A sailor ran past her, grabbed the infant, and continued running into a thicket. When she caught up with him he knocked her down and jumped atop her and the infant. They survived, though nine in Turtle Grove were killed, and the explosion brought an end to the indigenous settlement that had existed since the eighteenth century. The blast shattered tens of thousands of windows into clusters of glass daggers that flew into walls, into wood, into flesh, and into eyes—into the many eyes of those who had been watching the drama in the harbor through windows that winter day. Windows shattered fifty miles away. One girl sitting at her desk in Halifax's Catholic school saw the windows bend toward her like sails just in time to duck the shower of shards that followed. Houses were smashed into piles of splinters, and people were trapped or crushed underneath. The rain of black grease covered many of the people out of doors, making them almost unrecognizable to family members who met them on the streets, or in the hospitals, or went looking for them in the impromptu morgues.

Six-year-old Dorothy Lloyd was walking to St. Joseph's Catholic School with her three sisters when a woman ran toward them, hair flying back, shouting, "Go back! Go back!" They saw a mountain of smoke in the sky, stopped in their tracks, and were thrown to the ground by the force of the explosion. Smoke filled the air.

"Dolly, look at the stovepipes flying in the air," Dorothy said.

Her sister corrected her. "Those aren't stovepipes. They're sailors." The men were streaming by, and the blast then picked up the two schoolgirls and separated them from their other sisters. They came to earth in a vacant lot surrounded by fallen birds. The blast tore the clothes off some of the people that December morning, even tight-laced boots and buttoned coats, depositing them naked or partially clothed as far as a mile from where they had been walking or standing and watching the ship on fire in the harbor. The steep slope of the city rising up from the water prevented many from falling any great distance when the blast was done carrying them, and several people survived extraordinary airborne journeys. Fireman Billy Wells had been racing toward the harbor on the fire engine *Patricia*. The next thing he knew was that he was standing naked far above where he had been, and his arm was hacked to the bone. A wave full of debris from the harbor followed him uphill and washed him into a field. Wells recovered, but not everyone was so lucky. The other seven members of the fire crew were killed, and when Wells walked away from where he had landed he saw corpses hanging out windows and draped over telegraph wires.

Many of the injuries were grotesque. Twelve-year-old Irene Duggan had been thrown into the air and impaled through the flesh of her arm on a metal stake that left her dangling above the ground. A soldier got her down, and the Duggan brothers and sisters who had not been buried under the partially collapsed house dug out their severely injured mother and sister. A soldier just back from the battlefields of the First World War said the event "affected me far worse than anything I saw in France. Over there you don't see women and children all broken to pieces." Though he'd been sent back to recuperate from a punctured lung, he made twenty-three trips to a hospital carrying the wounded.

One of Dorothy Lloyd's sisters had been trapped under a school gate until a soldier freed her; the other was entirely unharmed. The four girls went back to a home whose windows had been blown out, but the family stayed there waiting for an older child until a soldier drove them out at gunpoint. They walked to the Halifax Commons with their neighbors, and on the way the missing boy pulled up alongside them driving a wagon. The stunning scenes were not over for Lloyd, though. She went to see a ring of nuns holding their habits out from their sides and found they were screening a woman giving birth on the grass on that cold day.

The night express from New Brunswick was approaching Halifax as the explosion hit, and the engineer slowed the train to a crawl until debris stopped it, and then crew and passengers took on wounded and homeless people and delivered them to nearby Truro. An earlier train approaching the area with three hundred passengers was spared because a railroad dispatcher, Vincent Coleman, rushed back into the telegraph office near the harbor despite the mortal danger to send a warning and a farewell up the tracks: "Hold up the train. Ammunition ship on fire making for Pier 6 and will explode. Guess this will be my last message.

Goodbye boys." His telegram stopped the train and sent out an early call for aid. He died in the explosion and is still remembered in Canada. Harold Floyd, a nineteen-year-old boy who stayed behind to telephone safety information, died as well. Jean Groves, the telephone operator at the exchange building near the dock, stayed behind in the shattered site to call for nurses, doctors, firemen. She had to be carried from the building. Doctors, nurses, and volunteers worked around the clock to save the lives of the injured. Trainloads of supplies and of volunteers, including medical teams and skilled laborers, poured in, and from the day of the explosion onward, the injured, orphaned, and homeless were dispatched by train to where their needs were met.

Uninjured locals stepped up to the emergency as well. A young businessman named Joe Glube slept through the explosion, awoke to find his mother and sister bleeding from superficial wounds, set off with them for the Commons when told to do so, and then detoured to board up the windows of his stationery store. There he realized how horrific the disaster had been and how great the need and again abandoned his task to take his secondhand Ford to the grocery warehouses. They had been opened, and volunteers were busy distributing their contents to the public. He began setting out with supplies and hauling the injured in to where they could be aided and later became the driver for a veterinarian who paid house calls to the injured. Such improvisation—new roles, new alliances, new rules—are typical of disaster.

Dorothy Lloyd's family was not alone in being bullied by the military—the supervisor of the Children's Hospital stood before her staff with a cut on her face and announced that she would not allow the hospital to be evacuated to the Commons, where the children might die in the cold. The nurses all supported her. An armed guard was set over the damaged area, and only people with passes were allowed to enter. But overall, recovery went smoothly, perhaps because of the relatively small size of the city or the wartime sense of common purpose already in place. Because of the war, the Germans in town were harassed, but no one seems to have been shot or seriously persecuted.

The San Francisco earthquake had happened in soft spring weather, though rain afterward made camping out-of-doors uncomfortable. The blizzard that brought snow and frigid temperatures to Halifax after the disaster did far more, and the differences between the two disasters were many. The wartime city had become a garrison town full of soldiers, but these armies immediately set to work aiding the populace and did not interfere with the civil authorities or citizens (though they did guard the devastated zones, making it difficult for some people to return to search for property and bodies). But the soldiers were as often useful and generous. They were ordered to shoot looters, but comparatively little seems to have come of this overreaction: the chief of police reported on December 9, three days after the explosion, that he had heard of only one case of attempted burglary. Clashes between competing authorities or between authorities and the public were few. The culture and civic temperament were different, so that though there was much generosity and courage, there does not, from the records, appear to be much of anything resembling the black humor and boisterous good cheer of San Francisco. The death toll was much higher as a percentage of the local population, and the winter wartime explosion as a result of human error was grimmer in many ways than a spring earthquake natural at least in origins.

Money, supplies, and volunteers came from around the world, and Boston in particular distinguished itself for the generosity of its aid. In the terrible weather, finding shelter was urgent. People sheltered in boxcars, in army tents, in the intact room or two that remained of their houses, behind boarded-up windows. Residents in the surrounding countryside and towns across Nova Scotia took in many. Orphaned children and children with severely injured parents were put up for adoption or foster care, and offers to adopt came in from all over the continent. As Halifax native Laura MacDonald writes in her history of the explosion, "Halifax, with its rigid class structure—divided by religion, class, and country—briefly integrated. English Protestant mothers, who two days before would not have stepped foot in Richmond, suddenly welcomed poor Irish Catholic children into their homes. Whole families were invited to live in the parlors of wealthier citizens. Soldiers and sailors, who created so much moral apprehension in the middle classes, were transformed into heroes. They were important not only because they were organized and prepared but because they did not have the responsibility of their own families. Teenagers and young adults also proved particularly useful. They took instruction, worked for hours on end without sleep, and were free of the usual responsibilities."

The Sociologist

The Halifax explosion is remembered by sociologists for one man, Samuel Henry Prince, a Halifax resident whose book on the explosion is considered the rough beginning of the revelatory field of disaster studies. Prince had been born in nearby New Brunswick in 1883, got a master's degree in psychology at the University of Toronto but also studied for the Anglican priesthood at Wycliffe College. When the explosion tore apart Halifax, he had been a curate at St. Paul's Church there for seven years and had already seen the aftermath of one disaster. After the *Titanic* had collided with north Atlantic ice and sunk, he had gone to sea on the S.S. *Montmagny* to search for and bury bodies. After the harbor explosion five years later, the hall at his church became a refuge for 350 homeless citizens, and the organization served more than ten thousand meals that first month. The church was close enough to the explosion that shrapnel hit it; some of which is said to be still visible in its walls.

Perhaps the aftermath of the explosion begat more intellectual curiosity in Prince, because sixteen months later he was studying for a doctorate in the new field of sociology at Columbia University in New York City. His 1920 dissertation, *Catastrophe and Social Change*, is an odd mix of stilted Victorian language, unexamined conventional ideas, and acute observations. Its premise is that disaster begets social and political change, and he opens with a set of assertions about the nature of that change. "The word 'crisis' is of Greek origin, meaning a point of culmination and separation, an instant when change one way or another is impending." He compares the crisis in an individual life to that of a society in disaster: "Life becomes like molten metal. It enters a state of flux from which it must reset upon a principle, a creed, or purpose. It is shaken perhaps violently out of rut and routine. Old customs crumble, and instability rules." That is, disasters open up societies to change, accelerate change that was under way, or break the hold of whatever was preventing change. One urban-planning adviser who came to Halifax commented, "The disaster simply had the effect of bringing to a point certain things which were pending at the time."

The nature of this change, these things pending, is not made clear in Prince's opening manifesto, though he does admit, "catastrophe always means social change. There is not always progress." The long-term changes in the Halifax area included improvements in public health services, education, and housing and more involvement by both citizens and civic authorities in the life of the city—and the hiring of women conductors on the trams. Beyond these practical phenomena, he noted "a new sense of unity in dealing with common problems." Just as the sinking of the *Titanic* had prompted changes in shipping and nautical communications policy, so the explosion begat new Canadian and international maritime standards, laws, treaties, and harbor regulations. The scramble to care for the terribly injured led to advances in pediatric medicine, emergency medicine, ophthalmology, reconstructive surgery, and other areas. Some of the economic and social development of the city may have been the result of the upheaval of the war rather than the explosion, but Prince tends to credit it to the latter. He doesn't examine the psyches of the citizens or look at how they themselves might have changed individually or collectively, politically or psychologically, or what the practical consequences of such changes might be. Halifax was a conservative, quiet town, where it was easy to believe that change rarely comes about but by crisis.

Joseph Scanlon, the scholar to study Prince in greatest depth, concludes that the priest turned sociologist was first of all a Christian. "The underlying basis for his thesis is actually theological. He believed Christ's death on the cross showed salvation comes from suffering. He linked the idea that suffering is necessary for salvation to the idea that catastrophe leads to social change, adversity leads to progress." And Scanlon quotes from Prince's *Titanic* sermon: "A world without suffering would be a world without nobility." Certainly Prince sees the Halifax disaster as both a death and a resurrection, quoting one local authority to the effect that "sad as was the day, it may be the greatest day in the city's history." And at another moment he consciously paraphrases the New Testament, writing, "At first it was a very general consciousness which seemed to draw all together into a fellowship of suffering as victims of a common calamity. There was neither male nor female, just nor unjust, bond nor free." (In Galatians 3:28, St. Paul says, "There is neither Jew nor Greek, there is neither bond nor free, there is neither male nor female: for ye are all one in Christ Jesus.") At the very end of his book he reiterates his credo, "Progress is not necessarily a natural or assured result of change. It only comes as a result of effort that is wisely expended and sacrifice which is sacrifice in truth."

Beyond this theological bent, Prince was muddled. Sometimes he reports social harmony; other times he mentions "friction and crises . . . which were only stopped short of scandal." At times he hails the constructive efforts of the ordinary citizens in caring for themselves; at others he deplores "volunteers . . . who could not be expected to understand the nature of scientific relief service." Though his conclusions are based on the long process of recovery, his most interesting reporting is on the first hours and days of the disaster. Prince's own observations and those drawn from direct sources tend to be positive about the people of Halifax. But he also used the manuscript of a Dartmouth journalist, Dwight Johnstone, who retold the usual disaster stories about looters and "ghouls"—those who plundered the dead. Even the language shifted from dry to dramatic when he described "the nightly prowlers among the ruins, who rifled the pockets of the dead and dying, and snatched rings from icy fingers." Ring snatchers are a major component of urban disaster myths, and in the 1906 earthquake also there were rumors of thieves who filled their pockets with fingers severed to get the rings they wore and bit off the earlobes of dead or injured women wearing diamond earrings.

In addition to referring to Johnstone's manuscript, Prince leaned on conventions of medical and psychological literature of the era, writing that disaster provokes "the abnormal action of the glands" and frees up "the primitive instincts of man," including "fear, fighting, and anger" and "food-getting." An equally inflammatory source was Gustave Le Bon's 1894 book translated from French as *The Crowd: A Study of the Popular Mind*. It may be why Prince portrayed the Halifax explosion as generating irrational behavior and "social disintegration." But he also drew on the ideas of a thinker as unlike Le Bon as almost anyone in nineteenth-century thought could be, referencing twice the anarchist philosopher and revolutionist Peter Kropotkin. The conjunction brings us back to the philosophical underpinnings of all disaster response, practical and intellectual. Beyond them lie larger questions about how human beings behave in the absence of coercive authority and what kind of societies are possible.

The Revolutionist and the Reactionary

Le Bon was born a year before William James and Peter Kropotkin, and though their conclusions were wildly different, all three were preoccupied with similar problems about violence, human nature, and social possibility. At the end of his teens, Le Bon moved to Paris to study medicine and stayed on for seven decades, until his death in 1931, as a prolific writer of books popularizing and sometimes entirely bastardizing the science of the day. Kept at arm's length by the university scientists who covered the same ground, he grew bitter about that—though he seems to have started out cynical. Even his early writings contain harshly dismissive statements about women, the poor, and nonwhite people. He speculated that South America was doomed to incessant revolution "because these populations have no national soul and therefore no stability. A people of half-castes is always ungovernable." Like many in the era immediately after Darwin's *Origin of Species* appeared, he mutated evolutionary theory into self-aggrandizing fantasy. He believed ardently in psychologies rooted in race and inherited mental states among races and classes and pursued popular pseudoscience methodologies. Behind his writing seethes a European male's incessant anxiety about being overtaken by other categories of human being. Science moved on, but Le Bon did not, and only one of his books ever had wide currency, so wide that in many ways we have never recovered from its argument.

In his highly influential *The Crowd*, he proposed that when individuals gather, they lose themselves and are swept along by primordial forces: someone in a crowd "is no longer himself, but has become an automaton who has ceased to be guided by his will. Moreover, by the mere fact that he forms part of an organised crowd, a man descends several rungs in the ladder of civilisation. Isolated, he may be a cultivated individual; in a crowd, he is a barbarian—that is, a creature acting by instinct. He possesses the spontaneity, the violence, the ferocity, and also the enthusiasm and heroism of primitive beings, whom he further tends to resemble by the facility with which he allows himself to be impressed by words and images—which would be entirely without action on each of the isolated individuals composing the crowd—and to be induced to commit acts contrary to his most obvious interests and his best-known habits."

To believe this is to believe that the very act of agglomerating into groups makes humans go mad and that the public is inherently dangerous. Before Le Bon, insurrectionary crowds were denigrated for being made up of people of criminal propensity or the deranged or imagined as being tinder lit by a demagogue's match. Le Bon's argument was that instead the crowd itself produced a form of irresponsible madness, a whole far worse than the sum of its parts. Because disasters push the population out into the streets and into collective solutions—community kitchens, emergency shelters, bucket brigades—disaster produces some of the crowds that made Le Bon and his ilk so anxious toward the end of the nineteenth century and into the twentieth. That anxiety never quite dissipated. As in San Francisco in 1906, some of them saw in any assembly of people an incipient mob. Crowds did have power, including the power to change policies and sometimes governments. In his book on revolution, Le Bon claimed such upheavals degenerated into "the effort of the instinctive to overpower the rational. This is why the liberation of popular passions is so dangerous. The torrent, once escaped from its bed, does not return until it has spread devastation far and wide." Like Hobbes, Le Bon believed the authorities reined in an essentially savage humanity. Prince subscribed to this kind of thinking too when he wrote of "the primitive instincts of man." The belief that we have a bestial nature refined by the march of civilization was a key tenet of the nineteenth-century European world, anxious to justify colonization of indigenous and tribal peoples and to see their own achievement as more than material progress.

Disaster produces crowds by amassing people in the streets and in shelters and defines them as a crowd by giving them a shared loss and destabilization to which the remedies are often collective. Crowds are not always a benign phenomenon. Though altruism usually prevails in the moment of disaster, scapegoating sometimes follows. The most appalling such postdisaster incident was after the Great Kanto Earthquake that struck central Japan at noon on September 1, 1923. More than 125,000 died in the catastrophe, many by fires caused by broken gas mains and overturned cookstoves in that land of wooden houses crowded together. Additionally, the massive quake made many wells go cloudy. Rumors that the fires were arson and the wells were poisoned by radicals or by Koreans led to hideous massacres. About six thousand Koreans and people mistaken for Koreans were killed by vigilante groups, along with some socialists. In some cases, these people were protected by the military and by police; in others these authorities colluded or led the murders and encouraged the rumors that devastated the unpopular groups. Military police who claimed to fear that anarchists would take advantage of the disaster to overthrow the government kidnapped the anarchist writer Sakae Osugi, his six-year-old nephew, and his lover, Noe Ito, beat the three to death, and threw their bodies down a well. After disaster, savage crowds sometimes appear, but as in San Francisco, the most brutal acts in the aftermath of the Kanto earthquake were not to sabotage the status quo but to preserve it, with the collusion of or at the hands of the authorities. The same is true of lynch mobs in the old South and the Nazi crowds of Kristallnacht—they were the majority brutally enforcing their own privilege over the rights of the minority. Samuel Prince might have tested Le Bon against what actually happened in Halifax to question this fear, but he did not. He did, however, turn to someone who saw human beings individually and in the aggregate very differently.

Peter Kropotkin saw the state and coercive institutions as instead the source of social ills and believed in the essential goodness of unregulated humanity. He became one of the great revolutionaries of the turn of the twentieth century, though his route to that role was an unlikely one. He was born a prince into a society both elegant and barbaric. His aristocratic Russian father owned fifteen hundred "souls," as the serfs were called when they were described as property. Each large landowner prided himself on a medieval independence in a country far from the industrial capitalism of western Europe. On the great estates, almost everything from piano tuning to making harnesses for the horses was done by serfs and servants, and many masters had their own orchestras. Kropotkin's father had bought two fine first violinists "with their large families, for a handsome sum of money, from his sisters," forced serfs to marry against their wishes, and sent those men who defied him into the army. Kropotkin's mother died early, and the servants became allies in protecting the boy and his beloved brother Alexander against their stern father and even invited them to their dances.

The boys responded gratefully to these people. When he was still very young, his French tutor told him about Mirabeau, a moderate in the

French Revolution who renounced his aristocratic title, and Kropotkin was inspired to drop the honorific before his name. The sweet-natured and tenderhearted Kropotkin's politics might by his contemporary and countryman Leo Tolstoy have been called love. The two later became colleagues whose political affinities outweighed their differences; the Christian anarchist Tolstoy even corrected the proofs of an essay of Kropotkin's, and the two worked together to relocate the persecuted pacifist sect of the Doukhobors, or Spirit Wrestlers, from Russia to western Canada. The playwright George Bernard Shaw met the former prince later in life and wrote, "Personally Kropotkin was amiable to the point of saintliness, and with his red full beard and loveable expression might have been a shepherd from the Delectable Mountains."

After an education in the czar's Corps of Pages, Kropotkin turned down the opportunity to join an elite military branch in the capital and pressed to be sent to Siberia to explore. "The five years that I spent in Siberia were for me a genuine education in life and human character," he wrote afterward, adding, "Siberia is not the frozen land buried in snow and peopled with exiles only that it is imagined to be, even by many Russians. In its southern parts it is as rich in natural productions as are the southern parts of Canada, which it resembles." He traveled over fifty thousand miles by boat and horse, across unmapped mountain ranges, down the Amur River with convoys of winter supplies and convicts for crew, through forests, into remote outposts, and, in disguise as a merchant, across the border into Chinese Manchuria. He was already deeply discontented with his hierarchical society and passionate about amending injustice. During his years in the remote edges of the Russian empire, he lived and worked with peasants, prisoners, tribal peoples, and others far outside the usual acquaintance of most European aristocrats. He surveyed the Amur region of far northeastern Asia and later redrew the map of that continent—a prodigious achievement in geography and exploration. He might have had a good career as a scientist had his political passions not taken precedence. After an era as an explorer he became a radical, then a prisoner who made a daring escape, then an exile for many years, most of them in England. The Russian Revolution made it possible for him to return but was also a huge disappointment to him, a soaring moment of liberation that collapsed into a new authoritarian regime.

Mutual Aid Versus the Social Darwinists

In the middle of *Catastrophe and Social Change*, Samuel Prince suddenly references Kropotkin. "Catastrophe and the sudden termination of the normal which ensues become the stimuli of heroism and bring into play the great social virtues of generosity and of kindliness—which in one of its forms is mutual aid. The new conditions, perhaps it would be more correct to say, afford the occasion for their release," he writes on page 55, and on the next page he footnotes Kropotkin's 1902 treatise *Mutual Aid: A Factor of Evolution*. Two pages later, he adds, "Communication has transformed mutual aid into a term of worldwide significance. As at San Francisco, when from all directions spontaneous gifts were hurried to the stricken city . . . so it was at Halifax." Though that aid wasn't actually mutual; it was altruistic, given from afar by strangers who needed and expected nothing in return. Or perhaps it is mutual in a broader sense: such aid knits together a larger society in which standards of compassion and generosity are maintained. Those who give receive a sense of themselves as members of a civilized world in which they will receive aid when their need arises. But in Halifax itself the first aid was often directly mutual, when people who were themselves impacted reached out to others in need—Joe Glube, for example, distributing food and caring for the wounded while his home and business were smashed up and he himself essentially homeless. We often hear about heroes in disasters, but the window of time when acts of physical courage matter is often very brief, and those when generosity and empathy are more important to survival last for weeks, months, years.

Mutual aid means that every participant is both giver and recipient in acts of care that bind them together, as distinct from the one-way street of charity. In this sense it is reciprocity, a network of people cooperating to meet each others' wants and share each others' wealth. When the Mission District residents in earthquake-torn San Francisco refused to let institutional kitchens replace their community kitchens, they were refusing to let mutual aid give way to charity, which would define them as the needy with nothing to give rather than the community with everything to give each other. When Dorothy Day established the Catholic Worker, she endeavored to make the aid mutual by making the people they served active participants in the work projects. In flood-ravaged New Orleans, the radical group Common Ground Relief's slogan is "Solidarity, Not Charity." In Halifax, Prince noted, "the preference upon the part of the refugee for plural leadership and decision" and "the resentment which succeeds the intrusion of strangers in relief leadership." People preferred to care for each other rather than to be cared for by strangers or governed by others.

Altruism and charity are distinct if not in the acts themselves at least in the surrounding atmosphere: altruism reaches across with a sense of solidarity and empathy; charity hands down from above. The latter always runs the risk of belittling, patronizing, or otherwise diminishing its recipients in underscoring the difference between those who have and those who need. It takes away a sense of self while giving material aid. Giving and receiving can have strange reciprocities. In Burma, Buddhist monks traditionally live on alms. Being allowed to give confers a blessing on the giver, so much so that during the 2007 uprising in that nation some monks refused to accept anything from the military and their families, thereby cutting them off from the workings of spiritual advancement as surely as excommunication exiles a Catholic. It also means that the monks live on faith in the generosity of others (though poverty in Burma after the 2008 typhoon became so dire that some monasteries resorted to buying food, because the laypeople were themselves destitute and hungry). Giving is itself the gift, and there can be a deep mutuality between giver and recipient in the horizontality of altruism rather than the hierarchy of charity. More complex exchanges take place in the arts: is it the writer or singer who is giving the work, or the reader or listener who brings the gift of attention, or are they knit together in a mutuality whose give-and-take is complicated? Seen in a larger context, continual exchanges knit together a society, form the conversation of which it is made. This is the aid described by Kropotkin that is mutual and thereby foundational to community and society.

The term *mutual aid* has become standard language for disaster preparedness. In that context, it describes the agreements among agencies to assist each other in crises, often by crossing the jurisdictional or geographical lines of their everyday activities. In California, the statewide system is called "EMMA," Emergency Managers Mutual Aid, born out of the realization after the 1994 Northridge earthquake near Los Angeles that services needed to be coordinated. The nationwide EMAC, or Emergency Management Assistance Compact, is "an interstate mutual aid agreement that allows states to assist one another in responding to all kinds of natural and man-made disasters." Most typically, such mutual aid is represented by the out-of-state firefighters who gather at the site of huge wildfires and the experts in search and rescue and other specialties who gather at the sites of more urban disasters.

Kropotkin would have argued that the mutual aid evident in the aftermath of the Halifax explosion demonstrated not only ordinary human but broader evolutionary tendencies. He begins his book *Mutual Aid* by saying, "Two aspects of animal life impressed me most during the journeys which I made in my youth in Eastern Siberia and Northern Manchuria. One of them was the extreme severity of the struggle for existence which most species of animals have to carry on against an inclement Nature. And the other was that even in those few spots where animal life teemed in abundance, I failed to find—although I was eagerly looking for it—that bitter struggle for the means of existence, among animals belonging to the same species, which was considered by most Darwinists (though not always by Darwin himself) as the dominant characteristic of the struggle for life, and the main factor of evolution." In the late nineteenth century, Darwin's work had been taken as scientific confirmation that life was essentially competitive, each pitted against each for survival. (A century before, Jean-Jacques Rousseau had stood conventional belief on its head to argue that a decent original humanity had been corrupted by civilization.)

This was often extrapolated into what later was called Social Darwinism, the premise of which was that the conduct of contemporary human beings inevitably echoed their own primordial behavior and nature's essential bleakness. It justified callousness toward those who lost out in the economic struggle: they did so because they were unfit, ill adapted, and lazy, rather than because the system was unfair—a common justification of colonial rapacity, the deprivation of the poor, and basis for theories of racial inferiority. They deserved it, or they were at least doomed and could not be saved, if the forces that trampled them down were as inevitable as nature itself. Social Darwinists also tend to share Thomas Malthus's belief that life must almost inevitably be a scramble for the scarce resources of the earth, a scramble in which some must die because there is not enough for all. Capitalism's fundamental premise is scarcity, while a lot of tribal and gift economies operate on a basis of abundance. Their generosity is both an economic and an ethical premise.

Mutual Aid countered a whole worldview, but it was prompted in particular by a celebrated 1888 essay by "Darwin's bulldog," the English scientist Thomas Henry Huxley. In "The Struggle for Existence in Human Society," he argued that primordial humans "strove with their enemies and their competitors; they preyed upon things weaker or less cunning than themselves; they were born, multiplied without stint, and died, for thousands of generations, alongside the mammoth, the urus, the lion, and the hyena, whose lives were spent in the same way; and they were no more to be praised or blamed." It was a spectacularly grim view of human beings as animals governed by the rules of this stingy nature. That view is pervasive in contemporary society. It is behind, for example, the statement in a potboiler book on the Halifax explosion that "the elements of civilized society were broken down and for many all that remained was the jungle law of self preservation." Civilization was thought to be a veneer beneath which the beast still snarled, and early humankind and "primitive" peoples were usually imagined as living harsh, chaotic, desperate, and deeply isolated lives, enemies to each other in pursuit of a life that was inevitably described as struggle for survival.

Kropotkin challenged the foundations of this worldview: if animal life itself and earlier and simpler forms of human society were not ruthlessly competitive, then the justification for the selfish side of contemporary human society as natural or inevitable would crumble. He argued instead that cooperation is as or more important a factor in survival, beginning with mutual aid among insects, birds, and mammals. Subsequent chapters dealt with social contracts and structures among all kinds of peoples, including medieval and modern European society. He noted that rather than being individuals pitted against each other, most traditional and tribal peoples live in extended families, or clans, whose organization shapes all relationships and conduct, who share wealth, cooperatively maintain community codes of conduct, and collectively punish violations against them. "The very persistence of the clan organization shows how utterly false it is to represent primitive mankind as a disorderly agglomeration of individuals, who obey only their individual passions, and take advantage of their personal force and cunningness against all other representatives of the species. Unbridled individualism is a modern growth, but it is not characteristic of primitive mankind." Later he elaborated, "For thousands and thousands of years, this organization has kept men together, even though there was no authority whatosever to impose it."

His indignation was inspired by his great kindness as well as his observations in Asia's far northeast and his wide readings in the literature of travelers, ethnographers, and historians. And it was shaped by his political agenda, for by the time he wrote *Mutual Aid* he was one of the theorists of the political philosophy called *anarchism*. The word means, literally, in Greek, "the absence of government." It is often used nowadays as a synonym for mayhem, chaos, and riotous behavior because many imagine that the absence of authority is equally the absence of order. Anarchists are idealists, believing human beings do not need authorities and the threat of violence to govern them but are instead capable of governing themselves by cooperation, negotiation, and mutual aid. They stand on one side of a profound debate about human nature and human possibility. On the other side, the authoritarian pessimists believe that order comes only at the point of a gun or a society stacked with prisons, guards, judges, and punishments. They believe that somehow despite the claimed vileness of the many, the few whom they wish to endow with power will use it justly and prudently, though the evidence for this could most politely be called uneven. The cases drawn from disaster largely contradict this belief. It is often the few in power rather than the many without who behave viciously in disaster, and those few do so often exactly because they subscribe to the fearful beliefs of Huxley, Le Bon, and others.

Diggers and Survivors

That an Anglican priest like Samuel Prince was familiar with the writings of a self-proclaimed "revolutionist" shows how much more mainstream the political philosophy of anarchy was a century ago. William James mentioned anarchists offhandedly in his writings, and Dorothy Day was deeply influenced by the anarchist thinkers and activists so visible in her youth and was herself one in many ways. Among the many strains of radical thought in their time, anarchism was an important one.

The mainstream has forgotten it now, though it was never an ideology like state socialism or Marxism. Rather, many anarchists argue that they have merely described and analyzed the ancient and widespread ways people organized themselves for millennia, with an emphasis on equality and liberty for all. They were not inventing anything new but reclaiming something ancient.

This is why what happens in disasters matters for political philosophy: the hierarchies, administrations, and institutions—the social structure— tend to fall apart, but what results tends to be anarchy in Kropotkin's sense of people coming together in freely chosen cooperation rather than the media's sense of disorderly savagery. The debate is at least as old as the English Civil Wars that prompted the timid authoritarian Thomas Hobbes to imagine that the only alternative to chaos was a strong central authority. A precursor to the Social Darwinists, Hobbes argued from the premise that the primordial human condition was a war fought by each against each, so brutal and incessant that it was impossible to develop industry or even agriculture or the arts while that condition persisted. It's this description that culminates in his famous epithet "And the life of man, solitary, poor, nasty, brutish, and short." It was a fiction to which he brought to bear another fiction, that of the social contract by which men agree to submit to rules and a presiding authority, surrendering their right to ravage each other for the sake of their own safety. The contract was not a bond of affection or identification, not a culture or religion binding together a civilization, only a convenience. Men in his view, as in that of many other European writers of the period, are stark, blank, mechanical creatures, windup soldiers social only by strategy and not by nature.

What is curious for a modern reader about the society imagined by Hobbes and then the social Darwinists is that it appears to consist entirely of unaffiliated men. The relationships between lovers, spouses, parents and children, siblings, kinfolk, friends, colleagues, and compatriots are absent, though those are clearly among the more ancient rather than modern aspects of human life. The world they imagine looks something like an old-fashioned business district during a working day, when countless people venture out to do economic battle with each other. But even those people are formed into corporations and firms whose internal cooperation is as or more important to their functioning than external competition. In the Halifax explosion, the Lloyd family undermines that of Hobbes just because it acts like a family: two parents and seven children wait for one more child in a ruined house in a dangerous place. The soldier who drives them forth with a gun perhaps does illustrate the Hobbesian coercive order, or perhaps illustrates that such an order can seem a lot like the selfish disorder it's supposed to have replaced. But on 9/11, even near Wall Street, the employees of the big brokerage firms acted with mutual aid and more.

Three hundred and fifty years after Hobbes, the biobehavioral scientists Shelley E. Taylor and Laura Cousino Klein concluded that contrary to the longtime assumption about how human beings respond to danger, women in particular often gather together to share concerns and abilities. They conclude that "this 'tend-and-befriend' pattern is a sharp contrast to the 'fight-or-flight' behavior pattern that has long been considered the principal responses to stress by both men and women. For women, that didn't quite make any sense from an evolutionary standpoint. It's a rare female of any species that would leave her baby to fend for itself while she physically takes on an aggressor. Females are more likely to protect their children and bond with other females who can help provide protection in the process." In other words, crises and stresses often strengthen social bonds rather than breed competition and isolation.

It's worth remembering that as the solitary Hobbes was writing *Leviathan*, the Diggers were staking their claim to live collectively in England. The Diggers were a small group of poor rural people who in 1649 moved onto common land and began to cultivate it by hand to grow subsistence crops—hence their name Diggers—and to build shelters from the forest wood. Theirs was a supremely practical gesture—the majority of these peasants were hungry and displaced, though their spokesperson was the educated visionary Gerard Winstanley. A handful of other groups of Diggers arose elsewhere in England. As claimants to a few small parcels of land, they posed a minor threat to the local gentry, but as radically democratic utopians questioning the legitimacy of the current order, they posed a major one to state and hierarchy. They argued on biblical grounds against the dividing up of the public land into private plots in that era when the commons was trickling into the hands of the wealthy. They proposed instead communal ownership and "working together, and feeding together as Sons of one Father, members of one Family; not one Lording over another, but all looking upon each other as equals in the

Creation." The Diggers' original name had been the True Levellers, after the derogatory name for other rural rebels who wanted to level society. That these anarchic rebels appeared at exactly the same time that Hobbes argued that only an authoritarian state saves us from our own savagery suggests that his answers to crisis were far from inevitable conclusions.

One of the more amusing recent manifestations of Hobbes came as entertainment, starting with the 2000 American television series *Survivor* (modeled after a 1997 Swedish version that was also wildly successful). The shows seemed to reference *Lord of the Flies* and other epics of savage regression and primordial competition, but merely dropping a bunch of people in a remote location and asking them to cope might have produced uneventful cooperation or unpredictable improvisation. Instead, the show's creators and directors divided the cast into teams. The teams competed with each other for rewards. Eliminating fellow members was one of the competitive games they were obliged to play to increase insecurity and drama within teams. The goal was to produce a single winner rather than a surviving society, a competitive pyramid rather than a party of cooperation. Toiling for food and shelter was overshadowed by the scramble to win out in a wholly gratuitous competition based on arbitrary rules. Capitalism is based on the idea that there is not enough to go around, and the rules for *Survivor* built scarcity and competition and winners and losers into the system. These people were not in the wilderness but living under an arbitrary autocratic regime that might as well have been Los Angeles or London. The producers pretended we were seeing raw human nature in crisis conditions but stacked the deck carefully to produce Hobbesian behavior—or rather marketplace behavior, which amounts to the same thing here.

Another way to put it: the premise is that these people were surviving a disaster that consisted of being stranded in a remote place without the usual resources. They were in fact surviving a very different disaster that consisted of the social order enforced upon them from above and outside. Which is to say that the shows were in many ways an accurate model of the way things are, but from inside rather than outside the systems that usually contain us. We are nearly all forced to play arbitrary and competitive games that pit us against each other, and the consequences can be dire. A recent story on water in the arid nation of Yemen on the tip of the Arabian peninsula concludes, "Yemen's experience offers a cautionary tale that shows the limits of free-market solutions to environmental problems. Instead of conserving water as it becomes scarcer and more precious, more and more Yemenis are rushing faster and faster to extract it from the earth and capture it from rains for profit, pushing the country toward an ecological nightmare." The country is in danger of running out of water completely because a competitive market system has replaced the traditional cooperative regulation of water. Pure competition is in this situation a disaster, as it is less dramatically in many others.

Dissent from Hobbes came long before Kropotkin and far more powerfully than the suppressed arguments of the Diggers. Few believed more fervently that we could do without government than the revolutionist Thomas Paine, igniter of the American Revolution, critic of the elite that steered that revolution away from true liberty for all, and enthusiast for the French Revolution before that went more brutally astray. In the 1791 book inspired by that latter insurrection, *The Rights of Man*, he described how well people actually functioned when the institutional structure vanished during that heady period when there was no longer a British government and not yet an American government. He wrote that during the two years of war with Britain "and for a longer period in several of the American States, there were no established forms of government. . . . Yet during this interval, order and harmony were preserved as inviolate as in any country in Europe. . . . The instant formal government is abolished, society begins to act. A general association takes place, and common interest produces common security. So far is it from being true, as has been pretended, that the abolition of any formal government is the dissolution of society, that it acts by a contrary impulse, and brings the latter the closer together." It's a revolutionary statement: government represses the potential strength of civil society. He concludes confidently, "In short, man is so naturally a creature of society, that it is almost impossible to put him out of it." In other words, human beings are gregarious, cooperative animals who need no authority to make them so; it is their nature.

Almost any of us would, when asked, answer that the societies of the industrialized world are capitalist—based on a model of competition and scarcity—but they are by no means wholly so. The radical economists J. K. Gibson-Graham (two women writing under one name) portray our society as an iceberg, with competitive capitalist practices visible above the waterline and below all kinds of relations of aid and cooperation by families, friends, neighbors, churches, cooperatives, volunteers, and voluntary organizations from softball leagues to labor unions, along with activities outside the market, under the table, bartered labor and goods, and more, a bustling network of uncommercial enterprise. Kropotkin's mutual-aid tribes, clans, and villages never went away entirely, even among us, here and now.

In disaster, as Samuel Prince himself noted, they become visible and important. People in a disaster zone temporarily function by entirely different rules, but even those far away often become generous with gifts of time, goods, and money. You can argue about whether these other economies constitute a subversive underworld or a prop to the official free-market economy, but they exist everywhere and they keep alive much that would otherwise die out. The same argument could be made that in disaster the altruism and mutual aid of fellow city dwellers and of those from afar relieve the state of its duty to take care of its citizens. If you believe in such a duty—and neither anarchists nor conservatives do. Perhaps the most important point here is that a shadow or underground economy that could be measured in emotion as well as effect comes into the light in disaster.

In his *Catastrophe and Social Change*, Prince wanted to argue that disaster led to change. In Mexico City, the subject of the next section of this book, it did lead to or at least catalyze profound and lasting social and political change. But the change that matters is not down the road, the end of a chain reaction. It is present immediately, instantly, when people demonstrate resourcefulness, altruism, improvisational ability, and kindness. A disaster produces chaos immediately, but the people hit by that chaos usually improvise a fleeting order that is more like one of Kropotkin's mutual-aid societies than it is like the society that existed before the explosion or the earthquake or the fire. It liberates people to revert to a latent sense of self and principle, one more generous, braver, and more resourceful than what we ordinarily see.

Kropotkin's *Mutual Aid* argues beautifully that cooperation rather than competition can be key to survival. It does not explain desires that go deeper than survival. When the sailor grabbed the Mi'kmaq child and ran with it into the forest before the *Mont Blanc* exploded, there was nothing mutual about it. He was increasing his own risk for a stranger of another race and region. When the doctors and nurses crowded onto the trains, the same was true. And when Vincent Coleman rushed back into the telegraph office where he died, he could expect no direct or personal return, any more than could Harold Floyd, giving his life to make crucial phone calls. In the Halifax explosion, as in most disasters, some people risked their lives and sometimes gave them for others, and they gave of themselves in ways that would never be reciprocated. Some elements of this may last—for example, with the Halifax orphans who were cared for by relatives and strangers for years afterward.

Any configuration of humanity in disaster needs to include altruism as well as solidarity. Such altruism is present throughout ordinary life as well in the huge numbers of everyday volunteers feeding the hungry and caring for the sick and solitary and lonely, whether that means driving people to medical appointments (networks of such drivers exist across the United States), staffing soup kitchens, delivering Meals-on-Wheels, becoming Big Brothers and Big Sisters, tutoring at-risk youth, reading to the blind, caring for the aged, writing to prisoners, and far more, the kinds of support that organizations like Day's Catholic Worker specialize in. Such activity does much to mitigate the cruelties of a competitive system. There are amusing arguments to prove that it is all really self-serving in some obscure evolutionary capacity, but the most that can be said is that in taking care of others such altruists are taking care of their sense of self, their ideals, and their hopes for society.

After the psychiatrist Viktor Frankl survived the Nazi concentration camp Auschwitz, he asked himself what distinguished those who made it from those who didn't. He argued that finding and holding meaning matters most. He spoke of "a will to meaning in contrast to the pleasure principle (or as we could also term it, the will to pleasure) on which Freudian psychoanalysis is centered, as well as in contrast to the will to power." Many were murdered outright, but in the harsh conditions of the camp those who lost their sense of purpose more readily died; those who had something to live for struggled and sometimes survived. Frankl concluded that it is "a dangerous misconception of mental hygiene to assume that what man needs in the first place is equlibrium or, as it is called in biology, 'homeostasis,' i.e., a tensionless state. What man actually needs is not a tensionless state but rather the striving and struggling for a worthwhile goal, a freely chosen task. What he needs is not the discharge of tension at any cost but the call of a potential meaning waiting to be fulfilled by him. . . . If architects want to strengthen a decrepit arch, they increase the load which is laid upon it, for thereby the parts are joined more firmly together."

The evolutionary argument for altruism could draw from Frankl to argue that we need meaning and purpose in order to survive, and need them so profoundly we sometimes choose them over survival. The act of so doing bequeaths that meaning and purpose to the community at large—the moral equivalent of war that is already with us in myriad ways. Thus it is that a sacrificed hero is said to be immortal—which is sometimes a sentimental lie, sometimes a truth about the way a society is built out of such acts. In them, a more expansive idea of what it means to be human survives, and with it a stronger sense of society, those things that are killed by cowardice and selfishness. Or you could argue with Kropotkin that for those who feel a deep enough sense of connection to the larger community, sacrificing themselves to ensure its well-being makes perfect sense. The argument is often made that parents, particularly mothers, will sacrifice themselves to save their children. The usual explanation is about genetic survival, but a larger sense of social survival motivates the heroism seen in Halifax. Either way, it defines us as members of a larger whole.

The Halifax explosion was both a particularly hideous disaster and a particularly clear-cut example of such generosity beyond reason. And certainly there is more mutual aid and more than mutual aid in everyday life than has been accounted for. The real question is not why this brief paradise of mutual aid and altruism appears but rather why it is ordinarily overwhelmed by another world order—not eradicated, for it never ceases to exist quietly, but we miss it at the best of times, most of us, and feel bleak or lonely for its lack. Disaster, along with moments of social upheaval, is when the shackles of conventional belief and role fall away and the possibilities open up.

FROM THE BLITZ AND
THE BOMB TO VIETNAM

The Blitz

On September 7, 1940, flashes lit up the darkness of wartime London and the first of fifty-seven consecutive nights of aerial attack by the Luftwaffe began. The sky buzzed with fighter and bomber planes, the latter of which dropped more than a thousand bombs and incendiary devices, causing 250 acres near the London docks to burn, and igniting forty other major fires. The initial bombs targeted industrial areas, but during the Blitz, homes, shops, churches, offices, factories, warehouses, streets, and buses would be smashed and splintered, Buckingham Palace would be hit while the king and queen were in residence, and a vast archipelago of craters began to dimple the city. Civilian air-raid wardens would try to guide their neighborhood's denizens to safety; the newly formed civilian fire squads would rush to put out the fires, knowing that the bombers would use the flames as targets for another round; and ambulance teams would make their way to the sites that had been hit. Spotter lights raked the night sky; antiaircraft fire rattled. Over the course of the war about sixty thousand British civilians were killed in the attack on their island, and tens of thousands of buildings were destroyed. About half of the total losses in buildings and lives were in the London area, where more than eight thousand tons of bombs fell, and only a small percentage of buildings survived unscathed.

Military and government officials had worried for decades about how the civilian public would react to an air war and presumed they would react appallingly. As social scientist R. W. Titmuss summarized in 1950, "The experts foretold a mass outbreak of hysterical neurosis among the civilian population. . . . Under this strain, many people would regress to an earlier level of needs and desires. They would behave like frightened and unsatisfied children." Eighteen "eminent psychiatrists . . . privately warned in 1938 that in the coming war three psychiatric casualties could be expected for every one physical." By one estimate, this would have meant three to four million mental cases within months of the beginning of the Blitz. Certainly those directing the bombing raids on both Britain and Germany (and later, Japan) believed that the onslaughts would have profound psychological impact with important strategic consequences, and so the bombing campaigns were immense, taking a huge toll in human life—of both civilians and bomber crews—and city structures.

Benito Mussolini himself wrote, "Once a raid has been experienced false alarms are incessant and a state of panic remains in which work comes to a standstill." Churchill worried that a helpless, hopeless public would overwhelm the army with the chaos of their neediness. The historian Mark Connelly adds, "The British working class was thought to be particularly susceptible to panic and disillusionment in the face of an aerial onslaught. . . . When it came to shelters, the government considered it best to protect people in small groups. Communal shelters, it was argued, would create conditions for an agitator's field day. It would also encourage a 'deep shelter' mentality, leading people to become molelike tunnel dwellers who would never resume their jobs in vital war industries."

People did take to the tunnels, despite the discouragement, and did so communally. The London public began buying tickets to ride the Underground system but went down there only to shelter overnight. "Thousands more turn the tube stations into vast dormitories every night—a kind of lie-down strike which at first perplexed the authorities, who could not think what to do with passengers who paid their threehapence and then proceeded to encamp quietly on the platforms," wrote the journalist Mollie Panter-Downes in 1940. "The latest semiofficial ruling is that the practice can be continued. The Ministries of Transport and Home Security, however, have appealed to the public not to use the tube as a shelter except in cases of urgent necessity. The urgent necessity of many of the sleepers who doss down on the platforms nightly is that they no longer have homes to go to." They had been bombed out. Eventually, those in charge were obliged to install bunks, sanitation facilities, and more, though the Underground never held more than a small percentage of the London area's eight million. People found reassurance in the deep-underground station platforms and in proximity to others, though photographs from the time make it clear the concrete labyrinths were neither particularly comfortable nor clean. Some spread out to camp in forests, caves, and the countryside outside London. Many became so inured to falling bombs they chose to stay home and chance death for a good night's sleep. Connelly says, "The people's role in their own defense and destiny was downplayed in order to stress an old-fashioned division of leaders and led."

When unfamiliar explosions went off near the Bethnal Green Underground entrance, hurrying people slipped on a wet, dimly lit stairway and fell atop each other—and 173 were suffocated, including 62 children. (This was due not to panic or selfishness but to the poor design of the place and the physics of tightly packed crowds: those in the back cannot see what trouble is up front, and any movement is amplified and extended by the mass of people—as happens annually in the crush during the hajj in Mecca nowadays.) That story was long suppressed. There was trauma, crime, and opportunism, and people knew it—but most people endured the bombings without losing their minds, principles, or sense of purpose. Despite early fears, Churchill and the government found the idea of unshakable British morale useful and made much of it. A 1940 film showing the nocturnal bombing, the defense, and citizens in the morning carrying on daily life amid craters, rubble, and shattered windows was titled *London Can Take It*. It featured an American voice-over saying in tough tones, "The army of the people swings into action" and "There is no panic, no fear, no despair. London can take it." In recent years, the story of their resolve has been challenged from the left as right-wing propaganda, though the resoluteness can be spun many ways: as superior national disposition, as patriotic dedication, or as resilience that had nothing to do with nationalism, nationality, or deference.

As people strove to save themselves and their community, some lost conviction in the reality or the rightness of many hierarchies. Olivia Cockett, a government clerk in her late twenties, wrote at the time, "On the first night of the Blitz I put out an incendiary bomb, alone for some minutes, though help came after I had dealt with it. This incident has come back to my mind on unexpected occasions. I was being 'put on' by my boss, and had resented it for some time. After the bomb, I stood up to him, thinking, 'If a blasted incendiary didn't frighten me and I dealt with it, why should I be afraid of him?' This has resulted in a general boldness of thought and action." A mother of two Cockett's age wrote that after surviving the raids, "I feel much more certainty and self-confidence . . . as a result of the discovery that I am not the coward I thought, and have more good in me . . . than I would have believed." Drawn away from personal problems and old concerns, people entered the intensified present of disaster. Virginia Woolf's nephew Quentin Bell reported that "from the time when she literally came under fire, the talk of suicide ceased" and commented, "Fate provided a sort of cure, or so it seems, in the form of actual rather than imagined dangers." Woolf herself wrote on September 22, 1940, "This wet day—we think of weather now as it affects invasions, not as weather that we like or dislike personally."

Tom Harrisson, who was there at the time directing the Mass-Observation surveys of wartime behavior, writes in his history *Living Through the Blitz*, that there had "in particular, been a massive, largely unconscious cover-up of the more disagreeable facts of 1940–1. . . . It amounts to a form of intellectual pollution: but pollution by perfume." Still, he concluded that though the "blitz was a terrible experience for millions" it was not "terrible enough to disrupt the basic decency, loyalty (e.g., family ties), morality, and optimism of the vast majority." The Blitz is unusual as a disaster in which public behavior is remembered in a positive glow, though that memory singles out the Britons in wartime as anomalies rather than akin to those in most other disasters. Three weeks into the London Blitz, Panter-Downes wrote, "The courage, humor, and kindliness of ordinary people continue to be astonishing under conditions that possess many of the features of a nightmare." People adjusted to the horrific circumstances; wonderful or horrible, the extraordinary becomes the ordinary. One survivor said of the beginning, "Once you've been through three nights of bombing, you can't help feeling safe the fourth time. So the only real panic I saw was then."

Many felt private fear and enormous strain but braced themselves by putting on a good front, and one famous effect of the Blitz was the relaxing of boundaries between strangers and between types of people. Privilege mattered: the wealthy were often able to get out of harm's way, while the poor and often the middle class were not, but some divides softened. Cockett describes herself whistling on her way to work after a particularly bad night of bombing and going up to a porter who was also whistling to say, "The tune for today is *Serenade in the Night*, please," at which they both laughed. An American witness, Mary Lee Settle, noted that "the English were discovering each other with the freedom of strangers, lurched by war out of their silences, often friendly, sometimes with the direct belligerence of the stripped down." A British writer added, "New tolerances are born between people; offsetting the paleness of worn nerves and the lining of sorrow there occurs a marvellous incidence of smiles where smiles have never been before; an unsettling vista of smiles, for one wondered how unsympathetic life could have been before, one was ashamed to reflect that it had needed a war to disinter the state of everyday comradeship." Disinter—as if it were that something vital had been buried during peacetime and was resurrected amid carnage and ruin. The Blitz was like most disasters: one in which some were killed, many bereaved and injured, many escaped death by a hairbreadth, and the great majority were witnesses and survivors in a drama that left them relatively unscathed. By some accounts, the greatest trauma of the London Blitz was the mass evacuation of London-area children that tore apart families and placed children in unfamiliar, sometimes unfriendly, homes. Many, however, stuck it out in the epicenter of danger, some by choice, some for lack of choice.

One young woman sheltered with her boyfriend's parents in northern London on the third night of the Blitz. In the long account she wrote the next day, she complained that her hostess made them all tea "just for something to do" and added that "that's one trouble about the raids, people do nothing but make tea and expect you to drink it." The hostess, identified only as Mrs. R., would cry "Is that a bomb?" with every thud, and her husband would grunt back "No, s'a gun." (An antiaircraft gun.) The anonymous writer commented, "I felt all swollen up with irritation, a bloated sort of feeling, but actually it was fear, I knew very well. A horrid, sick sort of fear, it's quite different from worry." She and her boyfriend went out into the garden, sat on the long grass, and found that the warm, beautiful summer night was "made more beautiful than ever by the red glow from the East, where the docks were burning." She fixed the scene in her mind, knowing it was historic, and "I wasn't frightened any more, it was amazing. . . . The searchlights were beautiful, it's like watching the end of the world as they swoop from one end of the sky to the other."

A bomb fell two streets away. Another landed nearer as they raced inside, came near enough to buffet her with waves "like bathing in a rough sea." She found herself clutching the floor as if to keep from falling while dust was everywhere, her mouth was full of plaster, and Mr. R yelled out contradictory orders to stay still and do something. The house was wrecked, the front door jammed, and so they climbed out a broken window. When people around them responded with anxiety to their blood-streaked, dusty appearances, she realized, "I might have been hurt! Somehow, right up to that minute I had taken everything for granted, in a queer, brainless way, as if it was all perfectly ordinary." She was taken in by a neighbor who plied her with blankets and a hot-water bottle "for the shock," and when she said she wasn't in shock her hostess "referred darkly to 'delayed shock.'" And then she was left alone: "I lay there feeling indescribably happy and triumphant. 'I've been bombed!' I kept saying to myself, over and over again—trying the phrase on, like a new dress, to see how it fitted." She concluded, "It seems a terrible thing to say, when many people must have been killed and injured last night; but never in my whole life have I ever experienced such *pure and flawless happiness.*"

She was young, she'd survived with her love by her side, and she had fifty-five more nights of bombing to endure before London became only an intermittent target, but time and war did not change her memory. Thirty-five years later Harrisson, the Mass-Observation researcher who had surveyed response to the Blitz as it unfolded, followed up on her story. She had recently become a grandmother, and she looked back on her night of being bombed as a "peak experience—a sense of triumph and happiness" that she compared to the "experience of having a baby." Near-death experiences and encounters with one's own mortality are often clarifying, tools with which to cut away inessentials and cleave to the essence of life and purpose. Illnesses and accidents can produce the same reinvigorated gratitude and appetite.

After that night of heavy bombing, residents of West Ham, a slum neighborhood near the brightly burning London docks, were evacuated to a local school and told to wait for buses. The buses went to the wrong location one day, arrived during an air raid the next, so the evacuation was postponed, and the night after that the school was bombed and an unknown number—perhaps as many as four hundred—of men, women, and children were blown up. There were many Blitzes, some terrible, some fatal, at least one ecstatic. It seems to be because the virtues of the Blitz were so exaggerated that the counterversions have been so fierce in denouncing the positive aspects as myth. But they did exist, in the first-hand accounts of the moment and not only in propaganda, though they existed alongside privation, injustice, fear, loss, and death. The ways that war differs from disaster matter, but the similarities can be illuminating. And the Blitz stands alone as almost the only time when the way that most people behave in disaster has been highlighted rather than missed, though it was highlighted as something specific to wartime or to Britain rather than the way things usually go.

The Rebirth of Disaster Studies

A young Missouri-born soldier with a degree in sociology, Charles E. Fritz, was in Britain during the war. "As a captain in the U.S. Army Air Corps during World War II, I was stationed at several different air bases and command centers throughout England from 1943 to 1946," he wrote toward the end of his life. His words appear as the preface to his major statement on disaster, a riveting challenge to all conventional wisdom that was written in 1961 and never published (though it was released in 1996 as a university paper, a landmark the world passed by without noticing). By the time he arrived, Britain was five years into a war; there were chronic shortages of food, clothing, and housing; and tens of thousands of Americans had just arrived to further overstretch its resources. "Under those conditions, one might expect to find a nation of panicky, war weary people, embittered by the death and injuries to their family members and friends, resentful over their prolonged life style deprivations, anxious and disillusioned about the future, and, more generally, exhibiting personal and social behaviors indicating a state of low morale and esprit de corps. Instead, what one found was a nation of gloriously happy people, enjoying life to the fullest, exhibiting a sense of gaiety and love of life that was truly remarkable." Fritz had a splendid time, in part because "my access to British family life was greatly enhanced during those years by my courtship and subsequent marriage to Patricia Ware, a resident of Bath,

England, who worked throughout the war as a nursery school teacher." Bath was heavily bombed too.

At the end of the war, Fritz was assigned to the U.S. Strategic Bombing Survey, which prepared a monumental study on the effectiveness of the aerial bombing of Germany's civilians. The Germans had not been "demoralized" to any profound degree either, despite atrocities far worse than any England had endured, such as the firebombing that one night turned Dresden into an inferno in which more than twenty-five thousand people died. The study Fritz worked on concluded, "Under ruthless Nazi control they showed surprising resistance to the terror and hardships of repeated air attack, to the destruction of their homes and belongings, and to the conditions under which they were reduced to live. Their morale, their belief in ultimate victory or satisfactory compromise, and their confidence in their leaders declined, but they continued to work efficiently as long as the physical means of production remained. The power of a police state over its people cannot be underestimated." The aplomb of the British under bombardment was attributed to special national characteristics that became a matter of pride; the resoluteness of the Germans was attributed to grim subjugation. Fritz noted that their surveys revealed that "people living in heavily bombed cities had significantly higher morale than people in the lightly bombed cities" and that "neither organic neurologic disease nor psychiatric disorders can be attributed to nor are they conditioned by the air attacks." From there the survey went to Japan without him and reached similar conclusions about bombing's psychological effects there.

After his discharge, Fritz entered the University of Chicago to pursue graduate work in sociology and in 1950 became associate director of the Disaster Research Project of the university's National Opinion Research Center, the first organization to systematically study human behavior in disaster. The cold war had come quick on the heels of the world war, and the U.S. government was assembling a vast nuclear arsenal and worrying about how its own population would react in a nuclear war with the Soviet Union. These cold-war fears were the impetus for the earliest systematic studies of behavior in disasters, and such nuclear-related studies were commissioned into the 1960s. Since other than Hiroshima and Nagasaki in 1945 there were no urban nuclear calamities to study, the method was to look at natural and domestic disasters and extrapolate.

Thus began the little-known and remarkable field of disaster studies. At first, graduate students in psychology and anthropology were employed along with young sociologists like Fritz, but the sociologists soon took the lead and have ever since largely owned the field—and largely been ignored, despite their extraordinary conclusions. That is, they have had an influence on disaster preparedness and planning in some places and at some levels, but their conclusions have had little effect on the media, public opinion, and the bureaucrats and politicians responsible for developing disaster-response plans.

The initial expectations were grim; as with the British authorities twenty years earlier, the military commissioners wanted to know more about "Herd Reaction, Panic, Emergence of Leaders, and Recommendations for Guidance and Control of Masses." Writes one of the pioneering sociologists, "From oral histories obtained later from key officials involved, it is obvious that there was a strong belief [on the part of the Office of Civilian Defense] that the reaction would not be a good one, that there would be widespread 'panic' and a breakdown of the social order." The premise was that people were sheep, except when they were wolves, and the solution was to find out how best to herd them. But the sociologists would stand all this on its head. None was more glowing about the results than Fritz.

His conclusions began to appear in 1954, and a few more essays followed in 1957, but he hit his stride in 1961. That year, in an essay in a textbook on "the sociology of deviant behavior and social disorganization," he summed up his conclusions from the research he had conducted and directed throughout the 1950s. Like the long, unpublished report from the same year, it strikes a wholly new note, or rather picks up where William James had left off (and quotes James and Prince), but does so from the basis of methodical investigation of dozens of disasters. He described the conventional beliefs that in disaster "there are mass panics and wild stampedes. People trample one another and lose all sense of concern for their fellows. After panic has subsided—so the popular image suggests—many people are hysterical, or so stunned that they are helpless. Others turn to looting, pillaging, or other forms of selfish, exploitative behavior. The aftermath is widespread immorality, social conflict, and mental derangement." Later, he described another stereotype: "that disasters render people a dazed and helpless mass completely dependent on out-side aid for guidance and organization."

Those beliefs have yet to die. Naomi Klein's 2007 book *The Shock Doctrine* is a trenchant investigation of how economic policies benefit-ing elites are thrust upon people in times of crisis. But it describes those people in all the old, unexamined terms and sees the aftermath of disas-ter as an opportunity for conquest from above rather than a contest of power whose outcome is sometimes populist or even revolutionary. She speaks of disasters as creating "these malleable moments, when we are psychologically unmoored and physically uprooted" and describes one recent disaster as being akin to torture in producing "profound disorien-tation, extreme fear and anxiety, and collective regression." It's a surpris-ingly disempowering portrait from the Left and one that echoes the fears of the prewar British authorities, the apparent product of assumptions rather than research. In a public talk when the book appeared she said that in extreme crises "we no longer know who or where we are. We become like children, we look for daddies." If only she had read Fritz. But his treasure was buried 650 pages deep in a dreary textbook on deviancy and in a manuscript first released thirty-five years after it was written. His essays are essentially two versions of the same manifesto, though the unpublished one goes further in its conclusions. These conclusions have become standard thinking among disaster sociologists, though few put it as boldly as Fritz. Half a century later, his work conveys the thrill of a redemptive discovery, and though later sociologists have tamped down a little his exuberant optimism, they have largely confirmed his insights.

Fritz's first radical premise is that everyday life is already a disaster of sorts, one from which actual disaster liberates us. He points out that people suffer and die daily, though in ordinary times, they do so privately, separately. And he writes, "The traditional contrast between 'normal' and 'disaster' almost always ignores or minimizes these recurrent stresses of everyday life and their personal and social effects. It also ignores a histori-cally consistent and continually growing body of political and social anal-yses that points to the failure of modern societies to fulfill an individual's basic human needs for community identity."

Later he describes more specifically how this community identity is fed during disaster: "The widespread sharing of danger, loss, and deprivation produces an intimate, primarily group solidarity among the survivors, which overcomes social isolation, provides a channel for intimate communication and expression, and provides a major source of physical and emotional support and reassurance. . . . The 'outsider' becomes an 'insider,' the 'marginal man' a 'central man.' People are thus able to perceive, with a clarity never before possible, a set of underlying basic values to which all people subscribe. They realize that collective action is necessary for these values to be maintained and that individual and group goals are inextricably merged. This merging of individual and societal needs provides a feeling of belonging and a sense of unity rarely achieved under normal circumstances."

In other words, disaster offers temporary solutions to the alienations and isolations of everyday life: "Thus while the natural or human forces that created or precipitated the disaster appear hostile and punishing, the people who survive become more friendly, sympathetic, and helpful than in normal times. The categorical approach to human beings is curbed and the sympathetic approach enlarged. In this sense, disasters may be a physical hell, but they result however temporarily in what may be regarded as a kind of social utopia." What someone like Pauline Jacobson discovered as personal experience in the 1906 earthquake, Fritz affirmed as a general principle. He goes on to describe other ways disaster alters the psyche. He declares, "Disasters provide a temporary liberation from the worries, inhibitions, and anxieties associated with the past and future because they force people to concentrate their full attention on imme- diate moment-to-moment, day-to-day needs within the context of the present realities." They provide relief from that web of old griefs, habits, assumptions, and fears in which we are ordinarily caught: the effects are as psychological as they are practical. Temporary liberation is, again, strong language, and Fritz was bold in pressing his case for redemptive disaster.

Disasters, unlike everyday troubles but quite a bit like wars, pose straightforward problems to which solutions can be taken in the form of straighforward actions: "An essential feature of disaster is that the threats and dangers to the society come from outside the system and their causes can usually be clearly perceived and specified. This contrasts with many other crises where the threats arise within the system and it is difficult to isolate and identify a widely agreed-upon cause." The ability to address directly and clearly the troubles at hand provides a satisfaction hard to find in other times. Disaster loosens attachments to routine and convention: "Disaster provides a form of societal shock which disrupts habitual, institutionalized patterns of behavior and renders people amenable to social and personal change." Fritz sheds light on life during disaster, but the shadows cast on it are those of everyday life—of the alienation not just from each other but also from tangible solutions, heroic roles, and chances to begin anew that disaster provides. His essays hint that disaster is relatively easy, at least in knowing what to do and who to be. It is everyday life that is hard, with its complications and ambiguities, its problems to which no easy solution can be found, its conflicts between people because of economics and ideologies that become relatively insignificant in crisis.

The Bomb-Shelter Crisis

Fritz's 1950s disaster research was prompted by the threat of an all-out nuclear war between the United States and the Soviet Union, in which major cities and regions would be devastated and irradiated. Both sides wanted to believe that the apocalypse was survivable, by sheltering the population from radioactive fallout, if not direct hits, and preparing to rebuild everything afterward. The expectations at the time of Fritz's early work were grim, as grim as those of British officials before the Blitz. As the Truman-era Project East River put it, "The prevention and control of panics in time of attack are important tasks of civil defense. For the possibility always occurs that where people panic under attack, more death and injury may occur from that cause than from the direct effects of military weapons." In other words, the civilian population potentially posed a greater threat to each other and their own country than did the enemy's nuclear arsenal—an astonishingly grim conclusion, and one often repeated.

For more than a dozen years, the United States strongly encouraged its citizens to build their own fallout shelters. The idea was that after a nuclear war, survival would require sheltering for days, weeks, or months from the radiation before you surfaced to rebuild civilization. Some community shelters were constructed, and subterranean spaces were sometimes adapted to such use. Lavish, fully equipped large-scale shelters were built for the federal government's elected officials and key bureaucrats, who were convinced their own survival was crucial even as they gambled on everyone else's. While Soviets built collective shelters, American citizens were encouraged to build their own: destruction was the government's job, survival the citizen's. But the public stalled before the moral quandaries private shelters represented. The burning question was this: if you built a shelter for yourself and your family—an option available largely to families with backyards, not city dwellers or the poor—would you let the neighbors in?

During the aftermath of the 1961 U.S.-U.S.S.R. confrontation over Berlin, as the cold war threatened to become hot, this other moral crisis captured the national imagination. That fall, an episode of the television show *The Twilight Zone* featured a false alarm in which "the thin veneer" of civilization was once again ripped away as neighbors became enemies in a scramble for survival. *Time* magazine ran a scathing story on survival-by-any-means shelter owners titled "Gun Thy Neighbor" that opens with the quote: "'When I get my shelter finished, I'm going to mount a machine gun at the hatch to keep the neighbors out if the bomb falls.'" The would-be gunman from suburban Chicago was an exception, though, as was the Jesuit priest who tried to craft a theology of every-man-for-himself (or his family) survival. Las Vegas's civil defense leader provoked widespread outrage when he proposed assembling a five-thousand-man militia to keep bombed-out refugees from California from flooding the desert town. Preparing for this vision of war meant preparing to go to war against the neighbors in their hour of desperation. Twenty years later, one historian concluded that "slowly but surely millions of Americans were coming to the conclusion that private fallout shelters were morally indefensible."

It was a remarkable moment upon which few remarked: ordinary citizens balked at taking steps for their own survival at others' expense, even in a time of great fear of nuclear war and suspicion that collective solutions and solidarities smacked communism. Dorothy Day and the pacifist Catholic Worker community refused to participate in the statewide civil defense drills that began in New York in 1955. Instead they showed up defiantly at Manhattan's city hall while everyone else went underground. Day was sometimes arrested, sometimes ignored, during her group's annual public refusal to cooperate, until 1961, when two thousand people showed up to protest and the drills came to an end. This collective mulishness is one small beginning of the great upheaval that decade would bring. And this defiant altruism goes beyond mutual aid and evolutionary arguments: these citizens found that refusing such aid to neighbors was so distasteful they could not shop for survival on those terms, even while their leaders gambled with the lives of all humanity.

Disaster Without Redemption, Redemption Without Disaster

After the two little-seen landmark essays of 1961, Fritz himself largely disappeared from view for the rest of his working life. A lieutenant colonel in the army reserves, he went to work on military subjects, starting with the Institute for Defense Analysis. His collaborator on those pioneering studies of disaster, Enrico Quarantelli, recalls that he investigated the likely effects of bombing North Vietnam and, unsurprisingly, reached the same conclusions the World War II studies had. "The indirect effects [of] the bombing on the will of the North Vietnamese to continue fighting and on their leaders' appraisal of the prospective gains and costs of maintaining the present policy have not shown themselves in any tangible way," declared one report Fritz researched (declassified in 1996). Much of his work during that era remains classified, though he also led disaster research for the National Academy of Science and in that capacity wielded considerable influence on the developing field of disaster studies.

Perhaps the greatest damper in his paper on disaster and mental health is this statement: "The emergence of this community of sufferers is posited as a universal feature of disasters where the survivors are permitted to interact freely and to make an unimpeded social adjustment to disaster." Often they are not permitted to do so, and the communities Fritz imagined as homogenous and united may have been more complicated—think of the Chinese in 1906 San Francisco, of Koreans and socialists in Japan's 1923 Kanto earthquake, of the fact that many civil defense administrators in the American South advocated or planned for segregated fallout shelters. During the 2007 San Diego fires, preexisting animosity toward illegal immigrants prompted authorities to single out Spanish-speaking and Latino-appearing victims of the fire to deny them services and supplies and arrest and deport those who were undocumented when they sought refuge in the stadium and other sites provided. In Texas, similar plans to check legal status in disaster have been decried by disaster sociologists, since such measures would prevent people from evacuating or seeking services crucial to their survival. Most societies have such divides, and disaster can undermine or magnify them.

Contemporary disaster scholars speak of vulnerability—of the ways that disasters find existing frailties and weaknesses in the system and pry them open to victimize some more than others. In this respect, disaster does not democratize. Even if there is a shining moment of equalization, the values and discriminations of the old society reappear in the aftermath. Who gets shelter, supplies, aid, and sympathy is a political and cultural decision in which old biases surface. Even when malice is absent, middle-class people who maintain extensive documentation and are good at maneuvering through bureaucracies do better at getting compensation. (For example, in the 1989 Loma Prieta earthquake, aid was given to one family per house in the farmworker town of Watsonville, although poor Latino families often doubled and tripled up, while chronically homeless San Franciscans were not offered hotel rooms as suddenly homeless denizens of the affluent Marina District were.) Stories of relief administrators with a bias as to who is deserving are common. Such situations prompt outrage that the changed world did not last, that the old wrongs and divides come creeping back. That the old order was unjust means that disasters do not equally affect all members of a region to begin with: think of the frailty of mobile homes in parts of the country regularly hit by hurricanes and tornadoes, of who lives in the flood plains, of how fire departments—as geographer Mike Davis points out in his landmark "The Case for Letting Malibu Burn"—often go to extraordinary lengths to put out fires in remote but affluent areas while neglecting inner-city slums.

The ability to act on one's own behalf, to enter a community of mutual aid rather than become a castout or a recipient of charity, matters immensely. Fritz describes the satisfaction and the power that comes from membership and agency—and they don't always come. Another, later sociologist, Kai Erickson, studied in depth a rural community in the coal-mining country of West Virginia destroyed in 1972 when a mine dam of black water broke open to roar down their valley. The torrent

killed many residents and swept away most of the homes. He speaks of
the euphorias and utopias mentioned in other disasters only to say that
no such effects were felt at Buffalo Creek. One reason is that no community converged; people were uprooted and isolated, many of them
permanently, and much of the rescue work was done by uniformed outsiders. No sense of power or solidarity was gained in the aftermath, and
the aid was not mutual. Toxic and technological disasters in particular
breed this kind of "corrosive community," as doubts and divides multiply
over the years. All this means only that the effects Fritz celebrates are not
universal to either every disaster or for everyone in any disaster. But the
Blitz was as real as the Buffalo Creek flood, and the effects Fritz describes
matter, both for the particular moment and for the window they open
onto desire and possibility.

Disasters without redemptive moments raise the question of redemptive
moments without disaster. Many pasts and some presents have provided
a more simple, urgent, and cohesive life for individuals and communities. Hunter-gatherers and others who live close to the bone daily experience risk and daily remake the circumstances of their survival. They
are bound together by an urgent necessity that is also a satisfaction. This
is the clan and village life that Kropotkin celebrated. Though it is easy
to romanticize such ways of life and to forget that they impose limita-
tions on choice, pleasure, privacy, ease, and the individuality that is both
our privilege and wound, it also reminds us that if life was in some sense
once always a disaster, it must have been so in Fritz's sense, in which peril
came accompanied by solidarity and urgency. There are good reasons we
left behind that existence, but we left behind with it something essential,
the forces that bind us to each other, to the moment, and to an inherent
sense of purpose. The recovery of this purpose and closeness without crisis or pressure is the great contemporary task of being human. Or perhaps the dawning era of economic and environmental disasters will solve
the conundrum for us more harshly.

In contemporary life, firefighters in particular seem to have work
that is absorbing, affirming—both in the regular encounters with death
and the value of the work—and generative of enormous camaraderie
and solidarity, else they would not undertake such danger for what is so

often a mediocre salary at best. There are other professions providing such rewards and depth. And things other than professions. Recreational activities—notably the dangerous and demanding ones: white-water rafting, mountaineering—also expose people to danger, require close-knit teams, demand all attention be fixed on the present, and affirm ability and skill again and again. Though the pleasures attributed to such activities are most often within the realm of sports and scenic wonder, the most important ones are more social and psychological. Sports teams for both participants and fans bind people together in moments of intense uncertainty, even if only a goal or a run is at stake and the community is as virtual as the screaming fans on a TV screen.

We devote much of our lives to achieving certainty, safety, and comfort, but with them often comes ennui and a sense of meaninglessness; the meaning is in the struggle, or can be, and one of the complex questions for those who need not struggle for basic survival is how to engage passionately with goals and needs that keep such drive alive—the search for meaning that Viktor Frankl wrote about after Auschwitz. Much in the marketplace urges us toward safety, comfort, and luxury—they can be bought—but purpose and meaning are less commodifiable phenomena, and a quest for them often sends seekers against the current of their society. Fritz spoke of "the failure of modern societies to fulfill an individual's basic human needs for community identity." It is only because calamities provide as a side effect what is often unavailable otherwise that they become what he calls "social utopias." In a society where immediacy, belonging, and purposefulness are already ubiquitous, a disaster would be only a disaster. As for those close-to-the-bone hunter-gatherer societies, you can imagine life in them as an ongoing disaster of sorts, one in which there is much risk, much struggle, much strain, much need for cooperation, and much reward; we have traded that reward for ease, safety, and individualism. And the other, slower, less-visible disasters of alienation and anomie. Not that we bargained it away individually; larger decisions with unseen cumulative effects were undertaken collectively and sometimes steered by powers whose interests are not ours—as can be seen by the institutional alarm almost every time we do agglomerate as a civil society.

And then there's religion. Congregations in temples, synagogues, churches, and mosques form a tangible community of sorts, reaffirmed weekly. Whatever one's beliefs, regular attendance can convey both a sense of membership in that human society and a support network in times of crisis. But this is religion as another group to belong to rather than as a practice and set of beliefs. Religious beliefs can generate many kinds of reaction to disaster. In early modern Europe and other parts of the world—and for some in contemporary North America—disasters are regarded as God's punishment, which makes the emotional response profoundly different. Resourcefulness, altruism, let alone joy in those circumstances, could be seen as contrary to God's will, and such a religious interpretation can depress what in other circumstances are common responses. Early American Puritans sometimes considered disasters to be heaven-sent because they cleared away material goods and thereby materialism.

Reading Fritz, it becomes clear that disaster provides not only opportunities and communities but a changed sense of self that matters. As Fritz wrote, "Disasters provide a temporary liberation from the worries, inhibitions, and anxieties associated with the past and future because they force people to concentrate their full attention on immediate moment-to-moment, day-to-day needs within the context of the present realities." Here Fritz seems to venture close to another sense of religion, not as community or belief but as practice, as a craft of refining the self into something more adequate to the circumstances we face, more able to respond with grace and generosity, to achieve less temporary liberation. Most religions turn their adherents toward the things we are afraid to face: mortality, death, illness, loss, uncertainty, suffering—to the ways that life is always something of a disaster. Thus religion can be regarded as disaster preparedness—equipment not only to survive but to do so with equanimity and respond with calmness and altruism to the disaster of everyday life. Many religious practices also emphasize the importance of recognizing the connectedness of all things and the deep ties we all have to communities, from the congregation of the faithful to all beings everywhere. In so doing, they inculcate as everyday practice the mutual aid and altruism that disaster sometimes suddenly delivers.

The overlaps are interesting. Buddhism, for example, teaches that suffering comes from attachment, including attachment to past pains and future outcomes and to a sense of a separate self. Disaster encourages nonattachment to material goods as well as to past and future, or rather less attachment to abstractions and objects and more to other beings and states of being. People are set loose in an absorbing present of intense uncertainty. During California's horrendous 2008 summer of fire, Tassajara Zen Mountain Center, a community residence and retreat center in the rugged mountains of California's central coast, was threatened for weeks with incineration. As the last of the monks and residents evacuated that July, the abbot and four others decided to turn back and face the fire.

The danger was high. While reluctantly allowing them to remain in the evacuated zone, the Forest Service had asked for the names of their dentists, in case they needed to be identified by charred remains. Their account of the several days they lived surrounded by burning land in an otherwise depopulated region is remarkable for its aplomb and for their quest to find metaphors other than fighting for what they were doing with fire—and for their success in saving their community's home. For days as the fire approached, they cleared brush, kept watch, and maintained firebreaks and their sprinklers, pumps, and generators. The day that towering flames up to forty feet tall approached them from all four sides, they patrolled for sparks and flames and put them out to the best of their abilities (they had some firefighting training, protective clothing, and equipment). It worked.

One of them wrote in the center's online journal of the disaster, "What was most compelling during these hours, and which in reflection remains the most satisfying, is the constant vigilance and effort that the fire required. It was . . . a demanding schedule of pure presence in which one utterly let go of a known outcome. There were undeniable moments of fear and anxiety, especially when we understood the reality that the fire was descending into Tassajara fast and from all sides, rather than creeping down one slope at a time as had initially been suggested by several professional firefighters. But there was little time to entertain fear, so fear quickly gave way to our effort to fully meet our belated guest and the tasks at hand." Dave Zimmerman, the center's director, concluded a few days later, "And finally, deep bows to the fire, whose undeniable dharma teaching of impermanence has earned our awed respect and attention." The abbot, Stephen Stucky, later said in a lecture that this encounter with the fire gave force to the idea of "being prepared to meet whatever arises." Tassajara survived as an island of green in an ocean of blackened mountainsides and burned forests. The community in looking for lessons from the fire found many, and much to be grateful for: their Buddhist practice had equipped them to respond calmly (many were distressed at the possibility of losing a beloved place but recognized that nonattachment and equanimity were other lessons that might have to be learned). And they benefited immensely from being a community, with the ability to organize responses and draw on support and resources close at hand and far away.

The Vietnamese Buddhist community of Biloxi, Mississippi, didn't have the resources or the luck that Tassajara did, and they faced water, not fire. They were dedicating their brand-new temple the day that Hurricane Katrina hit the Gulf Coast, and the head monk from Vietnam, a visiting senior monk, about eighteen elderly women, a neighboring African American family, a Vietnamese American Texas doctor who studied with the monk, and several others took shelter in the attic after the waters of the storm surge rose to the ceiling of the temple. They did not know for the several hours that they were trapped there in the dark whether the water would continue to rise, but the monks chanted, everyone remained calm, and afterward the national Vietnamese community brought relief supplies and aid in rebuilding the temple (as did the Burners without Borders project started by participants in the annual Burning Man festival in the Nevada desert). The doctor who had been stranded there told me, "Everything is so impermanent. One day we're having a celebration and a grand opening and the next day it's all destroyed. So you just sit down and think deeply. It does shock me to go through that. But as for the people it's very hard. First of all they're poor to start with." But the temple was rebuilt, and the monk who heads it was more than cheerful about the disaster when I visited the rebuilt temple. "Very happy" were his parting words on the subject.

The language of religion might best explain that sudden joy in disaster. It's anarchic, a joy that the ordinary arrangements have fallen to pieces— but anarchic in that the ordinary arrangements structure and contain our lives and minds; when they cease to do so we are free to improvise, discover, change, evolve. Although religion has talked for millennia of the liberations of loss, and from Tibetan sages to Saint Francis of Assisi giving everything away has been a first step on the spiritual path, it is a dangerous thing to say that disaster is liberating. Dangerous because when thrust upon those who are unprepared or unequipped, rather than chosen or embraced, when it comes by surprise its effect is only loss and suffering. But a surprising number of people seem ready to make the most of this moment, including those who have lost much or are suffering. The same is often true of those surviving serious illness or nondisaster losses. Transcendence sneaks in everywhere as a survival response.

Contemporary language speaks of the effects of disaster entirely as trauma, or even more frequently as post-traumatic stress disorder, PTSD. The twin implications are that we are not supposed to suffer and that in our frailty we are not merely damaged, but *only* damaged by suffering. If suffering is a given, as it is for most religions, then the question is more what you make of it rather than how you are buffered from it altogether. The awareness of mortality that heightens a sense of life as an uncertain gift rather than a burdensome given also recalls religious teachings, and it is often shared by survivors of individual traumas. One professor of psychology, Ronnie Janoff-Bulman, writes, "The confrontation with physical and psychological annihilation essentially strips life to its essentials, and for many survivors becomes a turning point from the superficial to the profound. Life takes on new meaning and one's own life is often reprioritized. In our own work with survivors of life-threatening diseases, crimes, and accidents, men and women frequently reported that only now can they truly enjoy life because they no longer take it for granted."

Indeed, disaster could be called a crash course in Buddhist principles of compassion for all beings, of nonattachment, of abandoning the illusion of one's sense of separateness, of being fully present, of awareness of ephemerality, and of fearlessness or at least aplomb in the face of uncertainty. You can reverse that to say that religion is one of the ways crafted to achieve some of disaster's fruits without its damage and loss. That state of clarity, bravery, altruism, and ease with the dangers and uncertainties of the world is hard-won through mental and emotional effort but sometimes delivered suddenly, as a gift amid horrific loss, in disaster. Think of the exhilaration of Pauline Jacobson and William James; think of Samuel Prince seeing disaster as religious trial; of Dorothy Day's populist mysticism: "While the crisis lasted, people loved one another"; think of the young woman who suddenly realized she might have been hurt when her shelter crumbled around her in the Blitz but emerged to experience "pure and absolute happiness."

The conundrum we call human nature readily rises to the occasion of a crisis and as readily slacks off when the living is easy. During its decade of prosperity based on precarious financial schemes, Iceland grew politically apathetic and a little dull and demoralized. When its mismanaged economy crashed spectacularly in October 2008, furious citizens took action and a vibrant civil society emerged; it was the best and worst of times as the country lost its economic wealth and social poverty. A young member of the demonstrations that toppled the neoliberal government wrote to me of those days of bonfires and drums, "I felt as if Iceland was being born again." That the worst time becomes the best is interesting, but hardly ideal. That the best times, the safe and affluent ones, become the worst poses other challenges, of how to maintain a sense of purpose and solidarity in the absence of emergencies, how to stay awake in softer times. The religious language of awakening suggests we are ordinarily sleepers, unaware of each other and of our true circumstances and selves. Disaster shocks us out of slumber, but only skillful effort keeps us awake.

HOBBES IN HOLLYWOOD, OR
THE FEW VERSUS THE MANY

Warning: Hero in Foreground

New Orleans, 1950: A stowaway sneaks ashore one night in New Orleans, plays cards, wins big, but feels sick. Before the illness gets him, a thug guns him down near the waterfront. It's just an ordinary murder until the coroner discovers the man was infected with pneumonic plague, an airborne and highly contagious form of bubonic plague, the disease that as the Black Death once wiped out a third of all Europeans. This is where the public health officer steps in. To prevent an epidemic, he's got forty-eight hours to track down all the people who came into contact with the dead man and inoculate them—and he needs to keep the press silent, lest there be panic. A lot of officials are skeptical about the gravity of the situation, but a cop works with him—and to keep things quiet jails the reporter who's got the story. We're meant to believe that a free press and an informed public are a menace, because that public would behave badly were it to find out what dangers face it. That's why the movie is called *Panic in the Streets*.

Los Angeles, 1974: a graduate student at the fictional Seismology Institute has miraculously mathematically analyzed the geological data to predict a massive earthquake is imminent. He is eager to warn the public, but the institute's director squelches him, saying, "A public announcement now that an earthquake is imminent: that could create incredible panic. People climbing over people trying to leave the city. That could be worse than the earthquake itself." Just as human reaction to a nuclear bomb could be worse than the bomb, so it could be worse than the most exciting earthquake the movies can concoct: one with the soil seething as though monsters are going to burst out of it, tall buildings toppling, a dam breaking, and people running every which way and screaming, especially the women, who scream a lot. After the shaking, blazing, and crumbling in this version of disaster comes lots of looting, carjacking, and general rampaging. (Even if they were predictable, earthquakes don't actually call for leaving the region, merely for leaving unsafe structures and situations: you can weather almost any quake on open ground without anything to fall on you or collapse under you. One of the peculiarities of this movie, however, is that the great low-slung sprawl of Los Angeles is represented largely by a high-rise downtown district.) Imagine if the National Weather Service gave up hurricane warnings for fear of panic and evacuation. The seismologists settle for warning the mayor, who alerts the governor, and they deploy National Guard troops—to manage the panic in the streets when the unwarned public is suddenly shaken. Once again the public is the menace. Not much in the cinematic imagination has changed in the twenty-four years between *Panic in the Streets* and *Earthquake*, the blockbuster movie starring supermacho Charlton Heston and a smashed-up Los Angeles.

The Cascade Range, Washington, 1997: a volcano is about to bathe the idyllic small town at its base in molten lava, and only the rugged geologist Pierce Brosnan understands this. He wants to warn the townspeople to prepare for evacuation, but his boss refuses to let him, on the grounds that if it's a false alarm, they'll be liable for the economic losses. (In real life a similar argument was made about the tsunami that devastated the South Asian coast on December 26, 2004: "The important factor in making the decision was that it's high [tourist] season and hotel rooms were nearly one hundred percent full. If we had issued a warning, which would have led to an evacuation, what would happen then? Business would be instantaneously affected," said a Thai official.) "I know it was intense up there," the boss says of some of the strange things happening on the volcanic caldera, "but I don't want to cause a panic over a few tectonic plates and shakes." Brosnan himself tells the town council that "we don't want to start a panic." Tension builds for an hour of film time, and by the point the scientists finally warn the small town at a meeting in the high-school gym, the eruption is already beginning. They've started a panic. "Do not rush, do not rush," says the sheriff, and so the small-town hordes rush out of the meeting, knock one of their own over and nearly trample him, and jump into cars which they begin driving erratically in all directions. Inevitably, one of them smashes into a power pole, electrical lines fall and spark and snake, brakes screech, and wheels squeal. And then Dante's Peak, after which the film is named, starts pumping lava. Brosnan, like a human Swiss Army knife, keeps opening up new skills: he is the superhuman scientist–action–figure who recurs in movies such as 2004's climate change drama *The Day After Tomorrow*.

The setting is Washington, D.C., 1998: a young journalist starts to investigate why a member of the president's cabinet has resigned, suspects a scandal when she hears he was always talking about a presumed mistress named "Ellie," does some online research and realizes that it's actually an ELE—"extinction-level event." A six-mile-wide meteor is headed for the earth and may wipe out our species and a lot of others, but before she can tell anyone about it, she is kidnapped by government agents for a clandestine meeting with the president. The administration, of course, does not want to tell the public, lest there be panic in the streets, but she forces their hand and they strike a deal with her: if she holds the story until they're ready, she'll get the first question at the press conference. So she bargains away the right of the people to know the fate of the earth for a career boost on a probably doomed planet, and everything endorses her choice. After all, panic and mob behavior do follow, and we're shown it on the TV news shown on the small screens inside the big screen of the blockbuster movie *Deep Impact*: the mob justice of a crowd killing a backhoe operator extorting huge sums to dig shelters, looters setting fires to abandoned stores, Moscow crowds rioting over food and fuel shortages.

The Absence of Panic

We all know about the virtually interchangeable phenomena of panic and mobs. We've seen them milling and shoving and stampeding and trampling and generally taking leave of their senses, again and again, at least in movies. Most people believe that Le Bon's fears about crowds will come true during disasters, though he believed that crowds infected themselves with regressive appetite and we mostly tend to believe that mobs accrete into a seething mass through lots of individual irrational fear, selfish reaction, and hastily unwise action—the behavior we call panic. The basic notion is of people so overwhelmed by fear and selfish desire to survive that their judgment, their social bonds, even their humanity are overwhelmed, and that this can happen almost instantly when things go wrong—the old notion of reversion to brute nature, though out of fear rather than inherent malice. It presumes that we are all easily activated antisocial bombs waiting to go off. Belief in panic provides a premise for treating the public as a problem to be shut out or controlled by the military. Hollywood eagerly feeds those beliefs. Sociologists, however, do not.

Charles Fritz's colleague Enrico Quarantelli recalls that in 1954, "I wrote a master's thesis on panic, expecting to find a lot of it, and after a while I said, 'My God, I'm trying to write a thesis about panic and I can't find any instances of it.' That's an overstatement, but . . . it took a little while to learn that, wait a second, the situation is much better here" than anyone had thought. He defines panic as extreme and unreasonable fear and flight behavior. Flight behavior, however, is not necessarily panic: he points out that what can look chaotic from outside—people moving as fast as they can in all directions—is often the most reasonable response to an urgent threat. The thesis was another landmark in the study of human reaction to disaster, another piece of the news that chipped away at the old myths. Quarantelli, even more than Fritz, went on to become a dynastic head of disaster studies, working with Fritz early on, then becoming a professor and founding the Disaster Research Center at Ohio State University that is now at the University of Delaware.

Fifty-three years after the thesis without panic, Quarantelli added, "In fact, most of the disaster funding, even to this day, is based on the notion of how can we prevent people from panicking or engaging in antisocial behavior. So in the early days of disaster studies that was the reason for funding. They just assumed the real problem was the citizens and the people at large, even though the studies from the beginning argued against that." He added, "If by panic one means people being very frightened, that probably is a very correct perception of what occurs at the time of a disaster. Most people in contact with reality get frightened and in fact should get frightened unless they've lost their contact with reality at the time of the disaster. On the other hand it doesn't mean that if people are frightened, they cannot act appropriately." Studies of people in urgently terrifying situations have demonstrated—as Quarantelli puts it in the dry language of his field—that "instead of ruthless competition, the social order did not break down," and that there was "cooperative rather than selfish behavior predominating." Quarantelli states that more than seven hundred studies of disasters demonstrate that panic is a vanishingly rare phenomenon. Subsequent researchers have combed the evidence as meticulously—in one case examining the behavior of two thousand people in more than nine hundred fires—and concluded that the behavior was mostly rational, sometimes altruistic, and never about the beast within when the thin veneer of civilization is peeled off. Except in the movies and the popular imagination. And in the media. And in some remaining disaster plans. A different worldview could emerge from this.

Heroes are necessary because the rest of us are awful—selfish or malicious or boiling over with emotion and utterly unclear on what to do or too frightened to do it. Our awfulness requires and produces their wonderfulness, a dull, drab background against which they shine. Or so it goes in the movies. They themselves need heroes. It's almost a technical challenge: you need close-ups, you need story lines, individuals to follow, a star to attract audiences—even the ensemble disaster movies have multiple heroes who assume leadership, like *Towering Inferno*'s Paul Newman and Steve McQueen. The camera doesn't have the same fun with a large group of people behaving well, and Hollywood feeds on stars. And conventions: they are unwilling, generally, to make the Asian grandmother a leading hero of the disaster, though she might get a cameo. These films are deeply reassuring—for those who want to believe that no matter what happens to their city or world the old status quo of gender and power and individual initiative remains intact.

You'd think with the building on fire or the earth shaking or the meteor arriving, you'd have dramatic tension already, but the real conflicts in these movies are often between good and bad protagonists, along with the altruism in the foreground and the selfish and scared backdrop of humanity at large. Generally a romance builds and a personal conflict gets resolved: people in disaster movies are not distracted from personal business by imminent destruction, and so they busy themselves with the resolution and evolution of fraught particular relationships rather than embarking on the blanket empathy and solidarity real disaster often produces. Conventional disaster movies are fascinating and depressing for many reasons, not least being the tidy division of the world into us and them. The them that is humanity in the aggregate, the extras, panics, mobs, swarms, and fails. Also failures are the other nonprotagonist authority figures—the head geologist in *Dante's Peak*, the chief seismologist in *Earthquake*, the developer who used shoddy materials in *Towering Inferno*, the upper-echelon decision makers during the ebolalike epidemic in 1995's deadly-new-virus-drama *Outbreak*—who are complacent in their power and wrong in their outlook, and not very attractive to boot, the them who will be proven wrong, over whom the hero representing up-and-coming authority and us must triumph. And does. The movies are not antiauthoritarian so much as anti authorities other than us; it's a matter of getting the right guy in charge, the one we can identify with.

The problem with bureaucrats during crises may be the only thing disaster movies get right. Quarantelli remarks that the organizations rather than individuals are most prone to create problems during a natural disaster. "Bureaucracy depends on routine and schedules and paperwork and etc. If done right—in fact, the modern world could not exist without bureaucracy. The only trouble with that is that the bureaucratic framework is one of the worst things to have at the time of disasters when you need innovations and doing things differently. In fact the better they operate during nondisaster times, the less likely they are to operate well. They can't maneuver, they can't integrate, etc. On the other hand, human beings, and this cuts across all societies . . . rise to the occasion. Again, not everyone does, just like not all organizations react badly. But in terms of human beings they rise to the occasion whereas organizations, in a sense, fall down."

In *Deep Impact*, the conflict is only between the great wisdom and technological savvy of the federal government and the pretty young reporter who must be brought in line with its agenda. When Quarantelli wrote about disaster movies, he cited an unpublished colleague who wrote that they "reinforce our cultural belief in individualism and individualistic solitions to social problems." He adds, "Disaster movies . . . usually portray the problem as resulting from the human beings involved rather than the social systems in which they operate."

All these movies reaffirm traditional gender roles too, or rather the helplessness of women is part of what sets the male hero in motion. In the relatively liberal *Dante's Peak*, Linda Hamilton as the small-town mayor and Pierce Brosnan's love interest doesn't scream, doesn't do anything dumb, but doesn't do anything else either. Though only a few years earlier she was contending with the Terminator and flexing some quite remarkable muscles, in this one she doesn't leap, or lead, or hot-wire the truck, or paddle the boat, or lead the rescue of her own children. She's just along for the ride. And she's the best-case example; the others scream, panic, are frozen with fear while some rugged lug rescues and quite often literally carries them. Ava Gardner as Heston's unhappy wife in *Earthquake* literally drags her husband down the drain. A movie like *The China Syndrome*, in which a nuclear power plant begins to melt down and the media expose the arrogant negligence and information suppression of the plant management and government, stands all this on its head, particularly since Jane Fonda plays a lead reporter and an active heroine.

The China Syndrome is a maverick among disaster movies in other respects, championing the public and the media against insiders, elites, and experts. Its worldview was buttressed by the near-meltdown of Pennsylvania's Three Mile Island nuclear power plant thirteen days after the movie was released. Usually in the movies, big technological fixes tend to save the day. In the 1990s films *Armageddon* and *Deep Impact*, as in the contemporaneous science-fiction romp *Independence Day*, nuclear weapons deflect the evil that comes from outer space, be it meteors or aliens. In *The China Syndrome*, nuclear technology is the problem, not the solution.

Fear at the Top

Disaster movies represent many kinds of fantasy. They entertain our worst fears and then allay them—if our worst fear is of chaos, and our confidence comes from traditional sources of authority triumphing, for triumph they do, again and again, all those rugged men and powerful leaders and advanced technologies. Even on the brink of annihilation, this world is more comforting and reliable than our world. There's a subplot in *Earthquake* whereby Jody, the National Guardsman, abuses his power during the crisis to shoot down his jeering roommates, nearly rape a young woman, and generally abuse his new power. But he's portrayed as a long-haired martial-arts-obsessed nut—he's freaky them, not trustworthy us, even in a military uniform. The bleary, hard-drinking old-school cop played by George Kennedy blows him away in one of those classic

Hollywood moments when killing is deeply satisfying, entirely justified, and neatly done. Of course the National Guard was out to prevent looting and civil disturbances—the rarity of looting in almost all disasters is another thing the methodical research of the disaster scholars demonstrates but the movies didn't absorb.

In fact Hollywood movies are to actual disasters as described by sociologists something of a looking-glass world. Disaster sociologist Kathleen Tierney, who directs the University of Colorado's Natural Hazards Center, gave a riveting talk at the University of California, Berkeley, for the centennial of the 1906 earthquake in which she stated, "Elites fear disruption of the social order, challenges to their legitimacy." She reversed the image of a panicking public and a heroic minority to describe what she called "elite panic." She itemized its ingredients as "fear of social disorder; fear of poor, minorities and immigrants; obsession with looting and property crime; willingness to resort to deadly force; and actions taken on the basis of rumor." In other words, it is the few who behave badly and the many who rise to the occasion. And those few behave badly not because of facts but of beliefs: they believe the rest of us are about to panic or become a mob or upend property relations, and in their fear they act out to prevent something that may have only existed in their imaginations. Thus the myth of malevolent disaster behavior becomes something of a self-fulfilling prophesy. Elsewhere she adds, "The media emphasis on lawlessness and the need for strict social control both reflects and reinforces political discourse calling for a greater role for the military in disaster management. Such policy positions are indicators of the strength of militarism as an ideology in the United States."

From their decades of meticulous research, most of the disaster sociologists have delineated a worldview in which civil society triumphs and existing institutions often fail during disaster. They quietly endorse much of what anarchists like Kropotkin have long claimed, though they do so from a studiedly neutral position buttressed by quantities of statistics and carefully avoid prescriptions and conclusions about the larger social order. And yet, they are clear enough that in disaster we need an open society based on trust in which people are free to exercise their capacities for improvisation, altruism, and solidarity. In fact, we need it all the time, only most urgently in disaster.

Medical historian Judith Leavitt points to two smallpox outbreak cases to demonstrate the way that behavior of those in power shapes a crisis and the value of an open society. One, in Milwaukee in 1894, was made far worse by a public health officer who allowed middle-class and upper-class people to quarantine themselves, "whereas, in the poor immigrant sections of the city, he used forcible removal to the isolation hospital. And you can imagine that discrimination there was not helping, so the smallpox . . . spread citywide. There was this phrase, 'the scum of Milwaukee' in the newspapers quite a bit, and the people who lived on the south side of Milwaukee felt that that's the way the rest of the city viewed them, as the 'scum of Milwaukee' and, therefore, it didn't matter what you did to them, so there was definite unequal application of the policy. And the immigrants responded by not reporting cases of small-pox, by hiding them when people came to the door. And ultimately, by rioting against forcible removal, and against vaccination." Suspicion of the vaccination's safety and effectiveness was the other unfortunate fac-tor, along with class conflict and elite panic.

In 1947, smallpox came to New York City very much the way that bubonic plague came to New Orleans in *Panic in the Streets*, but the insti-tutional response was utterly different. The public was treated as an ally. Leavitt recounts, "There were signs and buttons around everywhere, 'Be safe. Be sure. Get vaccinated.' There were multiple daily press con-ferences and radio shows about the diagnosis when it finally came, the spread of it, every case was announced, and there was a perception, and I would argue also a reality of honesty and justice from the Health Depart-ment and from the city government at this time, because people felt they were being informed as things were unfolding. In two weeks, five million New Yorkers were vaccinated." Coercion was used elsewhere: "The drug companies were a little less cooperative until Mayor O'Dwyer locked them into City Hall and said you are going to produce more vaccine, and you're going to do it very quickly, or you're not leaving this building, and they surprisingly agreed. . . . It was a voluntary vaccination program so those people standing in line were there in a voluntary fashion. Public compliance was incredibly high. Now I don't have to remind you that this is immediately post–World War II, and that did have something to do also with the level of organization in the city and the cooperative effort."

Even so, in 2005, federal officials in the United States from the pres-ident to the head of the Centers for Disease Control and Prevention speculated that a militarily enforced quarantine would be required were a new epidemic to break out: they were planning to go the route of Milwaukee, not New York City. And when the Indiana National Guard decided to simulate a radioactive disaster in a 2007 training exercise, they hired civilians to play rioters and looters charging at medical personnel and even stealing stretchers. ("It'll make a good snowboard" one stretcher thief remarked unconvincingly, apparently trying to rationalize his puzzling role.) Elite panic and the mindset behind it are hard to eradicate. They were half the disaster that San Francisco faced in 1906 and that New Orleans faced in 2005.

Quarantelli was Tierney's professor, but the phrase "elite panic" was coined by her peers, Rutgers University professors Caron Chess and Lee Clarke. Clarke told me, "Caron said: to heck with this idea about regular people panicking; it's the elites that we see panicking. The distinguishing thing about elite panic as compared to regular-people panic, is that what elites will panic about is the possibility that we will panic. It is simply, more prosaically more important when they panic because they're in positions of influence, positions of power. They're in positions where they can move resources around so they can keep information close to the vest. It's a very paternalistic orientation to governance. It's how you might treat a child. If you're the mayor of a city and you get bad news about something that might be coming your way and you're worried that people might behave like little children, you don't tell them. You presume instead that the police are going to maintain order, if the thing actually comes: a dirty bomb, a tornado, a hurricane into lower Manhattan. As we define it, elite panic, as does general panic, involves the breaking of social bonds. In the case of elite panic it involves the breaking of social bonds between people in positions that are higher than we are. . . . So there is some breaking of the social bond, and the person in the elite position does something that creates greater danger.

"In Three Mile Island, there was an evacuation of nearly 150,000 people. It was mainly a self-directed evacuation. The officials weren't in charge of it. By all accounts it was quite orderly." Yet Clarke is often asked, "'Well, what about the panic at Three Mile Island?' That wasn't panic, the elites panicked there. They didn't know what was going on inside the reactor, [neither] the people on-site nor Governor Thornburg. And finally the governor issued a declaration and he advised women, especially of child-bearing age, and children to evacuate. Scientifically for good reason, their bones and fetuses are more vulnerable, but all those other people who are not those things said, "hey, I'm going to go too. It seems to make good sense to me." And we later discover that the reactor was perhaps thirty minutes away from breeching containment, half of the thing melting down. So what happens? The elites in that case, they're afraid people are going to panic so they hold the information close to the vest about how much trouble the reactor is in." Imagining that the public is a danger, they endanger that public.

Praising Tierney's work, Clarke wrote, "Disaster myths are not politically neutral, but rather work systematically to the advantage of elites. Elites cling to the panic myth because to acknowledge the truth of the situation would lead to very different policy prescriptions than the ones currently in vogue. The chief prescription is, she notes, that the best way to prepare for disasters is by following the command and control model, the embodiment of which is the federal Department of Homeland Security. Thus do panic myths reinforce particular institutional interests. But it is not bureaucrats who will be the first-responders when the next disaster, whether brought by terrorists or some other agent, comes. It won't even be the police or firefighters. It will be our neighbors, it will be the strangers in the next car, it will be our family members. The effectiveness of disaster response is thus diminished to the degree that we overrely on command and control. This is another case where political ideology trumps good scientific knowledge about how the world works."

Tierney moderates her critique of institutions to say that the United States at least has civilian systems of response, relief, and recovery. This, she adds, is an advance upon the era when recovery was considered to be a job for private philanthropy, while emergency response in other countries is often still delegated to the military (as it ultimately was in Hurricane Katrina in the United States). She approves, too, of the growing ranks of trained emergency managers. Many disaster scholars concur that if public awareness on disaster behavior is lagging, institutional planning is changing for the better. And it's important to break up the monolith of the state into the various departments with various responses that constitute institutional behavior in any disaster: in 1906 San Francisco, the police conducted themselves far more reasonably, perhaps because they were rooted in the communities they served; in Halifax, most agencies behaved well; on the morning of 9/11 the Centers for Disease Control responded rapidly and appropriately; in Hurricane Katrina the Coast Guard distinguished itself for performing a maximum of rescues with a minimum of fuss and fear. Responses vary.

Asked how decades of studying disaster had influenced her political beliefs, Tierney responded, "It has made me far more interested in people's own capacity for self-organizing and for improvising. You come to realize that people often do best when they're not following a script or a score but when they're improvising and coming up with new riffs, and I see this tremendous creativity in disaster responses both on the part of community residents and on the part of good emergency personnel— seeing them become more flexible, seeing them break rules, seeing them use their ingenuity in the moment to help restore the community and to protect life, human life, and care for victims. It is when people deviate from the script that exciting things happen."

Her trust in human beings in the absence of governance is at odds with that of most who govern. After all, the elites of Britain before World War II anticipated that the citizenry would fall apart, while the American leaders plotting nuclear wars astonishingly concluded that the survivors posed more of a threat than the bombs themselves. My own impression is that elite panic comes from powerful people who see all humanity in their own image. In a society based on competition, the least altruistic often rise highest. In staying there, they play out a drama far more akin to the scenarios of Social Darwinism than anything Kropotkin found in Siberia. Those in power themselves are often capable of being as savage and self-serving as the mobs of their worst fears. They also believe that they are preventing crime when they commit it. General Funston having citizens shot as looters believed he was somehow saving the city, and the officials and vigilantes in Hurricane Katrina unloosed even more savage attacks on the public because that public was portrayed as a monster out of control—a collective King Kong or Godzilla, as we shall see. At large in disaster are two populations: a great majority that tends toward altruism and mutual aid and a minority whose callousness and self-interest often become a second disaster. The majority often act against their own presumptive beliefs in selfishness and competition, but the minority sticks to its ideology. Disaster cannot liberate them, even while many others find themselves in an unfamiliar world playing unfamiliar roles. Certainly it was so in San Francisco in 1906, in the big Mexico City earthquake of 1985, and Hurricane Katrina in New Orleans. But in Mexico, the majority mattered most, with extraordinary consequences.

III

CARNIVAL
AND REVOLUTION:
MEXICO CITY'S
EARTHQUAKE

POWER FROM BELOW

Shaking Inside and Out

One disaster utopia lasted. During the 1985 Mexico City earthquake, citizens discovered each other, their own strength, and the superfluity of what had seemed like an omnipotent and pervasive government, and they did not let go of what they discovered. It reshaped the nation. The real disaster began long before the earthquake, just as the utopia of social engagement and community strength lasted long after— and existed more vigorously than in much of the United States before as well. Utopia itself is rarely more than an ideal or an ephemeral pattern on which to shape the real possibilities before us. Mexicans tasted it and took steps to make it a larger part of everyday life.

Marisol Hernandez was a young single mother taking her son to day care on her way to work as a seamstress in a Mexico City sweatshop on the morning of September 19, 1985. Twenty-two years later, she said, "I wasn't at work yet because we came in at 8:00 a.m. and I was taking my child to the nursery; he was two years old. We were in the metro—I was in there with him when it happened." As people so often do, she continued onward as though everyday life still existed. She worked in the Pino Suárez neighborhood of sweatshops and garment factories just south of the Zócalo, the huge plaza at the heart of the immense sprawl of Mexico City, the symbolic center of the nation. Though she is no longer young and her life was never easy, the only sign of time on Hernandez's smooth oval face is that she looks no particular age as she speaks intently of that moment of rupture. "I went to the nursery to leave my son and went walking because the metro and the transportation wasn't functioning, but the ground was all broken up and the buildings had collapsed. I walked to Pino Suárez, but already everything had collapsed. I think I was at the point of losing my reason as I was seeing all of that. A long time passed where I couldn't believe what I was seeing."

The earthquake that hit that morning at 7:19 lasted an endless two minutes, while buildings swayed and shook and cracked and millions were awakened, startled, shaken, or crushed at the beginning of their day. Among the buildings that toppled or fell to pieces were many recent structures built badly under corrupt regimes. The builders had used substandard materials or skimped on reinforcing steel, and the officials in charge of safety had looked the other way. Particularly hard hit was the central city—its ground is the old lake bed that had surrounded the Aztec island city of Tenochtitlán, drained for expansion long ago but not quite terra firma even now. Most of the collapsed structures were south of the Zócalo, on the poorer side of the city, though one of the worst disasters was the collapse of the huge Nuevo León apartment building at Tlaltelolco in the north. It tipped over on its side like a grounded ship beached in its own rubble, once-horizontal floors tilted to the sky. Nearly five hundred people died inside it. Also collapsed were the central telephone exchange downtown, through which most of the city's phone calls were routed, the communications tower of the Televisa television station, two large hospitals, several downtown hotels, the buildings housing the ministries of labor, communications, commerce, and the navy, and many large apartment buildings. Ham radio operators were among the first to get news out to the world. Several hundred buildings were destroyed, more than two thousand irreparably damaged, and countless thousands more somewhat damaged. Though the percentage of buildings damaged was small—Mexico City was one of the world's largest cities—what was lost was central, literally and figuratively, for the administrative, commercial, communication, and transportation systems of the region and the nation.

A cloud of dust rose up to coat everything in pallor and choke those who moved through the ravaged streets. Eight hundred thousand people had almost instantly become homeless, at least temporarily. Estimates of the dead range from ten to twenty thousand, though many were not yet dead, just trapped and maimed by the collapse. Some would cry out for aid for days. Some would be rescued from ruins quickly or after volunteers tunneled for days through unstable heaps in which the smell of those who did not survive became terrible in the warm September air. A maternity ward collapsed, and twenty-two babies were eventually extracted from the heap it became. Eight infants were rescued from the ruins days after the government had ordered the collapsed structure bulldozed.

Students lay down in front of bulldozers so that the search for survivors could continue. But many were lost. Judith Garcia, who lost two small children and a husband when her apartment building collapsed and lived only because the quake threw her out the window, said bitterly, "I want to state that the people who died didn't die because of the earthquake; that is a lie. People died because of poor construction, because of fraud, because of the criminal incapacity and the inefficiency of a corrupt government that doesn't give a damn about people living and working in buildings that can collapse. The government knows that many buildings are death traps." The earthquake was a force of nature, but the disaster was not a natural disaster. The devastation was terrible, but the response was remarkable.

Marisol Hernandez was walking into one of the worst-hit districts. Pino Suárez has a beautiful old church at its center, but the rest of the neighborhood is a grid of nondescript slablike buildings made of the ubiquitous cement of Mexico City, taller and more regular than the houses and hovels of other parts of the city. The popular Super Leche restaurant was already serving customers when the earthquake flattened it and the apartment next door, killing hundreds. Garment-industry buildings weakened by being overloaded with heavy equipment and goods crumpled. One eleven-story complex turned into a three-story building. Those already at work were crushed in the collapse. A twenty-five-year-old worker, Margarita Aguilar, said that she "ran on the stairway and a wall came on us because the warehouse collapsed. The wall fell across our path and blocked our exit. My legs and one arm were trapped in the rubble, but one hand and my head, the most important things, were free. I climbed on a piece of furniture and broke a side window. I cut my hand and came out. Many compañeras ran toward the windows, and those were the ones that were saved because the part of the building that crashed down as if in a spiral was its center. But the windows to the street were free, so I looked out and shouted—or should I say that I wailed—"help" to the people who were down on the street. They sent us a rope." Another group of seamstresses threw bolts of fabric out the factory window and slid down those, abrading their skin as they slid and tumbled, but escaping. Citizens who were not injured or trapped came to the collapsed buildings and began organizing rescues immediately after the earthquake.

Hernandez was lucky she was not yet at work, and Aguilar that she escaped. An unknown number of seamstresses died that day. Unknown in part because the police prevented families from trying to dig loved ones out of the rubble, in the name of preventing looting or because the ruins were unsafe. In one notorious case, they also provided protection for an owner who wanted to salvage not the trapped women crying out for rescue but his equipment. Accounts suggest many owners did the same. Some of the buried had no one to dig for them because they were single mothers of young children. Some were themselves children in their teens. Sixteen hundred garment workers died according to one estimate. Eight hundred businesses were demolished. And somewhere between forty and seventy thousand garment workers were suddenly unemployed. By law, their employers owed them their wages and severance pay, but many of those bosses made themselves scarce. So the seamstresses started round-the-clock vigils at some of their work sites. "Looking back, the seamstresses pinpoint the day they watched their bosses remove machinery over the bodies and screams of their co-workers as a turning point in their lives," writes Phoebe McKinney. "It was then, they say, that their political consciousness was raised, and they realized it was time to demand the legal right to organize to protect themselves as workers." Out of the rubble was born the first independent women-led union in recent Mexican history. Marisol Hernandez changed that day. So did her country.

When police and soldiers were sent out into the city, they were ordered to protect property from looters—and in many cases, they became looters. There was little institutional assistance in rescuing or rebuilding, and people so distrusted the government that had overseen the creation of the doomed structures that they preferred to do it for themselves. The earthquake literally cracked open the facade of the ruling Institutional

Revolutionary Party, or PRI, and revealed the corruption underneath: in the ruined basement of the attorney general's office were found the bodies of six men who had been tortured, two of whom had died from their wounds; another tortured body showed up in the trunk of a car in that basement. Attorney General Victoria Adato shrugged, "It's absurd to suggest we tortured them. They had already confessed." Donated foreign aid was siphoned off; tents and supplies went astray; search-and-rescue teams from abroad were kept from saving lives—the Spanish had their equipment held up in customs, one group of French was given no guides or maps, and another was taken to a nice hotel when they wanted to go to work. (Some disaster scholars point out that search-and-rescue teams often arrive too late to rescue the living, who are more likely to be saved by the neighbors. Because the media often arrive when the neighbors have already done their rescuing, they naturally focus on the professionals.)

The Nuevo León building at Tlaltelolco was a particularly grim case. Tlaltelolco, or the Plaza de las Tres Culturas—Plaza of Three Cultures—was built around an old Spanish church and Aztec ruins, a reminder of the conflicts that had riven Mexican society since conquest, conflicts that survive in the majority of the population, who are mestizo, or mixed: descended from both Spaniards and indigenous people. Tlaltelolco had been the site of another conflict, the most infamous clash in modern Mexico, the massacre of students demonstrating in the plaza in October of 1968, just before the city was to host the Olympics. It crushed the student movement at the time, but the government massacre in which hundreds or thousands died is considered to be the moment in which the PRI lost its legitimacy, particularly with young and progressive constituencies. Dissatisfaction simmered, but nothing substantial happened afterward until the earthquake broke the stalemate between government and society. When the Nuevo León collapsed, it already bore a banner denouncing the inadequate repairs made after an earlier earthquake. The army troops that showed up at the building did nothing to rescue the residents within. Survivors from the Nuevo León and surrounding buildings went to the agency that managed the complex of dozens of multistory buildings and were told that the officials were too busy to meet with them. The next day hundreds of residents marched, only to be told that the man in command had to wait for instructions—the top-down bureaucracy was paralyzed. As the meeting grew heated, a large second earthquake hit, the protestors fled, and hundreds trapped in the ruins of the Nuevo León were crushed as the rubble settled. But soon a citywide housing-rights movement was born.

Similar battles over housing went on in other poor neighborhoods as the residents realized that even many standing buildings were dangerously damaged. With that they became the *damnificados*, the damaged people, and they numbered in the hundreds of thousands. Most camped outside their former homes, concerned that if they left the area they would lose their right to return—and the PRI proposed moving many displaced people far away, as they had feared. The earthquake could have become a pretext for a large-scale displacement of the poor and for gentrification. Many poor Mexicans had long benefited from rent-control measures that reduced their monthly payments to figures so low that some landlords didn't bother to collect and had little incentive to make repairs. By October 24, the citywide housing-rights movement had a name, the Unified Coordinating Committee of Earthquake Refugees (Coordinadora Única de Damnificados). They began to win battles to secure housing rights. In many cases tenants were able to purchase the homes they had long rented. Through their struggle after the quake, they did not merely preserve their existing situation but improved it.

Alessandro Miranda was fifteen that morning when his home—two rooms he shared with his parents and two others—collapsed around him. His father, who cut hair in the open-air market nearby, dug them out and then went to Super Leche to begin trying to rescue others in their Pino Suárez neighborhood of modest homes and sweatshops. The son said in 2007, "The streets were cordoned off by the army; we couldn't get out to too many places. People would arrive with water, provisions, and sandwiches, and they would offer us these things, as there were no resources. There were very many people of noble heart, with a clean way of looking at things. That's the good side." The bad side was looting—but he said that given the direness of people's poverty, it was not surprising that citizens stole too. But he saw as much generosity as greed and he still remembers the refugee camps positively. "During that time there was a beautiful community, the people of the barrios, the people from below began living really well, there was a lot of good coming from the people from below; they were very noble. There were fiestas, posadas, there was a lot of integration. We went at night to the park of San Miguel and there were cafeterias and we would order a sandwich and a coffee; whatever you needed they would give you. If you needed clothes, they gave you clothes, also breakfast, lunch, dinner. You didn't have to pay anything." His family's building on Regina Street was expropriated, and his parents became homeowners, as did many of the neighbors. They still live there, modestly, in a few neat rooms opening onto a communal courtyard where children and pets play. Miranda was traumatized by the earthquake and still responds swiftly to any intimation of another one, but he also became an architect dedicated to the role of design in radical social possibilities.

In many arenas, groups began to coalesce and take action, creating a citizenry stronger than it had been before. While the damnificados were finding common ground, Marisol Hernandez and other seamstresses were forming their union. She recalled, sitting in a little cement apartment in a raw, blank blue-collar edge of the city, with clusters of apartment buildings scattered across the pale soil, "From many sectors, from all over, many people were supporting the seamstresses. I can't say anything without being grateful, because definitively, they never left us alone." She still sews for a living now, but at the modest home she owns, with no commute and time to take care of her grade-school-age daughter. Laura Carlsen, an American-born activist who came out to organize with the seamstresses of Mexico City and stayed for good, recalls, "They began to have sit-ins at the homes of the owners, and the owners themselves became visible, much to their chagrin, because they would bring out flyers of their faces that said 'Wanted: Owner of This Shop' for failing to rescue, for not paying the legal compensation to these workers, and they went to their homes to say this." In the early days of the union, there were huge marches, and behind the scenes the members organized to chart the workers and places of employment, to make visible the invisible industry in which they had worked and their sisters had died. Carlsen adds, "When the stories started coming out, people on the Left, feminists, and even civil society on the whole began to get involved in this. They had people from all over the world coming and visiting to talk about the experience to see how their organizing was going. They were heavy times. First there was a period of the sit-ins and the marches and the militant actions." Then came the less dramatic phase of actually registering the union members, eight to ten of whom became union employees. "In many cases these were women who didn't have more than maybe three years of grade school. So they were also going through these crash courses in basic leadership and literacy." They were for a time "the moral center" of the earthquake, or rather of the society galvanized by that earthquake. Support came from all over.

As time went on, outside pressures—including the globalized garment industry's "race to the bottom" in search of the lowest wages on earth—undermined the union. But the women were forever changed. Many became homeowners through the movements they got involved with, and many gained a sense of their own rights and power they had lacked before. Hernandez now says, "At the beginning before we organized, I thought that Mexico, our nation, was all sweetness, that we didn't have problems, that everything was equitable, and after I am very clear that that is not true. There is a lot of injustice for all the workers, especially because they want to use cheap manual labor. At the personal level, I feel I am not the same, and I will never be able to be the same, because I learned a lot and it was a great learning." Gains from the earthquake were as tangible as a union and housing, but they went far beyond that. Mexico changed, on a scale as personal as principles and agendas and as grand as government and society. Citizens found a communal power to remake their world, and they did not let go of it. Carlsen says, "One of the seamstresses told me—and she was confused when she told me this— that her son one day said to her: 'Mom, I think when the earth shook it left it shaking inside you.' He was seeing a completely different person as his mother now."

This Country Awakened

Samuel Prince had written, "The word 'crisis' is of Greek origin, meaning a point of culmination and separation, an instant when change one way or another is impending." Another popular definition cited is in Chinese, where the written word for crisis is made up of the ideograms for disaster and opportunity. A crisis, says one dictionary, is "the point in the progress of a disease when a change takes place which is decisive of recovery or death; also, any marked or sudden change of symptoms, etc." The 1985 earthquake was a crisis in that sense, though the disaster was in many ways not the quake itself but the system that had been like a disease of sorts, to which the crisis of the quake would prompt a partial cure. Since 1929, Mexico had been governed by the PRI, the Institutional Revolutionary Party, whose very name is a contradiction. The PRI made Mexico a one-party country with an odd mix of free-market and government-controlled enterprises and massive corruption at every level. The PRI had seemed omniscient and inevitable to most Mexicans, though minority parties toiled in the wilderness outside its massive machinery, and many poor people regulated their own lives and barrios or villages with little or no government oversight.

When the earthquake hit, President Miguel de la Madrid was nowhere to be seen. He toured the ruins but didn't meet with the people or speak in public until late on the evening of the twentieth, and his televised speech seemed detached and distant. He came to seem superfluous. Afterward, he began focusing on macroeconomic measures to shore up the national economy rather than on providing relief for the sufferers. The country was in the grip of economic "liberalization" measures guided by the International Monetary Fund and the World Bank. Their measures were supposed to bring economic development funded by huge loans, but mostly brought instead huge debts and economic-austerity programs to pay for those debts. When First Lady Nancy Reagan showed up with a check for a million dollars, de la Madrid gave it back to her, asking her to credit it to the national debt "since during the time that it took to get the pen out and sign, the debt grew by $12 million because of interest." The country was already in a recession augmented by a fall in oil prices and the adoption of neoliberal policies that would increase poverty—policies it is fair to call a disaster.

As the emergency subsided, citizens who had done without the government when it came to rescuing their families and neighbors, feeding and sheltering each other, organizing relief brigades, cleanup crews, and more, didn't lose their increased sense of power, connection, and possibility. The quake marked the rebirth of what Mexicans call civil society. A skinny young man who became one of the moles who tunneled through the rubble to bring aid and rescue trapped survivors sums up something of what that experience was when he says that he "participated in that brigade and learned that being an anonymous human being can be, like, a very great satisfaction, and that you can grow inside, and that is better than to be recognized by the whole wide world pointing at you and saying, 'You did this, you did that.'" In finding a deep connection with one another, people also found a sense of power, the power to do without the government, to replace its functions, and to resist it in many ways. They began to do so, with astonishing results. The era of the earthquake was akin to that of the civil rights movement in the United States, when what had long been the status quo was found to be intolerable. When that happens, change follows.

On the grand scale, Mexico City, which had been governed directly by the PRI, with a mayor chosen by the president, by 1987 gained the right to elect some of its representatives, though it would take a decade more before they elected their first mayor directly. The shock of the earthquake freed them from the sense that the PRI was inevitable. By 1986, a political earthquake had riven the party over economic policy and internal corruption. One party member, Cuauhtémoc Cárdenas, demanded that the process of nominating a presidential candidate become more democratic, and in 1988 he broke with the party to become the candidate of six left-wing opposition parties. The son of Lázaro Cárdenas, one of the least corrupt and most beloved presidents in Mexican history, he was himself a reformer advocating for economic justice, more accountability, and less corruption. Much evidence shows that he won that presidential election less than three years after the earthquake, but the PRI announced that *"se cayó el sistema"*—the system has crashed, a phrase that became notorious—and stopped the computer tally of votes. Days later the party announced that their candidate had won. Few believed them, and millions rose up in the streets to protest, but they lost.

By 2000, the stranglehold of the PRI had been broken, and Mexico was a multiparty democracy of sorts, even if Vicente Fox of the PAN (Partido Acción Nacional, or National Action Party, a powerful conservative party) was not much more of a populist or reformer than the PRI's candidates had been. Meanwhile, Cárdenas became the first elected mayor of Mexico City, a position of considerable power, and his successor and party-mate Andrés Manuel López Obrador appeared to have won the 2005 election—only to have it apparently stolen again, this time by the PAN (some disagreement about the real outcome of that election exists). Once again, Mexicans rose up, and the Zócalo at the center of the country and its surrounding streets became the site of a massive encampment of a million outraged citizens. The uprising failed to change the election, though an earlier march of a million through the city had prevented the PAN from disqualifying López Obrador from running in the first place. Electoral politics and reform at the national level were disappointing, though simply making Mexico a multiparty state was a huge achievement.

Less easily measured is what gets called *civil society*. The term is as popular nowadays as it is slippery. As Michael Edwards writes in his investigation of the idea, it can mean nongovernmental associations and organizations, or it can mean society in general when it flourishes, or it can mean the public sphere and public life. In Mexico it most often means the first version of the term: the grassroots and citizen organizations that are independent of and often counterweights to the government. "I am clearly convinced that the country changed after 1985," the activist and theorist Gustavo Esteva declares, twenty-three years later. Esteva was involved with the black-marketeers' barrio of Tepito, not far from Tlaltelolco, which defended its housing rights and strengthened the ties that made it one of the most tight-knit communities in Mexico City. After the quake, he saw the term *civil society* emerge in Mexico at the same time that it became important in the Soviet Bloc countries to define the society, or the public, that could counter the monolithic governments of communism—and of Mexico in that era of global change. "As far as I can see, at the beginning of October, someone asked, 'But who are you?' Someone said, 'We are the civil society.' They really represented a radical change, a different way of thinking. The organization of the colonias/barrios was clearly strengthened. There was this feeling you had the world in your hands, beyond army or government. We created something like an alternative government. . . . Really, this country awakened after the earthquake—ordinary men and women can take things in their hands. Suddenly we saw that the people themselves were having real agency. In the late 1980s they were doing marvelous things." The housing movement and the seamstresses' union were only two manifestations of a widespread new engagement.

Former playwright, political prisoner, and then president Václav Havel, who was instrumental in the 1989 liberation of Czechoslovakia by a carefully cultivated independent civil society, defines *civil society* as "a society in which citizens participate—in many parallel, mutually complementary ways—in public life, in the administration of public goods, and in public decisions. . . . The functions of the state and of its structures in such a society are limited only to that which cannot be performed by anyone else, such as legislation, national defense and security, the enforcement of justice, etc." You could say that civil society is what unimpaired mutual aid creates; or that civil society is the condition and mutual aid the activity that produces it. In Mexico City in 1985, mutual aid is what people first set out to provide as they rescued and aided each other; as the tasks became less urgent and more politically engaged, civil society is what they built up.

Definitions of civil society often imply it is at odds with government, though the success of civil society can be measured by how effectively it shapes government to its needs and desires or, in Havel's terms, whittles government down to a minimum. Esteva, Kropotkin, and Thomas Paine, among others, would argue that a sufficiently potent civil society could render formal government superfluous or create a genuinely grassroots government, a true direct democracy. In many ways civil society performs the work of government, of providing vital services and decision-making structures. Barrios like Tepito had long regulated themselves informally, with a fluid but direct process more accountable and more truly democratic than electoral politics, in which a bare majority may choose a candidate but be unable to hold him or her accountable. In places across the world where government fails—remote parts of Africa, for example—a civil society often arises to serve the functions of regulating and providing basic services.

No one tells the story of the Mexican capital's civil society rebirth more ardently than Mexico's foremost cultural critic, Carlos Monsiváis. He wrote, "During the months of September and October, Mexico City changed. To the presidential residence in Los Pinos marched the seamstresses, nurses, the neighbors of Tepito, the neighbors of Tlatelolco, and doctors. This pressure changed many decisions . . . and for the first time many people learned to speak in assemblies and meetings." What he tells is the by-now familiar story of disaster: "Not even the power of the state . . . managed to wipe out the cultural, political, and psychic consequences of the four or five days in which the brigades and aid workers, in the midst of rubble and desolation, felt themselves in charge of their own behavior and responsible for the other city that rose into view." This was the city of power that came from below, of the earthquake of popular will that shook loose the grip of the PRI and began to remake the country. The earthquake is a mythic moment in Mexican history, and civil society is the phoenix that rose from its rubble.

Edwards points out that civil society is shaped by culture, writing that "norms of participation are different among whites and African Americans in the USA, for example, with the latter more likely to take part in protest and campaigning activities as part of an oppositional culture that characterizes many of their associations. Islamic and Confucian cultures think differently about belonging, solidarity, and citizenship, in part because of a stress on the collective rather than the individual." The differences between Mexican and U.S. or Canadian culture matter here. Mexicans often put a higher value on public life of the most immediate sort, on strolling, gathering, and celebrating in public; they have inherited a public architecture of plazas, monuments, and open marketplaces; these things are part of society there in a way that they are not in most places farther north. (Urbanists know that when a U.S. neighborhood or city Latinoizes, its public and pedestrian life often flowers.) Public life still plays a strong role in many Latin American countries as both a pleasure and a source of political power, and Latinos have a stronger recent history of political organizing outside and against institutions. The United States before the Second World War was very much more such a society, before suburbanization and McCarthyism, among other postwar forces, launched a great withdrawal. Some of this is simply the way that traditional cultures have long functioned, with assemblies and informal decision-making structures, some of it the way the overlooked poor care for each other, but some the legacy of a radical tradition that values popular power. Another way to frame it is to say that Mexicans are often better versed in Dorothy Day's other loves.

Thanks to a long legacy of corrupt and opportunistic governments, Mexicans are less likely to trust authorities to perform well or in the public interest and more likely to improvise other systems of support and decision making. Membership matters. So does, for many if not all Mexicans, a revolutionary romanticism that is far removed from the quotidian cynicism of the United States, where people believe either that little or nothing can change for the better thanks to human nature (the right) or the overwhelming power of government and capital (the left). Throughout Latin America, political volatility gives most citizens cultural memory of both insurrection and dictatorship, things to both fear and hope for from the political process. The long stability of the two northernmost countries in the hemisphere provides no such sense of risk and possibility. Revolution has a different legacy here, and the idea of radical change a different currency. It is as though they had an ability to recognize that disaster utopia, name it, connect it to other experiences, and make something of it. In other places, the unnamed qualities of a richer civic life and deeper ties often slip away for lack of a language and framework to prize them. It remains an orphan experience, unconnected and ultimately lost.

All these factors gave Mexico City's citizens the power to act outside their government and to pressure it to change. But they weren't only tools to apply to the state. They were pleasures Pauline Jacobson had celebrated, a few weeks after the destruction of her city in the 1906 earthquake and fire: "The individual, the isolated self was dead. The social self was regnant. Never even when the four walls of one's own room in a new city shall close around us again shall we sense the old lonesomeness shutting us off from our neighbors."

It's easy to see in Mexico City that the city of physical structures is paralleled by another city of social ties, affections, and commitments—or not paralleled, for the one can be strong where the other is weak, and the ties are often strongest in the poor neighborhoods. The community of Tepito had met with 150 other communities and organizations in the week after the earthquake, forming a dense net of information, alliances, and services to help itself through the disaster. In 1906 San Francisco the conscious pleasure in the sense of community and affection cropped up in individuals. In Mexico City in 1985 those individuals coalesced into communities that lasted. Elite panic in Mexico City wasn't panicky at all; the government seemed to fear the citizens hardly at all and instead to sweep them aside in pursuit of the usual interests. Elite selfishness or elite callousness might be a better term here. But the citizenry were also resolute, and in facing down the government and the institutions of power in this disaster they won many battles. A great many of the participants were young men who seemed to be living out William James's "Moral Equivalent to War" in making of their strength and freedom to act a force to salvage their community and solidify civil society. One such young man told me of how he left his house with a camera but never took a picture, didn't go home to sleep, and became part of the brigades, as they were called. These *brigadistas* did so much while the policemen and soldiers did so little that the people on the streets ignored the officials and concentrated their support on the young volunteers who went into the ruins, directed traffic, ran messages, organized resources, and demonstrated solidarity and commitment.

Society matters. A decade later, in another huge city far to the north, Chicago, an intense heat wave killed more than seven hundred people, twice as many as died in the Great Chicago Fire of 1871. The city government ignored the problem and then tried to minimize it and then blamed the victims. The majority of the victims were impoverished seniors who died in domiciles without air-conditioning or with inadequate air-conditioning. In his book *Heat Wave*, sociologist Eric Klinenberg looked carefully at who died and why. Though Latinos were nearly a quarter of Chicago's population, they represented only 2 percent of the deaths, a number much lower than whites as well as African Americans. African Americans in one poor neighborhood were ten times as likely to die as Latinos in the equally impoverished adjoining neighborhood. Klinenberg concluded that the difference was in the quality of the neighborhoods themselves. The highest casualty figures were in a high-crime area losing population and often described as appearing to be "bombed out"—other African American neighborhoods had much lower mortality rates. The adjoining Latino neighborhood with low death rates had "busy streets, heavy commercial activity, residential concentration . . . and relatively low crime."

He concluded that these factors "promote social contact, collective life, and public engagement in general and provide particular benefits for the elderly, who are more likely to leave home when they are drawn out by nearby amenities." Those who left their overheated homes for open space or air-conditioned shops, diners, or fast food restaurants or who sought and received help from neighbors were more likely to survive. That is, heat was only one factor in determining who died. Fear and isolation were others, keeping people in their homes even when their homes were unbearable. This too was far from a natural disaster. People lived or died because of the level of social amenities and social space in their neighborhoods—by whether or not the neighborhood itself was also home. "Residents of the most impoverished, abandoned, and dangerous places in Chicago died alone because they lived in social environments that discouraged departures from the safe houses where they had burrowed, and created obstacles to social protection that are absent from more tranquil and prosperous areas."

In 2003, the avoidable tragedy of the Chicago heat wave was repeated on a vastly larger scale. A spell of broiling weather killed thirty-five thousand people across Europe. In France, where fifteen thousand elderly people died, the deaths were blamed on the isolation of many of the victims, on a society that shuts down regularly in August, so that doctors and family members—and the minister of health—were on vacation as the crisis unfolded, and on society itself. Another kind of disaster comes entirely of this social failure: the famines that have killed so many millions. From the Great Potato Famine in Ireland in the 1840s to many South Asian and African famines of recent decades, the problem has not been absolute scarcity but distribution: there was enough food for all, but social structures kept it out of reach of some. And so they died and die of divisiveness and lack of empathy and altruism (though others were kept alive by such forces, often reaching out from great distances). If a disaster intensifies the conditions of everyday life, then the pleasures of everyday affection and connection become a safety net or survival equipment when things fall apart. In Mexico City, those social ties led first to the rescue, feeding, and sheltering of the damnificados, then to the organizations to defend homes and jobs, but ultimately to a stronger civil society reborn from the earthquake.

LOSING THE MANDATE OF HEAVEN

Contemplate This Ruin

More than three thousand years ago, the Chou dynasty defeated the Shang and became rulers of China for almost a thousand years. To justify their usurpation of power, they proposed that rulers rule by *t'ien ming*, the "mandate of heaven." The principle suggested that earthly rulers are part of the cosmic order, endorsed by the harmony they presumably provide or protect. The word *revolution* in Chinese is *ge ming*; *"ge"*—to strip away—and *"ming"*—the mandate. A revolution not only removes a regime but also tears away its justification for governing. So does a disaster: since the Chou dynasty, earthquakes in China have often been seen as signs that the rulers had lost the mandate of heaven. Even in modern times, many interpreted in this light the death of Chairman Mao two months after the colossal 1976 Tang Shan earthquake killed hundreds of thousands. And the extreme care the Chinese government took after the big 2008 earthquake may have been out of fear of losing credibility and support at a volatile moment when the citizenry and the world were watching closely for callousness and corruption (which were amply present in the badly built schools that killed so many children).

Much about this Chinese worldview seems remote from ours—but disasters in the Western world and present time also threaten the powers that be and often generate change. This is how disaster and revolution come to resemble each other. In some ways a disaster merely brings the existing tensions, conflicts, and tendencies in a society and its government to light or to a crisis point. If the government fails to meet the urgent needs of its people, if it is seen to be self-interested, incompetent, or possessed of interests that serve an elite while sabotaging the well-being of the majority, the upheaval of disaster provides an opportunity to redress this failing that disaster has brought to light. Political scientists A. Cooper Drury and Richard Stuart Olson write, "Disasters overload political systems by multiplying societal demands and empowering new groups on one hand while disarticulating economies and disorganizing governments (as well as revealing their organizational, administrative, and moral deficiencies) on the other." And as Quarantelli points out, bureaucracies aren't good at the urgent needs of disaster because they don't improvise rapidly or well—as do many citizens' groups, including the emergent groups that arise to meet new needs—and because their priorities are sometimes at odds with those of the citizenry.

This suggests another explanation for why elites, in the term coined by Caron Chess and elaborated by Lee Clarke and Kathleen Tierney, panic. They are being tested most harshly at what they do least well, and suddenly their mandate of heaven, their own legitimacy and power, is in question. Earlier disaster scholars tended to imagine that in natural disaster, all parties share common interests and goals, but contemporary sociologists see disasters as moments when subterranean conflicts emerge into the open. Tierney said, "Elites fear disruption of the social order, challenges to their legitimacy." Disasters provide both, lavishly.

Often in disaster, the government is at least inadequate to the crisis; not infrequently, it is so disarrayed as to be irrelevant or almost nonexistent. Some of this is simply scale: a city may have civil servants adequate to respond to an ordinary day of fires, injuries, and accidents, but not when such daily crises are multiplied a thousandfold. Then the citizens are on their own, as they are when bureaucracy and red tape keep institutions from responding urgently enough. In the absence of government, people govern themselves. Everyone from Hobbes to Hollywood filmmakers has assumed this means "law of the jungle" chaos. What in fact takes place is another kind of anarchy, where the citizenry by and large organize and care for themselves. In the immediate aftermath of disaster, government fails as if it had been overthrown and civil society succeeds as though it has revolted: the task of government, usually described as "reestablishing order," is to take back the city and the power to govern it, as well as to perform practical functions—restoring power, cleaning up rubble. So the more long-term aftermath of disaster is often in some sense a counterrevolution, with varying degrees of success. The possibility that they have been overthrown or, more accurately, rendered irrelevant is a very good reason for elite panic if not for the sometimes vicious acts that ensue.

Of course a government that is reasonably popular and responds reasonably well faces a very different situation. During the 1989 Loma Prieta earthquake, the Bay Area suffered relatively little loss of life because decades of good building codes and enforcement resulted in few vulnerable structures. Where structures collapsed, local volunteers and officials worked well together. The major calamity was the Nimitz Freeway collapse—the elevated structure had been built on soft ground. The first responders, as usual, were the locals—including factory workers who brought heavy equipment and stayed for four days to try to rescue the living and retrieve the dead. The radical group Seeds of Peace set up a kitchen and essential services, and officials joined the effort. There was little to resent about the behavior of the government and virtually no social change as a result, though many hailed the removal of the much-hated Nimitz, which had chopped an inner-city neighborhood in half, and San Francisco's damaged Embarcadero Freeway, an eyesore hiding the eastern waterfront. Less popular governments and more violent disasters are a volatile combination, however.

The first great modern disaster was the Lisbon earthquake of November 1, 1755, which destroyed much of that capital city of Portugal—and then did far more politically. It was modern, argues disaster sociologist Russell Dynes, because it was widely treated as a natural occurrence rather than a divine manifestation. Nevertheless it led to sweeping change both in Portugal and across Europe. It struck midmorning on a Sunday, when much of the population was at Mass. Stone churches collapsed onto their congregations. The royal palace and many stone mansions crumbled. The ocean pulled back to expose the rubble on the floor of the harbor, and then a tsunami scoured the waterfront portions of the city. Fires began that burned for several days. Tens of thousands died. It was a huge earthquake, centered on the Atlantic floor, estimated at nine on the Richter scale, devastating as far away as Morocco, felt as far away as northern Europe, with tsunami waves that reached Ireland and North Africa.

Pombal, one of the king's chief ministers, seized more power as the detached King José I and his court moved to tents outside the city. He used that power to modernize Lisbon, update its building codes, and evict the Jesuits with whom he had been battling (in part over how the colonies and their indigenous populations in South America would be governed, in part over how much power the church would have in Portugal). While Pombal battled the Jesuits at home, European intellectuals fought over the meaning of the earthquake abroad. Many argued against the divine theory of disasters or an all-powerful Providence. One, the philosophical writer Voltaire, immediately used the earthquake as the prime evidence against an optimistic worldview in his "Poem on the Lisbon Disaster" and later in his comic novella *Candide*. In the former he began:

> Come, ye philosophers, who cry, "All's well,"
> And contemplate this ruin of a world.
> Behold these shreds and cinders of your race,
> This child and mother heaped in common wreck,
> These scattered limbs beneath the marble shafts—
> A hundred thousand whom the earth devours. . . .

The Lisbon earthquake is usually considered to be one of the starting points of the European Enlightenment, a movement away from authority and religiosity toward individual reason—and doubt. Upheaval in disaster can be as immediate as political change, as intangible as ideological shift. A disaster like the 1985 earthquake in Mexico City produced both.

A Shock to the System

That disasters open the way for change is nowhere more evident than in the earthquake that, thirteen years before the Mexico City quake, devastated Nicaragua's capital and helped bring on a revolution. Not a large quake in objective terms, it was a shallow one directly beneath the city. It reduced to rubble much of the central city and killed several thousand. A large portion of the population lost homes and jobs. For decades afterward the heart of the city was a vast ruin populated by squatters, a negative monument to loss and politics. Dictator Anastasio Somoza could profit more from developing the urban edge than rebuilding the city center, so he attempted to remake the city for his own purposes. To facilitate doing so, he declared martial law and gripped anew the power he had been on the brink of reluctantly relinquishing after many decades of dictatorial rule—the Somoza dynasty had been in power since 1930.

Gioconda Belli, a daughter of Nicaragua's elite, a poet, and an early member of the Sandinistas, the group that would overthrow the government after the earthquake, remembers it vividly. "As the earth shakes so does the sense of security," she recalled thirty-five years later in Los Angeles, where she now lives. "It is such a shock to the system, to the body, and to the sense of place, to the sense of security. All of a sudden a lot of things that you took for granted cease to be for granted and you also realize what is important for you. What fascinated me about the earthquake was how the collective began to function as a whole. Usually it's very dispersed. And all of the sudden the grief and the pain and the fear and all of that, it kicks in. But what I found fascinating was how people networked and there was no higher authority. We were left to our own devices. And so we all knew we were dependent on each other and everybody helped each other."

Lavish from her mane of curly hair and rich voice to her many romantic and political involvements, Belli lights up describing what those days were like, still enthused about that social moment, still outraged about Somoza's actions: "All of a sudden you went from being in your house the night before, going to bed alone in your own little world to being thrown out on the street and mingling with neighbors you might not have said hello to very much or whatever and getting attached to those people, minding them, helping, trying to see what you could do for one another, talking about how you felt. There's no authority, you kind of stop believing in God for that moment. It's hard to process that there is a God when you're living through such horrors: seeing your city go up in flames and all the destruction. So that's what I remember, that kind of solidarity, and of course what happened was that we began to get—you know, it was December twenty-third at midnight, and we usually celebrate Christmas on the twenty-fourth, so the date was also very emotional. It was a family day. It's a very Catholic country. Aid began pouring in pretty quickly, but we began to see that the aid was not being channeled appropriately. It was being given to the military and the military families. You could drive on the highway and see outside their houses they had put up tents for their families because everybody was afraid to go indoors, because the aftershocks were quite intense. And also Somoza took over again, he named himself president of the emergency committee. The next day he was in command. You know this greed that decided to show itself, plus the military measures that were taken, the state of siege and curfew and censorship of the press, all of that happened. People basically felt that this government had forsaken them, and that's when things began to turn."

Somoza seized control of assets and industries with such rapacity that even the affluent and powerful who had previously tolerated him turned on him, and he alienated the Catholic Church as well. These wealthy Nicaraguans—Belli aside—were not the ones who made the revolution, but their disaffection with Somoza and what was called his "kleptocracy" helped open the way for it. Nor did the disaster inevitably result in a revolution; the revolutionaries themselves did the hard work of bringing it about, but the earthquake was a shift that helped. Other, later, events mattered: the 1978 assassination of the moderate but independent newspaper (*La Prensa*) editor Pedro Chamorro was a final outrage. But the shift in atmosphere came with the disaster on the night before Christmas Eve of 1972, and it lasted. Belli recalls, "June or July, I went back to Managua and there was still that sense, it was like—how could I explain it—like we were going back to the city, like we weren't going to give the city up. There was a lot of talk of moving the city somewhere else, people that swore they would never go back. So there was a sense of community in the neighborhoods. There was so much of a sense of having survived a catastrophe that really does bond people together. You never look at your neighbor the same way because after you go through something like that, you really land in reality in a different way.

"Life now is changed back, but I think that's also what [then] allowed revolution to become stronger, because, really, you had a sense of what was important. And people realized that what was important was freedom and being able to decide your life and agency. We had a sense of agency in those days that we were able to decide and to do. Two days later you had this tyrant imposing a curfew, imposing martial law, all those kinds of things. The sense of oppression on top of the catastrophe was really unbearable. And once you had realized that your life can be decided by one night of the earth deciding to shake: 'So what? I want to live a good life and I want to risk my life because I can also lose my life in one night.' You realize that life has to be lived well or is not worth living. It's a very profound transformation that takes place during catastrophes. It's like a near-death experience but lived collectively. It makes such a big difference. I think that's what brings out the best in people. I've seen it over and over, when you cease to think about yourself only. Something kicks in and you start worrying about the tribe, the collective. That kind of makes life meaningful." What's clear from Belli's and other accounts is that the experience is profoundly subjective: it cannot be measured by scismometers, casualty counts, fallen buildings, or anything so quantifiable. The disaster as we usually understand it is tangible, but its psychic consequences are both intangible and often its most important effect.

Scholars agree about the profundity of the rupture. Richard Stuart Olson writes, "Legacies of the Managua 1972 disaster and its aftermath persist to this day, including the emigration of thousands of Nicaraguans of all classes to the United States. Increased pluralism, social mobility, political opportunity, and, in the end, democracy are the most important and enduring. In fact, the 1972 disaster still abruptly divides Nicaraguan history and collective memory." The revolution did not come right away, but the insurgency grew, as did popular support for it. The Sandinista Revolution that took over Nicaragua in June of 1979 was the last of the old-style leftist revolutions, the last socialist revolution but also one of the last in which a small armed group overthrew a government in the name of justice and the people. And it was perhaps the last revolution in which the old idea of state socialism triumphed; a decade later the Berlin Wall would fall and a revolution in the nature of revolution would follow—but that is another story. Belli devoted much of the 1970s to working toward the revolution. Seven years after the earthquake, the revolution swept the country and the Sandinistas approached Managua in triumph.

Belli remembers, "Those first few days were like a dream because—just that feeling I remember of driving down the road toward Managua and people coming out to get the paper: their faces and the happiness. Yes, everyone was exultant and organizing. . . . This whole system of government disappears from one day to the next and you are left with this country, and you get to do it from the bottom up. It's quite an amazing energy. Everybody came to volunteer and bring things. The peasants would come with corn and whatever they could find. People would give you things and do this and that and would contribute things. It was this outpouring of love and goodwill, and wherever we went were these crowds that would come and they would kill a pig and have a big feast for us." Where disaster brought fear and grief, the revolution brought triumph—and bloodshed, but also a sense of radical uncertainty, shared fate, and urgency that brought on generosity and an atmosphere of mutual aid.

The Sandinistas in power did many splendid things—there were literacy campaigns and measures to bring economic justice and alleviate poverty—and some things that were less than splendid. They never resolved, for example, their relationship with the Miskito Indians who lived on the Honduran border, and the ways they confiscated the property of the rich was often vindictive or self-serving. But what the Sandinistas might have done is impossible to know, because "the Reagan Revolution" overtook the United States in 1980, and the Reagan administration, in those late years of the cold war, sought to extirpate all signs of socialism in Central America. The administration surreptitiously funded the Contras, the anti-Sandinista guerrillas who made sallies from the Honduran border to attack small rural communities struggling to raise food and realize the reforms. The Contras stiffened the Sandinistas' positions and sapped the economic vitality of the country, and it was in part to put an end to this hemorrhage that the people elected a non-Sandinista government in 1990.

Since then, much of the Sandinista achievement has trickled away, and the widespread poverty has become more dire—though some achievements of the 1970s still matter. Nicaragua is not a dictatorship anymore. Belli went back to her country after Hurricane Mitch in 1998 and says of those who had been hit hard, "They were amazing. I was so happy to see it. It was a product of the revolution. These people had organized themselves into this group, this community had organized themselves so they had their demands and what they needed, but not just asking; they had their own plan. The way they talk, they are so articulate and amazing, it's great to watch. They had that sense of purpose, of strength, and of dignity, which was not there before."

Revolutionary Weather

Less than nine months after the Mexico City quake, the nuclear reactor in Chernobyl, Ukraine, melted down and eventually dragged down an empire with it. In 2006, the man who had been head of the Soviet Union, Mikhail Gorbachev, reflected, "The nuclear meltdown at Chernobyl twenty years ago this month, even more than my launch of *perestroika,* was perhaps the real cause of the collapse of the Soviet Union five years later. Indeed, the Chernobyl catastrophe was a historic turning point: there was the era before the disaster, and there is the very different era that has followed." Part of the catastrophe was due to the secrecy that was by then habitual to Soviet bureaucrats, which endangered millions, and to the overall sense of unaccountable, incompetent, and callous governance. The forces that emboldened the civil societies of the Soviet satellite states in Poland, East Germany, Hungary, and Czechoslovakia to liberate those nations are not directly related to Chernobyl, but they benefited from a superpower that did not crush them when they rose up, a power that had mutated beyond recognition. Gorbachev asserts, "The Chernobyl disaster, more than anything else, opened the possibility of much greater freedom of expression, to the point that the system as we knew it could no longer continue. It made absolutely clear how important it was to continue the policy of *glasnost,* and I must say that I started to think about time in terms of pre-Chernobyl and post-Chernobyl."

The relationship between disaster and revolution has seldom been explored, though it crops up throughout the history of revolutions. Catastrophic weather across France in the summer of 1788 brought on the crop failures and bad harvests that led to the rising bread prices, shortages, and hunger that played a major role in triggering the French Revolution the following year. The 1870–71 siege and occupation of Paris in the Franco-Prussian War brought on the sense of daring and solidarity that made possible the Paris Commune—several weeks of insurrectionary self-government Kropotkin and anarchists everywhere have cherished ever since. Belli spoke of Nicaraguans feeling after the earthquake that since they could lose their life, they wanted to make it mean something, even if that involved risks. Disaster and crisis can stiffen resolve, as did disarming a bomb single-handedly for that young woman in the London Blitz who then felt emboldened to confront her boss. Sometimes they work by making a bad situation worse to the point of intolerability; they create a breaking point. Sometimes they do so by making obvious an injustice or agenda that was opaque before. Sometimes they do so by generating the circumstances in which people discover each other and thereby a sense of civil society and collective power. But there is no formula; there are no certainties. Leftists of a certain era liked to believe that the intensification of suffering produced revolution and was therefore to be desired or even encouraged; no such reliable formula ties social change to disaster or other suffering; calamities are at best openings through which a people may take power—or may lose the contest and be further subjugated.

Still the resemblances and ties between disaster and revolution matter. If a revolution is a disaster—which many who oppose them would heartily endorse—it is so because a disaster is also a utopia of sorts; the two phenomena share aspects of solidarity, uncertainty, possibility, and the upending of the ordinary systems governing things—the rupture of the rules and the opening of many doors. Naomi Klein's *Shock Doctrine* explores one side of the impact of disaster: the scramble for power on the side of the powerful, of authorities, institutions, and capitalism. It is a scramble because multiple parties or facets of society are contending for power and legitimacy, and sometimes the other side—the people, civil society, social justice—wins. Not easily—in Nicaragua, Somoza strengthened his hold temporarily, but the same earthquake that gave him his opportunity intensified resolve and brought on the revolution. The destabilization of disaster is most terrifying to those who benefit most from that stability. (Perhaps future historians will regard 9/11 too as an event that initially strengthened right-wing power in the United States but led to the election of Barack Obama and long-term change.)

Historian Mark Healey writes of natural disasters: "Insurrections by a 'nature' that had seemed subdued, they unsettle, disrupt, and potentially overthrow apparently natural structures of social power. Because the existing arrangements of power are so often justified as 'natural,' the unexpected reshaping of the 'natural' can call many of those arrangements into question. Such theaters of 'outrage and blame' test the authority of states and technical elites: they can serve to challenge or undo that authority, but also to justify or reaffirm it." This declaration comes in his essay on the 1944 San Juan earthquake and the rise to power of Juan Perón. The temblor that hit San Juan at the foothills of the Andes on a summer evening was the worst natural disaster in Argentine history, killing ten thousand and destroying the housing of half the people in the province. Secretary of Labor Perón led the rescue and reconstruction effort and through it achieved the national visibility that helped launch him to the presidency. (Then U.S. secretary of commerce Herbert Hoover attained a similar prominence with his relief efforts in response to the great Mississippi flood of 1927, likewise sometimes credited with bringing him to the presidency.)

Perón ruled the country for eleven years, and his blend of authoritarian populism is still known as Peronism there. "The provision of relief by outsiders can undermine the recovery it is intended to produce. As the gratitude of the moment faded, the disaster revealed and produced widening fissures within San Juan," writes Healey. The top-down disaster relief produced alienation and despair: bodies were incinerated in great heaps without being identified; children were evacuated without careful records being kept so that many of them too were lost to those who loved them; the sale of food and goods was forbidden, and though supplies were given away, not enough were available to forestall want. People became helpless and hopeless, denied a role in their own survival. And Perón rose to an extraordinary career as Argentina's most charismatic politician to date, so much so that more than six decades later Peronism is still an important force in that country's politics, though other strains matter more in this millennium. Many trusted authorities and centralized power more in that era when even most of the alternative visions included Socialist or Communist governments with pervasive control. In Argentina that trust is gone.

On December 19, 20, and 21 of 2001, Argentines launched an unprecedented uprising in response to that country's financial crisis and growing political disgust. In the election that October of 2001, citizens were so disgusted that nearly half did not show up or cast blank or spoiled ballots—putting pictures of Osama bin Laden in the ballot envelopes was one popular response. Three months later, the economy collapsed, victim of the neoliberal policies of "free trade" that brought in a rush of cheap imports that undermined many Argentine companies, privatized formerly public services and companies, caused massive foreign debt, and pegged the peso to the dollar in ways that destabilized the currency and the economy. Spreading poverty and unemployment had dogged the country in the 1990s, and the economy finally crashed in the South American midsummer of 2001. All personal bank accounts were frozen, and the middle class found themselves nearly as penniless as the chronically unemployed. The president resigned, the public rose up, chanting *"Que se vayan todos!"* ("Out with all of them!"), and within the next two weeks, the country went through three more presidents. On New Year's Eve of 2001 the American secretary of state tried to put through a call to the Argentine president, only to be told that there wasn't one at the moment.

An economic disaster is on the face of it not at all like a natural disaster. What has been wrecked is immaterial and abstract, but its consequences are more than tangible: it creates hardships, even emergencies, upends everyday life, throws people together in unexpected ways, changes their status, and often prompts them to take collective action. That first night, people everywhere were out in the streets banging pots and pans, and others saw them on television and went outside themselves to join them. One Buenos Aires inhabitant was on the phone with his brother when he heard over the line a racket from his brother's downtown neighborhood. A moment later he heard the *cacerolaza*, the banging of pots and pans, in his own neighborhood and hung up to join it. "What began angrily, with people coming out on the street in a rage, quickly turned joyful. People smiled and mutually recognized that something had changed. Later came euphoria," he told historian-sociologist Marina Sitrin.

Tens of thousands took over the streets of the city and fought the police for their right to be in public—a few died in the struggle, and many were teargassed or beaten, but they did not surrender. "I also remember the feeling of walking back after everything was over. That feeling of returning with so many people, walking openly on Corrientes, a main avenue in Buenos Aires, with the satisfaction of having played a part; feeling that we were in charge of ourselves," says that man who hung up the phone to head out into the street. Another recalls, "When you went out with the cacerolaza on the nineteenth, you saw your neighbors also *caccrolando*. And you said, how crazy! Because I never speak to this person, or we see that one in the street and only say good morning, or not, and here my neighbor is also banging a pot. Or, my neighborhood butcher is cacerolando! The neighborhood pharmacist! How strange . . . it was a reconnection with something that was lost. Many ways of being social had been lost."

Some of those things had been lost during the years of terror from 1976 to 1983, when those even suspected of subversion or dissent were tortured and disappeared; some during the frenzy to survive the economic pressures and privatizations that came after. As a result, people had withdrawn in fear from civil society, from a sense of membership in the body politic. The 2001 meltdown created something akin to disaster's sense of community. It was a revolution in spirit as well as in practical things. In fifty years of bad government, including a few murderous military regimes, Argentines had become deeply distrustful of politicians and state power, and most had abandoned public life. This time, they sought to withdraw from and reduce government's sphere, turning not to left-wing movements but to each other, relaunching a vital civil society. What they created was so new it required new words—*horizontalidad*, or horizontalism, to describe the nonhierarchical way many communities made decisions; *protagonism* to describe the new agency many found; *politica afectiva* to describe the politics of affection. The examples of Argentina in the earthquake of 1944 and the financial crash of 2001 demonstrate again that disasters are ultimately enigmas: it is not the disaster but the struggle to give it meaning and to take the opportunity to redirect the society that matters, and these are always struggles with competing interests.

These moments in which revolution resemble disaster utopias are strange. On the one hand, the revolution seems to have already, instantly, fulfilled its promise: all men are brothers, everything is possible, anyone can speak, hearts are full, solidarity is strong. The formation of a new government historically reallocates much of this potency to the state rather than civil society. On the other hand, much of this moment's glory is often regarded as a side effect, an incidental, and the revolution moves on to set up better education or economies but loses this fellowship and openness. Something trickles away.

The real revolution may be the period between regimes, not the new regime (and Jonathan Schell points out that, contrary to what we usually believe, the French and Russian revolutions terminated the old regimes without significant bloodshed; it was establishing the new one that was so violent). Certainly the period immediately after, or during, the revolution comes closest to the anarchist ideal of a society without a state, a moment when everyone has agency and no one has ultimate authority, when the society invents itself as it goes along. What makes the Argentine uprising remarkable is that the people seemed to recognize that ephemeral spirit and sought to cultivate it and see it as an end in itself rather than a means or byproduct. It was a revolution not to create a new state of government but a new state of being as free of government as possible, a revolution to embrace the richness of civil society and social possibility. Though like all revolutions it subsided, some of its effects are indelible—and influential elsewhere. It demonstrated that societies can change themselves, suddenly and for the better. The way the imagination of the possible changed is a longer story that continues into the present in Mexico, again linked to that earthquake of 1985.

STANDING ON TOP OF GOLDEN HOURS

The True Feast of Time

Falling in love is easy. The experience carries you along effortlessly for a while, everything is harmonious, and the possibilities seem endless. Then one day you wake up in the same room as another human being with his or her own needs and views and the interesting process of actually finding common ground and forming a resilient and lasting bond begins . . . or fails. A disaster is as far from falling in love as can be imagined, but disaster utopias are also a spell when engagement, improvisation, and empathy happen as if by themselves. Then comes the hard business of producing a good society by determination and dedication. Civil society has moments when it falls in love with itself or celebrates its anniversaries, when those ties again become enchantments rather than obligations. That era when the connections were made, the possibilities were exciting, and joy came readily matters afterward. Memory of such moments becomes a resource to tap into through recollection and invocation, and celebrating those moments revives and reaffirms the emotions. Thus it is that we celebrate birthdays, the dates on which couples met or were married, on which revolutions began, battles were won, on which a god, saint, or hero was born, performed a miracle, left the earth, and more. The enchanted time can be reclaimed and renewed by memory and celebration, and most cultures have a calendar of such occasions, when the linear time of production pauses and the cyclical time of celebration appears.

Disaster and revolution both create in some sense a carnival—an upheaval and a meeting ground, and there are carnivalesque aspects to disaster. We could think of revolutions as carnivals, for whatever good they create in the long term it is only in the moment that they create the sense of openness to each other and to possibility that is so exhilarating. That is, imagined as moments of renewal and reinvention rather than attempts to secure some good permanently, we could see the ephemeral utopia they create with new eyes. And certainly carnival and revolution have long been linked. (Though the word is used more generally in the English-speaking world, Carnival is most specifically the festivities that occur before Lent—in other words, a series of celebrations in the span of time between Christmas and Easter.)

Carnival makes sense as revolution too: an overthrow of the established order under which we are alienated from each other, too shy to act, divided along familiar lines. Those lines vanish and we merge exuberantly. Carnival is a hectic, short-lived, raucous version of utopia, one that matters because it is widely available, though just as carnival is scheduled and disaster is not, so carnival has known limits and consequences and disaster does not. Still, the resemblances are significant—carnival, for example, often features grotesque images, motifs of death, role inversion and transformation, and much chaos, as well as the basic ingredient of people living together in a shared space and going beyond their usual bounds. Carnival is in some sense a formalized disaster, a ritual to reap disaster's benefits with a minimum of disaster's tragic consequences. You could call it disaster made predictable, both in when it happens and what it wreaks. Fritz spoke of "the failure of modern societies to fulfill an individual's basic human needs for community identity" and concluded that "disasters provide a temporary liberation from the worries, inhibitions, and anxieties associated with the past and future because they force people to concentrate their full attention on immediate moment-to-moment, day-to-day needs within the context of the present realities." He could have also been describing what carnival provides in the more safe and structured break from ordinary time.

Some ancient calendars had three hundred sixty days; the five at the end of the year were categorically outside time, so that the ordinary rules did not apply (similarly, Halloween was initially a Celtic year's-end festival when the dead could travel through the gap between the old year and the new). A sense of being outside ordinary time, of disorder and inversion, governs saturnalias and carnivals. They are *liminal* in an almost literal sense, since that word means crossing lintels or thresholds. The Roman Saturnalia was a year-end winter festival of freedom: gambling was permitted in public, everyone wore the wool caps of freedmen, slaves were relieved of their duties and masters sometimes waited on slaves, a lord of misrule was chosen (and in some accounts, this holiday of Saturn was assimilated into that of Kronos, the god of time and the Golden Age). The festival lasted a few days and then several days, but long after it was over it must have left a lingering sense that the everyday order of things was not the inevitable one; it must have, like disaster and revolution, opened up the possibilities.

Scholarship nowadays denies a direct relationship between the Roman Saturnalia and Christian Carnival, but there are many similarities, including a lord of misrule and acts of inversion of ordinary power relations. In his book *Carnival and Other Christian Festivals*, Max Harris recounts the theological basis for the inversion of hierarchies, the passage in the Magnificat where Mary says (in Luke 1:22), in celebration of the impending birth of her son, "He hath put down the mighty from their seat and hath exalted the humble." And he quotes Peter Burke, who wrote that the whole Christmas season was "treated as carnivalesque, appropriately enough from a Christian point of view, since the birth of the Son of God in a manger was a spectacular example of the world turned upside down." Carnival, which was originally part of the Christmas season rather than the prelude to Lent, could include impersonations of the clergy; cross-dressing actual members of the clergy; comic blasphemies, including parodies of the Mass and risqué humor; ritual enactments of historic battles (particularly in the New World) in which the losers were no longer necessarily the losers; masks; dances; fireworks; spectacles; uproar; and chaos. The Russian critic Mikhail Bakhtin goes further in his famous description of carnival: "Carnival celebrated temporary liberation from the prevailing truth and from the established order; it marked the suspension of all hierarchical rank, privileges, norms, and prohibitions. Carnival was the true feast of time, the feast of becoming, change, and renewal. It was hostile to all that was immortalized and completed. . . . People were, so to speak, reborn for new, purely human relations. These truly human relations were not only a fruit of imagination or abstract thought; they were experienced."

Looking back from the perspective of disaster and revolution,

Carnival seems not merely to punctuate the calendar of ordinary time but to puncture it as well, as if with airholes to breathe through, or to let pressure off, or to let outside possibilities in. Carnival is often spoken of as liminal, as a moment of suspension between two states, of openness to transformation and difference, a moment when the rules are no longer in effect (though the disorder that Carnival creates and celebrates has its own strict parameters). Europe's Protestant Reformation, in eliminating so many festivals and celebrations, did not merely increase work time but also undid the dialogue between ordinary time and its festive interruption, an interruption that is also an assertion of civil society, of memory, of collective liberation. And so one way to regard uprisings and maybe even disasters is as unseasonal outbreaks of carnival, assertions of civil society, community, and the breakdown of categories and boundaries. Covert new erotic unions are a staple of old stories about masked Carnival, but the public union of each to each is its point.

Many traditional carnivals feature subversive and mocking elements: parodies of the church and religion, status reversals, reenactments of historical moments—such as the conquest of Latin America—in ways that reclaim power and voice. There is a permanent debate over whether carnival is truly subversive or the way an unjust society lets off pressure that allows the status quo to stand, but the only possible answer is that it varies, as do carnivals. The only great carnival rites in the United States include segregated balls and the public parade of New Orleans's most powerful people in masks and hats that vaguely resemble the pointed caps of the Ku Klux Klan. When the City of New Orleans mandated in the early 1990s that the parades no longer be racially exclusive, some of the old elite white krewes canceled their public events rather than integrate.

The last surviving oligarchical public parade, Rex, still follows Zulu, the blackface African American parade that was founded as a parody of both Rex and African American stereotypes a century ago. Each year Rex and Zulu acknowledge each other in an uneasy truce while all the rest of the city revels, dresses up, dons masks, promenades, and drinks a lot. Mardi Gras is a strange festival, balanced between asserting the status quo and letting loose, between hierarchy and subversion. After all, the great majority excluded from the elite carnival balls have their own balls, parades, street revels, and parties, some of which include biting social commentary. Traditional carnivals continue throughout Europe, India, and the Americas, notably in Brazil, the Caribbean, and Bolivia, while the feast days and festivals of Mexico and indigenous New Mexico continue another version of the rite.

Disaster belongs to the sociologists, but carnival to the anthropologists, who talk of its liminality. That is, like initiation rites, carnival takes place in a space betwixt and between familiar, settled states; it is a place of becoming in which differences diminish and commonalities matter, a separation from what came before. The anthropologist Victor Turner noted that liminal moments open up the possibility of *communitas,* the ties that are made when ordinary structures and the divides they enforce cease to matter or exist. The celebration that is carnival often resembles disaster in being made of turbulence and destruction: of people throwing colored powders in India or candies and meringues in Spain or beads in New Orleans; of creating huge messes in the streets and leaving piles of debris behind; of shouting, rushing, dancing, spinning; of mingling with strangers who are for the moment less strange; of images of the grotesque, the morbid, and the unsettling.

To make fellowship, joy, and freedom work for a day or a week is far more doable than the permanent transformation of society, and it can inspire people to return to that society in its everyday incarnation with renewed powers and ties. The anarchist theorist Hakim Bey famously coined the term *temporary autonomous zones* to describe these phenomena, neither revolution nor festival, in which people liberate themselves for pleasure and social reinvention. He saw their ephemerality as a survival technique, a way of arising, affecting, and vanishing before any move to repress arose: "The TAZ is like an uprising which does not engage directly with the State, a guerilla operation which liberates an area (of land, of time, of imagination) and then dissolves itself to re-form elsewhere/elsewhen, *before* the State can crush it." The goal is not permanence or confrontation, and the moment of liberation can be re-created, so that its lapse is not necessarily a defeat.

The First Day in History

At the beginning of the long vacation-time walk during which he would establish his poetic vocation, the twenty-year-old William Wordsworth landed in Calais, France. He and his traveling companion arrived on

July 14, 1790, the first anniversary of the dawn of the French Revolution, an anniversary that has been a festival almost ever since. It was a year since outraged Parisians had stormed the Bastille. A subsequent series of events, some violent, some festive, had upended the ancient political system and opened up what seemed, then, to truly be an era of liberty, equality, and fraternity. Revolutionary France was reinventing itself in accord at first with ideals and then with the undercurrents of power and fear—but in 1790, all was still bright. On that anniversary, as Wordsworth described it in his long autobiographical poem *The Prelude*, revolution's dawn recurred as festival:

> *But 'twas a time when Europe was rejoiced,*
> *France standing on the top of golden hours,*
> *And human nature seeming born again.*
>
> *Bound, as I said, to the Alps, it was our lot*
> *To land at Calais on the very eve*
> *Of that great federal day; and there we saw,*
> *In a mean city and among a few,*
> *How bright a face is worn when joy of one*
> *Is joy of tens of millions. . . .*

It's a remarkable moment in history, a festival that is also the reiteration of a revolution, a symbolic reenactment of its promise that is also a fulfillment.

> *Southward thence*
> *We took our way, direct through hamlets, towns,*
> *Gaudy with relics of that festival,*
> *Flowers left to wither on triumphal arcs*
> *And window garlands.*

They traveled on:

> *And found benevolence and blessedness*
> *Spread like a fragrance everywhere, like spring*
> *That leaves no corner of the land untouched . . .*

Unhoused beneath the evening star we saw
Dances of liberty. . . .

Wordsworth captures some of the key ingredients of such a moment: a joy magnified by its shared condition; the suspension of ordinary time; and the sense of a transformed human nature that opens up tremendous, hopeful possibility. Historian Mona Ozouf writes, "It was the great national thaw, already sensed by the Marquis de Ségur when he returned to France from Russia in 1790. He found that people spoke freely: in every public square 'groups of men were talking in lively fashion.' The old fear and circumspection had gone from their eyes: even 'individuals of the lower classes' had a proud, direct gaze. Everywhere there was noise and an 'extraordinary sense of movement.'" The revolution began with a sense of openness and egalitarianism; it degenerated into a bloodbath and the erection of new hierarchies. And French society would never again be subjugated the way it had under the absolutist monarchies and stark class divides of the ancien régime.

And that ephemeral liberation emerged again and again. During the Paris Commune of 1871, the painter Gustave Courbet said in a letter, "Paris is a true paradise. . . . all social groups have established themselves as federations and are masters of their own fate." During the Spanish Civil War, George Orwell wrote of loyalist-controlled Barcelona's transformation, "Down the Ramblas, the wide central artery of the town where crowds of people streamed constantly to and fro, the loudspeakers were bellowing revolutionary songs all day and far into the night. . . . Above all there was a belief in the revolution and the future, a feeling of having suddenly emerged into an era of equality and freedom." Eleanor Bakhtadze, a student during the French upheaval of 1968, which began as a student rebellion and ended as a powerful national strike that toppled the de Gaulle regime, said, "Paris was wonderful then. Everyone was talking." Of the Czechoslovakian uprising the same year, the photographer Josef Koudelka remembers, "Everbody forgot who he was. . . . Miracles were happening. People behaved like they never had before; everyone was respectful and kind to each other. I felt that everything that could happen in my life was happening during those seven days. It was an exceptional situation that brought out something exceptional from all of us."

Ariel Dorfman reports something similar from the dawn of the left-wing Allende administration in Chile in 1970. He spoke of people told they were powerless all their lives grasping this moment of victory and reports that he himself "felt life quicken and accelerate, I felt the giddiness of those few great moments in your existence when you know that everything is possible, that anything is possible. I felt as if I were the first man on Earth and this was the first day in history." Giaconda Belli writes that July 18 and 19, 1979, when the Sandinista rebels overthrew the Somoza dictatorship in Nicaragua, were "two days that felt as if a magical, age-old spell had been cast over us, taking us back to Genesis, to the very site of the creation of the world." An editor who was in South Africa when the apartheid era came to an end described to me the same sense of openness to an unknown future and each other and joy in liberty. Over and over again appears this sense of people having stepped together into the rosy dawn of greater possibilities, into a place where they feel their own power, the possibility of connection and concerted effort, and with those, hope. This is not only an idea but a feeling, a surge that has everything to do with making history. It's a liminal time, a time between worlds that is a world of its own. Wordsworth wrote elsewhere, in praise of the French Revolution,

> The whole earth the beauty wore of promise, that which sets
> The budding rose above the rose full blown.

It was not the achievement of the revolution but its air of possibility that was so radiant to Wordsworth.

Disaster's message that anything could happen is not so far away from revolution's exhortation that everything is possible. Revolutions beget a similar moment when the very air you breathe seems to pour out of a luminous future, when the people all around you are brothers and sisters, when you feel an extraordinary strength. Then the revolutionary moment of utter openness to the future turns into one future or another. Things get better or they get worse, but you are no longer transfigured, the people around you are no longer quite so beloved, and private life calls with its small, insistent whisper. (And privacy is what we are happy to go home to after communing with strangers and neighbors in carnival or friends at a party; the trick is knowing how and why to join again in due time.)

There was a carnival of sorts that sought this renewal specifically, the jubilee that has always hovered as a promise and never been executed as an actuality unless you call a revolution a jubilee. The jubilee described in Leviticus is supposed to happen every fifty years and "proclaim liberty throughout all the land," free the slaves, cancel debts, return the land to the original owner (who might be God or no one), let the fields lie fallow, and bring about a long reprieve from work. Slaves sang of jubilee; early-nineteenth-century revolutionaries embraced it as a great redistribution of wealth, a starting over even; and the British group Jubilee Research (formerly Jubilee 2000) seeks the cancellation of third-world debt as jubilee's contemporary equivalent. The idea of jubilee is a revolution that recurs as a festival.

A disaster sometimes wipes the slate clean like a jubilee, and it is those disasters that beget joy, while the ones that increase injustice and isolation beget bitterness—the "corrosive community" of which disaster scholars speak. Some, perhaps all, do both. That is to say, a disaster is an end, a climax of ruin and death, but it is also a beginning, an opening, a chance to start over. (It is also a way to start over for capitalism, creating markets for the replacement of what has been destroyed and more.) And in this light, we can regard the Puritan work ethic as a force of privatization, not only the spiritual privatization of Protestantism but also the privatization of what was hitherto public civic life. The moments of carnival, community, and political participation are in those terms nonproductive, wasted time, even—if you think of the seventeenth-century New England Puritans punishing those who celebrated Christmas—violations of belief. The widespread distrust of the life of unpoliced crowds, manifested in urban and particularly suburban design in the United States, in the bans by dictatorships on public gatherings, in the writings of Le Bon and the plans for disaster are measures against carnival and popular power.

The utilitarian argument against fiestas, parades, carnivals, and general public merriment is that they produce nothing. But they do: they produce society. They renew the reasons why we might want to belong and the feeling that we do. The product is far less tangible than everyday goods and services but vital all the same—if absent from many contemporary societies. A festival is a sowing of wildness and a harvest of joy and belonging. An endless fiesta would be exhausting and demoralizing: the pleasure would go out of it, the masks would disguise only fatigue and apathy, and there would eventually be nothing to celebrate. The ordinary and the extraordinary need each other, or rather everyday life needs to be interrupted from time to time—which is not to say that we need disaster, only that it sometimes supplies the interruption in which the other work of society is done. Carnival and revolution are likewise interruptions of everyday life, but their point is to provide something that allows you to return to that life with more power, more solidarity, more hope.

The City Belongs to Everyone

Lucha libre means Mexico's theatrical version of wrestling, but the word *lucha* is less specific than the English word *wrestling:* it means struggle and it is used in a political sense all the time. Lucha libre, free struggle, the enormously popular Mexican sport, serves as entertainment with symbolic and political dimensions, a carnival of masculine power and imaginative adventure. Like most sports, lucha libre serves as a drama with an unknown outcome for the conflicts between the *tecnicos*, good guys who play by the rules, and *rudos*, who cheat and generally embody evil. The wrestlers are always masked, anonymous, with stage names that have no ordinary names behind them, and so they parade like the figures in a carnival, dressed as gods, heroes, animals, and myths of the past. Among the best-known names are Blue Demon, the Black Shadow, and Thousand Masks. To unmask a wrestler is to defeat him definitively, and wrestlers sometimes compete for their tight-fitting, face-covering headpieces with letters, emblems, or colors that reflect the superhero names of the wrestlers. Ripping another wrestler's mask off is grounds for disqualification.

The most celebrated of all Mexican wrestlers was the silver-masked El Santo, the Saint, whose career spanned four decades, countless victories in the ring, fifty-two films, mostly science fiction and monster movies, and a lot of comic books. A week before he died, he pulled his mask back to reveal his face on television, but he was buried with the mask on. Lucha libre is the most carnivalesque of sports, depending on disguise and transformation, embodying metaphysical concerns about power, ethics, and justice.

Until 1987, many wrestlers' careers overflowed the ring into pop culture, but one wrestler came from far outside the ring to wrestle with injustice. Super Barrio emerged from the ruins of the 1985 earthquake, or rather from the lucha, the struggle that came out of the earthquake. When politicians cut ribbons or staged other public events they hoped would reflect well on them, Super Barrio would show up and pressure them to do better by the poor. He confronted landlords; showed up at evictions, meetings, and demonstrations; inspired the strugglers to feel more powerful and confident. He became famous as a sort of latter-day Robin Hood of the urban poor, and he lives on more than two decades after he first appeared. He is credited with stopping ten thousand evictions, and when he appeared on camera in a recent documentary he spoke about his politics in such phrases as, "We have asserted that the city belongs to everyone" and "The credit goes to the people. Who is behind the mask matters least" and "Super Barrio is all of us." Though the only one in costume, he placed everyone around him in carnival mode and opened up the possibilities.

Several men have worn the tight red-and-yellow outfit with the big SB on the chest, but only one man is publicly identified with Super Barrio: ex-revolutionary, former prisoner, *La Jornada* columnist, tenant organizer, and restaurateur Marco Rascón. His restaurant is a little fish joint in a fairly nice part of Mexico City, and he himself is kind, burly, grizzled, and hospitable, even to would-be interviewers with lousy Spanish who show up at closing time. When he spoke of the origins of Super Barrio, he spoke of himself, but also of El Santo. He recalls, "When we initiated the work of working with tenants in the center, in the historic region of Mexico City, there was a landowner who threatened the tenants with eviction. At that time El Santo had just died, so I proposed that the saint of the tenants appear to defend the tenants—it would be the ghost of the saint. At that time we were still very square militants, where playing with humor and with theatrical forms and performance was concerned. Now it is common but back then, we're talking 1983 and we had very rigid ideas. The people who struggled had to show we suffered, that people were exploited, the people had to be sad, the iconography was people that were very angry or very sad; those were the forms of the militancy and social struggle of the Left. I tried to insert humor, but there was no support in that moment.

"Another thing that existed in 1985 was that the lucha libre was very looked down upon; it was a thing for the poor and for vulgar people—it was vulgar. We went to save a woman so that they wouldn't evict her from her house—we went to defend her and upon our return I told them the story of El Santo, and we were walking with many people . . . and then we began to say we could do Super Barrio, so one woman said 'Yes!' So some went to buy the tennis shoes, and we were saying let's make it red and yellow because those are the colors that we most wanted; another went to buy the mask, another to make the shield on her sewing machine. The next day, when we had a protest, twelfth of June of 1987, Super Barrio appeared for the first time at a protest at the Angel de Independencia Polanco, where there were some offices."

Rascón continued, "Super Barrio is a personality whose credibility exists while he has a mask on; without the mask, he doesn't exist. There's a similar element to earlier national heroes such as El Santo or Zorro, as well as an echo of the pre-Hispanic origin of masks, the warriors in pre-Columbian times who donned animal masks to adopt their qualities. One of the things that has helped maintain Super Barrio's credibility is that the government has had to deal with him as a confrontational force. In addition, he has never allowed himself to be separated from his popular origins. When he speaks in public, he speaks in such a way that the average person can understand him. What he's expressing is the feelings of the people, especially those who get lost in the political discourse. That's why he's been able to achieve remarkable things. . . .

"The first time he showed up at a demonstration, he joined the neighborhood commission when they went in to meet with the municipal authorities, who were shocked when they saw a masked figure sitting across the table from them. Nowadays it's not that surprising, of course, but back then, the fact that they had to face a masked man gave us an important weapon. With Super Barrio, we dominated on their own territory. They got into such a defensive position that they couldn't say no to us on many matters which they had previously opposed." A year after the superhero's birth, he was a player in national politics. Rascón recalls how Super Barrio showed up next to the populist alternative presidential candidate "Cuauhtémoc Cárdenas, with his face of a statue, with a masked man at his side. The most serious of politicians with a masked man next to him and these pictures were all going all around the world. Cuauhtémoc, the day of the election, the reporters asked him to say who he voted for. And when he came out of the booth, he said, 'I voted for Super Barrio.'" The fiction had become real, and the carnival had possessed Mexican politics, for a carnival that arose from disaster to foment revolution is one way to describe Super Barrio.

Since Super Barrio stepped onto the stage of world politics, political activism around the world has become more festive—more carnival, you could say. But the superhero in the red tights didn't invent it; it was arising everywhere. Eastern Europe's civil society tested and stretched the boundaries of the possible with theater, music, and carnival celebrations. Václav Havel convened many of the forces of Czechoslovakia's "velvet revolution" in his Magic Lantern Theater, though the resurgence of Czech civil society did not really begin with theater but with a band, the Plastic People of the Universe, in 1976, whose liberatory gestures met with repression that triggered more such gestures and a real opening. Celebration of the canonization of local saint Agnes of Bohemia became another step in galvanizing the country's liberation, just as Mardi Gras antics helped trigger Poland's insurrection.

Since then, culture and politics, revolution and carnival have grown far closer. For the past twenty years, U.S. radicals have been speaking of "the politics of prefiguration": of the idea that you can and must embody whatever liberty, justice, democracy you aspire to, and in doing so in your self, your community, or your movement you achieve a degree of victory, whatever you do beyond that. Thus political demonstrations around the country have become less like complaints and more like celebrations. Several groups toward the end of the 1990s took this to carnivalesque extremes, which was only reasonable: if you were protesting against alienation, isolation, and privatization, festivity in public didn't merely demand but cultivated and reclaimed what was at risk. In the 1999 shutdown of the World Trade Organization (WTO) in Seattle, for example, giant puppets, costumes, banners, and, famously, people dressed as endangered sea turtles all played a role. It was both a blockade as potent as that of any general strike in the 1930s and a festive demonstration of what the alternatives look like. Similarly, four years later at the WTO meeting in Cancún, Mexico, a coalition of Mexican campesinos, Korean farmers, and activists from around the world gathered with banners, traditional costumes, musical instruments, parades, and theatrical props. One Korean man, a longtime international activist, committed suicide on the barriers to dramatize the mortal threat to small farmers the proposals held. Thousands of women pulled down barriers with carefully placed ropes. The activists again influenced the course of history—poor nations and nongovernmental organizations (NGOs) inside were inspired to stand up to the first world and corporate powers. When the talks collapsed inside, the people outside went wild with joy. Thus it is that one contemporary revolutionary has remarked, "The means are the end."

A Carnival of Revolution

That aforementioned revolutionary was Subcomandante Insurgente Marcos of the Zapatistas. Perhaps the greatest melding of carnival, disaster, and revolution came with Mexico's next round of masked heroes, indigenous revolutionaries from the southeastern mountains and jungles of Mexico, the Zapatistas. It is hard to say what the disaster was. It was the 501 years of colonialism, extermination, and discrimination against the indigenous people of the Americas. It was the long decades of impoverishment and repression under the PRI, which had turned the 1910 revolution's hopes of *libertad y tierra,* "land and liberty," into disappointment as the old tyrannies and deprivations continued. And it was the new threat posed to the survival of small farmers, rural communities, and the poor as a whole by the North American Free Trade Agreement (NAFTA) that triggered the uprising, since NAFTA went into effect that New Year's Day of 1994. Simply surviving with much of their culture intact was already a struggle and a form of resistance for the indigenous peoples who became the Zapatistas. The uprising was not the first uprising in these communities, and yet it was unlike anything the world had ever seen before.

A little more than eight years after the earthquake, the Zapatistas made their presence known with a traditional armed insurrection in which they seized six towns in Chiapas, including the old capital city, San Cristóbal de las Casas. Twelve days after their appearance on the world stage, armed conflict ended and they began to use their other weapons. A demonstration of a hundred thousand supporters in Mexico City helped make the transition. Then the unimaginable and unprecedented happened: they metamorphosed into a revolution whose weapons were words and ideas. They often speak of "the fire and the word," the fire being armed revolution, the word being the spread of ideas and conversations—nonviolent social change. They were the Ejército Zapatista de Liberación Nacional, the Zapatista National Army of Liberation, taking their name from the revolutionary leader Emiliano Zapata (1879–1919). From the beginning the Zapatistas wore masks, mostly ski masks, though some appear in bandannas. They served the same purpose they always have for outlaws and rebels—and revelers—the protection of identity, but as the years wore on they became a costume of anonymity, making the Zapatistas everyone and no one, like Zorro and Super Barrio.

All the comandantes, male and female, and nearly all the rest of the Zapatistas were indigenous, but one taller, paler figure stuck out, Subcomandante Marcos, whose manifestos, missives, and parables grew into a marvelous new literature combining political analysis, poetic language, anecdote, and humor. He often spoke for the Zapatistas and drew from their lore and worldview, but he contributed his own humor and verve. His "real" identity became an obsession of journalists after the uprising, and when one journalist took him at face value that he had been a gay waiter in San Francisco, he wrote, "Marcos is gay in San Francisco, black in South Africa, an Asian in Europe, a Chicano in San Ysidro, an anarchist in Spain, a Palestinian in Israel, a Mayan Indian on the streets of San Cristóbal, a Jew in Germany . . . a pacifist in Bosnia, a single woman on the metro at 10:00 p.m., a celebrant on the zócalo, a campesino without land, an unemployed worker . . . and of course a Zapatista in the mountains of southeastern Mexico." This gave rise to the carnivalesque slogan "*Todos somos* Marcos" ("We are all Marcos"), just as Super Barrio claims to be no one and everyone.

Though deeply rooted in indigenous tradition, the Zapatista revolution was a brand-new realization of what revolution could be. The revolutionaries spoke to a global civil society coming into being, sending out dispatches on the Internet that quickly spread and were translated. Laura Carlsen, who moved to Mexico after the 1985 earthquake to work with the unionizing seamstresses, says, "The Zapatista movement proved the power of language to weave global webs of resistance at the same time that it rejected the language of power. Unlike previous revolutionary movements, they did not announce plans to take power and install a new state. . . . The Zapatistas have deepened their commitment to building alternatives from the grassroots rather than controlling, competing for, or often even confronting the formal power of the state. Building autonomy is central to this process. Before the Zapatista uprising, the Mexican indigenous movement had already formulated a concept of autonomy that focused on recuperating traditional forms of self-government in the community."

If the Zapatistas arose from many long disasters, the society they created in their autonomous regions of Chiapas and that they propose in their globally circulated slogans and writings greatly resembles disaster communities. There is an emphasis on improvisation. *"Caminando preguntamos,"* they say, or "We walk asking questions." Rather than dogma, they have inquiry as a core principle. There is an intense critique of hierarchy and *mandar obediencia,* or "govern by obeying," is also a recurrent theme, imperfectly realized. At the entrance to one of their communities is a sign that could be at any of them: "Here the people govern and the government obeys." It is in many ways the society of mutual aid and self-government Kropotkin, among many others, dreamed of. It attempts to render permanent what disaster fleetingly provides: a realm in which people care for each other in the absence of entrenched and alienated authority and the presence of mutual aid, altruism, and love.

Another version of it arose in 2006, when what began as a teachers' strike in the largely indigenous state of Oaxaca turned into a mass uprising when the teachers were violently attacked. The city of Oaxaca, like Paris during the legendary commune of 1871, was taken over by its citizens, and the police were kept out. Young people guarded the barricades, women took over radio and television stations and created a public forum to discuss society, justice, desire, and possibility. That uprising was crushed, but only after a disaster utopia of improvisational and collective self-governance unfolded. It lasted several months.

Imagine an era when disaster is only disaster, not opportunity, because people already have a powerful and profound role in their societies. Such a society will never arrive as a jubilee, a perfect state, but it has come closer in recent years. The Zapatistas had their revolutionary carnival, and the world fell in love with them, but then came the long, hard job of making a revolution of everyday life, at which they continue to labor. The utopias achieved amid disaster are perhaps the once and future ordinary arrangement of things. And they do not appear only among remote and traditional peoples. They have arisen in the great cities of the twenty-first century, even briefly in the global heart of capital, a stone's throw from Wall Street.

IV

THE CITY
TRANSFIGURED:
NEW YORK IN
GRIEF AND GLORY

MUTUAL AID IN THE MARKETPLACE

Forget everything you heard about September 11, 2001, forget about Al-Qaeda, about the Bush Administration, about terrorism, about air-traffic control, about Saudi Arabia, Afghanistan, Islam, jihad, crusade, and oil geopolitics. Set aside how the hijacked airliners crashing into two buildings in southern Manhattan spiraled out into wars and laws and the erosion of the Bill of Rights and into prisons, bombs, torture, and the transformation of the world in many complex ways. All of these things matter, as do the planes that crashed into the Pentagon and that field in Pennsylvania, but they obscure other things that also count. These subjects turned faces toward global roots and implications and blocked any direct gaze at the city in crisis. Aspects of that disaster became international immediately, because the United States' air-traffic control shut down all flights in and out of the United States, because Wall Street was evacuated and markets were affected and alarm spread everywhere, because the world paused to watch and analyze and contemplate this most globally visible spectacle of all time.

Put all that away and look at it as a local disaster, as the fiery collapse of two colossi and the shattering of sixteen densely inhabited acres, with that strange toxic cloud of pulverized architecture, computers, asbestos, heavy metals, and human lives spreading around the city, the storms of office papers drifting over water to come to ground in Brooklyn and New Jersey, and refugees streaming in all directions, and the local effects of disrupted transit and work, health concerns, and rescue efforts. Only then can you see what the media in their rush to go to the centers of power and the labyrinths of Middle East politics and the stock of clichés about rescuers and victims largely missed: the extraordinary response of the people of that city.

When the towers crumpled and people nearby were plunged into the pitch-black darkness inside the fast-moving cloud of pulverized buildings, many of them thought they had died. And yet even after the most unimaginable event possible, even after being showered with debris and immersed in midmorning darkness, after that vision of 220 floors, each an acre in size, coming down, after witnessing commercial airliners become firebombs, after inhaling that terrible choking dust that would damage so many permanently, people for the most part got back up and tried to take care of each other en route to safety.

About twenty-five thousand people in the towers aided each other in an orderly evacuation without which the casualties would have been far higher than the 2,603 that resulted. (That many had not yet arrived at work, because of the time of the collisions and because of the citywide election, also kept down the numbers who died; an evacuation of twice as many would have been far more difficult.) The great majority of the casualties were people trapped above the fires, including more than 1,300 above the ninety-first floor of the north tower. Had the firemen who valiantly marched up the stairs while thousands were pouring down had better radio communications equipment, far fewer than 341 of them might have perished. Had the people in charge of the buildings ordered evacuations immediately rather than urging people to return to their offices or stay put in the south tower, more rescuers and workers might have survived. Of course what happened was unprecedented, and that the structures would collapse was initially unthinkable.

Evacuating the whole southern tip of Manhattan became urgent as the area became toxic and chaotic, and the towers' workers were joined in flight by residents, workers in surrounding businesses, passersby, schoolchildren, and others. A spontaneously assembled armada of boats conducted in a few hours an evacuation far larger than the fabled ten-day Dunkirk evacuation of the Second World War (that evacuation was done under fire, but the civilian boats approaching the dust cloud enveloping southern Manhattan had no way to know whether the attacks had ended after the two planes hit). Citizens on the streets aided wounded, overwhelmed, exhausted, and stranded evacuees, and concentric circles of support ringed the disaster site. Later, spontaneously assembled collection sites, commissaries, and supply chains supported the workers on what they called the Pile and the media would call Ground Zero. Many of those workers, particularly in the beginning, were also volunteers, some of them specialists—engineers, construction workers, medics, welders. Priests, ministers, rabbis, masseuses, medics, and other caregivers swarmed the site, and one of the largest disaster convergences in history transpired. Some of those who came without plans found or created useful roles and worked as part of the response for months. Many nonprofit agencies, notably those working with Muslims, immigrants, and the poor, sprang into action. Some new organizations were born. The city's less urgent functions were largely halted at first, and people paused to contemplate, mourn, argue, comfort, read, gather, pray, stare, and to act, sometimes powerfully, sometimes ineffectually, on their overwhelming desire to give and be of service. There were racists who wanted to attack any Muslim or Arab and people clamoring for war, but they were a minority in that city that suddenly came to a dreadful, thoughtful halt.

The evacuation of the towers and nearby areas had been calm at first, then anxious, and then urgent. When asked who the heroes were, emergency services policeman Mark DeMarco, who'd been at Ground Zero, replied, "I said, 'The people who were in the towers, who actually initiated the rescue before the police or fire department got there.' I said, 'They initiated it, they started it, they were helping each other.' I said, 'Everybody who was helping each other,' I said, 'to me they were all heroes.' And in hindsight, when we came walking out of the building, there wasn't any panic, there wasn't anybody running."

Michael Noble, a big, calm-looking midwesterner who'd risen to become a senior executive at Morgan Stanley, was on the sixty-sixth floor of the south tower when the first airplane hit the north tower. One of his coworkers who'd seen the plane fly right at him and remembered the 1993 attack on the towers ran out of a private dining room shouting, "They're back." Noble and several of his coworkers decided on their own initiative to evacuate and took the elevator down to the forty-fourth floor, only to find that the elevators had been closed and someone with a bullhorn from Port Authority—the agency that ran the buildings—was telling people to go back to their offices. "I just started down the stairs for no particular reason. It just seemed at the time that it was a good idea to get out of the building. So I went into the stairwell, and the stairs were crowded. People were two abreast, someone on every stair going down calmly, and I remember thinking as I was going down—there was a woman who was overweight in front of me and having a hard time—and remember at this time there's no emergency in our building—and I remember thinking: what do you do here? Do you move around her? She was now backing up quite a few people and I guess to her credit she just kind of moved aside, she was tired, she was out of breath, and she moved aside and people just kept going down and past her, as did I." On the nineteenth floor, there was another call for people to return to their offices, but he calculated how long it would take to return versus leave and decided to continue. The people who heeded the call to return and got into elevators mostly died, because the burning jet fuel from the plane that would shortly thereafter crash into the south tower turned the elevator shafts into infernos.

Noble continued, "So I go to my normal exit from the lobby and the signs are up saying use the revolving door, and there was so much debris that I couldn't budge the revolving doors. So I go to the other doors, where there's signs saying don't use these, and there was a young woman there and debris, and I'm getting ready to shove open this door when a huge chunk of debris falls from the sky right in front of us. I assume it was part of the building's facade, and both of us were kind of taken aback by that but we knew we had to get out, so I remember grabbing her hand and saying, 'Let's go.' We pushed out and we ran across away from the building, south toward Liberty Street, and she ran off in a different direction. . . . There was a parking lot for a Greek Orthodox church, and that's where I went. As I looked around, every car was on fire. It looked like a war zone. I remember looking down, and this was before I looked back up at the building, and there was an arm, severed at the elbow, with a wedding ring on, the same type of wedding ring as my own, and that shocked me a little bit to see a body part, and as I looked around there were body parts pretty well all around and lots of clumps of flesh, just blood and goo, not recognizable as a body part. I saw things that day that no civilian should see. . . . So I started walking up what I think was called the West Side Highway, and of course it was hard not to be looking up . . .

and I looked up and saw this speck in the sky and it caught my attention and it was a man who had jumped. I remember his arms and his legs just trying to grab at air and I watched him fall and I remember thinking, *How can I help this man? Is there some way I can communicate with him as he is about to die?* I don't know . . . it's what I thought. And for the last fifteen floors he fell I watched and tried to hold his hand, to be somehow in communication with him." He wished afterward that he had retrieved that wedding ring for the widow. For the next few days, he joined other senior management people in his firm, making phone calls to employees' homes to try to track down who had survived and where people were. Morgan Stanley had recently merged with Dean Witter, but before the crisis the two communities had remained distrustful. Afterward, Noble says, "It was open arms, how can we help, anything you need is yours."

John Abruzzo, a paraplegic accountant who worked on the sixty-ninth floor of the north tower, was carried down all those flights of stairs to safety by ten of his coworkers in relays, using an evacuation chair designed to skid down the stairs that had been provided after the earlier attack. Zaheer Jaffery, a polio survivor from Pakistan, worked on the sixty-fifth floor of one of the towers and remembers the long journey down the stairs: "We had to stop several times during our descent because of injured people being brought down. For example, you would hear, 'move to the right, move to the right' and everybody would move to the right, so that the injured could be taken down. And this happened, three, four times. People in a groove and then they had to reposition themselves. And people would actually: 'No, no, you first.' I couldn't believe it, that at this point people would actually say, 'No, no, please take my place.' It was uncanny." Eventually he got to the bottom of the stairs. "I was walking, very, very slow by now because I could barely walk. In the concourse level I was going so slow that two or three times people offered to carry me and I said, 'No, no, maybe someone else needs help.' You know the water was this much, up to my ankles, and it was slimy and slippery. My shoes were new and they were slipping. And by that time I knew that it was very serious because people were actually now beginning to run and you could hear the volunteers saying, 'Get out of the building before it falls. Get out of the building before it falls.'" One of the firefighters in Jules and Gedeon Naudet's documentary about 9/11 recalls people saying to the ascending firefighters, "What are you doing? Get out!"

John Guilfoy, a young man who'd been a college athlete, recalled, "I remember looking back as I started running, and the thickest smoke was right where it was, you know, a few blocks away, and thinking that, like, whoever's going to be in that is just going to die. There's no way you could—you're going to suffocate, and it was coming at us. I remember just running, people screaming. I was somewhat calm, and I was a little bit faster than my colleagues, so I had to stop and slow up a little bit and wait for them to make sure we didn't lose each other." He spoke of slowing down as though it was an ordinary, sensible thing to do—but to keep pace, in flight from imminent danger, not even with family or beloved friends but with coworkers is not what we imagine we ourselves or those around us would do. It exemplifies the extremes of altruism and solidarity in disaster. A young immigrant from Pakistan, Usman Farman, was also running from the cloud when he fell down. A Hasidic Jewish man came up to him, took into his hand the pendant with an Arabic prayer on it that Farman wore, and then "with a deep Brooklyn accent he said 'Brother if you don't mind, there is a cloud of glass coming at us. Grab my hand, let's get the hell out of here.' He was the last person I would ever have thought to help me. If it weren't for him, I probably would have been engulfed in shattered glass and debris."

Errol Anderson, a recruiter with the New York City fire department, was caught outside in that dust storm. "For a couple of minutes I heard nothing. I thought I was either dead and was in another world, or I was the only one alive. I became nervous and panicky, not knowing what to do, because I couldn't see. . . . About four or five minutes later, while I was still trying to find my way around, I heard the voice of a young lady. She was crying and saying, 'Please, Lord, don't let me die. Don't let me die.' I was so happy to hear this lady's voice. I said, 'Keep talking, keep talking, I'm a firefighter, I'll find you by the response of where you are.' Eventually we met up with each other and basically we ran into each other's arms without even knowing it." She held on to his belt, and eventually several other people joined as a human chain, which he delivered to the Brooklyn Bridge before returning to the site of the collapses. The Brooklyn Bridge became a pedestrian route, and a river of people poured for hours to the other side. New Yorkers were well served by their everyday practices of walking the city, mingling with strangers, and feeling at home in public. It is hard to imagine many of the more suburbanized and

privatized American cities responding with such resilience, resourcefulness, and public-spiritedness, and so the everyday qualities of true urbanism may too be survival skills in crisis. The denizens of many other cities
may have even had difficulty imagining that a mass evacuation could be
conducted on foot, that the human body that seemed so frail under attack
could nevertheless cover several miles or more to safety and to home.

A thirty-five-year-old financier named Adam Mayblum escaped with
several coworkers from the eighty-seventh floor of the north tower, just
a few floors below the airplane. In an account widely circulated on the
Internet, he wrote about their descent down the staircases as things
around them fell apart: "We could not see at all. I recommended that
everyone place a hand on the shoulder of the person in front of them and
call out if they hit an obstacle so others would know to avoid it. They
did. It worked perfectly." Later in his e-mail account, he added, "They
failed in terrorizing us. We were calm. If you want to kill us, leave us
alone because we will do it by ourselves. If you want to make us stronger,
attack and we unite. This is the ultimate failure of terrorism against the
United States. The very moment the first plane was hijacked, democracy
won." Maria Georgiana Lopez Zambrano, who was born in Colombia
and went blind after emigrating to the United States, had a newsstand
at 90 Church Street. Nearly sixty when the catastrophe began, she felt
shaking and heard rumblings and distressed people, and while she was
still confused about what had transpired, two women, strangers to each
other and to her, each took one of her arms and walked her north to
safety in Greenwich Village and then paused. One lived in New Jersey,
the other in Connecticut, and they were torn beween desire to get home
and reluctance to abandon Zambrano. "They say, 'No, I don't let you go
by yourself. We still here together. We help you.'" Eventually a woman
from Queens who recognized Zambrano joined them and took her to her
door there by foot and by taxi, and the other women proceeded on to
their families.

Fireman Stanley Trojanowski had tried to put out the fires that had
started in some cars—leaking jet fuel and the cascade of papers on fire
had ignited many vehicles. "A couple of young kids, maybe in their teens
or maybe their early twenties, tried to help me get the line from under
all the debris to get some water on the fires. They were just civilians.
There were a lot of cops sitting there dazed, all full of debris. I couldn't

get their attention." Many policemen and women and firefighters were valiant that day, but so were the others in the crowd. Joe Blozis, an investigator for the police department, recalls, "Something else that I won't forget is that the civilians, the pedestrians on the streets and sidewalks, were actually directing traffic to help us get through. Not only us, but all emergency vehicles. Streams of people, lines of people, were stopping other pedestrians and clearing trafficways to get the emergency vehicles in. If it weren't for the pedestrians doing this, it would have been a nightmare getting emergency vehicles down to that site." A private security director, Ralph Blasi, said, "I have the greatest admiration for the private security officers, guys who are making around twenty-five thousand dollars a year. We had often asked security guards, prior to 9/11, what they would do if a bomb went off and they saw a couple of dead bodies. The consensus was always that they would run. But on September 11, I had sixty guards working with me and not one ran." The owners and workers in small businesses around the epicenter pulled people inside for safety and breathable air when the collapses happened.

Ada Rosario-Dolch was the principal of Leadership High School, a block away. That morning she was concerned about her sister who worked in the towers, but "I can honestly say that one of the first miracles was that I didn't think about my sister again for the rest of the day. She worked at Cantor Fitzgerald and she did die in the World Trade Center that day, but at the time all I could think about was the kids." It's an extraordinary thing to say—that one's sister died, and that it was a miracle not to think of her until later. Rosario-Dolch continues, "I had two girls in wheelchairs. . . . I asked the elevator operators to go upstairs and get them, because I knew exactly where they were. When they brought them down I told all of them, 'Start going toward Battery Park. Meet me at the corner.' I then told my A.P. [assistant principal] to go up to the fourteenth floor and start the evacuation, floor by floor. I wanted everybody out, custodial workers, kitchen workers, everybody. I mean, these people were phenomenal. Nobody panicked. . . . We got everybody out and we went to Battery Park. . . . We knew the problem was north. We needed to go south. The two head security officers from the American Stock Exchange made sure that the street was clear and open, so that as the kids walked out they could walk out freely toward Battery Park. I waited by the exit door, and as each kid came out, I told them, 'You hold hands.

This is like kindergarden. Find a partner. Don't be alone. This is a good time to make a friend.'" All her students were successfully evacuated. In many cases, teachers took students home or evacuated on the boats with them to New Jersey and Staten Island. Parents were terrified when their children could not be located, but no students were harmed (except by inhaling the toxic air).

Many people were caught between the destruction and the water's edge, and hundreds of thousands were evacuated by water. Three hundred thousand is a moderate estimate. Ferries whose captains spotted the smoke or collapse turned around to dump their passengers out of harm's way, and then their captains and crew made fast repeat trips to haul away everyone they could. A historic-fireboat crew heard the Coast Guard call for all available boats and took 150 people, twice their normal load. All kinds of boats were involved, cruise ships and pleasure boats, water taxis, sailboats, municipal tankers, ferries, yachts, and tugs, some responding to the Coast Guard, many on their own initiative. A forty-one-year-old policeman named Peter Moog remembers, "One of our harbor boats pulled in, and I knew a guy on it, Keith Duvall. He said, 'Grab a sledge-hammer. We'll break into one of those yachts and take it.' There were about a thousand people there, all waiting to get the hell off the island. Keith and I broke into a boat. I said, 'Rich people always leave the keys in the boat.' So we ended up finding the keys and Keith got the boat started. I think he made about ten trips back and forth to Jersey with this big boat, taking about a hundred people a trip."

Many boats pulled up alongside the waterfronts, but there were no docks calibrated to their heights: people had to jump or climb on board. A fireman on one of the city's fireboats remembers, "People were just diving onto the boat. We were trying to catch them, trying to help them get on. Mothers and nannies with infants in their arms were dropping the children down to us. At one point we had four or five of them wrapped in little blankets, and we put them in bunks down in the crew quarters. I put four of the babies in one bunk, like little peanuts lined up in a row." They helped the mothers and nannies into the boat, hauled out one jumper who missed and landed in the water, and had to go in after another woman who'd fallen in and was too exhausted to haul herself out. A waterfront metalworker who went on board a ferry to help says, "Everyone did what they needed to do. No one had to tell anyone what to do. The mechanics who usually repair the boats hopped on boats to work as crew mates." And of his own experience he recalled, "I only had time to act. I didn't have time to react."

Ellen Meyers, who founded the nonprofit Teachers Network, was just getting off the subway at Canal Street when she saw the first plane hit. She became one of the first batch of people heading south while the thousands were streaming north, because her eighty-year-old mother lived in Battery Park City. She ran into an old friend named Jim, and the two joined forces. They got to her mother and were inside a utility room with fifty other people when they heard the second tower collapse. Meyers recalls that her mother said, " 'Maybe by now I have a river view.' So I'm laughing. Jim says, 'I haven't lived with HIV for twenty years to die right now.' I'm laughing more. He's laughing. We are laughing hysterically, and what goes through my mind is, 'There's no other two people I'd rather be with at this moment.' And that's my thought. I said, 'Okay. This is it. But boy, am I glad I'm with Jim and my mother.' I'm a person who likes company, and I realize, even in death I want to have company, you know, in that moment. I said, 'Well, this is it, and I want to go with them.' It feels okay. It feels okay." They lived, uninjured, packed her mother onto one of the boats, then got on boats themselves, and as soon as they docked went back to helping out.

Marcia Goffin, an executive in her fifties who worked in a law firm next to the towers, formed a series of emotional bonds as she moved through the calamity. She came running out of her building hand in hand with her assistant, Anne, and joined a small crowd trying to protect from the sea of runners a man who was down and bleeding, until a policeman took on the task and told them all to "get out of here." She didn't see anyone being trampled: "It seemed like a steady surge. People kept coming and coming and coming." She comforted a stricken man shaking in the subway, put her hands on his shoulder and made sure he was okay to move on. He told her, "I just ran down eighty flights and I'm alive." You could imagine that caregiving was particularly in her nature if it were not that so many people were doing the same that apocalyptic morning. She took the subway herself before the system was shut down and felt intensely connected with the other people on the car, though she never saw any of them again. She then got on a bus and sat down next to an African American woman with whom she held hands for much of the ride uptown, and when the two women and all the other riders were kicked off the bus—it was going back downtown, Goffin surmised, to evacuate more people—she brought the woman home with her to her Upper East Side apartment to rest and regroup and figure out how to go farther north to her own home. After a few hours the stranger left. Fleeting emotional connections were typical of this and many disasters, though there are exceptions—not only friendships but marriages would be launched amid the ruins of the towers in the months that followed.

Astra Taylor was in her early twenties, a tall young woman from Georgia working at a left-wing publishing house in TriBeCa, and she went out into the street with hundreds of others to watch the extraordinary spectacle not so far away. "We were all trying to figure this out together. What was happening to us, should we go home, and what should we do? A few people were crying, but I felt like they were the special kind of person who had the special capacity for empathy, to really empathize. We were just sort of in the streets, and there was this flood of people coming north, people covered in dust running for their life and not stopping. There are still hundreds of us in the streets feeling oddly insular." Her sixteen-year-old brother was with her, and they walked to the Village, had a beer—lots of people were having beer, waiting to find out whether life would go on, what had happened, and what they should and could do next. The Taylors gathered with the thousands on Delancey Street being held back from the Williamsburg Bridge because the police were worried that it too might be a target on that morning when no one was sure whether there was more in store for New York. Finally the throngs were allowed to walk, and they turned that bridge, like the Brooklyn Bridge earlier that day, into a broad pedestrian avenue to safety.

"We were probably milling around for two hours, waiting to cross the bridge, getting hot, and that was the moment where you were feeling your small softness. You're just this small, soft human amongst all these others just wanting to cross this water. Finally we were allowed to cross the Williamsburg Bridge, and the people who met us on the other side were the Hasidics [members of the ultratraditional sect of Jews centered in Brooklyn]. They met us with bottles of water. The feeling on the street was a sense of community and calmness. There was a sense on the street on September 11 of calm, of trusting in the people around you—kind of being impressed with how intelligently the people around you were handling the circumstances. There was camaraderie, no hysterics, no panic, you felt that people would come together. That's obviously what happened in the towers, there was a lot of heroism that day. But then suddenly you're back in your apartment and you're isolated and you're watching the news and it's this hysterical . . . they were so overwrought and they're just showing the image again and again of the plane hitting the tower and the tower collapsing. The experience on television was so different than the experience on the street.

"I felt connected to the people on the street and I felt impressed by them. I also felt that reality is not what I thought it was, I still have a lot to learn. The reality that people would do this, commit this act of terrorism but also the reality that people in the street are trustworthy, that people would help you and that you would help. Work—I really hate work—and it gets in the way so much: we're rushing to work and we're at work and rushing from work. We didn't go to work for a few days, and you had all this time to talk to people and talk to your family." Taylor had a lot of family on hand: two of her three younger siblings were with her in her warehouse home in Brooklyn. Her wheelchair-bound younger sister wasn't frightened by the attacks either. She was terrified that her parents would make her come back home because of them, and she'd lose her newfound liberty. She didn't, and the usually reclusive Taylors put on an exhibition for the neighborhood in their home. Taylor summed up Brooklyn that week as an anarchist's paradise, a somber carnival: "No one went to work and everyone talked to strangers."

THE NEED TO HELP

It was as though, in the first hours after the World Trade Center towers were hit, the people in and around the impact site became particles flung outward, away from danger. Thus did a million or so people evacuate themselves safely. Simultaneously there began a convergence on the site that grew all that day and week, tens of thousands of skilled professionals from medics to ironworkers and countless others just hoping to help. Many stayed to become integral parts of the long process of dismantling the monstrous rubble piles and searching for the dead, or took care of the workers who did so. The desire to help was overwhelming for a great many people, and because the attacks were perceived as an attack on the nation, not on the city, and because the media covered everything about them exhaustively, the convergence and contributions were on an unprecedented scale. Volunteers came from all over the country and Canada, and donations and expressions of solidarity came from around the world. "Nous sommes tous Americaines"—"We Are All Americans"— was the headline of *Le Monde*, one of France's leading newspapers.

Charles Fritz had identified the phenomenon of convergence in 1957, writing, "Movement toward the disaster area usually is both quantitatively and qualitatively more significant than flight or evacuation from the scene of destruction. Within minutes following most domestic disasters, thousands of people begin to converge on the disaster area and on first-aid stations, hospitals, relief, and communications centers in the disaster environs. Shortly following, tons of unsolicited equipment and supplies of clothing, food, bedding, and other material begin arriving in the disaster area." He identified various converging parties, from skilled and unskilled volunteers to the merely curious to opportunists. In New York, souvenir sellers and proselytizing Scientologists were among the most frequently noted in the latter category.

Families also began to converge, particularly the families of those who worked in the towers, many of them from outside the city. Flyers advertising for missing people began to wallpaper the city, posted by those with the forlorn hope that there were survivors in the rubble or hospitals or otherwise somehow missing but alive. (Undocumented workers disappeared with far less ceremony; their families were far away or afraid to seek them publicly.) The photographs on the flyers were often vacation snapshots or other incongruously cheery images, put out during those days of uncertainty. Distraught partners, parents, offspring, and others walked around asking if anyone had seen the person whose photograph they carried, asked hospitals for lists of people present, and generally thronged lower Manhattan. They became part of the community volunteers took care of, with kindness, with practical assistance in fielding new bureaucracies, with food, and other forms of assistance. The hospitals too had hoped to care for the injured, and medical teams all over the city waited in vain.

Temma Kaplan, a historian at Rutgers University who had participated in the civil rights movement's 1964 Freedom Summer, recalls, "Everybody wanted to respond. I went back to my block and some of my neighbors were on a street corner raising money; we didn't know what [for] but they thought that people would need things, and so they started raising money." They raised about sixteen thousand dollars from passersby in a few hours. She stayed out-of-doors, among the people who were almost all outside together. "By afternoon, Amsterdam Avenue had become like a river. People covered in dust were walking up the avenue—up Broadway, Amsterdam and Columbus avenues. It was as if they were getting as far away from the World Trade Center as possible and just walking north. It was a very warm day, like a summer day, but everybody was mourning, and people were in shock. The afternoon went on and on like a series of sequences of people trying alternately to comfort each other and get information about where people were and what we could do. Word would go out: somebody in the street said the rescue workers needed boots and they needed masks. Signs went up listing things workers needed and where, at what church, you could drop them off. Then a sign went up about cough drops. The rescue workers were choking on the smoke. Everybody cleaned out all of the drug store. People set out as if on a treasure hunt to find things."

She concluded, "On 9/11 I just needed to reaffirm that there was left a community, that people believed in things that were good, that we could go on and that there would be a going on. I felt that everybody was holding on to each other in order to try to brace and embrace each other, and it was both a horrible and wonderful experience at the same time. I felt that sense of collectivity I've experienced only rarely in my life, and it's always been in the face of tremendous horror. For a short time, during the first few days after 9/11, I felt that 'beloved community' that we talked about in the Civil Rights Movement." The next night she went downtown and handed out bottles of water to rescue workers, grateful she could be of use. For search-and-rescue teams, welders and others, there were urgent and specific tasks, but most New Yorkers milled around raising money, laying flowers in front of firehouses, giving away what they could, talking, making small gestures of care, solidarity, and generosity to each other when they couldn't reach the epicenter and its workers. As in Halifax, the generosity went beyond mutual aid: altruism itself became an urgent need.

In her book on altruism and democracy, *The Samaritan's Dilemma*, Deborah Stone writes, "From the voice of altruists, a more remarkable paradox emerges: Most people don't experience altruism as self-sacrifice. They experience it as a two-way street, as giving and receiving at the same time. When they help others, they gain a sense of connection with other people. Giving and helping make them feel a part of something larger than themselves. Helping others makes them feel needed and valuable and that their time on earth is well spent. Helping others gives them a sense of purpose." The difference in disaster is how many become altruists and how urgent their need becomes. The streets of New York were flooded with people desperate to find something to give, to do, someone to help, some way to matter. In a sense they were taking care of themselves, but a society in which this was how people ordinarily did so would be a paradise indeed, one in which every corner of suffering and lack would have been scoured by generosity.

Ilene Sameth, who worked at a gay and lesbian synagogue in the West Village, went south to volunteer, ended up first placing fresh flowers around a church altar and keeping the candles there lighted, then working in a tent that provided food for the workers at the Trade Center site. "I left there having felt like I did something incredibly important, even though it was just feeding people and giving them comfort in some way. I felt like I had seen something that very few people had seen, and certainly at that point, very few people had seen it. It gave me a way of moving on, because it gave me—I did something that gave me a sense of control. My partner, Amy, and I went that Saturday out to Jersey, and we bought a hundred sweatshirts and we bought twenty-five pairs of work boots, and we piled them up into our car and drove back into the city." Sameth concluded, "And as we were unpacking them, people were coming off the site, hearing that we had gotten the supplies they needed, and they were coming in with boots that were burnt, you know, melted and broken, and pulling them off and putting on new boots and grabbing sweatshirts. It was great to feel like we were really doing something."

Restaurants, cooks, volunteers who ended up working with food for days to months converged in impromptu kitchens, canteens, and dining rooms; bodyworkers and therapists converged to offer support; ministers, rabbis, and priests offered their services on the site; a group of bike messengers became couriers and delivery experts on-site. Most people were unable to do anything so direct. A young Asian American blogger aptly named Edmund J. Song gathered a group of singers from New York University and they strolled the city singing "Amazing Grace" and "America the Beautiful." A group of music students from Oakwood College in Huntsville, Alabama, took out their instruments when it turned out they too could not gain entry to Ground Zero as volunteers. Many people struggled to get past security to the Trade Center site, urgently wanting to be where they could be of use. They needed to contribute, and so any task, no matter how obscure or grueling, met their own needs as well as others'. A volunteer up in the middle of the night ended up helping a woman he didn't know push a cart of food to Ground Zero. They passed a woman standing alone in the night tearing pieces off bedsheets to give people as primitive respirators against the still-terrible dust and smoke. She had found her niche. Out of fear of further acts of violence and a desire to create order, the authorities—there were many of them, and they too were chaotic at first—attempted to keep all unauthorized people out of a slowly shrinking perimeter area. Many people sneaked in and became so valuable they stayed on for days, weeks, or months, given official recognition and passes or hired on in some capacity. A temporary community arose around the site of the fallen towers. But communities arose elsewhere in the city as well.

Emira Habiby Browne, a Christian born in Palestine and raised in Cairo, ran the Brooklyn Arab American Family Support Center, and she and her staff were at work the morning of September 11. They were doubly horrified—that the atrocity had happened and that it was going to have dreadful consequences for their communities. They immediately took the sign off their door and started getting threatening phone calls. Four staff people quit, Browne relates, "and at that point, we realized that people were very frightened, that nobody wanted to go out of the house, that women didn't want to walk in the streets, that children were not going to school, that the community was just terrorized. First of all they were very traumatized by what had happened like every other New Yorker and every other American because it was such a shock and it was so horrible." And they were afraid for themselves and their families. "So we sent out an SOS, so to speak, on the Internet, asking for volunteers who would be willing to escort children to school, women outside, and we were just deluged. I mean there was an unbelievable response. We had like twelve hundred people. We had to stop because we didn't know what to do with all these people who were saying they wanted to help. It was just amazing. It was really beautiful. I mean, I've never seen anything like it."

Within two days of the attacks, others began organizing against the war they feared, rightly, would come. One of the organizers wrote me, "We in New York did not see the world or anyone as our enemy and that same sense of solidarity and mutual aid within the city also extended to our wanting with all our might to prevent war and further killing in the world." For years afterward, New Yorkers raised some of the loudest opposition to the wars in Afghanistan and Iraq. It was an argument about foreign policy and sometimes about the legitimacy of war and violence, but it was also an expression of empathy for the civilians on the other side of the world who would bear the brunt of it. So while some took care of people standing next to them, others in that extraordinary upheaval in New York reached out across the globe.

The Forum

Desire to help and grief at the loss of life were the overwhelming responses, but some saw the attacks not as crimes but as an act of war and called for vengeance—mostly against Al-Qaeda, but some also wanted retaliation against Afghanistan or other parts of the Middle East. Those who believed in collective guilt wanted revenge on Islam or on Islamic or Arab émigrés in the United States. The latter were a minority, but enough to cause considerable danger and dismay for anyone who was or looked Middle Eastern. Thinking about the attacks and their consequences also became a public process. During that long pause when everyone roamed the streets and everything south of Fourteenth Street was shut off to those without a picture identification proving they were residents, Union Square, just north of that border, became the city's great public forum. For three weeks, it exemplified what cities can be at their best, a place where strangers come to meet, discuss, and debate, to be present in the public life of their city and country. There, people became citizens in a way they rarely do in this age. Urbanist and lifelong New Yorker Marshall Berman wrote of his city, "Many of its grand old places were born again. My favorite was Union Square, which overnight became the kind of thriving agora it was said to have been a hundred years ago."

It was largely a spontaneous gathering in the southernmost accessible open space in the city in those first days, but a group of young people nurtured the public life there. They didn't make it happen or control it, but they tended it like gardeners, weeding out conflicts and invasive media, encouraging expression to bloom, providing supplies and support. The central figure in this activity was Jordan Schuster, a rave organizer from the San Francisco Bay Area, attending New York University, living in a dorm facing the square, and experimenting with the social possibilities of the events he organized. A cheerful, intense, fast-talking young man even six years later, he was only nineteen when the planes hit the towers. His weeping drag-queen roommate woke him up, and they watched TV for a little while. Like thousands of others, Schuster went out and spent a few hours going to hospitals trying to help, putting his names on lists with everyone else. Then he turned his attention to his own front yard,

Union Square, and his particular talents for encouraging social events to flourish.

Schuster recalls of the crowd, "It was the first time that I had been in NYC that nobody knew where they were going. I mean, *nobody knew where they were going.* Everybody's walking around but nobody had an intention. . . . People were aimless. It was a really eerie time. So I was in Union Square and I had called my friends to show up in Union Square, and I was with five of the people that I knew, deejay people who had helped me with parties, just good solid people, and I was like, 'Look, we can't volunteer because there's not enough space and they don't know how to handle all the people, there's not enough structure in place for handling it and they don't know what to do. We can't sit and do nothing, and I hate TV, so I'm not going to sit at home and watch TV. So let's figure out something to do that we can just do, maybe other people will join or whatever.'"

He thought of the AIDS Quilt that began in San Francisco and became a huge international project, one large square to commemorate each victim of the disease in a tapestry that eventually covered acres. The analogous collective artwork for the moment, he decided, would be a mural. He dispatched one member of his crew to get donations from the drugstores and office supply stores nearby, and they soon had rolls of butcher paper taped up around the square and piles of markers for people to write with, and people began to write out their fear, their grief, their speculations, their messages to the lost, and more. The panels filled up quickly on that first day; the crew kept adding more; "and by the end of the day, we'd filled up half the square." The walls of writing begat conversations, and as it became dark people brought candles by which to see each other and the sheets of paper. Clusters of candles as memorials became one of the symbols of the public memorial that was one face of 9/11, and small shrines of flowers, candles, flags, and other offerings also proliferated across the square. Schuster recalls that another addition to the site was the talking stick, introduced by a social worker named James to moderate the heated conversations that arose. "Eventually they became art themselves, people would draw on them and there would be these conversation pockets all over the square. You had to have a stick if you wanted to respond, otherwise people would be, like, 'It's not your turn.'"

Everyone came to Union Square, the full range of ages and races in Manhattan, bringing griefs and gifts, and the people who were already there, says Schuster, found a new sense of belonging. Fifteen young homeless people became vital members of the teams tending the place. "The keepers of Union Square at the time were homeless people between the ages of fourteen and thirty. I knew without them it couldn't have happened. They were on the ground maintaining, they were the support for this whole scene. And when I wasn't there to help guide a decision about what was happening, they were the ones that were doing it and they did it brilliantly." Referencing Hakim Bey, he concludes, "It was a very successful pirate utopia, or whatever you want to call it. It was like the golden age for the homeless people because they'd never seen so much food and resources." For once, they didn't have to hustle for food and they had a valuable social role: "And for them it was really healing to be able to give."

Elizabeth Grace Burkhart, a therapist and photographer, sneaked into Ground Zero to take pictures that she displayed in Union Square. She recalled, "The George Washington statue was covered with graffiti reminiscent of the '60s, and there were Tibetan prayer flags everywhere. There were thousands and thousands of candles, probably thousands of bouquets of flowers. People would come— There was a Buddhist contingent that came and took over a quarter of—a corner of the park, lit butter candles and did chanting, and had the prayer flags up. It was really remarkable. There were kids playing the guitar and people proselytizing about Jesus and the end of the world. It was, you know, New York City. Then there was this wonderful woman, Jennifer Stewart, who gets dressed up as the Statue of Liberty, and she raised, single-handedly, twelve thousand dollars cash for the fire department. Besides taking myself down there and digging with my own hands, or sitting in the hospital, what else could I do, that I knew?" People crowded around Burkhart's photographs, eager for information, and one woman told her, "This is the closest I'll ever get to my ex-husband again." They formed a bond. The historian Temma Kaplan met a couple of people in their midtwenties who had lost a friend in the collapse, and they were giving away homemade cookies and brownies and asking for donations for their friend's widow. Kaplan remembers that they were sad and that "people kept coming by taking cookies, and giving them money. People wanted to hear their story, which they wanted to tell as a way to keep the memory of their friend alive." As so often happens in disaster, people need to give, and giving and receiving meld into a reciprocity that is the emotional equivalent of mutual aid. People shifted imperceptibly from needing to do something practical in response to the disaster to needing to participate, belong, and discuss, and Union Square became one arena where that need was met.

Kate Joyce, a nineteen-year-old from New Mexico whose plane had landed in New York as the towers were collapsing, spent much of the next few days at Union Square and remembers, "The city was veiled in the simultaneous chaos and quiet of disaster, and there there was an overarching and unspoken desire (almost hunger) to provide ears, eyes, voices, and bodies that would first and foremost nurture one another as we spoke passionately of the contemporary and historical conflicts, contradictions and connections affecting our lives. We stayed for hours, through the night, and into the week, riveted and expressive, in mourning and humbled, and in the ecstacy of a transformative present." About three and a half weeks after September 11, the parks department arrived during a lull in the crowds and carted away the candles and the layers of paper. New fences went up around the square, putting much of the space off-limits. The present was no longer transformative, or it was transformed back to ordinary life.

Blood and Food

You can imagine concentric circles of impact, disruption and participation spreading from lower Manhattan. The response was global, and nationally it was intense for weeks afterward. All over the country, people were seized with the urgent desire to give or somehow help. I was in a gym in San Francisco that morning, and a bodybuilder urged us all in a voice thick with emotion to go to the nearest blood bank. In New York itself, hospitals prepared for a huge influx of wounded, and a triage center was set up on the Chelsea Piers, but the disaster had been so brutal and absolute that there were only the living and the dead and few in between, including some burn victims at that point. (Perhaps memory of the 1993 World Trade Center bombing affected this reaction; in that incident there were only six deaths but more than a thousand injuries.) The armies of medical personnel were not required, which was hard for them at that moment when everyone's greatest need was to help: the staff waiting in hospitals and newly established medical sites was one of the peculiarly melancholy aspects of that day. People all over New York and all over the country lined up to donate blood, even though there was no particular need for it.

And the blood donations continued anyway—half a million donors, by one count, 125,000 gallons of donated blood, though far more people volunteered than donated. The Red Cross urged the White House's inhabitants to donate, and so they did, and so did many U.S. politicians, and even Palestinian leader Yasir Arafat, in a symbolically compelling and utterly useless gesture. (Blood is carefully screened, the United States has stricter criteria than many nations, and donations from abroad did not meet these standards.) People offered this stuff from their own bodies as though such a deep gift of life could somehow mitigate all that death. At St. Vincent's Hospital in the West Village, the lines of would-be donors wound around the block and eventually crowded the surrounding streets, becoming yet another way people passed the first hours and days out in public.

Many were turned away there and elsewhere, but the nation's blood banks were glutted with blood that would later be thrown away, in part because screening standards had been compromised—and in part because it wasn't needed at that time and the new supply far exceeded storage capacity. By December blood banks were back to making appeals for donors. Indeed, that moment of crisis had varying durations. Even across Manhattan, those at the northern end of the island had radically different experiences than those who worked or lived near Ground Zero. For most New Yorkers life returned, in many ways, to normal that week or month, or to normal routines and systems, even if they were profoundly disrupted psychologically and politically. For those working on the Pile, the ordeal would last for months. For residents in the area, their lives would be disrupted for upward of a couple of years. For those who were bereaved, widowed, orphaned, or severely injured or traumatized, there was no end in sight, though the word *closure* was invoked constantly by the media. And though few came to the trauma centers, thousands acquired more insidious injuries that would manifest later—respiratory damage from breathing the asbestos, heavy-metal, and otherwise toxic dust of the towers' collapse and the smoldering site afterward. And nightmares.

Tobin James Mueller was a writer and musician in his fifties who'd been up late the night before and was woken up in his Village apartment by the first plane. He in turn woke up his bellhop son, and they went to Washington Square to mull and mill, then to give blood. The next morning Mueller found a table on the West Side Highway at Seventeenth Street, where people were handing out coffee and doughnuts, and joined them. He wrote about what happened soon after: "I began as one guy behind a table of coffee and donuts, stationed on a sidewalk alongside a temporary ambulance dispatch mobile home unit. After three days' time, I find myself the coordinator of an army of 200 volunteers who have transformed the entire Pier 59 warehouse into a makeshift mini-mall for rescue workers on break. In addition, we staff a thriving deli-sized food station that feeds hundreds of firemen and ambulance personnel along the West Side Highway. We stock an amateur distribution center that fills a Police Harbor boat every 20 minutes (with respiratory masks, goggles, medicines, clothes, shovels, food and anything else we can find) destined for the Hudson River side of the World Trade Center."

Mueller added, "Everyone here was rejected by the city's official sites. I accept anyone who wants to help and anything anyone wants to donate. We find a place for everything and everyone. A hopeful would-be volunteer comes up to me and asks if there is anything she can do. I give her a task, and that's the last direction I need to give. Each volunteer becomes a self-motivated never-say-die powerhouse who does whatever it takes to get the job done. Then they find a hundred more jobs to do. There is so much to do. It's so much fun to participate in, I forget to sleep. Many of my volunteers have been working for over 36 hours. It is difficult to bring oneself to go back home. The thought of closing my eyes makes me tremble."

What began as a doughnut dispensary expanded phenomenally during the next few days. A security guard looked the other way as they took over a warehouse on the Chelsea Piers and quickly filled it with goods and services. The volunteers began to put out the call for supplies over the media, and people came with respirators, boots, socks, tools, cigarettes,

Gatorade—whatever was needed. As new volunteers arrived, they were drawn into the expanding operation, which found a use for almost everyone. Years later he described how it worked: "No one is turned away, my one rule. I never said no. That's one of the reasons it became a utopia." His authority was only to coordinate and appoint people, then let them take charge, his power only to give others the power to act. Someone advised about food spoilage and was appointed to take charge of the food. When people driven out by the devastation surrounding Ground Zero arrived to ask about housing, Mueller invited a new volunteer to work on it; the volunteer recruited others, who began calling hotels to ask for donated rooms, and they soon had a flourishing housing service.

He added, "We grew until Friday night without any interference from anyone. We were all going without sleep and all crazed. . . . I realized *this is a little heaven*. Everyone is walking around hollowed out by grief, they need to do this, you don't think beyond it. . . . Every twenty minutes we would fill a boat for Ground Zero—the Ground Zero area became a site of its own. 'Boat in' would be called, and about two hundred to three hundred workers would yell 'form a line'—a bucket brigade." They would load the boats, which also continued to be part of the massive volunteer operations. Across the Hudson River, volunteers in Jersey City created a similar operation.

Daniel Smith, a young architect, ended up at the piers too. He remembers that there were "in any given ten-minute period" about a hundred people donating goods. Of the other volunteers, he said, "You met great people. People had a good sense of humor. People were working really well together. There was a tremendous cross-section of people. I mean, you had people who very clearly English wasn't their first language, working with people who were, you know—obviously, you know—spent their Sundays doing the *Times* crossword. You had people who were not American citizens, that were feeling just as welcome as people who had lived in New York City for two or three generations." Like Mueller, he was struck by how well the commissary worked in the absence of a centralized authority.

Smith told Columbia University's oral history interviewer that within a few days, professionals who sought to run things appeared. The highly functional bottom-up organization of the commissary clashed with the top-down structure of these organizations. Smith says, "Everyone was in charge. The National Guard came. They were in charge. The army came. They were in charge. There wasn't—on the upper levels, there wasn't a lot of coordination in a lot of ways. In some ways, that may sound like it was frustrating, but actually, what it enabled us to do is cut through all the red tape and get work done, since we weren't connected with FEMA or the OEM [New York's Office of Emergency Management] or the Red Cross, the Salvation Army, the National Guard. We were able to just go in and do work. Basically, everyone that I met was really gung-ho about doing what they wanted to do, and like me, they didn't take no for an answer.

"I mean, we had security, food, housing, communications, counseling, massage therapy, which sort of fit in with counseling. There was the data processing center, the donations for medical supplies, and then also non-medical supplies." Contributions of food and material goods so outran need that they had to begin turning donors away. That Sunday the official agencies shut down the unofficial operation. In Mueller's account, they were not only shut down, but treated with suspicion. It had been a brief run, and a rewarding one for volunteers like Mueller and Smith, who were amazed by the harmony and productivity they achieved. Tricia Wachtendorf, a disaster sociologist who spent considerable time in New York during the aftermath of September 11, comments that convergent volunteers often irk officials because "the appearance of these groups suggests the inadequacy of official response efforts." She describes how goods managed by groups like Mueller's and Smith's were called "rebel food" and "renegade supplies." The improvisational skills of volunteers and emergent groups often outstrips that of institutions, she notes, and so they almost always function well first and are then eclipsed by the official relief agencies and established volunteer groups, which have resources and continuity on their side. The initially guerrilla effort became increasingly managed and professionalized as time went on, though a number of volunteers stayed on in their original roles or in salaried positions developed later.

The Heavenly Banquet and the Smell of Death

For Mueller, the Chelsea Piers commissary had been a utopia; for Temma Kaplan, the city had become the "beloved community" that Martin

Luther King and the civil rights movement dreamed of; for Kate Joyce, Union Square provided "an ecstatic present." For others, it was a far more overtly religious paradise. Father James Martin had left the business world to become a Jesuit priest thirteen years before 9/11, and he worked as an editor for the national Catholic newspaper *America*. But when the towers collapsed, he joined the convergence to see what he could do and became a chaplain at Ground Zero. Occasionally he gave blessings, and a few times he celebrated Mass, but mostly he just listened, comforted, and talked to the people at the site, particularly the many Catholic firemen.

A month later Martin reflected, "I do think, however, that it's made people a lot more—I think 'contemplative' is the best way to say it. I think people are really forced to ponder a lot of things that they might not have thought about: death, life, suffering, evil, all the big issues that might have been easier for people not to look at. I think that people are forced to look at those things now. I have to say, for me, working down there has been the most profound experience of the Holy Spirit that I've ever had. It's a feeling, of course, but it's also a very strong feeling, and it's an experience that I've not really had before. Essentially, for me, even from the first day, I felt this enormous sense of unity and friendship and concord and amity and everyone working together. For one thing, you have all these firefighters who gave their lives, firefighters and police officers and rescue workers who lie in the rubble. So that informs everything. Second of all, you have all the volunteers, all the rescue workers who were there donating their time, essentially. Not only the people from New York City but people who had come from all over the country. I talked to one firefighter who said he drove up from Florida. So there was this tremendous sense of just charity. On top of that, everybody was kind and patient and generous and helpful. I didn't hear one argument the whole time I was down there. It was really striking. You just got the sense—for me as a Christian—of the Kingdom of God. This is the Kingdom, this is the notion of everyone working and living together and eating together and pulling for a cause—totally other-directed, totally selfless and, frankly, very self-deprecating.

"So there's that feeling of unity. Then there were signs to me of God's presence. You walked on this boat that everybody ate on. There was a cruise line that I subsequently found out had sent their boat up from Virginia to be docked at the World Financial Center and provide food for everyone, with donations from area restaurants. Everyone ate on that boat: firefighters, rescue workers, police officers, steelworkers, welders, ironworkers, EMS people, search-and-rescue teams, nurses, doctors, priests. You walked on that boat and you saw this great crowd of people eating together, which was a very Eucharistic image for me, everyone eating together, everyone breaking bread together, in a sense, the heavenly banquet. It was very powerful." Another Jesuit, Father Steve Katsouros, joked with a colleague, "Osama bin Laden has done a lot to get Catholics to go back to church. I think that there is something very redemptive that has happened for so many people, and I think that they are looking at their world, their values, through different lenses."

Pat Enkyu O'Hara was the head, or *roshi*, of the Village Zendo, a Zen Buddhist center, when the Trade Towers collapsed. A calm older woman with short gray hair and an air of great and tranquil sweetness, she remembered some years later, "From that day, for a month it seems like, everybody was present to everybody. It was a transformation that was just striking, on the subway eyes met eyes that never would have. There was a camaraderie that was incredible, it was palpable, it was wonderful. And there was a kind of open vulnerability that people felt. There was this sense that suddenly, particularly with young people and people that have troubles with police often, that there was a changing in attitudes. These people in uniform were here to serve, and it was no longer the old-fashioned power imbalance, but it was something else. It was like they were the guardians, and that was so refreshing to see. It was a humanizing of the authority figures. And someone like Giuliani—if you were on the Left he was this monster figure, and suddenly he opened his heart and said that it was an unbearable situation, I think his expression was. That affected all of us because it showed humility and vulnerability, a side he wouldn't often show."

For Martin, the meals on the ship were "the heavenly banquet." Roshi O'Hara found another, more somber communion in the very air of New York: "The smell didn't go away for several weeks and you had the sense that you were breathing people. It was like the smell of gunpowder or the smell of explosion. It was the smell of all kinds of things that had totally disintegrated, including people. People and electrical things and stone and glass and everything. And the smell was just everywhere downtown. I remember talking to a group and encouraging them to experience the fact that we were actually breathing parts of other people. This is what goes on all the time but we don't see it, and now we can see it and smell it and feel it and experience it. Yes, so we had this wonderfully open moment where maybe there would be some really good questioning about the world we live in and our responsibility for it and that kind of thing, and then it seemed to close down and get into a reactive, contracted state. If you can think of the ego, when it's truly active, it's very contracted, it's a holding of 'just me.' And before that it had been: 'I am also all these people. I am the mother of a policeman. I am the daughter of a fireman, I am all these people.' And then suddenly there's this contraction and I'm back into a reactive state. It seemed to take a few weeks as I recall."

Nothing quite like this spectacle of sudden large-scale death had happened before in American history, but the immediate response has happened again and again, that odd mix of heaven and hell that disaster brings, that sudden shift into a deeper kind of life with urgency, empathy, and awareness of mortality. But if the popular aftermath was a festival of mutual aid, altruism, improvisation, and solidarity, then the institutional aftermath was elite panic at its most damaging. And that slower response largely overpowered the carnival of compassion that had taken place on the streets of New York.

NINE HUNDRED AND ELEVEN
QUESTIONS

The Parade of Clichés

Everyone said that the events of that day were both unimaginable and like something out of a movie. It was an astounding spectacle. A Rand Institute analyst had remarked in 1974, "Terrorists want lots of people watching, not lots of people dead." That was a year after the World Trade Towers had been completed, the year the movie *Towering Inferno* came out, suggesting how unsafe extremely tall buildings could be, simply for the evacuation problems they posed. (In the movie, people were evacuated from the roof; on 9/11, fleeing workers found that management had locked the doors to the roofs.) In 1981, the opening scenes of a science-fiction action movie, *Escape from New York*, actually featured a passenger plane hijacked by suicidal left-wing domestic terrorists who flew it past the Trade Towers and crashed it into another skyscraper. The Al-Qaeda terrorists had appropriated the destructive iconography of Hollywood and created a stunning spectacle that, by the time the second airplane crashed into the south tower, was already mesmerizing many millions. Bringing down the towers had been the goal even of the 1993 bombing. Eight years later, Al-Qaeda succeeded in creating spectacle and devastation far beyond their expectations. For weeks footage of the disaster would saturate almost all news media everywhere.

Lifelong Manhattan resident Tom Engelhardt wrote, "Only relatively small numbers of New Yorkers actually experienced 9/11: those at the tip of Manhattan or close enough to watch the two planes smash into the

World Trade Center towers, to watch (as some schoolchildren did) people leaping or falling from the upper floors of those buildings, to be enveloped in the vast cloud of smoke and ash, in the tens of thousands of atomized computers and copying machines, the asbestos and flesh and plane, the shredded remains of millions of sheets of paper, of financial and office life as we know it. For most Americans, even those like me who were living in Manhattan, 9/11 arrived on the television screen. This is why what leapt to mind—and instantaneously filled our papers and TV reporting—was previous screen life, the movies."

The U.S. media were intent on making the event far more like the movies, and in doing so the truth and the richness of what ordinary New Yorkers had achieved that terrible day were lost. Newsmakers described the response to the disaster as though it had been one of those disaster action movies in which what mattered was accomplished by masculine heroes. In the resultant stories, these uniformed heroes were exceptional, they were professionals, they were men of action, and most of all they were men. Lost in this epic version was the fact that most people effectively evacuated themselves from the towers and from the area without much uniformed assistance, and those who rescued others included unathletic gay men, older women executives, school principals, Hasidic Jews in distinctly unheroic outfits, a gang of accountants carrying a paralyzed coworker down sixty-nine flights of stairs, young men who stepped up while police were overwhelmed, homeless people, nurses, and chauffeurs. Everyone, in other words, as usual in disaster.

The public recognized what they ought to have known all along: that firefighters not just in New York or on that day make a living doing dangerous things with courage and aplomb, and that their job is as much rescuing people as putting out fires. And though the firemen were lionized, the fact that many of them were sent into danger without adequate communications equipment or coherent orders was deemphasized. As a former city detective working for the 9/11 Commission stated, "If anybody kept a record of which floors were searched, they wouldn't have needed half those firefighters." Sent up endless flights of stairs that warm morning carrying a hundred pounds of equipment and clad in thick protective outfits, some firemen were experiencing chest pains before long, some were lying prone, panting to recover from their ascent, given water by office workers fleeing without their help. Their chiefs had already determined that it was impossible to fight the fires, so there was no reason to carry fire hoses and other equipment. (And fire hoses were installed at regular intervals throughout the buildings.)

The 343 firefighters who died were brave and selfless, and many did help people evacuate. They were victims of terrorism but also of an uncoordinated, unprepared, and ill-equipped system. They viewed their own role with ambivalence and were uncomfortable with how it was mythologized. Ruth Sergel, a documentary filmmaker involved in the *This Is New York* photography project that arose from 9/11, said, "I know a lot of the firefighters were very upset that their stories—you know, they were telling their stories as honestly as they could, and then they felt they were being edited and presented as hero stories."

The media also made a hero out of New York City mayor Rudy Giuliani. He certainly filled the role of an action hero, striding fearlessly around lower Manhattan that day, dusted with the same pale stuff as the fleeing office workers, speaking boldly and feelingly, taking decisive action then and in the days that followed, later attending endless funerals and reaching out to the bereaved. On the one hand Giuliani seemed to have had, like so many private citizens in disaster, a moment of profound self-transcendence. The spiteful, self-serving, scandal-ridden figure was gone, and in his place was someone brave, empathic, inexhaustible, and omnipresent. But the old Giuliani came back soon enough to try to advance his own career on his performance and dismiss or suppress inconvenient facts about that day and his decisions before and after. He often lauded his own preparedness in creating an Emergency Operations Center, though that center was located in 7 World Trade Center and was quickly evacuated on September 11. The space was leased from a landlord who afterward became a major campaign donor to the mayor. Years earlier, his own advisers had fought his plan to locate the center at what even then they called Ground Zero.

As Wayne Barrett and Dan Collins put it in their book investigating Giuliani's 9/11 performance, "Giuliani, however, overruled all of this advice. Rejecting an already secure, technologically advanced city facility across the Brooklyn Bridge, he insisted on a command center within walking distance of City Hall, a curious standard quickly discarded by the Bloomberg Administration, which instead put its center in Brooklyn. . . . Giuliani wound up settling in 1997 on the only bunker ever built in the clouds, at a site shaken to its foundation four years earlier by terrorists who vowed to return. It was at once the dumbest decision he ever made and the one that made him a legend. If the center had been elsewhere, all the dramatic visuals that turned the soot-covered Giuliani into a nomad warrior would instead have been tense but tame footage from its barren press conference room." As the 9/11 Commission Report more quietly put it, "Some questioned locating it both so close to a terrorist target and on the twenty-third floor of a building (difficult to access should elevators become inoperable). There was no backup site." Had the center survived to coordinate the response, many more emergency personnel might have survived as well.

Other things went terribly wrong that day, thanks to lack of pre-paredness on the part of the city during Giuliani's reign, which lasted from shortly after the first bombing of the World Trade Center to shortly after the second attack. The 911 emergency call system was quickly overwhelmed, and operators without information on the disaster gave standard-issue advice to those in the towers who reached them—most often, to stay in place. They were unable to tell people whether the fire was above or below them. Many people were unable to get through to 911, were placed on hold, or were transferred to other operators who made them tell their stories again and again while time to escape slipped away. (The operators were often deeply humane in those conversations, but not helpful with practical matters.) The fire and police departments never transcended their old rivalries to work together, nor did they ever develop an information-sharing system or shared communications tech-nology. The police had working radios and knowledge that evacuation was urgently necessary while the firefighters continued to plunge inward and upward with noble, fatal futility.

Afterward, many immediately recognized the terrible toxicity of the air from the pulverized buildings. Asbestos, heavy metals, burning PCBs, and plastics were all fueling a deadly miasma that those on and around the site would breathe for months. The Bush administration edited the Environmental Protection Agency reports on air quality to turn alarm-ing science-based news into reassuring press releases, and Giuliani went along with the censorship and propaganda. It was a callous and deadly decision. Though safety experts made it clear that everyone on the Pile should be wearing a respirator and exercising other precautions against contamination, few fully followed those guidelines, and the city did not press for enforcement or other safety standards. Wall Street reopened six days after the attack, though the air quality there as well was terrible. When journalist Juan Gonzalez reported on some of the atmospheric dangers of lower Manhattan in the *Daily News,* six weeks after the attack, a deputy mayor called the newspaper's editors to denounce the story. The firefighters were lauded as heroes again and again, but they were not protected, beforehand by a workable system and good equipment, or after, by sane health standards (and today they remain shockingly under-paid, so much so that many work second jobs and most live far from the places they serve). Many of the firemen and other workers on-site developed what was known as "Trade Center cough," and for some it would worsen into serious lung disease and damage and a host of other health problems. Seven years later, more than ten thousand exposed people had sought treatment just at New York City's designated treatment centers and the total number affected remain unknown.

Susan Faludi in her 2007 book *The Terror Dream* traces how the media rushed to portray the disaster as a triumph of traditional masculinity and to attack feminism. They found people to interview who suggested that the nation had been attacked not because it was strong—intervening in Middle East affairs, stationing troops in Saudi Arabia—but because it was weak and feminized. Pundit Camille Paglia told CNN several weeks afterward, "I think that the nation is not going to be able to confront and to defeat other countries where the code of masculinity is more traditional." Faludi points out that though the terrorists were deeply misogynist religious extremists, many in the media were happy to portray feminists as somehow in league with them in weakening America.

A *National Review* article claimed that equal rights in the armed services had trumped "combat effectiveness." Feminism had "slid further into irrelevancy," said columnist Cathy Young. It is less clear how much the public, as distinct from their media, was truly influenced by this regressive narrative. Some did yearn for strong leaders, and Giuliani and Bush both benefited from that desire. Others disdained both; one woman who lived a block from the fallen towers referred to "Giuliani's homo-erotic death cult." Women took decisive action in the minutes, hours, and days of the disaster, and men and women worked together closely.

Of course masculinity mattered most in this narrative if warfare was the answer to the attack and the source of safety in disaster (at least if masculinity equals belligerence and militarism). The scramble on the part of these leaders was in part to avoid the obvious fact that the attacks had been neither prevented nor prepared for, despite many warnings to the Bush administration and the previous attack on the Twin Towers. Though the attacks were highly localized and killed a lot of internationals as well as Americans, they were almost universally read as an attack on the nation as a whole, as a successful symbolic act. This is one of the reasons attention immediately strayed from the citizens who responded so effectively to the question of how the nation, or rather its government, would respond. The 9/11 Commission uneasily summarized, "The existing mechanisms for handling terrorist acts had been trial and punishment for acts committed by individuals; sanction, reprisal, deterrence, or war for acts by hostile governments. The actions of Al-Qaeda fit neither category. Its crimes were on a scale approaching acts of war, but they were committed by a loose, far-flung, nebulous conspiracy with no territories or citizens or assets that could be readily threatened, overwhelmed, or destroyed."

War too was a familiar story that people slipped into, a way of asserting nobility, potency, and purpose in the face of a disorienting and destabilizing attack. All William James's comments about militarism and romantic violence in his "The Moral Equivalent of War" were relevant. People yearned to sacrifice, to join, to be part of something larger. War was the mode they knew. Army enlistment went up. The war on terror seemed profound to many who fell into wartime's conformities, even if terror was not something you could declare war on, even though what most people were feeling before the administration began its campaign of inculcating fear was almost anything but terror—grief, outrage, numbness, an urgent need to help, empathy, questioning, but not much sheer terror. Terrorism expert Louise Richardson comments, "In responding to the attacks on 9/11, Americans opted to accept Al-Qaeda's language of cosmic warfare at face value and respond accordingly, rather than respond to Al-Qaeda based on an objective assessment of its resources and capabilities relative to their own. There is no doubt that the sheer spectacle of the crumbling towers certainly appeared consistent with a view of cosmic warfare. But in point of fact, three thousand casualties, in a country long accustomed to more than five times that many homicides a year, might have elicited a more focused and more moderate reaction."

Trauma and Toughness

The federal government had also failed dramatically. Nineteen men armed only with box cutters were able to attack the symbolic center of American economic power and strike the administrative heart of the mightiest military the world has ever seen more than three quarters of an hour later. The only successful defense that day appears to be that of the passengers of United Flight 93. As their own plane was hijacked and they were forced to the rear of the plane, they began to make phone calls to spouses and parents and to airline and telephone administrators. Family members told them of the attacks on the Twin Towers, and they surmised that their plane was also intended to be used as a bomb. In the small amount of time they had, they gathered information, decided to thwart the terrorists' aims, made collective decisions on strategies to take back the plane, and in some cases said their good-byes, knowing that their deaths were almost inevitable. It was an astoundingly fast collaborative improvisation. They then staged an attack on their hijackers that may have forced the plane into a crash landing in Pennsyvania rather than allowing it to become the fourth missile attacking a significant target. The media turned the counterattack into another triumph of machismo, though nothing suggests that the female flight attendant preparing boiling water to throw on the hijackers was less brave or instrumental a part of that effort than the male passengers who also communicated their intent to attack. The only person known to have to struggled against the hijackers inside the cockpit was also a woman, probably a flight attendant.

Nearly three years later, the *Washington Post* wrote, "A painstaking re-creation of the faltering and confused response by military and aviation officials on Sept. 11 also shows that the fighter jets that were scrambled that day never had a chance to intercept any of the doomed airliners, in part because they had been sent to intercept a plane, American Airlines 11, that had already crashed into the World Trade Center." The *Post* cited a report that concluded, "The jets also would probably not have been able to stop the last airplane, United Airlines Flight 93, from barreling into the

White House or U.S. Capitol if it had not crashed in Pennsylvania." And it goes on to quote that report: "'We are sure that the nation owes a debt to the passengers of United 93,' the report's authors wrote, referring to an apparent insurrection that foiled the hijackers' plans. 'Their actions saved the lives of countless others, and may have saved either the U.S. Capitol or the White House from destruction.' The stark conclusions come as part of the last interim report to be issued by the staff of the National Commission on Terrorist Attacks Upon the United States, which is racing to complete a final book-length report by the end of next month." A somewhat less speedy decision-making process than that of the passengers on Flight 93 on September 11.

One of the most incisive critiques of what happened that day came from Harvard professor Elaine Scarry, who looked at the ways that the vast military machine failed and the small band of passengers succeeded. (She had previously written eloquently about torture, aviation, and other subjects.) She raised the question of nuclear-strike capacities that were supposed to make the country able to respond within minutes and the way such speed had long justified an administrative branch and military that bypassed more democratic decision-making processes: "By the standards of speed that have been used to justify setting aside constitutional guarantees for the last fifty years, the U.S. military on September 11 had a luxurious amount of time to protect the Pentagon." She points out that two hours went by between when the FAA discovered that planes had been hijacked and the Pentagon was struck, almost an hour after the first tower was hit. And she reached distinctly anti-institutional conclusions: "When the plane that hit the Pentagon and the plane that crashed in Pennsylvania are looked at side by side, they reveal two different conceptions of national defense: one model is authoritarian, centralized, top down; the other, operating in a civil frame, is distributed and egalitarian. Should anything be inferred from the fact that the first form of defense failed and the second succeeded? This outcome obligates us to review our military structures, and to consider the possibility that we need a democratic, not a top-down, form of defense. At the very least, the events of September 11 cast doubt on a key argument that, for the past fifty years, has been used to legitimize an increasingly centralized, authoritarian model of defense—namely the argument from speed." The mainstream narrative crafted from the ruins of September 11 did not recognize the enormous power of the unarmed public or the comparative helplessness of the world's mightiest military and of centralized institutions generally. Bureaucracies, as Quarantelli points out, do not improvise readily.

The mainstream story also tended to portray everyone remotely connected to the calamity as a traumatized victim. Once again, the language of a frail and easily shattered human psyche surfaced, as it had so influentially before the aerial bombing of the Second World War. The powerful phrase "post-traumatic stress disorder," or PTSD, was invoked, suggesting that everyone who survives or even witnesses an ordeal is badly damaged by it. The term arose from the politics of the Vietnam War, when antiwar psychiatrists and others wished to demonstrate the deep destructive power of an unjust and ugly war. As one British psychiatrist put it, the new diagnosis "was meant to shift the focus of attention from the details of a soldier's background and psyche to the fundamentally traumagenic nature of war." The risk for PTSD is far higher, unsurprisingly, for those who are already damaged, fragile, inflexible, which is to say that events themselves, however horrific, have no guaranteed psychic outcome; the preexisting state matters.

The term PTSD is nowadays applied to anyone who is pained at or preoccupied with the memory of a calamity, rather than only those who are so deeply impacted they are overwhelmed or incapacitated by suffering or fear. On September 14, 2001, nineteen psychologists wrote an open letter to the American Psychological Association, expressing concern over "certain therapists . . . descending on disaster scenes with well-intentioned but misguided efforts. Psychologists can be of most help by supporting the community structures that people naturally call upon in times of grief and suffering. Let us do whatever we can, while being careful not to get in the way." One of the authors of the letter told the *New York Times* soon after, "The public should be very concerned about medicalizing what are human reactions." That is, it is normal to feel abnormal in extraordinary situations, and it doesn't always require intervention. Nevertheless, an estimated nine thousand therapists converged on lower Manhattan to treat everyone they could find. The *Washington Post* called the belief that PTSD is ubiquitous among survivors "a fallacy that some mental health counselors are perpetuating in the aftermath of this tragedy." It was another way to depict survivors as fragile rather than resilient. Kathleen Tierney remarked, "It's been very interesting during my lifetime to watch the trauma industry develop and flower. The idea that disasters cause widespread PTSD is not proven, is highly disputed. It is also highly disputed that disaster victims need any sort of professional help to get better rather than social support to get better."

A less well known psychological concept is "post-traumatic growth," a phenomenon that applies to personal as well as collective experience. One of the major books on the subject explains, "Inherent in these traumatic experiences are losses such as the loss of loved ones, of cherished roles or capabilities, or of fundamental, accepted ways of understanding life. In the face of these losses and the confusion they cause, some people rebuild a way of life that they experience as superior to their old one in important ways. For them, the devastation of loss provides an opportunity to build a new, superior life structure almost from scratch. They establish new psychological constructs that incorporate the possibilty of such traumas, and better ways to cope with them. They appreciate their newly found strength and the strength of their neighbors and their community. And because of their efforts, individuals may value both what they now have, and the process of creating it although the process involved loss and distress. Groups and societies may go through a similar transformation, producing new norms for behavior and better ways to care for individuals within the group." Trauma is real. It isn't ubiquitous. And what people do with trauma varies. As Viktor Frankl remarked, "Often it is just such an exceptionally difficult external situation which gives man the opportunity to grow spiritually beyond himself."

Business as Usual

New York City was not Mexico City or Buenos Aires. Though individual transformations were profound, no great collective renewal arose from those extraordinary days of mourning, volunteering, and connecting. There was little language, there were few models for people to say *This is how life could be, this is what I desire my society to be;* society is what was strongest that day, stronger than individual human life, than professional skill, military might, terrorist rage, or government power. Curiously, no one commented on the ways that the old Hobbesian/capitalist models of competition had been replaced by an intense and creative cooperation, a marvel of mutual aid within blocks of Wall Street. Of course civil society was powerful enough to describe what had happened in Mexico in 1985 on its own terms; in 2001, the media and the government colluded in telling a very different story, one that harked back to the movies and their romance with authoritarianism and exceptionalism.

It was a national disaster in the sense that people across the country were drawn into an intensified present of questioning, openness, altruism, a pause from which many conclusions might have been reached, many directions taken. In a strange way, a lot of people valued the sense of urgency, solidarity, and depth, the shift away from an everyday diet of trivia to major questions about life, death, politics, and meaning. Or not so strange, if you regard ours as a serious species, craving meaning above all—as Friedrich Nietzsche once commented, "Man, the bravest animal and the one most inured to trouble, does not deny suffering per se: he wants it, he even seeks it out, provided it can be given a meaning." The nation was poised for real change, for rethinking foreign policy, oil dependence, and much more. It was the classic disaster state of immersion and openness to change that Fritz had spoken of: "Disaster provides a form of societal shock which disrupts habitual, institutionalized patterns of behavior and renders people amenable to social and personal change." It was as though the country hovered on the brink of a collective post-traumatic growth into something more purposeful, united, and aware, but the meaning of the event itself got hijacked, again and again, and in its place came all the cheap familiar stories.

It's possible to imagine a reality that diverged from September 11 onward, a reality in which the first thing affirmed was the unconquerable vitality of civil society, the strength of bonds of affection against violence, of open public life against the stealth and arrogance of the attack. (These were all affirmed informally, in practice, but not institutionally, and they constituted a victory of sorts, a refusal to be cowed, a coming together, and a demonstration of what is in many ways the opposite of terrorism.) From that point, the people yearning to sacrifice might have been asked to actually make sweeping changes that would make a society more independent of Mideast oil and the snake pit of politics that goes with it, reawakened to its own global role and its local desires for membership, purpose, dignity, and a deeper safety that came not from weapons but from a different role in the world and at home. That is to say, the resourcefulness and improvisation that mattered in those hours could have been extended indefinitely; we could have become a disaster society in the best sense.

This spirit of brave resolve and deep attention, this awakened civil society, seemed to alarm the Bush administration, which immediately took measures to quell it. Bush's initial dumbfoundedness, slow reaction, and flight all over the country constitutes one form of elite panic; his administration's anxiety to dampen the surge of citizenship was another. People were encouraged to stay home, to go shopping to stimulate the economy, to keep buying big cars, and to support the wars, first in Afghanistan, then in Iraq. The "America: Open for Business" campaign equated consumerism with patriotism, and a torrent of red, white, and blue merchandise issued forth. By the following summer, the administration would suggest that people spy on their neighbors, sowing suspicion and divisiveness, while failing to supply practical training to cope with disasters. They constantly spoke of more terrorist attacks, of a vulnerable nation, of terrible things that might happen, spoke with a certainty designed to inculcate fear and with it obedience. The preposterous five-color terror-alert system was created, and during the several years afterward, the United States, as anyone passing through an airport was routinely reminded, was almost continuously on "threat level orange."

The government emphasized that only armed men and professionals were ready to respond, though the only effective response that fateful day had been by unarmed civilians on United Flight 93. They seemed desperate to push people back into an entirely private life of consuming and producing. And despite the extraordinary atmosphere of those first weeks, they largely succeeded in destroying the disaster atmosphere of courage, improvisation, flexibility, and connectedness. Government officials and newly minted terrorism experts began to air endless scenarios for destruction by sophisticated means, from dirty bombs to airborne biological warfare, despite the lack of evidence of intention or ability by Al-Qaeda to use such means. The attacks had been carried out with box cutters, after all (and the largely forgotten anthrax attacks that soon followed turned out to be committed by someone with privileged access to the United States' own bioweapons labs). Soon enough every place from the Golden Gate Bridge to New York City's Pennsylvania Station was patrolled by men in camouflage with automatic weapons.

In contrast with many previous disasters, the public itself on the streets of New York was not treated as an enemy. Elite panic manifested elsewhere. The adminstration demonized anyone who remotely categorically resembled a terrorist, by ethnicity, country of origin, or religion, and the human and legal rights of Middle Eastern men vanished as they were kidnapped, tortured, and imprisoned without charges or rights. Victims included American and Canadian citizens as well as immigrants, and soon after 9/11, men and boys seized in Afghanistan and other places around the world. The Bush administration in an unprecedented move claimed that neither domestic nor international law protected these prisoners and introduced a new era of torture, lawlessness, and unrestrained executive power unprecedented in American history. As with events such as the Great Kanto Earthquake, citizens were sometimes inspired to take justice into their own hands, and intimidation and assault of people associated with Islam and the Middle East followed. An equal and opposite reaction of individuals and organizations arose to protect these people and their rights.

In a sense the Bush administration made its own disaster movie, with the United States as victim, the government as John Wayne, and images and narratives fulfilling all the clichés and familiarities of the genre. Most notable, of course, was the fighter jet that delivered Bush, after a dramatic 150-mile-per-hour landing, on the deck of an aircraft carrier shortly after the war on Iraq was launched. Though he was not the pilot, he swaggered in a flight suit with a bulky crotch to announce major combat operations were concluded before a banner reading "Mission Accomplished." As the war spiraled out of control for years afterward, they must have regretted the image, but in those early days, questioning the administration was a dangerous thing to do. Like Giuliani, they had taken back the mandate of heaven the disaster might have snatched from them, and it would require a far larger disaster to rip it from their grasp, four years later. But in those first weeks and months, they were riding high. (Of course, Al-Qaeda collaborated on the movie clichés, supplying the Arabian fanatics, the opening spectacle, and the flowery language of jihad as global war.)

Soon after 9/11, the broken nation of Iraq, which the United States had never stopped bombing since its first war there, was portrayed as a potent regime possessing "weapons of mass destruction" and intent on using them. While President Franklin D. Roosevelt had told Americans during the Second World War that we have nothing to fear but "fear itself," fear, or terror, was constantly cultivated. Indeed, the war on terror became one of the great Orwellian oxymorons of the age: actually eliminating a tactic—terrorism—from the world was impossible, and the war the administration launched was not quelling but inflaming fear, or terror. Curiously, New Yorkers remained among the least terrified during the subsequent years, marching in the hundreds of thousands against the war on Iraq, voting against the Bush administration in 2004. Within six months of the attacks, the families of some victims founded or joined Not in Our Name, one of many antiwar groups that sprang up in the wake of 9/11. Within days of the attack, some were organizing against war as a response.

Many individual lives changed. Jordan Schuster, who had helped catalyze Union Square's moment as a great public forum, chose to become an activist for social justice when he graduated and was still one when we met in 2007. Mark Fichtel, who was the president and CEO of New York Board of Trade, Coffee, Sugar, Cocoa Exchanges that morning, had a hair-raising, or rather knee-scraping, escape that morning, though a "little old lady" got him on his feet after he was knocked down by the fleeing crowd. Nevertheless, he was able to get home rapidly that day, "and actually within an hour I had talked to all my senior executives. We had a disaster recovery plan for the New York Board of Trade in place." He got his organization up and running immediately. Six months later he quit his job, studied Islam for "800 hours," and began to teach classes on the subject.

Tom Engelhardt, quoted previously, was a book editor and lifelong New Yorker in his later fifties when 9/11 happened. He found the news coverage so distressingly inaccurate that he began to assemble alternative versions from his own online reading of international newspapers and other sources and send them out to a handful of friends. Soon his commentaries atop these clippings grew into eloquent, impassioned full-length essays of his own, and he had hundreds, then thousands, of subscribers. Thus he began TomDispatch.com, which seven years later provided about three long political essays a week, half by writers he was already associated with—Chalmers Johnson, Jonathan Schell, Mike Davis—and others who found him or he found through his new life as an essayistic news service. The commentaries and reports were picked up by many other Web sites across the world and by newspapers from the *Los*

Angeles Times to *Le Monde Diplomatique*. I contacted him about eighteen months after 9/11 with an essay on hope and history that I wanted him to circulate and became a regular contributor to TomDispatch.com. The site allowed me to speak directly to the issues of the moment and made me more of a political writer with a more far-reaching voice at a time that seemed to demand such urgent engagement. And its editor became a close friend. Such are the ricochets of history.

Many became more political, though the Bush administration's response more than 9/11 itself prompted the majority. There was no one pattern of response, however. I met one couple who lived with their two young children in a beautiful loft apartment in a converted office building a block from the Twin Towers. They had fled that morning carrying library books and some recently purchased clothing to return to the seller. They had to stay away until the following January, when their house was finally purged of the toxic dust that covered everything from the French toast left on their breakfast table to the children's toys, their clothes, their books, and everything else, and the infernal fires in the Pit had stopped burning. For many the disaster lasted for weeks, or for a few months. For this family, as for many of the forgotten residents in what was widely portrayed as a nonresidential business district, it lasted for years. By the end of it, the husband in this couple had become a pessimist who spoke of his grinning face in family photographs before the world around them collapsed as "innocent" and saw himself as suffering from PTSD. "I'll never be happy again the way I was then. I'm always looking over my shoulder." Uncertainty undermined him, but his wife came to embrace it.

She became an optimist, though her route there was circuitous. A political insider, she at first attempted to use all her contacts to figure out when the next attack would be, to be in control of what was happening. "And then all of a sudden one day I realized I just wasn't going to know. The cloud lifted, I felt better. . . . One day it all went away and I don't know why. I couldn't control the environment and I wasn't going to know. My neighborhood I had worked so hard to rebuild is a huge scar; I had my children thinking, half the people thought I was a freak, the other half thought I was a hero, which was also a problem. One night I sat down here and realized we had these incredible sunsets [where the towers had been] and everything was fine. The return to normal was a return to chaos." She added that one of her "mythologies" had been "that I was born too late for a cause—and here I was given one." The neighborhood organized to fight for its rights, for realistic safety standards, for compensation, and in doing so came together. She was a participant but not one who assumed public leadership or came to depend on that leadership for identity. She also suffered a near-fatal illness. After the two experiences, "I became a person of faith. You realize what horror awaits and are grateful it didn't happen. Three thousand were murdered but 25,000 were saved. It was 3,000 and not 3,004, and we're still here. I think it's very easy to be compassionate when it's abstract. People say it's how people behave when things are bad that matters. But that's easy. It's how they behave when things are good."

In the immediate aftermath of 9/11, there were civil servants in abundance: firefighters, police, city workers, and volunteer civil servants converging to deal with failed systems. Citizens themselves were making the major decisions, from evacuating the Trade Center buildings despite the advice to stay put from the Port Authority to organizing massive relief efforts. While the Pentagon failed to act, citizens took dramatic action inside Flight 93, possibly because of the passengers' quick collective decisions and actions. It was not only a moment of mutual aid and altruism but also a moment of participatory democracy at the forum in Union Square, at the dispensaries, impromptu kitchens, and volunteer efforts all over the city. People decided to do something, banded together—usually with strangers—and made it happen. It was anarchy in Kropotkin's sense of self-determination rather than of chaos. It was also typical of what happens in disaster, when institutions fail and civil society succeeds. It demonstrated that both the will and the ability to make a vibrant society in the absence of authority can exist, at least briefly. Once they gathered their wits, the Bush administration's most urgent campaign was not to take America back from terrorists but from its citizens. That campaign was largely successful.

In some ways that matter, 9/11 was an anomaly, and the refrain after it happened was that everything had changed. In other ways, it was a classic disaster complete with a revitalized civil society of rescuers, mutual aid, and public forums and with many forms of elite panic. If the people of

Mexico had won the postdisaster contest of power against their government, or at least won significant battles, Americans lost most of the battles after 9/11 and got instead a militarized society with fewer rights and less privacy. If Argentines three months after 9/11 had made of a sudden economic disaster a chance for social rebirth, Americans missed the chance. The country's romance with right-wing solutions was in full flower, and militarism, individualism, and consumerism drowned out the other possibilities. Argentina had been at the end of a long road of authoritarianism, repression, and foreign intervention when it rose up. The language to describe, let alone celebrate, what had arisen in the ruins of the Twin Towers was missing, and so was the vision of what role this mutual aid, altruism, collaboration, improvisation, and empowerment could play in a society free to invent and direct itself. The logic of wartime was used to inculcate a patriotism that was akin to deferential obedience. Civil society had triumphed in the hours and days after the attacks, but it failed in the face of more familiar stories told by the government and retold by the media, again and again. Four years later the balance would shift a little.

V

NEW ORLEANS: COMMON GROUNDS AND KILLERS

WHAT DIFFERENCE WOULD IT MAKE?

The Deluge and the Guns

At the last minute, her daughter was unable to pick her up for the drive to Atlanta, so Clara Rita Bartholomew, a strong, outspoken woman of sixty-one, went into the closet of the house she'd inherited from her sister to escape Hurricane Katrina's wind. She'd been awakened by the howling gale at six that Monday morning, August 29, 2005. She sheltered first in the bathroom, where she could see the wind rip chunks off the neighbor's house, then in that closet, the safest place in the house. The gales died down, she left the closet, looked out the window, and saw the water was at the level of a nearby stop sign. A foot of water had come into her home, even though it was high off the ground. She was in St. Bernard Parish, next to New Orleans Parish, and in her parish exactly four houses would escape flooding. She didn't know it at the time, but the levees had broken all along the Mississippi River Gulf Outlet. This man-made shortcut from the sea for commercial ships was nicknamed the Hurricane Highway, since it invites hurricane storm surges to charge in straight from the Gulf. As the water began rising up her legs, she pulled down the latch for the stairs to the attic and climbed higher.

There Bartholomew saw that the storm had ripped part of the roof off the attic. And even up there she wasn't out of reach of the waters. "And I'm screaming and hollering, 'I don't want to die, Jesus save me, please. What have I done?' And by the time I closed my eyes, a big wave . . . two big waves just met and covered me, and when it sprayed, it just sprayed on top of all the other houses, because this house was up high, and finally it just sprayed it, and the wind kept blowing, the wind kept blowing. I could reach down and touch the water. The water was pretty, it was nice and white. And I'm screaming and hollering, 'Please God, don't let me die. Please God, don't let me die.' And then finally all different types of animals I've never seen before in my life came into the house. Finally I did have nerve enough to look down. Every ceiling in the house was gone, every window was gone, the back door was gone. All kinds of animals [were] making all kinds of noise, and I was running, because they was coming to my feet. It was horrible. So finally I'm thinking it's over, and it came and shook the back side of the house, and I'm praying to 'God, Lordy, Lordy, you know I can't swim,' and then finally for about four hours it beared down and so finally I'm standing on the stairs to the roof, and I'm tired, Lord, I'm tired, but if I fall asleep I'm going to drown. So here come the wind again, and then finally it must have been about three o'clock and it stopped. A white couple drowned in front of me, they were trying to get to the river." That is, they were trying to get to the high ground by the Mississippi River, where they might crawl out of the water. Bartholomew cheered them on as they struggled.

"And like a big wave, a surge, just came and took them under. Oh, the little girl hollered. She just screamed and screamed and screamed. In the meantime the wind is still blowing you still got that fine misting rain. Then a body passed right in front of me. Then I'm looking around the attic to try to get something to pull it up to me, and then there was a big old alligator following the body. Oh, I froze, I couldn't even move, and then after it calmed down the rain stopped. I thought my neighbor was on the roof, so I hollered and all of a sudden beautiful seagulls came and pelicans. [My neighbor] didn't have a shirt on, so they was eating him up like he was dead meat, and so he got a shotgun and started shooting at them. And then the wind started up again. Oh, it blowed and blowed and blowed. I was getting tired." She found her sister's Bible and read a psalm. She repented of her sins. She saw a beautiful boat without anyone in it float by and took it as a sign from God. She waited to die.

A lot of people waited to die in Hurricane Katrina, and more than sixteen hundred did so, though some of them were so unwell they never knew what got them, or they died not of the hurricane or the flood but of thirst, heatstroke, lack of medicine, or murder in the days after the waters had settled and the wind had passed. It's hard to say that Bartholomew was lucky, but she lived. She stayed on that torn-up attic a while longer and saw coffins and bodies, livestock and wildlife, alive and dead, go floating by. A boat went by with a young white couple in charge. "So finally I heard the white girl say, 'I hear someone hollering,' and he said, 'No it's just the water going down.' She said, 'No, turn the motor off.' When he turned the motor off, you know what I did? I hollered, 'I'm Clarita, I'm alive.' When he came to the opening of the roof and he saw me, 'How did you live through that?'"

She got into the boat, where one rescued neighbor told her of seeing alligators swimming in the flooded neighborhood, another told of fleeing from rooftop to rooftop as the water rose. They passed St. Rita's Nursing Home, where thirty-five elderly and disabled people drowned in the suddenly flooded building. Clarita's rescuer, who worked for the parish, and his wife saved about a hundred stranded people with their boat, she recalls. An armada of volunteers went out in small craft that week and ferried uncounted thousands, tens of thousands, to dry ground. Bartholomew herself got dropped off at a high school and slept on the floor that Monday night. From there, she was evacuated to the Astrodome in Houston, Texas, and when I met her, she was trying to make a home of an empty apartment in San Francisco and keep tabs on when she would be allowed to return to fix her house. She endured something like the apocalypse, more so than most people can imagine, but her ordeal had comparatively few stages. An ordeal of wind and water, an evacuation, an awful time in the Astrodome, and a long exile.

A lot of people who lived in New Orleans Parish went through more. Cory Delaney, a twenty-four-year-old from a one-story home in the outskirts of New Orleans, went with his father, his disabled mother, and a few other relatives to take shelter in his aunt's two-story house in the city. From there everything went wrong. The possessions on the ground floor began to float in the seeping water, and then the water began to climb the stairs. They were stranded, and a help sign on the roof brought nothing. They ran out of water to drink, and the helicopters flying by that they hoped would rescue them kept going, guns pointing out the window. On the third day as he began building a raft, a boat came. He carried his mother, while other relatives carried her wheelchair. At the staging area were more men with guns: a policeman with an M16 in hand who told them to walk to the top of the interstate and wait for a bus. They settled in with about two thousand people. Buses did begin to come by, but some didn't stop, and others took away the most vulnerable.

Delaney found himself in a group of about twenty-five that began to function as a social unit—a lot of people stranded by Katrina would become part of these improvised communities that took care of each other and made decisions together. But sitting on the shadeless blacktop of an elevated highway surrounded by water reflecting back the glare and humid heat was too much for his frail mother. One policeman came and gave them water, but the next round of police to come by "got out of their cars with their M16s and their AK-47s ready to shoot somebody. They told us to back up like we was all fugitives. They pointed their guns at us and told us, 'They not coming for ya'll. Ya'll got to fend for yourself. Try to walk to the Superdome' So we walked down there pulling my mama, and nobody tried to help. They just ride past—people riding past in boats taking pictures of us like we was just some homeless people, refugees or something. We stayed out there two more nights sleeping on the interstate, this is like five nights now. We was just all frustrated, didn't know what to do. I had to build a tent over my mama to keep the shade on her 'cause she was dehydrated. She wasn't eating and wasn't drinking too much. I mean, she was like going away. So we're praying, we got people coming up to us praying for my mama." He asked people for help, to no avail, until finally the National Guard got them on a truck to the suburb of Metarie, where his mother got priority for evacuation—and was whisked away, lost to the rest of the family for days. Eventually, the rest of the family got a bus to Texas. "We ended up in this concentration-like camp with barbed-wire fences and snipers, like we did something wrong." At the time of his interview, he was in Minnesota, about as displaced as a person could be without leaving his country.

He wasn't the only one to end up with a succession of guns pointed at him. Fed by racism and the enormity of the storm, the elite panic reached extraordinary levels in the aftermath of Hurricane Katrina. That generated a disaster of its own, whereby the victims of Katrina were regarded as menaces and monsters, and the response shifted from rescue to control and worse. Katrina was a succession of disasters, the somewhat natural disaster of the storm, the strictly unnatural disaster of the failing levees that flooded St. Bernard Parish and much of New Orleans, the social devastation of the failure or refusal of successive layers of government to supply evacuation and relief, and the appalling calamity of the way that local and then state and federal authorities decided to regard victims as criminals and turned New Orleans into a prison city, in which many had guns pointed at them and many were prevented from evacuating. Or killed. Or left to die.

Of course, as Kathleen Tierney pointed out to me, Katrina wasn't a disaster. It was a catastrophe, far larger in scale than almost anything in American history. An emergency is local—a house burns down, a hospital floods. A disaster covers a city or a small region. After the 1906 earthquake you could just cross the bay for sanctuary, and half the city remained standing anyway. After 9/11 you just had to evacuate lower Manhattan; the rest of the island and other boroughs were fine. On September 11, many people in New York City sat home ordering takeout and watching TV about "New York Under Attack." The day after the 1989 Loma Prieta earthquake my power was restored so that I could sit near the exact center of San Francisco and watch network news report on my city's destruction. After Katrina, 80 percent of New Orleans was flooded, all vital services were wrecked or suspended, and ninety thousand square miles of the coastal south were declared a disaster area. The most impacted areas of Mississippi, Alabama, and Louisiana had devastation far inland. The storm surge alone had pushed ocean water—a nearly thirty-foot-high wall of it in places like Biloxi—miles in from the coast. Places like New Orleans's Lower Ninth Ward were underwater for weeks, and basic services were not restored for months. Many places will never return to anything like what they were before August 29, 2005; many communities and extended families were permanently ripped asunder.

But much of what happened after the levees broke didn't have to. It was the result of fear. When Tierney was speaking about elite panic— "fear of social disorder; fear of poor, minorities, and immigrants; obsession with looting and property crime; willingness to resort to deadly force; and actions taken on the basis of rumor"—she was talking shortly after Katrina, perhaps the worst case of elite panic in the history of the United States. New Orleans had long been a high-crime city, but the mythic city of monsters the media and authorities invented in the wake of Katrina never existed, except in their imagination. That belief ravaged the lives of tens of thousands of the most vulnerable.

The Corpses That Weren't There

"What difference would it practically make to anyone if this notion rather than that notion were true?" William James had asked in his second lecture on pragmatism. In the hours, days, and weeks after Katrina, those with one set of beliefs were responsible for many deaths; those with another saved many lives. Fear fed by rumors and lies and lurking unexamined beliefs about human nature hit New Orleans like a second hurricane. Ray Nagin and Eddie Compass, respectively the mayor and police chief of New Orleans (and both African Americans), contributed to the atmosphere of fear and turmoil. About twenty thousand people had taken refuge in the downtown Superdome sports arena, which had been opened up as a shelter of last resort but was not stocked with anything near the needed quantity of food and water or backup power. The hurricane had ripped off part of the roof, the restrooms backed up and the plumbing failed, so that sewage seeped out into the rest of the facility, and without air-conditioning and adequate electricity the place became a dark, fetid, chaotic oven. Much of the area surrounding its raised concrete perimeter was flooded. People were not allowed to leave, prisoners of the fears of those in power. Rumors of savagery inside abounded. Compass told the television talk-show host Oprah Winfrey, "We had little babies in there. . . . Some of the little babies getting raped." He was overwhelmed by sobs on television and eventually had a breakdown. Nagin reported that there were "hundreds of gang members" in the Superdome, raping and murdering. During his Oprah moment, he told the national audience that people had been "in that frickin' Superdome for five days watching dead bodies, watching hooligans killing people, raping people."

Despite the assumption that the Superdome and Convention Center had become nests of vipers, the media focus was for a while on the retail outlets on dry ground reportedly being plundered. The hysteria about looting became so intense that two and a half days after the storm, on August 31, Nagin and Governor Kathleen Blanco called emergency responders—police and National Guard, mostly—off search and rescue to focus on combating looting. They had chosen protecting property over saving lives. Put that way, the decision sounds bizarre, but the word *looting* itself is maddening to some minds, creating images of chaos, danger, and boundless savagery. What difference would it make if we were blasé about property and passionate about human life? Governor Blanco said, "These are some of the forty thousand extra troops that I have demanded. They have M16s, and they're locked and loaded. . . . I have one message for these hoodlums: These troops know how to shoot and kill, and they are more than willing to do so if necessary, and I expect they will." Ninety-nine years later things had not changed from the San Francisco mayor's infamous "shoot to kill" proclamation that also focused on looting.

The media took its cue from these hysterical, gullible leaders. CNN declared, "On the dark streets, rampaging gangs take full advantage of the unguarded city. Anyone venturing outside is in danger of being robbed or even shot. It is a state of siege." No evidence exists that anyone was shot or killed by the supposed gangs, though certainly a lot of bullets were fired. Rumors of policemen being shot down were retracted, as were many accounts of snipers taking potshots at rescue helicoptors—a senseless act that fits the notion of regressive savagery and panicked mobs. The *New York Times* wrote, on September 1, "Chaos gripped New Orleans on Wednesday as looters ran wild . . . looters brazenly ripped open gates and ransacked stores for food, clothing, television sets, computers, jewelry, and guns." So did policemen, but that news broke later. The police were captured on national television raiding a Walmart. They also stripped a Cadillac dealership of its stock. Some were found driving Cadillacs as far away as Texas. With laconic southern humor, the dealership later reopened with a billboard that advertised its cars were "Driven by New Orleans' Finest."

Looting is an inflammatory, inexact word that might best be excised from the English language. It pools together two very different activities. One might be called theft; the other requisitioning, the gathering of necessary goods in an emergency—think of Salvation Army volunteers and affluent professionals breaking into drugstores in San Francisco during the 1906 earthquake to get medical supplies for the injured. Such requisitioning is an utterly appropriate response to extraordinary circumstances, a choice of survival and aid over the rules of everyday life. Almost no stores were open for business during the days after Katrina, and money was not relevant in many places; the only way to get essentials was to take them.

Peter Berkowitz, a lawyer who was bringing his son to enroll at Loyola University, got stranded along with thousands of other tourists and visitors. He became part of a large group of nonlocals who camped by the Riverwalk Mall adjacent to the Convention Center that also became first a large-scale emergency shelter and then the source of endless fear-filled rumors. In a widely circulated letter to his mother, Berkowitz writes that his group witnessed policemen toting duffel bags breaking into the mall, "and that really opened up the mall for us. We gathered food, drinks, and explored the stores. Some other tourists appeared and joined us. We took chairs and tables out of the mall. The police had 'opened up' Footlocker and other stores, so there were shoes and clothes available for the taking. I wandered through looking for bedding and ways to set up camp. I took the cover off some kiosks to use as a bed. . . . We went in systematically all day long, taking out food and provisions."

They, like tens of thousands of others, had no idea if and when relief would come. Media moved freely in and out of the city, but the promised evacuation was inexplicably slow, and many believed they had been abandoned either to die or to struggle to survive by new rules. Some seemed to have taken nonnecessary goods out of rage at the situation, some out of opportunism. It seems to be a small percentage who had time to think of things other than survival and aiding the more vulnerable. Survival required requisitioning. As the short-term emergency of the hurricane turned into the long week during which people were trapped in New Orleans, food, water, diapers, medicine, and more ran out and were replenished from stores. Left-wing media, people forwarding e-mail images, and eventually Soledad O'Brien on CNN pointed out that news photographs of African Americans gathering necessities were titled looting, while whites doing the same thing were "gathering supplies." Opportunistic theft and burglary are, historically, rare in American disasters, rare enough that many disaster scholars consider it one of the "myths" of disaster. Some such opportunism happened in Katrina. The first thing worth saying about such theft is who cares if electronics are moving around without benefit of purchase when children's corpses are floating in filthy water and stranded grandmothers are dying of heat and dehydration?

Since the answer is, apparently, quite a lot of people, including those who first determined the priorities and public face of the disaster, it's worth saying that the few significant previous examples of large-scale theft during disasters had been in Florida and the Virgin Islands. Quarantelli wrote about them, pointing out that in the Virgin Islands example, extreme poverty and social inequality made theft a quick and readily available form of mitigation in the upside-down world of disaster. In a 1994 piece about looting for an encyclopedia of criminology, he wrote, "In some communities there are normally very high everyday rates of stealing and weak social sanctions against such behavior. If a major disaster were to impact such a locality, just continuation of normal patterns would result in high rates." New Orleans had high crime rates already, and there was a lot of opportunistic theft in Katrina, though its scale remains unknown—was it a hundred, a thousand, ten thousand thieves? No one seems to have estimated this. Many trapped in the city believed they had been left to die, some believed that it was because they were black. There was some truth to those beliefs. Even television news commentators noted that an affluent white community would not have been left to suffer for so many days while the federal government dithered. The unfulfilled promises of evacuation and aid day after day turned Katrina into a social crisis that had something in common with civil wars and civil unrest, occasions when plundering is common. And that's enough on looting. Except to say that in disasters people often stay behind to protect their property from looters, so that an uncommon phenomenon shapes a common fear that generates risky behavior.

Many of the people left behind in New Orleans were elderly, ill, or otherwise frail, mothers and young children or extended families who couldn't bring themselves to split up for an evacuation or leave some members behind. Though much blame was heaped upon those who did not evacuate, many lacked the resources to do so: a car, or gas money, or a place to go. Many lived off monthly checks, and by late August their funds had run low or out. Thousands of tourists were stranded when their flights out of New Orleans were canceled. Some residents stayed behind to protect their property; others, including doctors and nurses at hospitals, stayed to take care of those who could not leave. A mandatory evacuation order was given late on the weekend before the hurricane arrived, but no resources to carry it out were provided.

By Wednesday, August 31, Katrina had evolved far beyond a natural disaster, or even a man-made physical disaster of levee collapse and urban flood. It was a sociopolitical catastrophe. The world watched as a largely impoverished, largely African American population suffered in the hot, filthy, ruinous city. Children cried, people begged for help, and a look of hopeless despair settled in on many faces. The most vulnerable, particularly the elderly, died unnecessarily, and their corpses were there live on-camera, outside the Convention Center and the Superdome, often with grief-stricken family around them. They had been truly abandoned, a huge crime and national shame. Abandoned or been trapped, but the way that New Orleans became a prison city will be told later. That some responded with rage, recklessness, and improvised attempts to aggrandize their resources is not surprising under the circumstances. Is social breakdown when thieves proliferate? Or when people are willing to kill those suspected of property crimes? Or when the most vulnerable are left to die? Or the most powerful prevent aid and evacuation?

All during those days, the Federal Emergency Management Agency was turning away volunteer rescuers, buses, truckloads of supplies, offers of help from powerful entities ranging from a huge military ship with a floating hospital, drinking water, and other crucial supplies to Amtrak (whose trains could have at any moment, and eventually did, move masses more effectively than buses). Often the excuse was that it was not safe to enter New Orleans. The job of supplying buses was contracted out to a Bush administration supporter who didn't actually deal with buses—his specialty was trucks, so he had to seek out and subcontract bus companies to dispatch to the disaster scene, an approach that created unbearable delay as well as unreasonable profit. Surely this cronyism is a form of looting, as were the contracts that paid exorbitant sums to major corporations for tasks like putting tarps on damaged roofs. FEMA had been folded into the new post–9/11 Department of Homeland Security, and the DHS had been so preoccupied with terrorists that it neglected all the other dangers facing the citizens it was supposed to serve.

The media itself did a better and a worse job than ever, rising to the occasion and falling apart in equal measure. For the media too shattered. There were on the one hand journalists in the devastated zone breaking out of their safe, bland roles to report with passion, with courage, with empathy, and soon with outrage and even fury at the layers of government that had failed to provide first evacuation, then rescue, then relief—water, food, medical care, even shade and sanitation, let alone transportation out of the hell New Orleans became. Among the journalists telling these stories were some of the biggest names in television journalism, as well as reporters for major newspapers. There were on the other hand endless editors and producers and more removed journalists and columnists eager to spread unsubstantiated stories about terrible crimes, about snipers, looters, pillagers, mass rapes, mass murders, hostages, about a sort of orgy of brutality. When the television stations and newspapers were repeating rumors, they were helping to create the profound social crisis Katrina became.

When Samuel Prince reported on what he had seen in explosion-torn Halifax, he saw generosity, courage, and need; when he quoted his journalist friend's fabrications, he came up with ghouls robbing the dying and the dead. Most of the stories about poor black people becoming savage marauders—raping, sniping, murdering, terrorizing—were quietly withdrawn later that September and into early October, at least in the newspapers. But the damage had been done. Thanks at least in part to the inflammatory stories, the city had been turned into a vast prison in which victims were treated as menaces—the old tragedy of San Francisco all over again, ninety-nine years later. People took rumors as facts. And they took the fake facts as confirmation of ancient realities.

As Jed Horne, metro editor for New Orleans's *Times-Picayune* put it, "Reporters, even from some of the big papers that for a decade had been exhaustively critiquing their own and their rivals' work for signs of racial and gender insensitivity, proved shockingly comfortable reviving stereotypes that were both unflattering and, as it turned out, false. Rumors of gang rapes and wanton murder needed to be repeated only two or three times before reporters decided the rumors had been corroborated, and repeated them in print. . . . Of course it did not help the cause of reliable journalism that, for reasons of their own, the city's mayor and his police chief were repeating some of these same rumors as fact." The rumors made it into the television and print media.

Commentators began to wax philosophical. Far away in Britain, political columnist Timothy Garton Ash was confident that it all confirmed Hobbes: "Katrina's big lesson is that the crust of civilisation on which we tread is always wafer thin. One tremor, and you've fallen through, scratching and gouging for your life like a wild dog. Remove the elementary staples of organised, civilised life—food, shelter, drinkable water, minimal personal security—and we go back within hours to a Hobbesian state of nature, a war of all against all. Some people, some of the time, behave with heroic solidarity; most people, most of the time, engage in a ruthless fight for individual and genetic survival. A few become temporary angels, most revert to being apes." Ash had even revived the Victorian cliché about civilization as a thin veneer. It was as though a levee had broken and a huge flood of deadly stereotypes was pouring in on the already beleaguered people of New Orleans.

On September 3, *New York Times* columnist Maureen Dowd summed up the popular viewpoint that New Orleans was "a snake pit of anarchy, death, looting, raping, marauding thugs, suffering innocents, a shattered infrastructure, a gutted police force, insufficient troop levels, and criminally negligent government planning." By that time, there were supposed to be hundreds of murder victims' corpses in the Superdome, stories of child rape were rampant, and armed gangs were allegedly "marauding" through the streets of the city. There were even rumors of cannibalism. People close to the situation believed many of these horrors, which magnified their fear and confusion. People far away believed them too, and the retractions came too quietly and too late.

The slander against an entire population was not readily erased. Many who believed the sensational front-page and lead-news-program stories of barbarism never noticed the retractions. Recently I met an English scholar who still believed the Ash and Dowd version, and I heard just the other day of a distinguished professor who was still reluctant to let go of the atrocity stories he had heard about the Convention Center from a New Orleans policeman who had abandoned his post. A policeman who didn't, thirty-year-old Dumas Carter, recalled afterward that during that horrific week his boss was panicking about the hotel where his officers were based: "Now the captain is saying, 'Okay, you all got to get out of the hotel. They're going to riot and they're going to burn the fucking hotel down. They're going to start this big massive thing, they're going to start killing people on Convention Center Boulevard, it's going to be a big massacre.' At this point it's like four days into it, and we're trying to explain to the captain, these people are so tired and thirsty and hungry they couldn't flip over a lawn chair if they wanted to riot. I won't say anything bad about my captain. My captain was making good decisions based on bad information."

On one occasion, Carter had a man or men apparently fire at him and melt back into the crowd he estimated at twenty thousand in and around the Convention Center. But the gunslingers were a tiny fragment of the population there, which was mostly peaceful, exhausted, and altruistic, and he was not hit: "Then came the military helicopters. They'd fly over the crowd, then fly seven or eight blocks away and drop food and water from about forty or fifty feet—high enough to bust the boxes and send bottles of water all over the concrete. There was a group of people, Good Samaritans, who pilfered the Convention Center for handcarts and walked out to where the food and water was and brought it back to the people. And the people got together as a group and disseminated it amongst themselves, without any riots, any fights, anything. And then these people put together a box of food and water and brought it to us. We didn't take it. We told them, don't worry about us, give it to the kids and the old people. But these people were looking out for us at this point! And the people at the Convention Center were left high and fucking dry. They survived, they pulled together, they sang songs all night. I mean, they would come and ask us: 'You're looking tired, are you feeling okay? Those were the people I swore to protect.'" So much for Hobbes.

Denise Moore went to Memorial Hospital, where her mother worked, to take shelter in the solid many-storied building, but was so offended when she and her family were booted from the room they were assigned in order to accommodate two white nurses who showed up late that she went home. Her home quite literally collapsed around her, and so she ended up at the Convention Center. She recalls, "And we were left there. Without help. Without food. Without water. Without sanitary conditions, as though it's perfectly all right for these 'animals' to reside in a frickin' sewer like rats. Because there was nothing but black people back there. And then the story became, 'They left us here to die, they're going to kill us.' By the time the rumors started that the National Guard was gonna kill us, I almost halfway believed it. The police kept passing us by. And the National Guard kept passing us by with their guns pointed at us, and because they wouldn't—when you see a truck full of water and people have been crying for water for a day and a night and the water truck passes you by? It was almost like they were taunting us. And then, don't forget they kept lining us up for buses that never showed up. I didn't see anybody get raped; I did see people die. I saw one man die, and I saw a girl and her baby die. But I didn't see anybody getting hurt."

The rumors were right about one thing: there were gangs there, if *gang* is the right word for inner-city men who grow up together and hang out together. Moore said that they "got together, figured out who had guns and decided they were going to make sure that no women were getting raped, because we did hear about women getting raped in the Superdome, and that nobody was hurting babies. And nobody was hurting these old people. They were the ones getting juice for the babies. They were the ones getting clothes for people who had walked through that water. They were the ones fanning the old people, because that's what moved the guys, the gangster guys the most, the plight of the old people. That's what haunted me the most, seeing those old people sitting in their chairs and not being able to walk around or nothing. They started looting on St. Charles and Napoleon. There was a Rite Aid there, and you would think they would be stealing stuff, fun stuff or whatever, because it's a 'free city' or whatever, according to them, right? But they were taking juice for the babies, water, beer for the older people, food, raincoats so they could all be seen by each other. You know, I thought it was pretty cool and very well organized." She compared them to Robin Hood. "We were trapped like animals, but I saw the greatest humanity I'd ever seen from the most unlikely places." Though undoubtedly not all armed men were as altruistic as those Moore reports on, there was more mutual aid and far less Social Darwinism inside the Convention Center and the Superdome than the media reported and the authorities imagined.

Newhouse News Service reported on September 26, 2005, that a doctor with FEMA—the organization that couldn't initially get relief into the city and kept a lot of supplies and rescuers out—had sent a refrigerated 18-wheeler and three doctors to process the bodies. They quoted the doctor saying, "I've got a report of two hundred bodies in the Dome." The actual body count was six, including four natural deaths and a suicide. The September 26, 2005, Newhouse story went on to conclude, "The vast majority of reported atrocities committed by evacuees—mass murders, rapes, and beatings—have turned out to be false, or at least unsupported by any evidence, according to key military, law-enforcement, medical, and civilian officials in positions to know."

Locked and Loaded

There were many ways in which the war in Iraq spilled over into Hurricane Katrina. Governor Blanco's troops fresh from the battlefields of Iraq, M16s locked and loaded, implied that New Orleans too was a war zone and that the job of the National Guard was to retake the city. The *Army Times* took this literally in a September 2 news article headlined, "Troops Begin Combat Operations in New Orleans" that began, "Combat operations are under way to take this city back in the aftermath of Hurricane Katrina." In other words, the stranded citizens were the enemy and the city was to be taken from them. New Orleans was not to be rescued, but conquered. Blackwater security forces, whose casual massacres in Iraq became notorious, were sent in. Jeremy Scahill reported for *The Nation* magazine that the four Blackwater commandos he talked to "characterized their work in New Orleans as 'securing neighborhoods' and 'confronting criminals.'" He reported further that "they all carried automatic assault weapons and had guns strapped to their legs. Their flak jackets were covered with pouches for extra ammunition. When asked what authority they were operating under, one guy said, 'We're on contract with the Department of Homeland Security.' Then, pointing to one of his comrades, he said, 'He was even deputized by the governor of the state of Louisiana. We can make arrests and use lethal force if we deem it necessary.' The man then held up the gold Louisiana law enforcement badge he wore around his neck." Eventually the U.S. Army arrived. National Guard units in fatigues and armored personnel carriers were still patrolling the city in 2007, per Nagin's request, since crime was high, and the police department continued to be in disarray. The belief that poor black people were going to attack, or were attacking, or had descended into some sort of maelstrom of animality, shaped the governmental responses and the media coverage. And it turned citizens into vigilantes. The real violence of Katrina deserves its own chapter, however.

For many of the tens of thousands stranded there for the better part of the week, the trauma was not merely the terrible storm and the flooding of their city, the waters in which bodies floated and poisonous snakes swam, the heat that blistered skin and killed many, the apocalyptic days in which people gave birth and died on freeway overpasses surrounded by unclean waters, in which many despaired of ever being taken from a city that had utterly collapsed into a wet and filthy ruin, or that people tried to give away their children so that they might be evacuated first. It was being abandoned by their fellow human beings and their government. And more than that, it was being treated as animals and enemies at the moment of their greatest vulnerability.

MURDERERS

It Made People Crazy

When I came to the Gulf Coast, I thought that my subject was the extraordinary communities of volunteers that had sprung up in the wake of Katrina and become funnels through which hundreds of thousands had come to the region, and that is one of my stories. But though no one seemed to be looking for the story of the murder of perhaps dozens of African American men, I couldn't avoid it. At first it was all secondhand. Or thirdhand. On my first trip to New Orleans after Katrina, I heard that an uptown woman had said her son had seen the forces patrolling the French Quarter shooting black men and throwing their bodies in the river. A friend who'd done extensive investigations himself in the immediate aftermath of the hurricane knew someone who'd witnessed a military escort on one of the rescue boats shoot down two young black men stranded on a rooftop. The black men had fired first, but probably into the air—much of what would be imagined as sniper fire or threats were shots fired to get attention. (It turned out that an astonishingly high number of New Orleanians of all classes and races seemed to own pistols, rifles, shotguns, and semiautomatic weapons. Even the most altruistic rescuers went out in boats with sidearms as well as life vests.) But the witness later committed suicide.

This was all hearsay, but it didn't arise from the kind of fears and stereotypes that the other rumors did. It was white people talking about the savage things other white people had done to black people. And then there was Jeremy Scahill's account in *The Nation* magazine of private security firms—part of the mercenary army that along with the official army overran the city in the wake of the storm—firing into the night at "black gangbangers." They were allegedly returning fire, though none of the hired enforcers had been hit. They left behind, in their own words, "moaning and screaming." The army showed up to check out the mercenaries, but no one investigated the injured then or after. A few days after the storm, middle-aged Danny Brumfield was shot in the back by police in broad daylight, in front of his son and daughter, outside the New Orleans Convention Center. He had a pair of scissors in his hand, and the police inside the car claimed their lives were in danger. His family said the scissors were for cutting up cardboard to make shelters for his grandchildren.

Sixteen months after the hurricane, seven policemen were indicted on murder and attempted-murder charges for the one incident that did become well known: the September 4, 2005, shooting on the Danziger Bridge that left two people dead and four wounded. The police claim they were responding to reports of snipers. Witnesses said there never were any snipers. One of the dead was a mentally retarded man, age forty, Ronald Madison. Madison's brother Lance said the two were walking across the bridge to the dental office of a third brother when shooting broke out. The police claim that Ronald Madison reached for a weapon in his waistband, but his brother, a longtime Federal Express employee who has no criminal record but was arrested that day for attempted murder, says they were unarmed. The retarded man got five bullets in the back, though the police report says he was shot only once. Nineteen-year-old James Brisette was walking with a friend's family to get groceries when the police opened fire. He died. One of his teenage friends was hit by bullets in the hands, elbow, neck, and stomach and now has a colostomy bag. The friend's aunt, Susan Bartholemew, had her forearm blown off. "My right arm was on the ground lying next to me," she recalled. Her husband was shot four times. The Bartholemews' daughter was unhurt. The policemen were out of uniform and had emerged from a rental van. The victims thought they were vigilantes. The indictments led to no convictions, though in late 2008, the United States Justice Department opened an investigation into the shootings at the request of some of the victims' families.

Michael Lewis, a native son of the affluent Uptown area, wrote a wryly humorous piece about his and his neighbors' experiences of Katrina and the fears that afflicted them. The few who remained behind in unflooded Uptown were mostly men convinced they needed to protect their property, turning each pretty old home into a fortress to be guarded with an arsenal. "Pretty quickly, it became clear that there were more than a few people left in the city and that they fell broadly into two categories: extremely well armed white men prepared to do battle and a ragtag collection of irregulars, black and white, who had no idea that there was anyone to do battle with. . . . The police had said that gangs of young black men were looting and killing their way across the city, and the news had reached the men inside the forts. These men also had another informational disadvantage: working TV sets. Over and over and over again, they replayed the same few horrifying scenes from the Superdome, the Convention Center, and a shop in downtown New Orleans. If the images were to be reduced to a sentence in the minds of Uptown New Orleans, that sentence would be 'Crazy black people with automatic weapons are out hunting white people, and there's no bag limit!'" Lewis can afford to be amusing because he assumes the people who sat on their porches armed to the teeth didn't actually use their weapons. That's probably true of Uptown. Elsewhere, crazy white people with automatic weapons were killing black men and joking about it.

There were vigilantes, and they committed the most heinous crimes during Katrina—well documented but not publicly acknowledged. The *Times-Picayune* won two Pulitzer Prizes for reporting on the devastation of its own city, but the newspaper didn't always ask tough questions. In the commemorative Katrina book the paper published, there's a photograph of a chubby, snub-nosed white man in an orange T-shirt sleeping on his side, an arsenal next to him. The caption reads, "On a balcony in Algiers Point, resident Gary Stubbs catches a couple of hours of sleep as part of a self-appointed posse that guarded the neighborhood against looters. The weapons, including an AK-47 assault rifle, five shotguns, a derringer, a flare gun, and a pistol, were donated by evacuees who had given the neighborhood defense force permission to enter their homes and take what they needed." CNN's Katrina picture book ran the same picture with the caption, "A New Orleans man grabs a couple hours of sleep next to an arsenal of guns. He and several friends rode out Hurricane

Katrina. . . . The guns were donated to them by out-of-town residents so they could protect everyone's property." Most people would come up with two questions immediately: did people menace that property? And did the vigilantes shoot them? The answers appear to be no and yes. The media didn't ask those questions, though the answers were pretty easy to come by.

New Orleans is both a city and a parish—the latter being the term Louisiana uses for its counties—and New Orleans Parish stretches across the broad Mississippi to claim Algiers, a small portion of what is usually called the West Bank. As the Mississippi snakes along to form the undulating southern edge of the city, it creates a bulge on the northern shore that is the community of Algiers, a mix of old and new houses with black and white inhabitants. At the top of the bulge is Algiers Point, a neighborhood of pretty pastel-painted cottages with gingerbread trim where some of the bloodiest crimes of Katrina took place. A native New Orleanian told me that there on the West Bank, the other side of the river—where no flooding and what appears to be the worst massacre took place—officials issued her cousin a bulletproof vest, a badge, and a gun and told him to "go shoot niggers." He may not have, but some did, and the confessions fueled by a sense of impunity and perhaps by guilt have seeped out everywhere. At the Common Ground clinic founded in Algiers shortly after the storm, everyone who came in for an injection or a dressing or medication also needed to tell their story, and the volunteers heard a lot.

Aislyn Colgan, a young medic who worked there in the early days, told me, "We made it a policy early on that everyone getting a [tetanus or immunization] shot had to get their blood pressure taken and their temperature taken and do the whole thing, which allowed me or whomever to sit down and have a conversation and that was mostly what we were doing. 'How's your house? How's your family?' Some of the hardest parts of it was hearing people talk about how they had lost everything. Just so many people, one after another: 'I've lost everything, I've lost everything.' That became the daily norm. . . ." She admired the religious strength that got many people through the loss of ancestral homes, of all their worldly goods, of family members.

But that young medic from Oakland, California, a sturdy fair-haired woman with a broad, honest face, also told me, "In Algiers, a lot of people in the white neighborhood formed vigilante groups. They got in their vehicles and drove around. More than one person told me, told me personally, that yes, 'We shot seven people and we killed them.' Or 'We killed five people and we don't know what happened to the other two.' Or 'It was four and three.' And people were saying that you would've done the same thing, 'You don't understand, they were coming for you,' because of the chaos and probably the rumors that the sheriff was spreading. But that was what was scary to me: people have this capacity for good but also this tremendous capacity for evil. One of the most intense conversations I had was with this woman who said: 'They were coming for our TV and we had to shoot them. If we hadn't shot them, they would have come back with their brothers and killed us.' I think the same thing that brought people to completely rearrange their priorities, to be like, 'Whatever I'm going to do, I'm going to rescue you, if that means I have to get this refrigerator to float and pole you back one by one I'm going to do it.' I think the same kind of response was 'You are not going to get near my house.' It made people crazy."

We Shot 'Em

The murders were no secret. There were plenty of rumors, but the evidence was there. When I mentioned them, some people looked at me as if I was a gullible, overwrought bleeding-heart outsider, and then paused thoughtfully and said, "Well, actually. . . ." Then they'd add a new detail, a new firm of mercenaries set loose in New Orleans, a new vigilante crime they'd heard about. That was the locals. I tried to enlist a Pulitzer Prize–winning journalist from another part of the country to investigate, and she said she was going to check out the story with her friends at the *Times-Picayune* to see if there was anything to it. I was furious. It wasn't a rumor or a theory. I had the evidence. So did much of the rest of the world. More than a million people saw the premiere of Spike Lee's 2006 HBO documentary, *When the Levees Broke*. It includes an interview with Donnell Herrington of Algiers, a sturdy, soft-spoken African American guy not nearly as tall as his basketball college scholarship would suggest.

Spike Lee found him and put him in *When the Levees Broke*. Standing on the levees near the Algiers ferry, he told just the story of how he was shot by vigilantes, not who he was and what he had done before, or what happened afterward. On camera in that film that was seen by so many millions of people, Donnell pulled up his shirt and said, "This is the buckshots from the shotgun." His torso was peppered with lumps. And then he gestured at the long, twisting raised scar that wound around his neck like a centipede or a snake: "And this is the incision from the surgery from the buckshots that penetrated my neck and hit my jugular vein." A man described his own attempted murder on nationwide television, and no one thought to investigate? Even Spike Lee, who had devoted a whole documentary to the murder of four little girls during the civil rights era, just cut away to news footage of Governor Blanco announcing that they were going to restore law and order.

Lee's film was the most widely available piece of evidence. But I'd also offered the journalist a copy of another documentary, Danish filmmaker Rasmus Holm's ironically titled *Welcome to New Orleans*, which focused on the events in Algiers Point. In it, longtime Algiers resident Malik Rahim showed the camera the body of a black man lying on his face near the street, bloated from the heat, abandoned. As he also told the nationally syndicated news program *Democracy Now*, "During the aftermath, directly after the flooding, in New Orleans, hunting season began on young African American men. In Algiers, I believe, approximately around eighteen African American males were killed. No one really knows what's the overall count. And it was basically murder. It was murder by either the police or by vigilantes that was allowed to run amok."

There were bodies lying on the street in the place that had never flooded, the comparatively undamaged place where no one was dying of thirst or heatstroke. A lot of people seemed reluctant to take the word of Rahim, an ex–Black Panther with dreadlocks halfway down his back, but there was that body on camera. There was Herrington's testimony, and the mute testimony of his savaged body. And on Holm's film there were vigilante confessions, if confession is the right word for cheery, beer-enhanced boasting. At a barbecue the Dane managed to attend shortly after Katrina, a stocky white guy with receding white hair and a Key West T-shirt chortled, "I never thought eleven months ago I'd be walking down the streets of New Orleans with two .38s and a shotgun over my shoulder. It was great. It was like pheasant season in South Dakota. If it moved, you shot it."

A tough woman with short hair and chubby arms added, "That's not a pheasant and we're not in South Dakota. What's wrong with this picture?"

The man said happily, "Seemed like it at the time."

A second white-haired guy explained, "You had to do what you had to do. If you had to shoot somebody, you had to shoot. It's that simple."

A third said, "We shot 'em."

The woman said, "They were looters. In this neighborhood we take care of our own."

And the last man to speak added, "You know what? Algiers Point is not a pussy community."

Here was the marauding, murdering gang the media had been obsessed with, except that it was made up of old white people, and its public actions went unnoticed.

Moved by his anguish over the murders, I vowed to Rahim that I would get them investigated and exposed. Eventually, I brought together the *Nation* magazine with the best and most fearless investigative journalist I know, A. C. Thompson, and handed over my evidence and contacts. A.C. is equally at ease with rogue cops and gang bosses and has broken a lot of crime stories in his day. The magazine supported many visits to look into records, launch a legal battle with the coroner (who was withholding autopsy information on all Katrina's dead and "lost" many of these public records), and interview the victims and the perpetrators. Nine months later, still waiting to get the coroner's records, A.C. sat at my kitchen table and riveted me with his accounts of whom he'd met and what he'd already figured out.

He'd become close to Donnell Herrington. And he'd talked to the vigilantes, who unlike even convicted killers doing life without parole he'd interviewed for other investigations, readily confessed to murder. Boasted of it, really. One guy who took him home to show him incriminating videotape and photographs of what he and his companions had done said, "People think it's a myth. But we killed people." The vigilantes told Adam that they'd shot three black men one morning and that they knew they were looters, because they had tote bags with them. The bags were full of nice sports apparel. Definitive evidence. A.C. wanted to tell them that when people attempt to evacuate their region, they often take clothes, their best clothes, and that if you know anything about inner-city

African American men between about fifteen and thirty-five, they wear sports gear a lot. What does it mean to assume that anything a black man carries is stolen? But it wasn't his job to educate them, just to let them talk.

And they talked. The vigilantes had gotten the keys of some of their neighbors who'd evacuated, set up barricades—even felling trees—to slow down people's movement through their area, accumulated an arsenal, and gone on patrol. Unfortunately, they were also between the rest of New Orleans Parish and the ferry terminal from which people were being evacuated; a lot of people had good reason as well as every right to walk through those streets. At one point they even demanded a black man leave the neighborhood, even though he lived a few blocks from where his neighbors threatened him. Suddenly, in that mixed neighborhood, blacks were intruders. The vigilantes were convinced that their picturesque neighborhood on the other side of the river would be overrun by looters, and they claimed the men they shot were looters, but they did not report the loss of even a garden hose or a flowerpot from a single front yard. "What difference would it practically make to anyone if this notion rather than that notion were true?"

The Ordeal of Donnell Herrington

One balmy September afternoon in 2008, A.C., Donnell, and I sat at a picnic table in New Orleans's City Park under the spreading oak trees with the ferns running up their thick arms and the Spanish moss dripping down their fingers. Big black butterflies flitted through the soft, humid air, and squirrels chased each other around the trees. A.C. found Donnell Herrington, the vigilantes' surviving victim, the hard way, since he was one of the myriad displaced and bounced around by the aftermath of the storm. He looked through obituaries for relatives, looked the relatives up in phone books, and they eventually led him to the man. Donnell told us in a soft, level voice what he had seen, done, and suffered during those three days. His story arcs through the best and worst of disasters and human behavior. Before Herrington was a victim he was a rescuer. He saved old people. He saved children. He saved family. He saved the neighbors. He saved strangers. The twenty-nine-year-old could have evacuated his hometown, New Orleans, as Hurricane Katrina approached, but he couldn't bring himself to leave his grandparents. Their home in the St. Bernard housing project out near City Park on the north side of town weathered the hurricane fine, but later that day the water began to rise, mysteriously, horrifically, until it had filled the first floor of the buildings all around and what had once been a city was a weird lake. No help appeared, but word spread that if you could get to the elevated interstate you could get evacuated from the flooded city. Some of the stranded people, like his grandparents, were frail; some couldn't swim.

Herrington was strong, and so he found an inner tube and got into the vile water to look for a boat. "Another cousin of mine, just when we were thinking there was no hope, came along with a boat. I told him, 'Let's get our grandparents.' That's when I started helping people throughout the neighborhood." Herrington stood in the prow of the small skiff, and he and a few friends poled the boat along through the murky waters with the submerged cars, stop signs, and other obstacles. They continued rescuing into the night, when the city without power became darker than he'd ever seen it before. On one of their night-rescue journeys, the one with his female cousins and their small children, they nearly flipped the boat, and Herrington recalls, "I was thinking, Lord, don't let it tip over because we had babies on board, and if the babies would've fallen into the water, we probably couldn't have saved some of them because it was too dark for us to see." He estimates that in the four hours they were in the boat, they transported more than a hundred people from the flooded neighborhood to the interstate.

At daybreak, he, his cousin Marcel Alexander, then seventeen years old, and their friend Chris Collins set out walking the several miles on the freeway to downtown New Orleans, hoping to find help for his grandparents, who were sleeping on the asphalt with everyone else. "I saw some crazy, crazy, crazy things. . . . One young lady was having a baby on the interstate. I saw people dead on the interstate, some older people who just couldn't—it was crazy. I was just passing people up. My heart was going out to these people." He wasn't even allowed to get near the Convention Center, where thousands of evacuees would end up stranded, or the Superdome, and he wasn't allowed to walk back up the interstate to check on his family. At that point he was close to the Crescent City Connection, the bridge across the Mississippi, and so Herrington decided to just walk several more miles to the Algiers home to which he and his girlfriend had moved a year earlier. Alexander and Collins came with him.

The apocalypse kept unfolding. Nothing was flooded over there, but a huge branch from the pine tree in front of his rented townhouse had smashed in the roof of the place, and it was not habitable. Most people had evacuated, and the place felt like a ghost town. One of the few remaining neighbors told him that people on the West Bank were being evacuated from the Algiers Point Ferry a few miles farther on. His cousin was worried about their family and on the verge of tears. "I kinda felt responsible for him, and I kept telling him, 'You gonna be okay. You gonna be all right.'" The three young black men set out for the ferry, though Herrington didn't know the way exactly. They ran into another man and struck up a conversation with him. He gave them directions, told them that he had a generator but was going to evacuate to Atlanta when he'd fixed a flat tire, and told them too that maybe the neighbors who miraculously had a working phone might let them use it. They did. Herrington called his family and assured them that he was okay, though in a few moments he would not be.

As they continued their journey, the guy with the flat said, "'Be careful because these guys are walking around the area with shotguns,' but I wasn't paying that no mind." A few blocks later, while Herrington had his head turned to talk to Alexander, a man he didn't even see stepped out and pulled the trigger on a shotgun. "It happened so fast I didn't even hear the loud boom. Like I said, I felt a lot of pressure in my neck and it lifted me off my feet and I hit the ground and I didn't know what actually happened and I kinda blanked out for a second and my vision was kinda blurry, and when I opened my eyes I saw my cousin standing over me and I looked down at my arms and everything and some of the shots hit me in my arms, my neck, my chest, all over my body." His jugular vein had been punctured and blood began to spurt out of his neck. Marcel stood over him, overwhelmed with horror, and Herrington looked past him to see the stout middle-aged man reloading and told his cousin to run. Facing death, he was still taking care of his family.

"So I'm looking at the guy walking toward me and he was walking pretty slow, and that was because he was trying to get the rest of the gauges in the shotgun. And at this point I'm on the ground and I'm praying, 'God, please, don't let this guy stand over me and shoot me, try and take my life.'" He got to his feet, but his way was obstructed by the branches the vigilantes in Algiers Point had scattered around when they decided to turn their neighborhood into a death trap. As he tried to hop over one of them, he heard another boom. The would-be murderer had shot him in the back, and the blow knocked him down again. He got up, walked on, and asked the first people he saw for help but they drove him off their porch. He managed to stagger onward. He asked some shirtless white guys in a truck for help, but they called him a nigger and one of them said, "We're liable to shoot you ourselves." He managed to stay on his feet long enough to reach the house of the guy who had warned him a few minutes earlier about the men with shotguns.

You had to believe, first, that all African American men are criminals and intruders and, second, that people in a disaster have a pressing interest in acquiring private property to act as the vigilantes did believe. Deciding Donnell was a looter was crazy. He was a Brink's truck driver routinely trusted with hundreds of thousands of dollars who was evacuating with a lot of money in his pocket and no interest in taking someone's TV on his way to the ferry. He was a rescuer who'd just saved many lives. He was a kind man who told us later on, "I prayed about this situation and everything, I asked God to forgive those guys that done this thing to me; it was kind of hard to even bring myself to that, but I know it's the right thing to do. But at the same time those guys have gotta answer for their actions." So far they haven't.

He had been a rescuer. Then he had been a victim. In the last act of his extraordinary journey through Katrina's flooded cityscapes and desperate people, he was rescued. While the man who'd warned him worked on his flat tire, his girlfriend and her mother took him into the house and tried to care for him while they figured out what to do next. Donnell recalls, "Your life is in your blood; when your blood is draining like that it's like your life is draining in a certain sense. I was actually fainting, you know, I was weak, I was pretty weak at that time; it's a strange feeling, then at the same time your heart is racing and your mind is telling you that you're about to die." The younger woman saw the vigilantes in the street looking for Herrington to finish him off. After Donnell was shot, two younger men with guns had terrorized Alexander and Collins with racial insults, death threats, and a pistol-whipping, and these vigilantes came by to finish off Donnell. The younger woman kept them off the property until her boyfriend, armed, stepped in, though maybe it was the woman's threat to contact the police that sent the vigilantes scurrying. The guy changed his tire in a hurry, and they got Donnell into the backseat. They drove to West Jefferson Medical Center and were told by a doctor in the parking lot that they were not accepting any more people. The young woman argued with them, a doctor took a look, signaled for a stretcher, and Donnell was on his way to the emergency room to get his jugular repaired, just in time. In his medical charts, the doctors estimate he had lost two liters of blood, nearly half the blood in the body of an ordinary human being. But he lived.

Maybe you can call him one of the lucky ones. The vigilantes confirm again and again that they killed several men, or rather each of the several sources A.C. found describes different murders. Talking to other sources, A.C. came up with another West Bank murder story. Henry Glover, age thirty-one, and his brother Edwin King were walking near a Chuck E. Cheese's place in an Algiers mall when shots rang out, and Glover was severely wounded. A man with a Chevy Malibu picked them up and decided the hospital was too far away. He thought perhaps the police would administer first aid and drove Glover to the elementary school, where a police tactical team was holed up. The police responded, Adam said, "by getting aggressive instead of rendering help." They beat up King and his friend, smacked one of them in the face with an assault rifle. "Meanwhile there's poor Henry in the back of the car bleeding, and no one's doing anything." The police took the men's wallets and marched them out of the area on foot. "The last they saw of Henry and the Malibu was an officer with flares in his pocket getting into the car and driving off. When they finally located the car and Henry, the car was on the levee a short distance behind the Fourth District Police Station, and the coroner had Henry's charred remains. There was no car left and very little left of Henry Glover"—just a skull, some ribs, and a femur, and a car "burned beyond belief." A.C. thinks someone took Glover's skull as a souvenir, because it was there in the police photographs but not in the coroner's report.

A homicide detective told A.C. that he was instructed not to investigate any homicides at that time. "We heard around the station that the guy had been a looter, shot for being a looter." He added that the tactical-unit people were crazy and that he thought someone in law enforcement burned up Glover's body, possibly with a flash-bang grenade taken from the nearby National Guard facility, when it began to smell. "Ever smell a dead body?" he asked. That detective quit the force because of everything that had happened during Katrina, he said to A.C., including shoot-outs between looting cops and law-abiding cops. Hobbesian man in uniform. The police had a substation in the mall, and perhaps they shot Henry. But no one in New Orleans was investigating some charred human ribs with a bullet in them behind a police station. Or a man who'd testified on national television about his near murder and shown the evidence written across his body. Or the suppression of hundreds of coroners' records of autopsied Katrina victims.

Like elites when they panic, racists imagine again and again that without them utter savagery would break out, so that their own homicidal violence is in defense of civilization and the preservation of order. The killing rage of the Klan and lynching parties of the old South were often triggered or fanned into flame by a story, often fictitious or exaggerated, of a crime by an African American man. Of course there were crimes committed by African Americans in Katrina, but to imagine that every black man is a criminal or to punish a whole group or unconnected individuals for a crime is racism at its most psychotic and vigilantism at its most arrogant. That force, driven by hurricane winds of fear and rumor and a flood of old stories, turned deadly. And because once again a disaster was understood in terms of all the familiar stories, what actually happened went almost unnoticed.

Death by Obstruction

The story I wasn't looking for and couldn't look away from changes the history of Katrina. And it fits the history of disaster. The version the media was all too ready to write in the days after the city flooded and the system failed was about out-of-control homicidal rampaging African Americans. They turned out to be largely mythological, and the hundreds of corpses rumored to be in the Superdome and the Convention Center dwindled into small numbers of people who mostly died of natural causes. Almost no one was eager to tell the other story of bands of heavily armed white men, affluent ones in Uptown, blue-collar ones in Algiers Point. If the facts don't fit the beliefs, murders in plain view can go largely unnoticed.

If you want to count indirect homicide, you could find a lot more deaths. Start with the lack of an evacuation plan for New Orleans. That was clearly a problem eleven months earlier, when Hurricane Ivan headed for and then missed New Orleans. Historian and geographer Mike Davis had written prophetically in 2004, "The evacuation of New Orleans in the face of Hurricane Ivan looked sinisterly like Strom Thurmond's version of the Rapture. Affluent white people fled the Big Easy in their SUVs, while the old and carless—mainly black—were left behind in their below-sea-level shotgun shacks and aging tenements to face the watery wrath." As in the Chicago heat wave ten years earlier, the greatest number of casualties were the aged. Indirect homicide could be Blanco and Nagin deciding to pull law enforcement off search and rescue to focus on looting. Indirect homicide is most certainly the Bush administration's downsized, crony-stuffed version of FEMA, which was so lackadaisical about getting people evacuated from New Orleans that you could have imagined it was sheer incompetence if that branch of Homeland Security hadn't also been aggressively turning away relief supplies and rescuers. Someday some researcher with access to those coroner's records may be able to estimate how many people died, in homes, in hospitals, on those highways, and in the two big public shelters because of the delays and blockades.

Not all of it was that indirect. Donnell Herrington had managed to cross the Crescent City Connection, the bridge leading from downtown New Orleans across the river to Gretna, the suburb next to Algiers. Not very many people would be able to follow him in the days to come, at least not on foot. The sheriff of Gretna and a bunch of unidentified men with guns closed the bridge to pedestrians. Most of the people in the Superdome and Convention Center could have walked away from the squalor, the shortages, the suffering, and been easily evacuated from the unflooded side of the river. The Convention Center was practically at the foot of the bridge. But they weren't allowed to cross the waters. The blockade was so monstrous that even a television anchorman from right-wing Fox News afoot in New Orleans, Shepard Smith, vented his own outrage at these authorities on camera: "They won't let them walk out. They got locked in there. And anyone who walks up out of that city now is turned around. You are not allowed to go to Gretna,

Louisiana, from New Orleans, Louisiana. Over there, there's hope. Over there, there's electricity. Over there, there is food and water. But you cannot go from here to there. The government will not allow you to do it. It's a fact." New Orleans was not just a catastrophe. It was a prison.

Larry Bradshaw and Lorrie Beth Slonsky are paramedics and long-time partners; they had been at a paramedic conference in New Orleans and, like Berkowitz, been stranded when their flights were canceled. Not long after the storm subsided, they were told that on the other side of the river there were buses waiting to evacuate people. So they and the newly formed multiracial clan they were part of set out for the bridge and a route out of the trouble. "When we left the hotel we were probably sixty to seventy percent white, but by the time we got to the bridge, we passed the Convention Center and all these locals are gathered around and they see a bunch of tourists marching very determined like we know where we're going and pulling our suitcases behind us. People would say, 'Where you going?' And some of our group didn't want to help these people very much, but it was 'Come on, safety is just across the bridge.' And some of the people told us, 'They won't let you cross the bridge.' We heard that and it didn't register. We thought, 'Are you kidding me?' It just kind of went in one ear and out the other." So they recalled many months later. At the time, they wrote an account of their travails in the swamped city: "The two hundred of us set off for the bridge with great excitement and hope. As we marched past the Convention Center, many locals saw our determined and optimistic group and asked where we were headed. We told them about the great news. Families immediately grabbed their few belongings, and quickly our numbers doubled and then doubled again. Babies in strollers now joined us, people using crutches, elderly clasping walkers and others, people in wheelchairs. We marched the two, three miles to the freeway and up the steep incline to the bridge. It now began to pour down rain, but it did not dampen our enthusiasm.

"As we approached the bridge, armed Gretna sheriffs formed a line across the foot of the bridge. Before we were close enough to speak, they began firing their weapons over our heads. This sent the crowd fleeing in various directions. As the crowd scattered and dissipated, a few of us inched forward and managed to engage some of the sheriffs in conversation. We told them of our conversation with the police commander and of the commander's assurances. The sheriffs informed us there were no buses waiting. The commander had lied to us to get us to move. We questioned why we couldn't cross the bridge anyway, especially as there was little traffic on the six-lane highway. They responded that the West Bank was not going to become New Orleans, and there would be no Superdomes in their city. These were code words for if you are poor and black, you are not crossing the Mississippi River and you were not getting out of New Orleans." Slonsky and Bradshaw were white, but they were not willing to abandon their nonwhite companions to try to negotiate their own salvation.

Across the river, the Jefferson exits were blocked with junked vehicles. Gretna was not interested in mutual aid. It was not interested in saving lives. Its officials were interested in keeping New Orleanians out by any means necessary, including pointing guns at desperate men, women, children, and babies. As the Reverend Lennox Yearwood said before a November 2005 civil rights march to the Crescent City Connection Bridge, "Can you imagine during 9/11, the thousands who fled on foot to the Brooklyn Bridge . . . ? What if they had been met by six or eight police cars blocking the bridge, and cops fired warning shots to turn them back?" Two years later, Gretna's police chief, Arthur Lawson, told the *Times-Picayune*, "I don't second-guess this decision. I know I made it for the right reasons. I go to sleep every night with a clear conscience." City officials blame their acts in part on the lack of an evacuation effort taking people from Gretna to the undamaged world beyond. The city was worried, they say, about being burdened beyond capacity. They claim they had no food, water, or shelter for the evacuees. Many on the West Bank had been petrified with fear of New Orleans's violent crime for decades and saw Katrina as the moment when that danger would surge from the east to their safe terrain. But even white Algiers Point residents attempting to push baby carriages across the bridge were pushed back at gunpoint. At least four civil rights lawsuits were pending as of 2008.

The whole world watched the obscene spectacle of people living and dying on freeway overpasses and the edges of the Superdome and the Convention Center. But few understood exactly why those people were stranded in heat, in filth, without food, without water, without medical care, without decent shelter. Even the hospitals were unable to evacuate. Katrina rolled in on a Monday morning. By midweek, most of the city's hospitals were flooded, without power and thereby without air-conditioning or basic life-support systems like respirators and dialysis machines, without provisions, without the ability to monitor severely ill patients or perform many medical services.

A National Guardsman clad for battle stepped out of an armored personnel carrier to tell a doctor at Charity Hospital, the vast central-city complex where the poor had done much of their birthing and dying for decades, that it was "too dangerous" to evacuate her patients. Across the city, at Memorial Medical Center, where water had filled the first floor of the building and things had become desperate, the same thing happened. Many evacuation efforts had failed by that Thursday, when the doctors, nurses, and hospital workers who had stayed behind finally rounded up boats and began shipping patients across the waters to where they could be evacuated from New Orleans. A muscular state trooper with a twelve-gauge pump-action shotgun told the doctors overseeing the evacuation, "Doc, we'll be closing down this loading ramp at five p.m. We just can't guarantee security around here after five." A doctor protested that he didn't see a serious security problem.

The trooper replied, "Doc, we'll decide what are security threats and what aren't security threats."

The doctor replied, "We can't spend another night here. A bunch more people will die." Ten people had died the night before, of heat, stress, and lack of medical resources. The trooper threatened to pull out entirely if the doctors disobeyed. They disengaged and managed to stage evacuations from the other side of the building. The doctor who wrote this account, Richard E. Deichmann, contrasted these bureaucrats preoccupied with notions of safety but unconcerned about human life with the volunteers who showed up. A Texas father and son who appeared that day in their flat-bottom boat figured out the evacuation route for the hospital. (A flooded city is full of underwater obstructions—street signs, fences—and shifting depths, so it's easy to get stranded if you're not careful, and the shallower the boat's draft, the better.) The father told Deichmann, "The thing is, they wouldn't let us put in once we got here. They tried to turn us around and make us go back. We wasn't coming all this way to turn back. We told the cops 'Okay.' Then just snuck our boat in somewheres else." Saving lives was an outlaw activity.

An armada of volunteers with boats—from inside New Orleans, from the surrounding Cajun countryside and from farther afield—had poured, often surreptitiously, into the city to be of help. These mostly white out-of-town boatmen (for they were also mostly men) counterbalance the murderous vigilantes. A remarkable photograph from soon after the storm shows bumper-to-bumper boat-trailer traffic heading into the city, as bravely altruistic as the fleet that rescued the stranded New Yorkers on September 11, 2001. (The Coast Guard and Fish and Wildlife Service also performed heroically, free of the fear and fantasy that snarled up the other government agencies.) On Thursday, September 1, FEMA officials suspended search-and-rescue operations, claiming it was too dangerous.

New Orleans sheriffs evacuated some prisoners well after the levees broke and abandoned others in the Templeman III complex altogether for days after the flood, leaving six hundred inmates without food, water, or power in a jail that flooded. Some of the surviving prisoners said others drowned in their cells. For days some adolescents were trapped up to their neck in the filthy water. Guards on the psychiatric ward were locked in to prevent desertion, prisoners themselves, and then ordered to shoot down any prisoner attempting to escape the hellish conditions. Other prisoners ended up evacuated to an overpass, where they lived for days with guns drawn on them. Many who had been arrested for minor and nonviolent offenses were lost in the system for months. Tom Jawetz of the National Prison Project said, "The Louisiana Society for the Prevention of Cruelty to Animals did more for its 263 stray pets than the sheriff did for the more than 6,500 men, women, and children left in his care."

Not every disaster features elite panic or failed evacuations. The 1973 volcanic eruption on Heimaey in the Westmann Isles off the coast of Iceland early in the dark morning of January 23, 1973, was a surprise. Even so, within six hours, the many boats docked near the town managed to evacuate all fifty-three hundred residents safely. Lava flowed for six months, buried a third of the town, and the community spent a few years in exile from the heat, damage, and fumes, then rebuilt and returned, with little of the social drama of other disasters. Iceland has a poor tradition of official political participation but a rich one of social connection, both due perhaps to the tiny size and rural background of the homogeneous population. An evacuation plan was in place when the volcano erupted, and people acted on it.

The island of Cuba is nearly the same size as Iceland but is in every other way profoundly different. It too has an effective civil defense system for the hurricanes that come more frequently but with far more warning than most volcanic eruptions. Cuba's government has instituted disaster education, an early-warning system, good meteorological research, emergency communications that work, emergency plans, and civil defense systems—the whole panoply of possibilities to ensure that people survive the hurricanes that regularly scour the island. In a major hurricane, the entire population is evacuated from the threatened coast to higher ground. Deaths are rare. Cuban civil society matters too: people check in on each other, urge holdouts to come along, and generally prevent the kind of isolation that stranded many in Katrina or in the Chicago heat wave. A Jamaican writing about the devastating Caribbean hurricanes of 2008 commented, "Cuba is organised as a mutual aid society in which every citizen has his responsibilities, his duties and his place. When hurricanes threaten Cuba, people move out of the way guided by the neighourhood Committees for the Defence of the Revolution—CDR. They move the old and the young, the sick and the healthy and their cats, dogs, parrots, their goats, donkeys and cows, to safe places. Here is a truly incredible fact. Last week the Cubans moved 2,615,000 people—a number nearly equivalent to the entire population of Jamaica—to safety. Four people died in the storm, the first fatalities for years. It is a remarkable statistic. Three years ago when Texas tried to evacuate a million or so ahead of hurricane Rita, more than 100 people died in the evacuation."

Those who talk about civil society sometimes call what makes Cuban disaster society work *social capital,* an odd term for the only avowedly Communist nation in the hemisphere, but this wealth of connection and care has been in Cuba, as in so many other places, critical to survival. In its 2004 report on Cuba's superb systems, Oxfam America concluded, "The Cubans have consistently built up their social capital to strengthen risk reduction, and have done this in times of rigorous economic scarcity. Their example raises the distinct possibility that life-line structures (concrete, practical measures to save lives) might ultimately depend more on the intangibles of relationship, training, and education" than on material wealth. Every disaster is to some degree a social disaster, and though a

strong and united society cannot prevent disasters, it can plan and prepare for them, protect the vulnerable or make them less vulnerable, and
make response and recovery work. New Orleans in the Katrina era was
a battleground between the forces that made it strong and those that
helped destroy it. The latter side has won many of the battles, but the war
is not yet over.

LOVE AND LIFEBOATS

Richer and Poorer

The media went crazy in Katrina, and so did a lot of people in power and a few groups of men with guns. They were by the numbers a small part of Katrina, but their disproportionate influence did much to shape the disaster, or rather to pile a series of man-made calamities atop a catastrophe. Even so, the majority of people reacted as they usually do in disasters, with generous improvisations to save themselves and others. Two things struck me most powerfully on my travels in New Orleans during the aftermath of Hurricane Katrina. One was those murders hidden in plain sight. The other was the love. There was a sweet emotional directness in many of the people in New Orleans unlike anything I've encountered elsewhere, and it was one of the many elements that made this city everyone knows is one of the poorest places in the USA one of the richest as well. People pouring my coffee or selling me string called me "baby" and "sweetheart," strangers were easy to talk to, people readily told their stories and in the telling laid bare their hearts with all the hopes and suffering within, and invited me to come back anytime with any need I might have.

A creole man who struck up a conversation with me in a café told me he tried living in Seattle, but no one would make eye contact and it was hard to meet people, so here he was, trying to move back. A friend of a friend of a friend invited me to stay with her the first time we met, and by the time I'd stayed with her a few times was a dear friend I flew back to see and celebrate Mardi Gras with. The neighbor who shared a porch with her told me that her sister said it was inevitable she herself end up in New Orleans because in Chicago she so often came close to getting punched out for her forthrightness with strangers. Nearly all the older houses had front porches and people still sat on them, enjoying themselves on warm evenings, of which there are many, and on hot nights people—poorer people, probably people without decent air-conditioning, but also my friend's more middle-class neighbors—sat out under the trees that lined some of the streets, or the shaded traffic meridians, held barbecues to which the whole block might be invited, and generally lived in public among each other. They lacked that shrinking fear of strangers and sacralization of privacy that governs much of the architecture of suburbia and the growth of gated communities, the sprawls where no one mingles or, it sometimes seems, gets out of their car except in parking structures. Theirs was an old-fashioned conviviality that could be too bacchanalian to meet the earnest desire for civic revival held by many social critics but was nevertheless vibrant and embracing.

The older African American women pierced my heart with their bold kindness. I interviewed a tough, cynical old widow in her FEMA trailer next to her ruined home in the Lower Ninth Ward. She wasn't on the high ground there, the Holy Cross region by the Mississippi River; she was right off St. Claude Avenue in the middle of the zone where the raging waters of the broken levee had pushed houses off their foundations and floated them down the street, where cars had ended up in trees and people in one-story houses had drowned or suffocated in attics, or been stranded on roofs, where bodies were still being found months after the terrible deluge. She sat in her stark white FEMA trailer, the kind of trailer that would later be demonstrated to exude carcinogenic formaldehyde fumes, and gave me a fairly grim view of human nature and her neighborhood's chances of resurrection. And in parting, she looked me right in the eye and said, "Just remember. Jesus loves you and so do I."

I had long wondered whether there was a society so rich in a sense of belonging and purpose that disaster could bring nothing to it, a society where there was no alienation and isolation to undo. I'd always thought I might find it in Mexico or a traditional indigenous community. I found a little of that in New Orleans. The disaster there was so horrific it begat little of the ebullience of many other disasters—though it created some remarkable disaster communities and even positive social change (as well as social destruction: deeply embedded communities were scattered to the corners of the country, and longtime institutions like Charity Hospital and the public school system were destroyed, intentionally, in the name of post-Katrina progress).

Of course, Katrina wasn't a disaster. It was a catastrophe, far more devastating in its effects and scale, far harder to recover from, since so many buildings, institutions, and the economy itself were shattered across a wide region (even leaving aside the intentional destruction, or disaster capitalism, that savaged long-standing public institutions post-Katrina). Many who had been scattered far across the country did not return, some by choice, some owing to lack of resources. Even Mexico City in 1985, despite the huge death toll, retained its population and a far higher percentage of inhabitable buildings. New Orleans was a watery ghost town for weeks, largely deserted for months after Katrina, and even today many homes, the majority of dwellings in some neighborhoods, remain uninhabitable or unrehabilitated.

The city had always lived with disaster, so much so that boarding up windows against hurricane winds was halfway to routine, partying through the storm was a tradition, and *hurricane* was also the name of a sweet rum cocktail served in a lot of French Quarter bars. New Orleans had always been threatened by hurricanes and floods and brutalized by the terrible summer heat (and, in the nineteenth century, by yellow fever). The great Mississippi flood of 1927 and the devastation of Hurricanes Camille and Betsy in the 1960s were part of collective memory in this place so rich in memory, because people tell stories, learn from elders, stay put, mock recent history in each year's Mardi Gras parades, or put it in songs.

New Orleans's poverty was easy for the media to explain in the aftermath of Katrina: it showed up in statistics about income, housing, illiteracy, crime, wages, and joblessness. This poverty was real, and it was harsh, trapping people in lives with few resources and limited horizons. It had a lot to do with the crime that was high before and after Katrina. And then there was the racism: this was far from Paradise. The white people of New Orleans had been steadily moving away for decades, leaving an urban core that was about two-thirds African American and a periphery of fear and hostility toward the city and its citizens, a geography similar to that of Detroit and its suburbs.

Overall population had been steadily declining from a high in the early 1960s; other than tourism, the port, and the universities, there were few jobs—and so the city did not have the financial momentum to rebuild after disaster that, say, San Francisco in 1906 had. Without Katrina, it would have been doomed to a long, slow decline. With Katrina, its fate took a strange turn—and remains uncertain in many ways years later. The poor were once again most injured and most likely to be dispersed by the calamity (and by the city's decision to board up and then tear down nearly all the huge housing projects across the city, which in many cases were not even damaged).

Even in decline, it is an extraordinary city. Its poverty is obvious. The ways New Orleans was and is rich are not so easy to measure, though a statistician could surely find out how deeply embedded in family, neighborhoods, associations, the annual cycle of celebration, and love of place a great many Orleanians are. New Orleans has an unusually low transience rate: a lot of people, rich and poor, live in the neighborhood, or on the street, or in the house where they were born and have a deep sense of belonging, to their networks of people and to the city itself—as though they had broad branches in the social present and deep and spreading roots in the historical past, like the magnificent live oaks that shade many of the older avenues of the city. Many live in a forest of cousins, aunts, uncles, and ties of blood and of people they grew up with and presumed they would know forever, along with places, institutions, rites, foods, music, and the other threads of the fabric of New Orleans. After Katrina, many were devastated by the loss of something most of the rest of us in the United States had never had. Our grandparents lost it in emigrating from the Old World or leaving the farm, or our parents in moving to the anonymous suburbs, or we ourselves in joining that free and lonely legacy—not tradition, for it is antitradition—of transience and rootlessness. This embeddedness can also be described as a diffuse love, an atmosphere of familiarity and affection in which many of its citizens bask.

Social Aid and Pleasure

New Orleans is also a town of festivals. Not only the rites of Mardi Gras but also of St. Patrick's Day, St. Joseph's Day, Jazz Fest—enough holidays that one parade the second Mardi Gras season after Katrina featured a long, long series of floats commemorating the annual cycle of holidays. Mardi Gras itself is not one day of parades, costumes, and revelry, as many outsiders imagine, but rather the whole ancient carnival season from Twelfth Night in early January to Fat Tuesday, the last day before Lent, a cycle of several weeks of intensifying celebration. Many plan and prepare costumes and floats all year, and the krewes who put on each parade are social organizations that function year-round. Second line parades may occur any day of the year. They evolved out of jazz funerals (and aspects of the jazz funerals apparently trace back to West African traditions that were not lost in the Middle Passage). The Social Aid and Pleasure Clubs that commission the second lines themselves evolved from the African American benevolent societies that came out of the postwar Freedmen's Bureau as a means to provide funerals and other forms of support as well as fellowship and security. They were one of the many forms mutual aid took in a more close-knit era that lingers on in New Orleans. Their very name acknowledges as little else does in everyday language that mutual aid and pleasure are linked, that the ties that bind are grounds for celebration as well as obligation.

Louis Armstrong, New Orleans's most famous jazz musician, remembered with great joy how early on in his life music gave him the diplomatic immunity to move relatively freely through New Orleans—while playing in parades through rival groups' neighborhoods and through the white districts otherwise off-limits. New Orleans is the birthplace of jazz and the capital of the Mississippi Delta, where the blues arose from sorrow and genius and mixed musical legacies. It is also a divided and dangerous city; but the wealth of music undid something of the profound impoverishment that is racism. Parades by definition travel, and the musicians, if not their followers, in the parades of Armstrong's youth, could go almost anywhere, which is why an early parade with the Tuxedo Brass Band was one of his happiest memories: "I really felt like I was somebody," he recalled, and his biographer Thomas Brothers writes, "With his 1921 success with the Tuxedo Brass Band, Armstrong believed that he had solved, through his growing musical ability, the problem of trouble-free movement through a dangerous city." In those frequent celebrations, New Orleanians renew their ties to tradition, place, and each other. In Spike Lee's documentary When the Levees Broke you can see one of the members of Black Men of Labor exult that their second line parade has let them come to Jackson Square in the heart of the French Quarter, which would ordinarily be out-of-bounds for them.

The second line parades continue, if not unabated. Nearly two years after Katrina, I followed the Hot Eight Brass Band through the areas upriver from the French Quarter, starting near the Walmart on Tchoupitoulas Street that during Katrina had been plundered by police as well as other locals. The members of the band mostly wore T-shirts, but the Social Aid and Pleasure Club members marching with them wore matching peach-colored short-sleeved suits and porkpie hats. The musicians played their instruments with joyous zeal, and the mostly black crowd in their wake danced exuberantly through the middle of the streets, joined by people trickling out of the old houses the parade passed. It was an hour or two of joy for no particular reason, under the spreading oaks of the residential streets and past the bleakness of dying industry. Such an event on a small scale does what carnival does on a large scale: the subtle work of making society.

New Orleans is extraordinarily rich, as well as appallingly poor, and it sometimes seems to be made up largely of contradictions. This social richness is shot through with crime, racism, fear, and apartheids. But the divides themselves are not easy to explain. The media in the wake of Katrina tended to equate race and class, but the city has a black bourgeoisie with deeper roots than any other on the continent, and plenty of poor white people. Progressives from other parts of the country sometimes assume as well that the white people there are all racists, but there are ardent antiracists among both the native white population and the many newcomers who were and are artists, filmmakers, lawyers, organizers, drag queens, environmentalists, and bartenders deeply smitten with the city. There are mixed-race alliances and the children that resulted, as well as a thriving Vietnamese community, a Latino community that exploded with undocumented workers doing demolition and renovation after the catastrophe, and deeply rooted indigenous communities in the surrounding countryside. The lines are not simple. The flood of 2005 overran the middle-class white neighborhood of Lakeview, as well as the black middle-class sprawl of Gentilly, the Vietnamese enclave in New Orleans East, the poor neighborhoods of the Ninth Ward, and the economic and racial mixed zones of the central city—and much of the rest of the Louisiana, Mississippi, and Alabama coasts.

Old and New Ties

Katrina tore apart many old ties and networks and begat new ones as well. These were no substitute for what was lost, but they matter all the same. When Katrina struck, people around the country immediately responded with an outpouring of grief, anxiousness to help, outrage at the government, and concrete support. Huge sums were donated. Within the week, the liberal political action group Moveon.org had set up a Web site, Hurricanehousing.org, on which nearly two hundred thousand people would volunteer housing, much of it in their own homes, to the displaced. These invitations to join households express something of the deep emotional response in those first days (even as the media were still describing New Orleanians as monsters but showing them as sufferers):

> We live in the downtown area so we are around anything you need (schools, the zoo, job opportunities . . .). Albuquerque is willing to do everything possible to help. We will be accepting women and children only. There is a mom, dad, and a teenage daughter. We have two potbelly pigs, and two cats. We are all new at this, but feel comfortable to call collect . . . you are more than welcome in our home. We are horrified by the scenes on the TV.

> Room available on second floor in a fairly large home with 2 ½ baths and a basement located in suburban Detroit neighborhood. Full house privileges included with use of phone after 7:00 PM weekdays and weekends. I am a single divorced father with a 14-year-old daughter that stays with me much of the time. We have two small dogs. God bless you. I will keep you in my prayers. Keep your faith as Job had done.

> My mom and I rent out our rooms usually, but in this case it would be free. We are in New York State, which is a ways away, but We are willing to help any way we can. we live in a beautiful town with a great community, in a safe environment. We are not wealthy, but will give all we can.

> *I live in a nice middle-class neighborhood. I am disabled and am at home all day, so I can watch child while mother and father look for job. My wife is a preschool teacher. Prefer nondrinking or drugs, elderly couple OK also. Pets OK, have big backyard. Prefer Christian.*

But there was also a pagan bisexual couple in their thirties in San Francisco. And a young married couple in Bozeman. And tens of thousands of others in a nationwide surge of altruism.

Communities of people thrown together by circumstance were everywhere. I met a gaunt older man, a housepainter by trade, named Keith Bernard Sr., in his neighborhood, the Lower Ninth Ward, and he told me his story of survival in a sweet, plaintive voice. Where he lived on the south side of the Lower Ninth "was a nice quiet neighborhood, it really was. Katrina ran all our best friends away, most of our neighbors were elders, as a matter of fact in a two-block radius all of our neighbors were elderly. They were beautiful. Talk about fine people, they were homeowners, they were nice people willing to help to give whatever they can." As for himself, "I stayed because I could've been of help to someone, which I was." The Lower Ninth is notorious for drugs and crime, but like most such neighborhoods the reputation is earned by a fraction of its population, and the majority of churchgoers, retirees, working people, children, and others lead ordinary lives. Bernard was a renter near the high ground of the Holy Cross part of the neighborhood, but not high enough when the storm surge burst into the area. His house flooded and the water chased him up into the attic. His only way out was to dive back into the house and through a broken window into the lake his neighborhood had become. He and his dog came across a boat and made it to a two-story house, where they sheltered for the first, worst brunt of the storm.

They were rescued by police who dropped them off on the St. Claude Bridge that crosses the canal that cuts off the Lower Ninth from the rest of the city. Bernard was able to walk to an elementary school, where many others had taken refuge. "It turned into a community effort. Everybody cooked. They fed one another. They scavenged the food that they had from stores that had been vandalized, whatever, but they were really, really nice. I saw people being compassionate about people that they never met, people that they never saw, people that they never knew reaching out to them, feeding them, giving them clothes. You know, we didn't have no use for money, so the basic was the clothes and the food. This was New Orleans everywhere. This was everywhere in New Orleans."

That might have been the school I visited six months later, when New Orleans was still something of a ghost town. Written on the green chalkboard in one of the upstairs classrooms was, in neat handwriting, "September 2nd, 2005, 9:15 a.m. We are sorry for the school, but the shelter was a blessing. We had to bring over 200 people here with no help from any Coast Guard boats. People died and are still in their house, we had to leave them, we asked the C. G. for help and got NONE. Thanks to Mickey, McKinley, Eric, Phil, Tyrone, Karl B., J-Roy, Richard, Cedric, Jeff D., Jeff, Ben, Big Greg, 10th Ward Al, Lance + Anthony. We saved the whole project. THEY LEFT US HERE TO DIE."

After the disaster, people in the devastated neighborhoods were scattered. NENA, the Lower Ninth Ward Neighborhood Empowerment Network Association, keeps a big map in its cement-block office—which was, in 2007, a former community center lent by St. David's Catholic Church next door—with a green pushpin for every returnee. The green dots were scattered everywhere, though they represent only a small percentage of homes and residents. NENA was founded by resident Patricia Jones, a former accountant, in June of 2006, to help people cut through the extraordinary red tape that surrounds the new building codes, the FEMA money, the Road Home fund from the state of Louisiana, the insurance regulations, and other bureaucracies returnees face, but it also fosters connections and community. Help came from all over the country, but there was plenty of mutual aid from within the city.

Pam Dashiell, a warm, easygoing political powerhouse, had been president of the Holy Cross Neighborhood Association (named after the Holy Cross School, it encompasses the southern stretch of the Lower Ninth and its highest ground). As members of the HCNA began to return, they held meetings several times a week. In the summer of 2007, they still met weekly, rather than monthly as they did before Katrina. The group has been potent for both its ambition and its coordination of many outside groups and funders. And while a lot of individuals and groups aspired to just restore what had been, the HCNA looked at how to make the Lower

Ninth better. The list of who came to help sounds like the setup for a joke: churches, the movie star Brad Pitt, graduate students, lots of young anarchists, and the Sierra Club.

Most of the returnees had lost family members to the Katrina diaspora, and the fabric of the neighborhood is still mostly holes. Dashiell evacuated to St. Louis with her daughter, daughter's partner, and grandchild. Only she returned, and she returned even though she was a renter who lost everything in her home. She set about to reclaim not only a home but a community in the Lower Ninth. A lot of people elsewhere bought the story that these places did not make environmental sense to reclaim and reinhabit, and Dashiell recalls that the developers who were part of the city's Bring New Orleans Back Committee were, like the businessmen trying to abolish Chinatown after the 1906 earthquke, "in reality looking at ways to not bring the Lower Nine back. To hear what they were really saying at that level and what they were doing was just unbelievable, and for me that was a catalyst. We had to do something. We organized. We developed a plan. We were everywhere we could be." Though the businessmen were arguing that rebuilding didn't make environmental sense, environmentalists were the ones "who provided the support," Dashiell said. The HCNA pursued a rebuilding effort that would address the ways New Orleans had chosen to violate the natural landscape. Unlike mostly middle-class white Lakeview or largely Vietnamese American New Orleans East, the Lower Ninth is not a new neighborhood or one on extremely low ground. Its ecological precariousness is relatively recent, the result of man-made waterways that brought storm surges into the area.

Pitt, who with his partner and children nominally moved to New Orleans after Katrina, helped organize and underwrote a competition to design sustainable housing for New Orleans and has since given millions to the rebuilding effort. Originally, the project was to have generated houses across New Orleans, but after Pitt met Pam Dashiell and the HCNA, he decided all the resources should go into the Lower Ninth. Members of the neighborhood group got involved in the competition to design an eighteen-unit apartment building, several single-family homes, and a community center that will include day-care facilities. In the summer of 2008, some of the architecturally adventurous houses Pitt had helped bring into being were nearly finished. They stood on tall stilts that contributed to their resemblance to just-landed spaceships, in the empty space near the levee breach where so many houses had been smashed up by the force of the waters. A lonely expanse spread around them with only a few inhabited buildings, including the two-story house Common Ground came to own and rehabilitate. That house in 2006 was full of silt and on it was spray-painted "BAGHDAD" in crude lettering insisting that this too was a war zone. Two years later, the building was clean, newly plumbed, and a hive of activity surrounded by gardens—and a shabby doghouse labeled "FEMA," a succinct visual joke about the government that had failed to help when it mattered most.

Housed, like NENA, in a building lent by a church, the Holy Cross Neighborhood Association is a key player in the rebuilding of the Lower Ninth. Founded in 1981, the HCNA had been working with the Sierra Club on environmental justice issues that posed serious threats to the neighborhood long before Katrina. So the club and the HCNA were already in place when Katrina hit; Common Ground (the funnel for volunteers cofounded by New Orleans native and former Black Panther Malik Rahim), Emergency Communities, NENA, the People's Hurricane Relief Fund, and other organizations—including many church groups— emerged in the wake of the storm. Existing ties mattered enormously. New ones arose. A tangle of organizations, connections, and networks— and will and love—held together the city that had fallen apart.

The semisuburban white enclave of Lakeview at the other end of New Orleans became far more gregarious; a daughter of that neighborhood working as an anthropologist told me that many there said to her, "If it wasn't for my neighbors, I wouldn't be here."

Picking Up the Pieces

In a city like New York—affluent, well run, fully functional for the great majority of its citizens—getting back to normal was a coherent goal. In a city like New Orleans that had been falling apart for decades, plagued with corrupt and incompetent policing, courts, and government generally, undermined by poverty and divided by racism, *back* wasn't necessarily the direction to go. The disaster was a chance for some to try to reinvent their community and their lives—a gamble, really, since it didn't always work. It didn't always fail either.

After the upheaval of the disaster came the long, hard task of rebuilding homes on the Gulf. Deciding to come back was complicated. It depended for most people on whether the neighbors were coming back. To have a home you needed a neighborhood around it. To have a neighborhood you needed a city and some of the basic services—water, sewage, schools, transit—they are supposed to provide. To have a city you needed some environmental action on New Orleans's shattered levees and other systems and maybe some confidence in solving larger environmental problems. Which meant you needed a nation that was committed. It wasn't, but people came back anyway, some with no guarantees whatsoever.

In a disaster like the 1906 earthquake, there was a great deal for people to do as soon as the shaking was over—rescuing, fighting fire, building temporary shelters and then those convivial community kitchens. Some felt more powerful as they took action, formed community, made decisions, functioned in the absence of the usual systems. That sense of agency was not so widespread in Katrina. The disaster did bring together many who stayed in the city. But most people evacuated, believing they would be gone a few days but then found themselves in exile. Staying in the city meant being utterly overwhelmed by the scale of the catastrophe, stranded by the water and seeing the authorities go berserk. Many felt helpless, even if they were not stuck in one of the terrible public shelters, and when they were evacuated, they were often put on buses and planes without being allowed to choose or even know their destination. Those who could evacuate under their own means controlled their destiny—where they went and when they returned. Those who couldn't didn't. Evacuees were often received kindly after their city was wrecked, but their few days away stretched into weeks and months. They were estranged, adrift, uprooted, recipients of charity more than members of a community of mutual aid. Organizing anything amid that diaspora was difficult, and so was staving off despair.

Earthquakes and fires are comparatively clean disasters; the flood of New Orleans left behind silt, mud, debris, and, indoors, toxic mold, while the unexpectedly long evacuation left food to rot in tens of thousands of refrigerators; bodies decaying in flooded homes; dead animals among the fallen trees and debris; contaminants and toxins carried by water that settled in odd places; a huge oil spill in St. Bernard Parish; a filthy, stinking, soggy mess dismaying to those who came back.

The most optimistic of all disaster scholars, Charles Fritz, had ascribed his positive disaster experiences only to those who are "permitted to interact freely and to make an unimpeded social adjustment." This was hardly what happened in the first days and weeks of Katrina, when many felt abandoned, criminalized, imprisoned, cast out, and then like recipients of charity—or hate. Many are still displaced years after the storm— the calculus is, "If you couldn't afford to evacuate, you probably can't afford to come back"—and rental housing in particular has evaporated from the city. The scale of the devastation and loss meant that mutual aid was not enough. Enormous amounts of assistance from outside were required, and they came in bureaucratically choked dribbles from government agencies and in unstinting waves from the huge quantity of volunteers who came from around the country to rebuild New Orleans, tens and then hundreds of thousands. Eventually a handful of visionary projects would be launched in New Orleans, bringing real if limited benefits to a troubled place.

Like the people in Mexico City in 1985, the people of New Orleans won a lot of battles. The early plan to just raze the low-lying areas that were often also the low-income areas was killed off by people like Pam Dashiell, and citizen pressure forced the city government to recommit money to rebuilding some of those neighborhoods. ACORN, the group that works on housing issues with poor communities around the country, is headquartered in New Orleans, and Wade Rathke, its founding director, told me, "Even if you take some of the most aggressive plans—to take away fiscal ability and land control from local officials—they didn't succeed." Public housing was largely razed, though some affordable housing was to be built on some of the sites—and Rathke points out that "it's impossible for me to pretend that we weren't losing it in city after city for twenty years. To win in New Orleans would have been to reverse what we've been losing everywhere else." He was not happy about the hundred thousand people who hadn't come back three years later, but he noted that the labor scarcity had meant a rise in wages for a lot of the city's service economy and other jobs and a rise in employment levels in a city that had long been hemorrhaging work. There were victories and improvements. But a lot of people were still uprooted and suffering. Rents were up, essential services—hospitals, day care—were greatly reduced, the homeless population doubled, and by the third anniversary of the disaster, the city had 71,657 vacant, ruined, and uninhabited houses. Many were permanently exiled, stranded in toxic trailers in remote locations, homeless, or overwhelmed by the task of trying to return. (The kind of bureaucracy that strangled official response is demonstrated by the rule that forbade FEMA to spend disaster-relief money on permanent structures; the toxic $70,000 trailers consumed money that in a less inflexible system could've been used for rebuilding or for sturdier, saner shelters.)

The commitment was extraordinary. When I first visited the Lower Ninth, six months after Katrina, it was eerily abandoned. No one lived there, and there were no streetlights. The storm seemed to have just happened. Cars were still tossed over fences, houses sat in the middle of streets, other houses existed only as splintered wreckage, and a lot of the street signs that weren't missing were homemade. Those signs said a lot about the people who'd come back in advance of their own government to try to bring the Lower Ninth back to life. Every time I returned, the place was different—wreckage disappeared, signs appeared, houses were reclaimed, yards mowed from the six-foot-high weeds that had sprung up, and more and more signs of life were apparent—but like so many other neighborhoods, it was still missing a huge portion of its people and its future remained utterly uncertain.

Waves of volunteers arrived in the city, many of them focusing on gutting houses and beginning the long, hard journey toward rebuilding a habitable city. Others provided food, counseling, medical care, and more. National organizations such as Habitat for Humanity and the Red Cross showed up to fulfill their mandate. Existing local organizations shifted their purpose or intensified their mission, as did the Holy Cross Neighborhood Association and many churches. Churches from around the country sent delegations down to do a week's work on a project; for many it was a profound experience. For a few years, thousands of college students went to rebuild New Orleans as an alternative spring break. New local organizations arose, from the radical People's Hurricane Relief Fund to the upper-class Women of the Storm, who used their access to bring in politicians to see the devastation firsthand. Counterculture groups played an important role, from descendants of the black power movement to hordes of young white anarchists. An extraordinary amount of love and work went into the effort to revive a city that had been pronounced dead shortly after August 29, 2005.

BELOVED COMMUNITY

Pitching a Tent

Thanks to Katrina, the Bush administration lost its mandate of heaven. Perhaps the president and his team should have lost it in the chaos of September 11, 2001, but they cannily framed that situation in a way that led to a surge of patriotic fear and deference and defined the administration as decisive, powerful, unquestionable—until the summer of 2005. Only then did the media and public begin to criticize the administration with the fearlessness that should be part of every era, every democracy. Many reporters standing in the ruins of the Gulf voiced unscripted outrage over the incompetence, callousness, and cluelessness of the federal government during the catastrophe. After Katrina, people who had been afraid to criticize the administration were emboldened to do so. It changed the tone nationwide, and Bush soon became the most unpopular president in American history.

On September 1, the president said, "I don't think anyone anticipated the breach of the levees." The media later obtained videotape of him being warned of that possibility on August 28. The public too began to speak out more fearlessly that summer. Poverty and race became issues again. MSNBC commentator Keith Olbermann was so outraged by Katrina that on September 5, 2005, he launched into a furious, widely circulated tirade against the Bush administration, the beginning of his Special Comments that were routinely the most hostile critique of the president in the mainstream media and one of the most noted. "It wasn't Iraq that did George

Bush in—it was the weather," he said in 2007. Bush's own pollster, Matthew Dowd, said later, "Katrina to me was the tipping point. The president broke his bond with the public. . . . I knew when Katrina—I was like, man, you know, this is it, man. We're done." By then a liberal black man with a background in community organizing had become a serious contender to succeed that president in the 2008 election—an unimaginable possibility not long before; and another Democratic contender for the White House launched his campaign in New Orleans and made poverty its central issue. The nation shifted, not only from deference to the president but from fealty to the politics of the far right, and Katrina was the turning point.

Bush had been on a five-week vacation at his ranch in Crawford, Texas, when the hurricane hit, and he waited a few days before deciding to return to work in the nation's capital. On the way, he had Air Force One swing low over New Orleans. Being photographed sitting comfortably looking out an airplane window at a city in which people were still stranded did not help his image. His vacation had been disrupted already, though. Cindy Sheehan, the mother of a soldier killed in Iraq a year earlier, had camped outside the presidential expanse to demand that Bush meet with her. Harrowed by grief at her son's death, she tried to make sense of it by demanding the president tell her "for what noble cause did my son die?" She thus became a major voice in the antiwar movement, a surprising role for a suburban mother of three and devout Catholic who had hitherto led a quiet life, surprising most of all to her.

At that moment in August of 2005, the rangy blond mom with her unstudied, heartfelt, and sometimes outrageous speech became the narrow point of a wedge opening up room to debate the war. She set up a tent in a ditch by the road to the presidential ranch in Crawford on August 6, and supporters began to gather, bringing their own tents and vehicles and building an impromptu village around what began as a small vigil. They named it Camp Casey, after her dead son whose image was everywhere. During a slow news month, this standoff between a bereaved mother sitting at the gates and a president who wouldn't show his face became a huge story. Her son's death had been her disaster; that she made something remarkable of her response to it was clearly her salvation.

I stopped by Camp Casey the day that Hurricane Katrina hit the Gulf and found a big camp and an extraordinary community akin in many ways to disaster communities. The rolling green landscape studded with small groves of oak trees was beautiful. The sky was strange, huge white clouds swelling overhead, the air stifling. A field of crosses, one for each American soldier dead in the war, stood in front of the huge shade tent with open sides and in which all the meetings, meals, and conversations were held. Someone had come the day before and decorated the crosses with roses of all colors that were wilting in the steamy air. Retired colonel Ann Wright—the career diplomat who resigned on March 19, 2003, the day the U.S. war against Iraq began—strode around making sure everything was going well at the camp. Tough, sweet, and enormously competent, she had directed the evacuation of the U.S. presence in Sierra Leone when that nation erupted in conflict and helped establish the embassy in Afghanistan in 2001. She radiated the same joy many others there did: that this was exactly the meaningful work they had always wanted, and the heat and disarray and discomfort mattered not at all compared to this great sense of arrival. Everywhere people were having the public conversation about politics and values a lot of us dream about the rest of the time, average-looking people of all ages from all over the country, particularly the heartland.

I met a woman who lost her teaching job in Indiana for saying something against the war to elementary-school kids and who was terribly worried about her navy son; a twenty-five-year-old from Kansas City, Missouri, on his honeymoon with a wife who pushed his wheelchair everywhere, because an explosion in Iraq had paralyzed him; an old man from Slater, Missouri, who had been in the marines from 1957 to 1963 and had been sleeping in his Ford pickup with 300,000 miles on the odometer during the encampment; four elders from the American Indian Movement, who said what everyone said, "I heard about it and I had to come." The dozen or so clean-cut, serious young veterans of the unfinished war were restless that day, worried that much of the Louisiana National Guard and its equipment was stationed in Iraq when their state needed them desperately. Immediately afterward, the camp broke up, and the group Veterans for Peace drove busloads of supplies to the Gulf, becoming one of the earliest relief efforts to arrive, responding directly from outside the gates of the president's vacation home while inside everything was stalled and confused.

Sheehan herself moved through the camp giving interviews, hugging veterans, receiving gifts, seemingly inexhaustible, as though grief had hollowed out all usual needs and left her nothing but a purity of purpose. She said to me at the end of that day, August 29, "This is the most amazing thing that has ever happened to me and probably that ever will. I don't even think I would even want anything more amazing to happen to me."

Reconciliations

Early in his work with the civil rights movement, Martin Luther King Jr. began to talk about the "beloved community." The movement was against discrimination, segregation, and other manifestations of racism. In King's eyes, it was not only against but also for—for a larger vision, a utopian ideal of fellowship, justice, and peace. Every activist movement begins by uniting its participants in important ways, giving them a sense of purpose drawn from the wrongs they seek to right and the shared vision of a better world. In 1957, King wrote that the ultimate aim of the Southern Christian Leadership Conference, a key player in the movement, was "to foster and create the 'beloved community' in America where brotherhood is a reality. . . . Our ultimate goal is genuine intergroup and interpersonal living—integration." Integration was no longer merely a practical matter of buses, schools, lunch counters, and workplaces. It was a metaphysic of solidarity and affinity, a condition of hearts rather than laws and facilities. The same year he declared that the nonviolent activist in this movement "realizes that noncooperation and boycotts are not ends themselves. . . . The end is redemption and reconciliation. The aftermath of nonviolence is the creation of the beloved community." Of course that was a movement that came out of the black churches of the South, and so it was religious from its roots on up. Other groups took up the term, notably the Student Nonviolent Coordinating Committee that organized Freedom Summer and introduced ideas about participatory democracy rather than charismatic leadership to the activists of the 1960s.

What begins as opposition coalesces again and again into social invention, a revolution of everyday life rather than a revolt against the system. Sometimes it leads to the kind of utopian community that withdraws from the larger society; sometimes, particularly in recent decades, it has generated small alternatives—cooperatives, organic farms, health-care projects, festivals—that became integral parts of this society. One of the fundamental questions of revolution is whether a change at the level of institutions and systemic power is enough or whether the goal is to change hearts, minds, and acts of everyday life. Someone like King wanted both: the end of the official apartheid and discrimination in the United States and the transformation of spirit and imagination in each and every citizen.

When we talk of social change, we talk of movements, a word that suggests vast groups of people walking together, leaving behind one way and traveling toward another. But what exists between these people is not movement but a settling in together that is the beginnings of community (though in other cases, notably that of the civil rights movement, a community quite literally got up and began moving, through streets, across states, into diners and voting places). This is one of the major rewards of activism—a new community offering a new sense of shared purpose and belonging, honoring the principles for which it fights, the conditions so palpable among the people at Camp Casey that August. Again and again, antiwar, environmental, social justice, human rights, and other movements generate new communities, often transcending old divides, and in the process bringing something of that urgency, purposefulness, suspension of everyday concerns, fellowship, and social joy also found in disaster. This, of course, is not always what happens: dysfunctional organizations with bad internal dynamics are legion, but much of the activism of the 1980s in particular focused on cleaning up the process—working toward egalitarianism, nondiscrimination, and accountability from the inside out. The affinities with disaster communities are obvious: activist communities come into being in response to what is perceived as a disaster—discrimination, destruction, deprivation—and sometimes generate a moment or fragment of a better world. As Temma Kaplan, a New Yorker who had been part of that movement in the American South, said, "For a short time, during the first few days after 9/11 I felt that Beloved Community that we talked about in the Civil Rights Movement."

After Katrina, existing communities had been devastated, both by the physical damage that scattered residents to the corners of the country and by the traumas of the social and political catastrophes. The volunteers who came from outside the area did something to restore those existing communities and in the course of doing so generated an ephemeral series of communities all their own. Religious groups played a huge role in the resurrection of New Orleans. In terms of sheer might, Catholic Charities and the Methodist Church did the most. (A Mennonite call to retired RV owners to congregate in the Gulf listed among the benefits of volunteering, "Becoming the 'hands and feet' of Jesus offers a very rewarding retirement activity; fellowship with other persons of a like mind as you become part of a team; bring back hope to those who have lost it; enjoy social times, potlucks, eating out together, accepting local invitations for meals." Though the Mennonites I saw were mostly in their prime and fiercely good as construction crews.) The tight-knit community around Mary Queen of Vietnam Church in New Orleans East organized the congregation whose early return and effective mutual aid made it possible for others in the Vietnamese American community to return as well.

And then there were the groups descended from the countercultures, the not-always-beloved communities of resistance of the 1960s, the Black Panthers and the Rainbow Family, as well as a lot of young anarchists connected to more recent movements around economic and environmental justice and human rights. Often while the big groups were still sorting out their business or entangled in bureaucracy, the small groups these radicals begat were able to move faster, to stay longer, to sink deeper, to improvise more fitting responses to the needs of the hour. The volunteers became their own culture. And much of the positive experience of disaster seemed to belong to them, not to the residents.

Six months after the hurricane, I stopped in at the Made with Love Café, in St. Bernard Parish, just across the line from the Lower Ninth. The dining room was a big tent where volunteers served three hot meals a day to hundreds of returnees. New Orleanians called it "the hippie kitchen." Behind a young woman in a bandanna and undershirt serving up food, a sign painted on cardboard in bright colors read, "To Emergency Communities Made with Love Café & all the amazing residents: WE WILL NOT FORGET YOU!" A black woman and white man were singing and playing music as people sat at long tables talking and eating. Around the main pavilion was a collection of tents, trailers, temporary buildings and other tarp-covered structures, a packaged food giveaway, a yoga site, and various other amenities. I struck up a conversation with one of the volunteers, Roger, who was walking his two elderly greyhound rescue dogs around the back of the complex. A white-haired white retiree with a thick Boston accent, Roger seemed almost transfigured by joy when he spoke of his work in this little community. He and his wife worked in the supplies site, handing out free stuff. They had found the volunteer opportunity on the Web, driven down to participate, and were, when I met them, six weeks into an eight-week stay.

Half an hour later, I met an African American man who'd been in New Orleans all his life. We were standing at the site where the infamous barge bashed through the levee to flood the Ninth Ward. Looking downcast, this substantial middle-aged man told me he had grown up at the levee breach in a house that had become a pile of splinters and rubble, though after Hurricane Betsy in 1965, his family had moved uptown. This day six months later was the first time he felt ready to come and look at the devastation. He had been evacuated from New Orleans, spent three months in Houston, come back, but he said it didn't feel like home anymore, and it never would. He was grieved and embittered by the way people like him had been treated in the eventual evacuation and upon their return. If he could win the lottery, he told me, he would leave New Orleans for good. This spectrum, from Roger's joy to the local's despair, was New Orleans early on.

The out-of-town volunteers were often very different from the locals, emotionally and culturally. But they weren't necessarily at odds. I asked Linda Jackson, a former laundromat owner who became a key staff person at NENA, the Lower Ninth Ward Neighborhood Empowerment Network, how the community felt about the assistance pouring in from around the world. She replied in her whispery voice, "They're stunned. They never thought the world would reach out the way they did. I'm not going to say that it makes up for [the initial, official Katrina response], but the help that we've been given from throughout the United States and the world, it makes us work that much harder. We say: you know what, if these people can come down here and take off of work, drop out of school for a couple weeks, there's no way, there's just no way we can have a negative attitude."

Over and over again I met volunteers who told me they initially came for a week or two but who three months, six months, a year later were still at work in New Orleans. One morning in June of 2007, I stopped at the Musicians' Village that Habitat for Humanity was building in the

Upper Ninth Ward—a whole neighborhood of small, tidy row houses raised well off the ground and painted in bright colors. I struck up a conversation with a small, dark man of unclear ethnicity and a very distinct Harley-Davidson motorcycle, Brian from Monterey, California. He told me that ten months earlier, in August of 2006, he had taken a detour to New Orleans from his journey to watch the leaves change in Vermont. "And I was going to stay for a month, but after a couple weeks they realized that I was the only trim carpenter they had. So they asked me to stay." Habitat for Humanity was founded by a wealthy couple who realized that their money wasn't giving them purpose or joy; it is a Christian group and one that has a strategy for integrating volunteers and locals. They call it "sweat equity": the future homeowners must work on the houses—though in New Orleans the houses were going up in such numbers that the homeowners would sometimes be chosen only later. Brian said that for him, it wasn't about saving New Orleans or social justice: "At first I thought it was, or I just wanted to help because it was such a mess. In New Orleans East, this elderly couple had been in this house thirty-five or forty years, very elderly, they couldn't get anybody to tear it down, they had no insurance, they had to get the lot leveled, so every day they would burn. They would tear off part of their house and burn it in the front yard. You see stuff like that and you just get angry. The money's there. The money is there, and like I said, at first I thought I was doing it for an idealistic reason, but I get more out of it than I put into it, a lot more. I get letters and postcards from people that have been here, and a lot of them just can't wait to get back. I'm doing it for the people here, the people I'm working with, and the volunteers. That's where I get my love from."

Finding Common Ground

It started out with shotguns on a front porch, transformed into young medics bicycling through the streets offering assistance to anyone and everyone who wanted it, and it ended up as dozens of relief and reconstruction projects around the city and thousands of volunteers. Malik Rahim, the former Black Panther who reported to anyone who listened that vigilantes were murdering African American men in Algiers, recalls, "Right after the hurricane I got into a confrontation with some white vigilantes in Algiers, and when I got into them I seen that I was over-matched. I had access to a couple of weapons, and maybe enough ammunition that I could withstand maybe two, three firefights with them, and that's about it. I made a call for some help. Scott Crow and Brandon Darby came to assist us." Crow and Darby were white activists from Texas who had worked with Rahim on the case of the Angola 3—former Black Panthers who had endured decades of solitary confinement on questionable charges. One of them, Robert King Wilkerson, had been exonerated and released, and the young Texans came to check in on him. Their adventures in eluding the authorities, launching a boat, exploring the city by water, and eventually being united with King were considerable, and at the end the two young white activists, the two older ex-Panthers, and Rahim's partner, Sharon Johnson, sat together in Algiers and talked.

As Rahim, a substantial, powerful, deep-voiced man with long dreadlocks, remembers it, "Scott on the morning of the fifth of September, he said it was time that we organize. And when he told us this, we sat down at my kitchen table and we started organizing Common Ground. The name came from Robert King Wilkerson. King said that what we have to do—because our main discussion was upon how come social movements, all social movements, in America start off with a bang and end with a fizzle—what he said was that we allow all our petty differences to divide us. And King said what we have to find then is that common ground that's going to bring everybody together. So with that we said, 'Hey, that's it, Common Ground, let that be the name.'" The response brought up another King, the one who had popularized the term "beloved community" and declared, "Hate cannot drive out hate, only love can do that."

Rahim continued, "After that I had twenty dollars, Sharon put up thirty dollars, and with that we financed Common Ground." Millions of dollars would follow. "And from there we was blessed that our phones were still working, so from there we started getting on the phone. We started calling around the country to everyone we knew, and started asking them for some assistance. After that here comes Veterans for Peace. The first to come up was the Veterans for Peace from Florida, and they brought up a bunch of supplies. The next thing you know people start coming. Cindy Sheehan came. And with her came a lot of help. By then we had opened up our health clinic, at least it was a first-aid station by then. A group from France came and helped us make the transition. We organized Common Ground Relief on the fifth of September, and on the ninth we organized a first-aid station. And then maybe three weeks later we made the transition from a first-aid station to a bona fide health clinic. But when it was a first-aid station, it was open twenty-four-seven; we must have been serving at one time from 100 to 150 people a day. Again, like I said, I'm a spiritual person and I truly believe that the Most High casts no burden on you greater than you could bear. My life has been a life of community activism, so I was always able to call upon some of the things that he had blessed me with to provide, to use now in this time of need. A food distribution center was easy for us to start with because this was what I learned how to do when I was in the Panther Party. The health clinic or the first-aid station: again, what we did in the Panther Party."

The Panthers had started out as an oppositional group to fight police brutality and discrimination in the inner city. The rhetoric of the Panthers was fiery, and the images of young African Americans with weapons and spectacular shoot-outs with the police (and ambushes by police in which Panthers died) were all too memorable. Much of the rest of the Panthers' achievements have been overshadowed by their outlaw glamour and "off the pigs" rhetoric. The year of its founding, 1966, the Party had come up with a "ten-point program" whose last point was, "We want land, bread, housing, education, clothing, justice, peace, and people's community control of modern technology." As the party spread to cities across the United States, the members went about providing some of those things. They fed breakfast to schoolchildren, tested for sickle-cell anemia, and escorted elders to the bank to cash their checks safely. They called these "survival programs." The term underscores how much the inner city felt like a disaster zone.

Common Ground started out with its own survival programs. And the truth of the organization's name was borne out by a clinic that immediately began offering medical services to everyone on the West Bank—including some of the vigilantes who confessed about the murders to the medics while receiving care. Rahim credits the medics who bicycled around the area with preventing an all-out race war in the volatile area. They went door-to-door checking on people, offering care, and softening the divides and fears. At first Common Ground was run largely out of Johnson and Rahim's modest one-story house, and then the storefront clinic nearby in Algiers was added.

In the Lower Ninth Ward, Common Ground set up a tool-lending station, and as the volunteers began to flood in, some were put to work gutting houses ruined by the floodwaters. Others began to work on bioremediation, on a soup kitchen, and on other projects. It was an ambitious organization that planned, in addition to basic survival programs, to replant the cypress swamps killed off by the salt water of the MR-GO canal on the north side of the Lower Ninth, to try to take over a big apartment complex on the West Bank to lodge many of Katrina's displaced, and to publish a small newspaper for a while. Sometimes its reach exceeded its grasp: the housing project fell through, after a lot of time and money were squandered on it.

The organization was sometimes criticized for bringing white people into black communities, for attempting to make policy as well as practical change, for the ambitious scope of its plans and programs, for its sometimes turbulent internal politics. Thousands of volunteers cycled through, bringing fresh energy—and chaos. A lot of the activists needed to be oriented on how to work across cultural and racial differences. Many came from groups that operated by consensus and wanted that form of direct democracy to be the modus operandi at Common Ground. Allowing transient volunteers to make major decisions without living with the consequences didn't make sense to Common Ground's leadership, and so a lot of friction resulted.

Still, the extremely informal methods often worked, and they allowed improvisation in constantly changing circumstances. Emily Posner, a white volunteer who came early on and stayed a long time, recalled, "After the disaster, it was amazing; the Red Cross had a hundred warehouses all over the place and their stuff was just sitting there. Sit, sit, sit, and then we would befriend some Red Cross workers and say: 'Come on, we need to drive our trucks in here.' So we would just get the stuff and get it out and distribute it all over the community. And we did this in not just Red Cross warehouses but all kinds of groups. We had a network of grassroots people working together all over the Gulf. 'We have all this chicken and no electricity yet—can we send a truck over to your community?' And that way the most amount of people would get something.

There's all kinds of communities within Common Ground. When you work with eleven thousand people [the number of volunteers who had passed through by early 2007], hundreds of people have taken up, at a certain point, long-term roles. While it's an informal thing, there are friendships that have been made that will last forever, and those friendships will be needed in the future for sure. We're a network of people now that if a storm happens we know what to do. And we'll all call each other."

When it worked well, people on both sides of the old racial divides went away with changed perceptions. The volunteers mitigated the racial violence and demonization of the first days after the storm. And they went back to their homes and communities around the country, often transformed in some ways by the experience, and spread the word. This kind of social change is incalculable but important. When he studied Common Ground's beginnings, disaster scholar Emmanuel David thought of Freedom Summer, the movement to register Mississippi voters in 1964, which brought a lot of college-age youth from around the country down to witness and combat racism and poverty. They then went home again bearing stories of what they had seen, galvanized to keep working toward some version of the beloved community. Freedom Summer is a landmark in American history, but the actual number of participants in rebuilding New Orleans is far, far larger—certainly in the hundreds of thousands at this point, but no one is counting. Of course, what transpired also made visible who had abundance and who was destitute—a nation of haves and have nots.

Rahim says the encounters his organization fomented "showed blacks that all whites are not evil or oppressors or exploiters because here that's the only thing that we ever had. And it showed the whites that all blacks here are not criminals, that there are good God-fearing people here." Volunteers stayed in rough barracks in the community, often in reclaimed buildings. "We work with solidarity. That means that if you work here, you going to have to stay here. You going to have to keep your presence in the community, and it breached those gaps. We was the first organization to reach out to the Native American community in Houma, we was the first organization to reach out to the Vietnamese community here." Common Ground's motto is Solidarity, Not Charity, an emphasis on working with rather than for that sets it apart from many national relief groups, however messy its realization of its goals. Projects begat projects.

The clinic split off to become a separate organization, Common Ground Clinic, which begat the Latino Health Outreach Project, which for a few years provided outreach and aid to the hordes of mostly undocumented immigrants who arrived to do the hard work of demolishing and rebuilding the city.

Aislyn Colgan, the young medic who had told me about vigilantes confessing to her about the murders, reflected on her nearly two years on and off with the Common Ground Clinic: "I was only twenty-five when I came down here, and I was in the middle age range. There were very few people over the age of forty, so no one had any experience and we were all learning how to be a leader without being forceful, and a lot of people had different ideas about that. I use the excuse all the time: it was so life and death, that chaos and crisis was propelling a lot of our actions. It took a long time for the clinic to transition. I don't think it was until right when I was leaving that we realized that we have to keep that spirit alive, the spirit that it was created in, that 'we have to just give everything we can.' We were open twelve hours a day, seven days a week the first three months and giving, giving, giving because that was the spirit that it was created in and how do you institutionalize that? How do you make it sustainable?

"It is so rare that you get an opportunity to put into action what maybe you've sat around the coffee table and talked with someone about. When do you ever see that the powers that be are failing at their duty, and when do you ever get the chance to move beyond being angry about it and actually do something very concrete and tangible and immediate? Like, you can't provide these people with health care, but we're here and we can do it. We would get calls from the Red Cross asking us if we had any gloves because they were out of gloves. You're the Red Cross, you just got billions of dollars donated to you and you don't have gloves? And here we are getting everything donated to us through all of these informal networks of organizations, and the National Guard was referring people to us. The systems that you'd expect to be in place were just not, and we were able to provide, to fill that gap. I was really surprised by—I don't know if the right word is *empathy*—but I was really surprised by just how far down you go with someone. I really built my life around the struggle the last year and a half. I gave every ounce of my attention to this city and it really has changed my whole way of thinking about things and viewing the world.

"On one level I'm a lot more scared that the government isn't going to come through. I don't have faith in the government, or even large organizational city bodies or anything to come through in a natural disaster, and I live in the Bay Area, so I'm really scared about earthquakes. I don't believe that anyone is going to come save me and that really freaks me out. Then also on a personal level I feel like the further down—I don't know how to describe it, but there's a depth to my understanding of pain and a depth to my understanding of joy. I was never a person who cried about happy things, but I find that I cry more often. I feel like I have a much stronger sense of the harshness of life and also the beauty. It's like they're one and the same."

Welcome Home

After the 1906 earthquake, San Francisco became a landscape of ruin, but also of improvised outdoor community kitchens, tents, odd piles of salvaged stuff, lavish giveaways in a largely nonmonetary gift economy, lowered social boundaries, and humorous signs—and heartfelt signs, such as the Mizpah Café's "One touch of nature makes the whole world kin." As one of the witnesses described the scene, "When the tents of the refugees, and the funny street kitchens, improvised from doors and shutters and pieces of roofing, overspread all the city, such merriment became an accepted thing. Everywhere, during those long moonlit evenings, one could hear the tinkle of guitars and mandolins, from among the tents." It resembles the campouts that have become a major part of counterculture gatherings since the 1960s, notably the biggest and longest-lived of them all, the Rainbow Gatherings held annually since the early 1970s.

They have bridged the gap between utopian experiment and traditional carnival, incorporating costuming, dancing, music, festivity, ceremony, and large-scale mingling. In creating an infrastructure to maintain weeks of communal life, the gatherings recall utopian communities, but in producing nothing practical and instead relying on resources garnered in the outside world, whether by Dumpster diving or putting it on a credit card, they are more like a festival. If you regard mainstream society as a disaster—some Rainbows call it Babylon—it makes sense to create the equivalent of a disaster community as an alternative and refuge from it. This is one of the arenas in contemporary society where revolution, disaster, and carnival converge into something namelessly new. The first Rainbow Gathering was in 1972, and it's said that Vietnam vets with experience in setting up field kitchens, latrines, and hospitals were instrumental in creating the infrastructure. This emphasis on autonomous systems of survival—as the back-to-the-earth movement, among other things—is one of the overlooked legacies of the 1960s, arising from a sense that the mainstream was already a disaster (and maybe from childhoods spent amid scenarios of postatomic survival). The right-wing survivalist equivalents are notably less gregarious, focusing on pioneer-style nuclear-family units holed up alone and armed against everyone else.

Rainbow Gatherings, which now bring together about thirty thousand people to a different national forest location each year, build a functioning temporary society quite literally from the ground up. Each site is chosen for access to potable water, and an often elaborate piping system brings waters from source to camp. A group arrives early to set up, laying out the grounds and digging latrines, hugely important in preventing disease from spreading and fulfilling the commitment to leave behind an undamaged landscape. Another group stays behind to do cleanup. There is no formal structure or hierarchy, but a great deal of informal oganizing—all decisions are by consensus, anyone may participate, and volunteer groups perform all tasks. (Those who have been around a long time and done a lot of the work accrue power, but it is hard to call this hierarchy.) In addition to the national gathering in the United States each July (with a day of prayer and meditation on the Fourth), regional gatherings, a worldwide gathering, and gatherings in Canada, Europe, New Zealand, and Australia are now established. I have been to a regional Rainbow Gathering, and my response was mixed—I'm not big on clouds of pot smoke, hugs from strangers, hybridized religious appropriations, and grubby personal style—but I saw the desire and partial realization of a goal of creating a mutual-aid gift-economy society and an impressive and moving atmosphere of sweetness, openness, and generosity.

A crucial aspect of Rainbow Gatherings that was not true of Woodstock in 1969 or Burning Man now is that it truly exists as far outside the monetary economy as possible. Burning Man, the huge annual desert gathering, charges a steep admission, patrols to keep the nonpaying out, hires a company to supply and maintain hundreds of chemical toilets, contracts a local hospital to set up a clinic on-site, and leaves all major decisions to the staff of the limited-liability corporation it has become. (Many of the paying attendees, however, create their own gift communities within their camps or with offerings of music, dance zones, drinks, and spectacle to the general public.) The Rainbow Family passes the hat, charges nothing, admits everyone, and food, sanitation, and medical care are all collective volunteer efforts (though the quality of care and cooking can be erratic). The kitchens are the hubs, and many Rainbows are devoted to their annual intensive of cooking and giving away food to strangers. It is a fuzzy but functioning version of the beloved community, an intentional version of disaster's inadvertent communities, and arrivals at gatherings are routinely greeted with "Welcome home."

When Katrina hit the Gulf region, the 2005 national gathering in West Virginia's Monongahela National Forest had been over for more than a month. But many participants kept in touch and some converged on the disaster zone. One named Hawker wrote on September 22 of that year, "As the magnitude of the disaster began to sink in I started receiving phone calls from around the country from my Rainbow friends suggesting we go down and feed folks. What a great idea I thought. If anyone knew about keeping people healthy in a primitive setting and dealing with creating refugee camps it was Rainbow. Add to that that we knew each other already and we seemed like a natural." His group settled in Waveland, Mississippi.

Hawker continued, "The whole town was wiped out by a 30-foot wave that took the town out completely. Almost nothing salvageable was left. Katrina was the great equalizer for this town, making poor and rich equals in the struggle for basic food, shelter, clothing and survival. . . . We arrived in the parking lot of a Fred's food store and met a local Christian relief group from Bastrop Texas called Bastrop Christian Outreach Center. They were down there, as they said, 'to just love on everyone as much as we can.' That sounds like Rainbow to me. We joined forces in a common goal to serve and help as much as we could. We were two totally different groups united by a common cause. The relationship couldn't have been better. We set up a common serving area but two kitchens, one of BCOC and one Rainbow. After time Rainbows went to the BCOC kitchens and BCOC folks came and helped in the Rainbow Kitchen. We become one together. We cooked, set up a 'wall-less mart' where people could get basic food, camping, clothing and other needs. We provided medical needs in our first aid tent (up the road Carolina Medical from Charlotte NC set up a larger mobile field hospital for more serious needs). But mostly we tried to give the town the love and support they needed. One of my favorite tasks was to sit down and eat dinner with locals each night. They usually couldn't wait to tell you their stories. The days were long and the heat tremendous. This was the hardest I have ever worked as I got up at 7:00 am to work till midnights each night with sweat pouring down me all day in the 95–103 degree sun. Yet the faces who came each morning and thanked us for giving them hope made it all worth it."

They were serving as many as four thousand meals a day, much of it food donated by the Organic Valley cooperative, in a geodesic dome tent donated by people from Burning Man. That a bunch of latter-day hippies found common ground with evangelical Christians is in some way typical of disasters; the crisis created circumstances in which their common goals mattered a lot and their divergent beliefs and lifestyles didn't. Some of the churches were doing good works a century ago and may well be doing them a century from now. Their stability has value. So does the instability of the counterculture groups, the ability to improvise and adapt. Disaster scholars like to talk about emergent organizations, organizations that arise in response to the needs of the moment. *Emergent* suggests one round of response—and often such groups appear to fulfill one task or one urgent round of needs and then dissolve. But Common Ground evolved from addressing something as urgent as medical care to something as long-term as wetlands reconstruction and still exists years later (and it is itself in some sense an outgrowth of the Black Panthers forty years before). What began as the Waveland kitchen would move from location to location, wherever the need was most urgent, broaden its offerings, adapt to its community, and shift both toward a formal non-profit organizational structure, on the one hand, and giving over the roles and resources to the communities themselves, on the other, and then dissolve.

Some volunteers had been doing such work for decades before Katrina and as American Rainbow Rapid Response would continue doing it in other sites around North America afterward, from the U.S.-Mexico border to Wisconsin, where small towns and farmers working with Organic Valley cooperative were flooded in the summers of 2007 and 2008. The ability to metamorphose adaptively may be as valuable as the ability to survive as a distinct entity or agenda. Both churches and counterculture groups have been able to work small-scale and improvise with the communities they serve, rather than dispensing the one-size-fits-all aid that often issues forth from the largest organizations. Government disaster planning often presumes that volunteer efforts would work better with more centralized coordination, but the opposite is often true.

After Katrina, Rainbow Gathering regular Felipe Chavez was tending another kitchen, the Welcome Home Kitchen that set up in Washington Square Park just east of the French Quarter in New Orleans shortly after Katrina and was soon driven out. Nearly two years later, I ran into him in the Upper Ninth Ward at St. Mary's of the Angels, cleaning the grill of a salvaged restaurant stove. St. Mary's had allowed Common Ground and other volunteer groups to set up a base there, and a lot of people were moving through. Chavez, a Yaqui Indian from Tucson, Arizona, told me, "It's unfortunate it takes disasters to bring people together, but in a way I feel like it was a miracle, and good things happen after that. One example of that is all these people coming to help and showing compassion. And in New Orleans, there's a lot of people walking the streets that need shelter, that need help. There's people that are off their meds and maybe dangerous, and there's no place for them to be, so they need help and they just end up in jail. There's still a lot of healing that needs to come to New Orleans." The Rainbow Gathering had given Chavez that sort of help decades before. He was an alcoholic whose friend took him to a Rainbow Gathering in the late 1970s. There he was overwhelmed, burst into tears, was comforted by strangers, and turned his life around, both by reconnecting with his own indigenous heritage and by beginning a life of service.

On December 1, 2005, the New Waveland Café closed down, and much of the equipment and many of the crew moved to St. Bernard Parish, just across the line from the Lower Ninth Ward, to establish the Made with Love Café. Like the New Waveland, it was a community center where meals drew people in to receive everything from washing machines to social support. One of the Waveland volunteers, Mark Weiner, had taken it upon himself to organize it as a nonprofit, so that as the free supplies dried up they could apply for funding, and so that as the goodwill and energy of the disaster aftermath slackened, he could maintain a viable structure. A stocky, red-haired, earnest young man who had recently graduated from Columbia University, Weiner told me that he and the other young man who formalized the organization had not been part of the Rainbow Family but had been impressed by what they were doing—and many Rainbows came with them to the new project. Two years later, none remained, but their influence lived on. For Weiner, the key idea was a kitchen as the hub of a community space that could offer other practical and intangible forms of aid.

So in December of 2005, Weiner created a registered nonprofit called Emergency Communities. The name "was our third choice, and the other two were taken by bands. It has various meanings, it could be a noun in the sense that we are building an emergency community, each site is an emergency community. Or it can be the creation of a community from an emergency. But the idea is to blur the lines between those that are helping and those that need help into a single community." It was a goal along the lines of Common Ground's Solidarity, Not Charity. The Made with Love Café moved in January 2007 across the line to the Lower Ninth, where there were finally enough people to make use of such a facility, and the Comin' Home Café opened. It was housed in a church building that had been gutted to a concrete floor, bare walls, and a roof, but it was on the main thoroughfare, St. Claude Avenue, and it had washers, dryers, computers, phones, and a big-screen TV on which Saints games were shown. In front were big oaks, full of screaming parrots, and a hand-painted Comin' Home sign. In the back were two refrigerator trucks, a screened kitchen made to be disassembled and taken to the next volunteer site, and various vehicles in which volunteers lived. There was a small library, bright murals of a marching band of alligators and an alligator in an Emergency Communities apron, cheerful tablecloths on all the tables, and young volunteers moving purposefully around the building and the visitors.

Weiner was good at the art of the possible. Because a group of local youths got out of hand and intimidated other community members, EC hired security services from a large corporation, a step not in keeping with a lot of radical ideas of community. The actual guards, however, were locals who got on well with both community members and volunteers. The anarchic consensus model of the Rainbow Family didn't last either. As with Common Ground, entrusting major and lasting decisions to transient members was problematic. Weiner thought that efforts like Emergency Communities had an ongoing future anywhere disaster hit. He wasn't so sure its internal organization was such a model. He called it a benign dictatorship and added, "I'm more into democracy than that. I just happen to be the benign dictator." Even so, his goal was to just provide aid and perhaps a catalyst for devastated communities to get back on their feet and take care of themselves—to give power away, not accumulate it. Emergency Communities also ran a community center in Buras, down on the peninsula south of New Orleans that got hammered as hard as any place by Katrina, and by the middle of 2007, the center had been handed back to the community to run, and St. Bernard had its own organizations in place. The Comin' Home Café ran through late 2007.

When I first met Weiner, I thought he represented a move back to the mainstream from what the Rainbow Family had launched—until I found out he was the son of Maoist revolutionaries from the 1960s. He didn't retain all his parents' beliefs, but he did keep a critique of the mainstream and a sense of the malleability of society and its radical possibilities. Emergency Communities went through a remarkable evolution during its more than two years after Katrina, from a Rainbow Family project in a rural area to a new nonprofit in an urban one, from one in which the volunteers shared a background to one marked by diversity. It was an extreme example of the improvisation disaster brings, the ability to respond to changing circumstances in ways the larger nonprofits rarely can. It comes out of both the emergency that generated it and the long legacies of the unrest of the 1960s. That it ceased to exist is also a response to changing circumstances; but the thousands who came through to give or receive support were in many cases changed by the interactions. Dispersed throughout the world, they continue their activist work.

As sociologist Emmanuel David wrote to me, "What seems so beautiful about these groups is that many of them emerged spontaneously out of the specific conditions of the event. Now that the organizational structures are in place, the groups can enter (and some plan to and have entered) into other disasters. But the question is: can these emergent groups turned established groups function with the same level of improvisation/creativity that once characterized their actions? Or will these groups formalize, create policies and procedures, the same kind of mechanisms that bogged down the Red Cross, FEMA, and other organizations?" The answer varies from organization to organization.

Weighing the Balance

The volunteers are evidence that it doesn't take firsthand experience of a disaster to unleash altruism, mutual aid, and the ability to improvise a response. Many of them were part of subcultures, whether conservative churches or counterculture communities, that exist as something of a latent disaster community already present throughout the United States and elsewhere. Such community exists among people who gather as civil society and who believe that we are connected, that change is possible, and who hope for a better earth and act on their beliefs. They remind us that though disasters can be catalysts to bring out such qualities, disasters do not generate them; they are constructed by beliefs, commitments, and communities, not by weather, seismology, or bombs. Some of these groups explicitly advocate for another kind of society; some are happy to repair and augment the existing one.

Years later, it is hard to weigh the balance. The original catastrophe of Katrina—the lack of an evacuation plan for the poor and frail, the ill-maintained levees—was the result of abandonment of social ties and investments. Yet despite the dire consequences of this social withdrawal, the answer to Katrina on the part of New Orleans mayor Ray Nagin and many others has been more abandonment, more privatization. They made of the catastrophe an opportunity to further conservative goals: they fired every public-school teacher in New Orleans and reinvented the school system as, largely, privatized charter schools less accountable to parents and taxpayers; they closed public housing in the city at a time when the need for homes was desperate, rents were escalating, and the huge projects were some of the most intact housing left in many neighborhoods; they let Charity Hospital, for generations the source of most health care for the poorest, stay dead; reduced public transit by 80 percent; and through lousy management increased the burden of return-ees by such acts as demolishing Holy Ground Baptist Church without bothering to contact the pastor or congregation, who were in the process of rebuilding the church. Some of these were fiscal decisions on the part of a hard-hit city, but the desire to privatize the system and shut out the poor was an ideological choice. In countless ways the state and federal government magnified and expanded these losses. In 2008 the billions of dollars of aid supposed to be available to rebuild were just beginning to be released. These were not responses to disaster, but expansions of it.

In the wake of Katrina, New Orleans was full of contrasts. There was a marked one between the volunteers who were free to come and go from the disaster zone and those who were trying to resettle it. But there was a more dramatic conflict between those who believe in civil society and the possibility of a beloved community and those who, along with Hobbes, Le Bon, and a lot of elites who panic, believed that their own selfishness was justified by a selfish world. As the dictionary defines it, a *crisis* is "the point in the progress of a disease when a change takes place which is deci-sive of recovery or death; also, any marked or sudden change of symp-toms, etc." Almost every disaster is a clash between opposing forces and visions of society. Even Mexico City had losses as well as wins; the ruling party proved as resilient as the communities that organized. And even New Orleans has victories. Some of them are as small as a friendship or a rebuilt church, some as large as new awarenesses and preparedness across the continent.

People were caught unprepared by Katrina—both by the material damage and by the enormity of the elite panic—in ways that will not hap-pen again anytime soon. The disaster discredited a regime at the height of its powers. Citizens and outside volunteers together won many vic-tories, though victory sometimes meant nothing more than keeping at bay the more destructive schemes to reinvent the city for the few. Friend-ships and alliances were formed across old divides, of which Brad Pitt's involvement with the Holy Cross Neighborhood Association and the Lower Ninth is only the most extreme example. Much that was tangible and important was achieved, from the clinics in the first days of the disas-ter to the ongoing reconstruction efforts. But the events of Katrina left many scars—Malik Rahim, for example, was so dismayed by the racism he encountered in the first days after the storm that three years later he was planning to leave the country. He feared a pandemic could bring an even worse response. Beyond that, Katrina's effects are still unfolding, in a devastated city and its citizens but also in the hearts of the hundreds of thousands of volunteers and in the new coalitions that arose.

This has been a book about disaster's recent past, but it also has a future, a future where knowledge matters and so do desire and belief.

EPILOGUE:

THE DOORWAY IN THE RUINS

Who are you? Who are we? The history of disaster demonstrates that most of us are social animals, hungry for connection, as well as for purpose and meaning. It also suggests that if this is who we are, then everyday life in most places is a disaster that disruptions sometimes give us a chance to change. They are a crack in the walls that ordinarily hem us in, and what floods in can be enormously destructive—or creative. Hierarchies and institutions are inadequate to these circumstances; they are often what fails in such crises. Civil society is what succeeds, not only in an emotional demonstration of altruism and mutual aid but also in a practical mustering of creativity and resources to meet the challenges. Only this dispersed force of countless people making countless decisions is adequate to a major crisis. One reason that disasters are threatening to elites is that power devolves to the people on the ground in many ways: it is the neighbors who are the first responders and who assemble the impromptu kitchens and networks to rebuild. And it demonstrates the viability of a dispersed, decentralized system of decision making. Citizens themselves in these moments constitute the government—the acting decision-making body—as democracy has always promised and rarely delivered. Thus disasters often unfold as though a revolution has already taken place.

Two things matter most about these ephemeral moments. First, they demonstrate what is possible or, perhaps more accurately, latent: the resilience and generosity of those around us and their ability to improvise another kind of society. Second, they demonstrate how deeply most of us desire connection, participation, altruism, and purposefulness. Thus the startling joy in disasters. After the psychiatrist Viktor Frankl survived Auschwitz, he concluded that retaining a sense of meaning and purpose was in many cases decisive in who survived and who did not. After 9/11, New Yorker Marshall Berman cited Nietzsche: "Man, the bravest animal and the one most inured to trouble, does not deny suffering per se: he wants it, he even seeks it out, provided it can be given a meaning." Frankl quotes another version of Nietzsche's pronouncement: "He who has a *why* to live for can bear almost any *how.*" When Dorothy Day gave up her lover, she gave up an intensely tangible private affection for another, broader love, of God, but also of purposefulness, meaning, involvement, and community, without which she had been miserable even in her ménage. She gave up her *how* for a *why.* The joy in disaster comes, when it comes, from that purposefulness, the immersion in service and survival, and from an affection that is not private and personal but civic: the love of strangers for each other, of a citizen for his or her city, of belonging to a greater whole, of doing the work that matters.

These loves remain largely dormant and unacknowledged in contemporary postindustrial society: this is the way in which everyday life is a disaster. For acted upon, given a role, this is a love that builds society, resilience, community, purpose, and meaning. Private life matters immensely, but the language for prizing eros and domesticity has never been stronger, and the language for public life more atrophied, at least in the mass-media mainstream of the English-speaking world. Around the periphery come crowds of ideas about gift communities, direct and participatory democracy, civil society, urban regeneration, beloved community, joy, and solidarity. People have never reached toward these things in more ways, and the many alternatives being tried out across the country from agriculture to decentralized decision-making systems matter, as do the broader examples around the world from Argentine alternatives and Mexican Zapatismo to greening European cities and solidarity networks stretching from India and South Africa to the West. Beliefs matter nowhere more than in the way citizens in many Latin American nations have been able to seize the moment of disaster and make something of it. It is the ability to describe and cherish the other loves that makes disaster's moments of mutual aid last. You may be able to rejoice in what you cannot name, but you can't cultivate it.

As I write, the election and inauguration of Barack Obama still seem extraordinary events. The great paradox is that the most powerful man in the world rose to that position with a vision of collective strength and grassroots power, forces his new role seemed designed to trump or thwart, though he may yet succeed in encouraging them. Or they may refuse to submit even to him. His "yes we can" language of populism and democracy was unlike anything that had appeared on the national stage in a long time. The forces that elected him and rejoiced in that election likewise represented something that had long seemed dormant in American society, a hopefulness, an idealism, a willingness to risk change, and a desire to participate and take power. Not coincidentally, the enormous disaster of the failure of global capital a month before the election played a signficant role in Obama's triumph, making his pragmatism matter and his promise of change desirable, while the patriotic rhetoric of his Republican rival came to seem increasingly irrelevant.

The election and inauguration of the nation's first African American president were awash in tears of joy and something deeper than joy, a feeling that ancient wrongs could be righted, that we could, in the phrase of Abraham Lincoln that was everywhere that season, live up to "the better angels of our nature," a feeling that seemed itself to belong to those angels. The world rejoiced with Americans; there were tears in Kurdistan, Iceland, and Kenya. Obama represented a meaningful departure from the status quo, and the atmosphere he arrived in felt disastrous in its openness to change and its sense of solidarity and possibility. And it was a time of deep economic disaster that promised to lay waste old possibilities and demand new arrangements. To what extent his electorate will keep pace with his promises and their own dreams or subside into disengagement and private life remains to be seen, though it is hard to imagine the moment could last. Yet, like a moment of revolution, it matters, and the world has changed.

Disaster may offer us a glimpse, but the challenge is to make something of it, before or beyond disaster: to recognize and realize these desires and these possibilities in ordinary times. If there are ordinary times ahead. We are entering an era where sudden and slow disaster will become far more powerful and far more common. When I began writing this book in 2007, floods were washing through central England and central Texas; fires raged in Greece, Utah, and California; heat waves baked

Hungary and parts of the United States while droughts afflicted other regions; and China faced drought, flood, fire, and heat waves all at once. Peru had been hit by a big earthquake, and the devastation of Pakistan's 2005 earthquake, the Gulf Coast's Hurricane Katrina, and the Indian Ocean's 2004 tsunami were far from over. As I rewrote this book a year later, central China was recovering from the huge Sichuan earthquake of May 12 that killed at least seventy thousand and left millions homeless; Burma's coastal regions had been devastated by a typhoon (and its people more so by a dictatorship that thwarted most attempts at aid); England and the upper Mississippi had flooded again; Benin, Togo, Ethiopia, Niger, and many other African countries had also flooded, as had the state of Tabasco in Mexico. Madagascar was hit by three cyclones; California had burned again on an epic scale; New Orleans had been sorely tested by another hurricane that had also destroyed or damaged ninety thousand homes in Cuba; people were stranded on their roofs after a hurricane that brought on floods and hundreds of deaths in Haiti and displaced or stranded millions in Texas; and more hurricanes were brewing in an unprecedentedly volatile year of hot storms in the Gulf of Mexico, including another that reached coastal Canada, where my inquiry had begun five years earlier in the wake of Hurricane Juan.

In late 2007 the humanitarian organization Oxfam reported, "Climatic disasters are increasing as temperatures climb and rainfall intensifies. A rise in small- and medium-scale disasters is a particularly worrying trend. Yet even extreme weather need not bring disasters; it is poverty and powerlessness that make people vulnerable. Though more emergency aid is needed, humanitarian response must do more than save lives: it has to link to climate change adaptation and bolster poor people's livelihoods through social protection and disaster risk reduction approaches." In speaking of poverty, Oxfam calls for material change, but powerlessness implies more subtle social conditions. What we know about the history of disaster and the plethora of disasters coming calls for obvious infrastructure and systemic changes and specific disaster preparedness. But it also calls for more metaphysical changes—first, to acknowledge how people respond in disasters and to reduce the institutional fear and hostility to the public, then to prepare to incorporate what the disaster scholars call "prosocial" behavior into disaster planning.

The current global economic depression is itself a vast disaster.

Grim though it is, it may also be a chance for decentralization, democratization, civic engagement, and emergent organizations and ways of coping—or perhaps it is more accurate to say that it may demand these things as means of survival. The more profound preparation for disaster must make a society more like that of disaster utopias in their brief flowering: more flexible and improvisational, more egalitarian and less hierarchical, with more room for meaningful roles and contributions from all members—and with a sense of membership. Civil society is what saves people and creates the immediate conditions for survival—rescue teams, field kitchens, concerned neighbors—and it is a preventative too, as the Chicago heat wave, Cuban hurricanes, and many other disasters have demonstrated.

Already, climate change is shaping up to be as unfair as disasters have ever been, impacting the vulnerable of the tropics, highlands, far north, and coasts while those most responsible for creating the turbulent anthropocene (or human-made) climate era stall on measures to limit and mitigate its effects. It too is a democracy question, about who benefits, who loses, who should decide, and who does. Surviving and maybe even turning back the tide of this pervasive ongoing disaster will require more ability to improvise together, stronger societies, more confidence in each other. It will require a world in which we are each other's wealth and have each other's trust. This world can be made possible only by the faith in social possibility that understanding ourselves in past disaster can give us and by the embeddedness in place and society that constitutes a sense of belonging.

When I began to discover the remarkable findings and conclusions of the disaster sociologists, particularly the profoundly positive views of Charles Fritz, they seemed to confirm a sunny view of human nature. But not everyone behaves well. Elite panic in disaster, as identified by the contemporary disaster scholars, is shaped by belief, belief that since human beings at large are bestial and dangerous, the believer must himself or herself act with savagery to ensure individual safety or the safety of his or her interests. The elites that panic are, in times of crisis, the minority, and understanding that could marginalize or even disarm them, literally and psychologically, as well as the media that magnify their message. This would help open the way to create a world more like the brief utopias that flash up in disaster.

At the end of 2008, a report by the U.S. Army War College proposed that the economic crisis could lead to civil unrest requiring military intervention. Treasury secretary Henry Paulson had himself suggested martial law might be required, and the Phoenix police were themselves preparing to suppress civil unrest, including that provoked by the economic downturn. Even as the Bush administration was fading from the scene, those in power continued to regard the public as the enemy.

Relieving those in charge of their entrenched beliefs will not be easy. Lee Clarke, the coauthor of the definitive essay on elite panic, told me that after 9/11 he found himself at a lot of conferences sponsored by the Department of Homeland Security and by FEMA. There he tried to tell the bureaucrats what actually works in disasters. "In a chaotic situation command and control is bound to fail," he'd say of the top-down management system many organizations deploy in crisis. He told the disaster administrators who wanted to know what message to give people in disaster that it is the people who might have some messages to give them on what's actually going on and what's actually needed. Clarke concluded, "They don't have a way to fold civil society into their official conceptions."

Federal bureaucrats under Bush weren't doing well with these new ideas, but at more local levels many planners and administrators have changed disaster plans and underlying premises. During the 1989 Loma Prieta earthquake, San Francisco houses built on the unstable landfill of the Marina District collapsed and caught fire, and firefighters were overwhelmed with the task of fighting the flames with broken water mains. Volunteers helped carry heavy hoses from the waterfront, where a fireboat pumped seawater to put out the flames. The San Francisco Fire Department's report on the quake says, "Hundreds of citizen volunteers assisted the Fire Department at the Marina District fire and the collapse of a building at Sixth and Bluxome streets. Some, acting under the direction of Department members, were instrumental in rescue and fire suppression operations. Clearly, the organization and direction of volunteers must be addressed." A more marked difference from the suspicion and divisiveness of such authority in the 1906 earthquake could not be found—though the writers of the report might have noted that the volunteers did well without being organized or more than haphazardly directed.

In the aftermath, the Neighborhood Emergency Response Team (NERT) program was created to train volunteers to take care of their neighborhoods and city in disaster. The fire department runs the program, which has trained more than seventeen thousand citizens. The city used the centennial of the 1906 quake to urge, via bus placards, billboards, and more, disaster preparedness in every home—not only the stockpiling of supplies but also the creation of emergency plans. The NERT program trusts citizens and distributes power to the thousands who have been trained in basic rescue, firefighting, and first-aid techniques and given safety vests, hardhats, and badges. What this city government has learned—or admitted—is that it is inadequate to respond to or control response to a disaster and that the only viable strategy is to invite citizens to take power. Nationwide, particularly since 9/11, citizen emergency response team programs are growing, and the disaster managers who have become part of city and regional government are generally free of the old clichés and fears about ordinary people's behavior in disaster.

The San Francisco Fire Department estimates that an 8.3 earthquake with wind at ten miles an hour could generate 71 large fires, which would require 273 fire engines—though the city has only 41. On the other hand, said firefighter Ed Chu at my NERT training in late 2006, "eighty percent of people saved in a disaster can be saved without specialized skills." He stressed that the timeliness of the rescue mattered most for those who were trapped, which is why neighbors are often more important than experts. At the end of the training, participants were divided into teams and given a list of emergencies to prioritize—nonfatally injured senior citizens, downed overhead electrical lines, and a small fire in a building in this town of densely packed wooden buildings where fire spreads readily. My team decided to put out the fire first, since it seemed like a chance to prevent greater harm, and were roundly scolded. The firefighters amazed me by saying, "In a disaster, property no longer matters. Only people matter." We had come a long way from San Francisco in 1906.

Property matters in another sense: San Francisco's government emphasizes that citizens are likely to be on their own for the first seventy-two hours after an earthquake, but the poor are unlikely to set aside the earthquake emergency kits and supplies, including food and water, the city urged all citizens to keep on hand. As for New Orleans,

Hurricane Gustav threatened the city three years after Katrina, and the event was a measure of what had changed and what was still rotten. Images of water lapping over the levees flanking the Lower Ninth Ward suggested that they were not nearly high enough. The Superdome had a gigantic lock on it, and no one was invited to shelter in place. This time Mayor Nagin ordered a mandatory evacuation in time, but for the estimated thirty thousand without resources to evacuate themselves, this meant lining up for a long wait for buses to unknown destinations. The evacuees were processed, given wrist bracelets, and bused to warehouses, where they were confined. Many were subjected to arrest and imprisonment after background checks—though thanks to New Orleans's shoddy record-keeping, many of them were arrested for charges that had been dismissed but not cleared. Background checks constitute part of the criminalization of disaster victims. An estimated half of all undocumented immigrants in New Orleans were trapped by fear of being denied services or deported and did not evacuate—and this population is deeply imperiled by such criminalization. Many who evacuated by means of the government vowed not to do so again.

It was hard this time around to say whether the problem was the system in that moment or the poverty that consigned so many to such a crude and criminalizing system. Many lessons had still not been learned. As the storm approached, CNN ran a teaser about rape, murder, and looting, and Nagin announced, in a threat played over and over, "Anyone who's caught looting will be sent directly to Angola"—the notorious former slave plantation and current maximum-security prison. "You will go directly to Angola Prison and God bless you when you get there." In the same speech he warned that the thousands of FEMA trailers from which those still displaced after three years had presumably been evacuated "will become projectiles" in the violent winds. New Orleans was vulnerable not only because of its setting—facing the great cauldron of hurricanes that is the Caribbean across an eroded buffer zone of wetlands in an era of climate change—but because of its social divides and injustices.

Fixing those wrongs and wounds in New Orleans and everywhere else is the work that everyday disaster requires of us. Recognizing the wealth of meaning and love such work provides is the reward everyday disaster invites us to claim. Joy matters too, and that it is found in this most unpromising of circumstances demonstrates again the desires that have survived dreariness and division for so long. The existing system is built on fear of each other and of scarcity, and it has created more scarcity and more to be afraid of. It is mitigated every day by altruism, mutual aid, and solidarity, by the acts of individuals and organizations who are motivated by hope and by love rather than fear. They are akin to a shadow government—another system ready to do more were they voted into power. Disaster votes them in, in a sense, because in an emergency these skills and ties work while fear and divisiveness do not. Disaster reveals what else the world could be like—reveals the strength of that hope, that generosity, and that solidarity. It reveals mutual aid as a default operating principle and civil society as something waiting in the wings when it's absent from the stage.

A world could be built on that basis, and to do so would redress the long divides that produce everyday pain, poverty, and loneliness and in times of crisis homicidal fear and opportunism. This is the only paradise that is possible, and it will never exist whole, stable, and complete. It is always coming into being in response to trouble and suffering; making paradise is the work that we are meant to do. All the versions of an achieved paradise sound at best like an eternal vacation, a place where we would have no meaning to make. The paradises built in hell are improvisational; we make them up as we go along, and in so doing they call on all our strength and creativity and leave us free to invent even as we find ourselves enmeshed in community. These paradises built in hell show us both what we want and what we can be.

In the 1906 earthquake, a mansion burned down but its stone portals remained standing. A photograph shows that suddenly, rather than framing the entrance to a private interior, they framed the whole city beyond the hill where the ruins stood. Disaster sometimes knocks down institutions and structures and suspends private life, leaving a broader view of what lies beyond. The task before us is to recognize the possibilities visible through that gateway and endeavor to bring them into the realm of the everyday.

GRATITUDE

Disasters take place on the scale of the personal as well, and for those who are lucky they muster a small version of disaster utopias and societies. I was lucky. Midway through the writing of this book, I underwent a short-lived but serious illness. The medical details don't matter here, but the social ones do. I had lived through the stories of many disasters, spent time with people who evacuated the Twin Towers or found themselves stranded on a roof during Katrina, been much affected by my own city during the Loma Prieta quake of 1989, been around floods and fires, but this was a more intense experience for me and very much one of disaster in miniature. With what I had learned from my researches, I regarded my own mental and emotional states with great interest. At one point I was so exhausted that much of what I ordinarily cared about didn't matter, and I was content to be rather than do. There was a strange serenity to this condition, a suspension of ordinary time and ordinary annoyances and ambitions. As Fritz had noted, "Disasters provide a temporary liberation from the worries, inhibitions, and anxieties associated with the past and future because they force people to concentrate their full attention on immediate moment-to-moment, day-to-day needs within the context of the present realities." So does illness. Going on being—surviving— was the task at hand, and it was entirely absorbing.

As the illness faded, I found that it had made me fiercer—less willing to waste my time and more urgent about what mattered. As Gioconda Belli had said about the Managua earthquake, "You realize that life has to be lived well or is not worth living. It's a very profound transformation that takes place during catastrophes. It's like a near-death experience but lived collectively." After the way the people around me rose to the occasion, I was left with confidence that the love and bonds that mattered had been and would be there. In a weak moment, I wished that life could always be like this and then realized that I didn't need such tender care the rest of the time but that it was always there, latent, implicit, a premise from which I could operate all the time. It made everyday life a little better. And it made me think the same latencies pertain to the society at large, not consistently, but in ways that can matter a lot.

This book is dedicated to the citizens of my own small disaster utopia, with love:

Tom

Tina

Susan

Sam

Rebecca

Pam

Mike

Marina

David

Antonia

Amy

This project began as the Raymond Williams Memorial Lecture at Jesus College of Cambridge University, commissioned by Professor Rod Mengham there, and became a talk at Yale's Agrarian Studies colloquium, where Professor James Scott provided brilliant commentary and encouragement. It then metamorphosed into an essay for *Harper's* magazine that went to press the day Hurricane Katrina hit the Gulf Coast. My splendid editor there, Luke Mitchell, insisted that my optimism about human nature would be proven right even while I quailed at the avalanche of stories claiming sheer savagery had been unloosed. Luke was right. I equivocated for a while, but the sorrows and secrets of Katrina made it seem important to continue a project that had begun almost as a whim, an investigation of the strange joy I'd found in my own 1989 earthquake experiences and elsewhere, and became a long excavation into unacknowledged social desires and possibilities. Thus, this book.

Over and over again, I went looking for the meaning of disaster and found friendship as well. Dan Bollwinkle, who came along early to transcribe dozens of interviews and to talk about his own good work on the tsunami in Thailand, was particularly generous, as was sociologist Michael Schwartz, who appeared via our connection at TomDispatch. com at the perfect moment to read the first draft and provide brilliantly insightful analysis and critique of the social and political ideas here and considerable encouragement. Also providing valuable readings of the first draft were Brad Erickson, Adam Hochschild, and Marina Sitrin.

The great disaster scholars Kathleen Tierney, Lee Clarke, and Enrico Quarantelli were generous with their time and knowledge, and this project owes a huge debt—as does, I think, this society—to their achievements in this field. Two years running I attended the University of Colorado's Natural Hazards Center annual disaster studies conference and benefited greatly from the presentations and conversation. In each of the places I visited and wrote about, I again received generosity and a plethora of ideas. Bob Bean, in Halifax, inspired me to investigate disasters more deeply after my 2003 visit there and let me question him further later on.

In San Francisco, a project on the 1906 earthquake with my friends Mark Klett, Michael Lundgren, and Philip Fradkin got me going, and as usual I relied on the San Francisco Public Library and Bancroft and the other libraries at UC, Berkeley and remain grateful to those institutions and their librarians.

My friend Nate Miller dropped everything to accompany me to Mexico City at the last minute and was a huge help; my dear friend Guillermo Gomez-Peña's ancestral home in the city served as our base, and Laura Carlsen, Marco Ramirez, Gustavo Esteva, John Holloway, Marisol Hernandez, Alejandro Miranda, John Ross, Jose Luis Paredo Pacho, and others were generous with their time, ideas, and memories. Guillermo was the first to tell me how profound a political upheaval the earthquake had been—he himself had participated in the relief activities—and Iain Boal sent along valuable readings on the subject early on.

In New York, the Columbia University Oral History Office's fantastic

9/11 interviews were a major source for the section on 9/11, and Tobin James Mueller and Pat Enkyu O'Hara kindly made time to talk to me, as did, back in California, Jordan Schuster, Michael Noble, and Astra Taylor.

On my first visit to New Orleans after Katrina, Jennifer Whitney and Jordan Flaherty were generous with their time and local knowledge, as was the sociologist Emmanuel David; on my second visit I crossed paths with Christian Roselund, who was also a big help; Rebecca Snedeker became a great friend and good guide who supplied important resources, encouragement, insight, and inspiration. So many people were generous with time and conversation at a difficult time for their city, including Malik Rahim; Linda Jackson, of NENA; Pam Dashiell and Sharon Lambertson, of the Holy Cross Neighborhood Association; Brian Denzer; Darryl Malek-Wiley, of the Sierra Club; Aislyn Colgan, formerly of the Common Ground Clinic; Brian from Habitat for Humanity; Emily Posner from Common Ground; Felipe Chavez; Kate Foyle; Mark Weiner from Emergency Communities; my fellow San Franciscans Larry Bradshaw and Lorrie Beth Slonsky; and Clara Bartholemew, whom I interviewed for Abe Louise Young's Austin-based Alive in Truth oral history project in November 2005, and Abe herself, who also became a friend.

Katrina vanden Heuvel, at *The Nation*, listened to me when no one else did about the unreported murders of the hurricane, and Adam Clay Thompson took up the story of the murders and nailed down all the facts and details with brilliant detective work over the next year. *The Nation* sustained a long lawsuit to access the coroner's records that should've been public but weren't, and the world owes them a debt for doing everything in their power to get the truth out and see justice done. Working with A.C. was a joy.

Donnell Herrington, the young man nearly killed by racist vigilantes in the aftermath of Katrina, spent three days with Adam and me three years later. My gratitude for his trust that we would do his story justice and my admiration for his gifts as a storyteller and his strength as a survivor in the face of horror are boundless. Time spent with him was an honor.

Thi, the monk in charge of the Vietnamese Buddhist temple in Biloxi; Dr. Don LaGrone; the Buddhist community of Biloxi; and Carmen Mauk of Burners Without Borders were likewise generous with their time and stories. So was Gioconda Belli during a wonderful afternoon at her house in Santa Monica.

Some of the second draft of this book was completed while I was a senior Mellon scholar at the Canadian Centre for Architecture in Montreal, and thanks go to them for support to focus on the work—and for giving me the opportunity to travel to New Orleans one more time.

I've now been working with my editor, Paul Slovak, at Viking, for a dozen years and with my agent, Bonnie Nadell, longer—more reasons to be grateful.

Rebecca Solnit
September 2008, San Francisco/New Orleans/Montreal

NOTES

Prelude: Falling Together

4   **The man in charge:** The man who had so much to say about the hurricane was Bob Bean, of Nova Scotia School of Art and Design.

I. A MILLENNIAL GOOD FELLOWSHIP: THE SAN FRANCISCO EARTHQUAKE

The Mizpah Café

13   **Mrs. Anna Amelia Holshouser:** In "The Great Fire of 1906" series on the disaster, *Argonaut*, May 14, 1927.

14   **There they spread an old quilt:** Many of these shacks and camp kitchens can be seen in photographs at the San Francisco Historical Photograph Collection of the San Francisco Public Library and at the Bancroft Library's online site, http://bancroft.berkeley.edu/collections/earthquakeandfire/index2.html/.

15   **"when the tents of the refugees":** Edwin Emerson, in Malcolm E. Barker, ed., *Three Fearful Days: San Francisco Memoirs of the 1906 Earthquake and Fire* (San Francisco: Londonborn Publications, 1998), 301.

16   **"in cordial appreciation of her prompt":** *Argonaut*, May 21, 1927.

18   **"A map of the world":** Oscar Wilde (quoting from Wilde's "The Soul of Man Under Socialism"), in Robert V. Hine, *California's Utopian Colonies* (Berkeley: University of California Press, 1983), 8.

19   **"Stalinists and their ilk":** David Graeber, *Fragments of an Anarchist Anthropology* (Chicago: Prickly Paradigm Press, 2004), 11.

21   **"The number of weather-related disasters has quadrupled over the past":** "Climate Alarm, 2007": *Oxfam Briefing Paper 108.*

Pauline Jacobson's Joy

24   **Mary Austen:** "The Temblor," in David Starr Jordan, ed., *The California Earthquake of 1906* (San Francisco: A. M. Robertson, 1907), 355.

24   **H. C. Schmitt:** *Argonaut,* May 8, 1926.

25   **Thomas A. Burns:** *Argonaut,* May 29, 1926.

26   **Maurice Behan:** *Argonaut,* June 19 and 26, 1926.

26   **A man from the business department:** *Bulletin,* May 25, 1906.

27   **The plumbers union:** Information at http://www.sfmuseum.org/1906.2/plumbers.html/.

27   **Charles Reddy:** *Argonaut,* July 31, 1926.

28   **William G. Harvey:** *Argonaut,* March 5, 1927.

29   **"The best thing about the earthquake":** Eric Temple Bell, in Barker, *Three Fearful Days,* 143.

30   **"Remarkable as it may seem,"** Jack London, in ibid., 134–35.

30   **Charles B. Sedgewick:** In ibid., 209.

30   **"Owing to the fact that every bank":** *Argonaut,* April 21, 1906.

31   **"a stock of face creams and soap and dresses":** Pauline Jacobson, "How It Feels to Be a Refugee and Have Nothing, By Someone Who Is One of Them," *Bulletin,* April 29, 1906.

33   **"Modish young women":** *Bulletin,* April 30, 1906.

General Funston's Fear

34   **"Without warrant of law and without being requested":** Frederick Funston, letter to the editor, *Argonaut,* July 7, 1906.

34   **General Sheridan:** In Dennis Smith, *San Francisco Is Burning: The Untold Story of the 1906 Earthquake and Fires* (New York: Viking, 2005), 90.

35   **as many as five hundred citizens were killed by the occupying forces:** Ibid., 157: "A miner, Oliver Posey, testified in a deposition that 'instant death to scores was the fate for vandalism; the soldiers executed summary justice.' Like all statistical evidence for the four days of fire, the number of civilians executed by soldiers varies widely from account to account. Funston himself admits in his narrative to three, and there are accounts that claim as many as five hundred were killed. Based on eyewitness testimonies collected with extraordinary care by the director of the San Francisco virtual museum, Gladys Hansen, the total number of people shot down by the military is estimated to be at least five hundred—one-sixth of the three thousand victims the virtual museum cites as having perished in the earthquake and fire. Any educated analysis of the period would suggest that the actual tally is much closer to Ms. Hansen's figure than to General Funston's." But he cautions, "If as many as five hundred people were shot by soldiers, it can be assumed that there would be many more firsthand accounts of these shootings than actually exist." The lower estimate is from Philip Fradkin, *The Great Earthquake and Firestorms of 1906: How San Francisco Nearly Destroyed Itself* (Berkeley and Los

Angeles: University of California Press, 2005), 140: "One researcher placed the number at 490. I doubt if the number exceeded 50 or 75 such murders, which was no small amount."

35   **"unlicked mob":** *Argonaut,* March 19, 1927.

36   **"The Federal Troops . . . have been authorized by me to KILL":** Widely cited and reproduced; a copy of the broadside may be seen at http://www .sfmuseum.org/1906.2/killproc.html/.

37   **"What Funston unwittingly set into motion":** Fradkin, *The Great Earthquake,* 63.

37   **"About noon the university announced":** Quoted in Stuart H. Ingram, "Impressions from Berkeley," *California Geology,* April 2006.

37   **"I have no doubt, and have heard the same opinion expressed":** Funston, quoted in Gladys Hansen and Emmet Condon, *Denial of Disaster* (San Francisco: Cameron and Co., 1989), 47.

38   **"The prompt appearance of our troops was all that saved the city":** William Stephenson, letter to the Bowdoin College class of 1877, in Bancroft online earthquake archive, http://content.cdlib.org/xtf/view?docId=hb6z09p1nj&br and=eqf&doc.view=entire_text/.

38   **"I was waited upon at my headquarters":** Charles Morris, in Hansen and Condon, *Denial of Disaster,* 76.

39   **A banker . . . witnessed soldiers:** In Hansen and Condon, *Denial of Disaster,* 71.

39   **Volunteers . . . broke the windows of drugstores:** Ibid., 57.

39   **James B. Stetson and his son:** "We took with us Miss Sarah Fry, a Salvation Army woman, who was energetic and enthusiastic. When we arrived at a drugstore under the St. Nicholas she jumped out, and, finding the door locked, seized a chair and raising it above her head smashed the glass doors in and helped herself to hot-water bags, bandages, and everything which would be useful in an emergency hospital." In "San Francisco During the Eventful Days of April, 1906," James B. Stetson, at http://content.cdlib.org/xtf/view? docId=hb4p3007dw&brand=eqf&doc.view=entire_text/.

39   **Another man was seen picking over the rubble of a ruin:** Hansen and Condon, *Denial of Disaster,* 162.

39   **The police invited Mormon elders to take supplies:** Fradkin, *The Great Earthquake,* 141.

39   **A grocer who charged extortionate prices had his goods expropriated:** *Bulletin,* April 21, 1906.

39   **A National Guardsman yelled at an African American man:** Fradkin, *The Great Earthquake,* 142.

40   **The cashier of a bank was shot as a looter:** Hansen and Condon, *Denial of Disaster,* 161.

40   **General Funston later wrote, "Market Street was full of excited, anxious people":** In Frederick Funston, "How the Army Worked to Save San Francisco:

Personal Narrative of the Acute and Active Commanding Officer of the Troops at the Presidio," *Cosmopolitan*, July 1906, http://www.sfmuseum.org/1906/cosmo .html/.

40　　**A drunken soldier had pushed his way into a tent:** Letter in "Selection from the Hooker Family Papers," Bancroft Library Presents the 1906 San Francisco Earthquake and Fire, http://content.cdlib.org/xtf/view?docId=hb7m3nb5f1& brand=eqf&doc.view=entire_text/.

40　　**Mary Doyle wrote a cousin on a scrap of brown-paper bag, "A large number of men and even women":** Smith, *San Francisco Is Burning*, 160.

40　　**An officer's daughter wrote a friend, "A good many awful men are loose":** Hansen and Condon, *Denial of Disaster*, 160.

40　　**"I saw one soldier":** Henry Fitchner, *Argonaut*, March 26, 1927.

40　　**"The terrible days of the earthquake and fire," General Greeley reported on May 17:** In Hansen and Condon, *Denial of Disaster*, 98.

42　　**Frank Hittell:** In Barker, *Three Fearful Days*, 247.

42　　**Jerome Barker Landfield lived at the north end of the city, and he wrote afterward, "Water was lacking, but the proprietress":** in "Operation Kaleidescope: A Melange of Personal Recollections," http://content.cdlib.org/xtf/ view?docId=hb2c6004p0&brand=eqf&doc.view=entire_text/. He also writes, "Not far away I saw Mayor Schmitz, surrounded by a group of prominent citizens and officials. The greatness of the disaster seemed to have unnerved them. I went up to Schmitz and begged him to stop the dynamiting. I told him that we had the fire under control and stopped at Greenwich Street, and that further dynamiting would imperil the rest of Russian Hill, which was now safe. But he would not listen."

42　　**A miller reported that ten of the Globe Grain and Milling Company's:** *Argonaut*, March 26, 1927.

43　　**A volunteer named Edwards worked for twenty-four hours without stopping:** *Argonaut*, October 30, 1926.

43　　**A mail carrier named Roland M. Roche . . . "This improvised bucket brigade":** *Argonaut*, January 8, 1927.

43　　**"The stories have but one beginning and one end":** In Henry Anderson Lafler, "How the Army Worked to Save San Francisco" (a riposte to General Funston's essay of the same title, unpublished manuscript, July 1906, Museum of San Francisco Online), http://www.sfmuseum.org/1906.2/lafler.html/.

44　　**the subcommittee on the permanent relocation of Chinatown:** See Fradkin, *The Great Earthquake*, 35–36.

44　　**Hugh Kwong Liang:** In Barker, *Three Fearful Days*, 119–23.

45　　**indignant citizens broke the Chinese porcelain:** Fradkin, *The Great Earthquake*, 293.

45　　**"The Japanese asked for very little relief":** San Francisco Relief Survey: The Organization and Methods of Relief Used After the Earthquake and Fire of April 18, 1906. (The Russell Sage Foundation, 1913), http://www.sfmuseum .org/conflag/relief1.html/.

45 **Phelan and Adolph Spreckels were competing:** See *Argonaut,* September 11, 1926.

46 **"Prior to the earthquake, Mr. Spreckels was directing a fight":** *Argonaut,* August 28, 1926.

46 **a waterfront man pressured by his banker:** Hansen and Condon, *Denial of Disaster,* 74.

46 **"there is pressing need for mutual concession":** Ruef, quoted in *Bulletin,* May 9, 1906.

46 **"the extreme scarcity of house servants":** *Argonaut,* July 21, 1906.

46 **"drones":** *Argonaut,* July 28, 1906.

46 **The *Bulletin* had run a more sympathetic piece:** Jane Carr, "The Dignity of Labor," *Bulletin,* May 25, 1906.

47 **"The great majority of refugees":** *Argonaut,* June 9, 1927.

47 **The *Argonaut* reports:** "The system, despite forceful and ubiquitous protests, was quickly extended throughout the entire city except the Mission, where the resistance was so vehement, and where any attempts to force the regime was so likely to produce disorder, that its adoption was not forced by the relief authorities" and goes on to quote "Colonel Fegiber," saying, "The influence of this contract method of supply . . . was almost immediately perceptible by the reduction of the number of persons applying for relief—an average of 80 percent, it was estimated, many declining with indignation to accept assistance in the form offered, and by outcries, more or less pronounced, demonstrating beyond the possiblity of a doubt, the intense unpopularity of this scheme. . . . In the meanwhile the number of indigents supplied daily had dropped from 313,145 (as on the 1st of May) to 15,353 on June 30." A decline clearly not due to people's acquiring housing and incomes so quickly.

47 **I heard . . . Michael Brown of FEMA** make this statement at the University of Colorado Natural Hazards Center annual conference, Boulder, CO, July 2006.

William James's Moral Equivalents

49 **"What difference would it practically make to anyone if this notion rather than that notion were true?"** William James, "What Pragmatism Means," Lecture II, in *Pragmatism and Other Writings* (Harmondsworth, England: Penguin Books, 2000), 25.

51 **"the University is absolutely Utopian":** William James to Ferdinand Canning Scott Schiller, letter of January 16, 1906, in *The Letters of William James,* Vol. 11, ed. Henry James [son of the philosopher, not brother] (Boston: Atlantic Monthly Press, 1920), 148.

51 **"It is verily the simple life":** Ibid., in a letter of January 28, 1906, to Harald Hoffding, 15.

52 **"The Utopian dreams of social justice":** William James, *The Varieties of Religious Experience* (New York: Penguin Books, 2008), 360.

52 **"The war against war is going to be no":** William James, "The Moral Equivalent of War" (see http://www.constitution.org/wj/meow.htm/).

52   "all the qualities of a man acquire dignity": Ibid.

53   "there were, instead of military conscription": Ibid.

53   "man's relations to the globe": Ibid.

53   "The martial type of character": Ibid.

53   "consisted wholly of glee": William James, "Some Mental Effects of the Earthquake," in *Memories and Studies* (New York: Longmans, Green, 1911), 211.

54   "Everybody was excited": Ibid., 216.

54   "My business is with 'subjective' phenomena": Ibid., 217.

54   "The crop of nervous wrecks may yet have to be reaped": *William and Henry James: Selected Letters*, ed. Elizabeth M. Berkeley and Ignas K. Skrypskelsis (Charlottesville: University of Virginia, 1997), 473.

54   "simply could not bring himself to empathise": Linda Simon, *Genuine Reality: A Biography of William James* (Chicago: University of Chicago Press, 1999), 342.

55   "Two things in retrospect strike me especially": In James, "Some Mental Effects," 221.

55   "like soldiering . . . always lies latent": Ibid., 223.

55   "the universal equanimity": Ibid., 223–24.

55   "I feel that I have collapsed, simply": Henry James, in Berkeley and Skrypskelsis, eds., *William and Henry James: Selected Letters*, 472.

55   "We never reckoned on this extremity of anxiety": William James to Henry James, ibid., 473.

55   "Surely the cutting edge of all our usual misfortunes": In James, "Some Mental Effects," 224–25.

56   "Never again": Pauline Jacobson, "How It Feels to Be a Refugee and Have Nothing in the World, by Pauline Jacobson, Who Is One of Them," *Bulletin*, April 26, 1906.

56   "The cheerfulness or, at any rate, the steadfastness": In James, "Some Mental Effects," 225.

56   "breaking through the barriers": William James, "The Energies of Men" (originally published in *Science* magazine and found at http://psychclassics .yorku.ca/James/energies.htm/).

Dorothy Day's Other Loves

58   "formation of a political machine": In Fradkin, *The Great Earthquake*, 328.

58   "The California Progressives": Ibid., 306.

59   God as "a great noise that became louder": Dorothy Day, *The Long Loneliness: The Autobiography of Dorothy Day* (San Francisco: HarperSanFrancisco, 1997), 20.

59   "a deep rumbling and the convulsions": Ibid., 21.

59   "What I remember most plainly about the earthquake": Dorothy Day, *From Union Square to Rome* (Maryknoll, NY: Orbis Books, 2006), 24.

60   "I did not want just the few": Day, *The Long Loneliness*, 39.

60   "One afternoon as I sat on the beach, I read": Ibid., 118.

61   "made me feel that from then on my life": Ibid., 38.

61   "There was a new baby that year, born in May": Ibid., 30.

61   "The love for my baby brother": Ibid., 31.

61   "I was in love now with the masses": Ibid., 46.

61–62 "I have always felt that it was life with him": Ibid., 134.

63   "They felt exhilaration in the constant light": Barry Lopez, *Arctic Dreams* (New York: Charles Scribner's Sons, 1986), 3.

64   Paine writes that nature "has not only forced man into society": In Thomas Paine, *The Rights of Man*, http://www.ushistory.org/paine/rights/c2-01.htm/.

65   "The enduring attraction of war": Chris Hedges, *War Is a Force That Gives Us Meaning* (New York: Anchor Books, 2003), 5.

66   "Although all disasters have their unique": Stephen Doheny-Farina, in "The Grid and the Village," *Orion*, Autumn 2001, online at http://www.orionmagazine .org/index.php/articles/article/90/.

66   "people have so great a need to reverence" and "How little, how puny": In Day, *The Long Loneliness*, 165.

67   "genius, a saint, an agitator": Dorothy Day, in William D. Miller, *Dorothy Day: A Biography* (San Francisco: Harper and Row, 1982), 228.

67   "the works of mercy": Day, *The Long Loneliness*, 185.

68   "sense of solidarity which made me": Ibid., 147.

II. HALIFAX TO HOLLYWOOD: THE GREAT DEBATE

A Tale of Two Princes: The Halifax Explosion and After

73   Gertrude Pettipas . . . "A great black ball of smoke": In Joseph Scanlon, "The Man Who Helped Sammy Prince Write: Dwight Johnstone and the Halifax Explosion," *International Journal of Mass Emergencies and Disasters* (March 1992): 189–90.

73   The description of the explosion comes from Laura MacDonald, *Curse of the Narrows: The Halifax Explosion of 1917* (Scarborough, ON: HarperCollins Canada, 2005), and the statistics from Janet Kitz, *Shattered City: The Halifax Explosion and the Road to Recovery* (Halifax, NS: Nimbus Publishing, 1989), 25; http:// www.cbc.ca/halifaxexplosion/he3_shock/he3_shock_destruction.html/.

74   The ship's anchor shank, weighing half a ton, was thrown two miles, and the barrel of a large ship-mounted gun nearly three and a half: Kitz, *Shattered City*, 25.

75   A native woman, Aggie March, stood . . . watching: MacDonald, *Curse of the Narrows*, 43.

75   "Go back! Go back!" and "Dolly, look at the stovepipes": In Megan Tench, "One Minute You're Leading a Very Normal Life. The Next Minute It's Chaos" (profile of Dolly Lloyd), *Boston Globe*, November 24, 2001.

76   Billy Wells: In MacDonald, *Curse of the Narrows*, 71.

76   **Twelve-year-old Duggan:** Ibid., 79–80, 121.

76   **A soldier . . . said the event "affected me far worse than anything":** Ibid., 63.

76   **Dorothy Lloyd's:** Tench, "One Minute You're Leading a Very Normal Life."

76   **"Hold up the train":** Vincent Coleman, as quoted by the Maritime Museum of the Atlantic. See http://www.museums.gov.ns.ca/mma/AtoZ/coleman .html/.

77   **Jean Groves, the telephone operator at the exchange building near the dock, stayed behind:** In Scanlon, "The Man Who Helped," 198–99.

77   **Joe Glube:** In Kitz, *Shattered City*, 62–63.

77   **the supervisor of the Children's Hospital:** Ibid., 54.

78   **the chief of police reported . . . one case of attempted burglary:** Ibid., 79.

78   **Halifax native Laura MacDonald writes in her history of the explosion, "Halifax, with its rigid class structure":** In MacDonald, *Curse of the Narrows*, 89–90.

79   **his church became a refuge for 350 homeless citizens:** In Scanlon, "The Man Who Helped," 192.

79   **"The word 'crisis' is of Greek origin":** Samuel Henry Prince, *Catastrophe and Social Change: Based upon a Sociological Study of the Halifax Disaster* (New York: Columbia University Press, 1920), 16.

79   **"Life becomes like molten metal":** Ibid., 19.

79   **"The disaster simply had the effect":** Ibid., 130.

79–80 **"catastrophe always means social change":** Ibid., 21.

80   **"The underlying basis for his thesis is actually theological":** Joseph Scanlon, "Disaster's Little-Known Pioneer: Canada's Samuel Prince," *International Journal of Mass Emergencies and Disasters* (November 1988): 225.

80   **"A world without suffering would be a world without nobility":** Ibid., 231.

80   **"sad as was the day, it may be the greatest day in the city's history":** Ibid., 122.

80   **"At first it was a very general consciousness which seemed to draw all together":** Prince, *Catastrophe and Social Change*, 63.

81   **"friction and crises":** Ibid., 98.

81   **"volunteers . . . who could not be expected":** Ibid., 84.

81   **But he also used the manuscript of a Dartmouth journalist, Dwight Johnstone:** See Scanlon, "The Man Who Helped." *International Journal of Mass Emergencies and Disasters* (March 1982): 189–206.

81   **"the nightly prowlers among the ruins":** Prince, *Catastrophe and Social Change*, 25.

81   **Scanlon comments on Prince's use of Johnstone:** In Scanlon, "The Man Who Helped."

81   **"the abnormal action of the glands" and frees up "the primitive instincts of man," including "fear, fighting, and anger" and "food-getting":** Prince, *Catastrophe and Social Change*, 36, 39.

82   **"because these populations have no national soul and therefore no stability"**: Gustave Le Bon, cited in Robert A. Nye, *The Origins of Crowd Psychology: Gustave Le Bon and the Crisis of Mass Democracy in the Third Republic* (London, Beverly Hills: Sage Publications, 1975), 43, and Gustave Le Bon, *The Psychology of Revolution* (New York: Putnam, 1913), 45.

82   **"is no longer himself, but has become an automaton who has ceased to be guided by his will"**: Gustave Le Bon, *The Crowd: A Study of the Popular Mind* (Kitchener, ON: Batoche Books, 2001), 19.

83   **"the effort of the instinctive to overpower the rational"**: Le Bon, *Psychology of Revolution*, 37.

84   **Kropotkin's father had bought two fine first violinists "with their large families"**: Peter Kropotkin, *Memoirs of a Revolutionist* (New York and Boston: Houghton Mifflin, 1930); previously serialized in *Atlantic Monthly,* 1898–99), 30.

85   **"Personally Kropotkin was amiable to the point of saintliness"**: In George Woodcock, *Anarchism: A History of Libertarian Ideas and Movements* (Cleveland: World Publishing Co., 1962), 185.

85   **"The five years that I spent in Siberia"**: Kropotkin, *Memoirs*, 168.

85   **"Siberia is not the frozen land"**: Ibid., 168.

86   **"Catastrophe and the sudden termination of the normal"**: Prince, *Catastrophe and Social Change*, 55.

86   **"Communication has transformed mutual aid"**: Ibid., 57.

87   **"the preference upon the part of the refugee"**: Ibid., 49.

88   **EMAC . . . is "an interstate mutual aid agreement"**: In http://www.fema .gov/government/grant/pa/9523_6.shtm/, VII, 4, and elsewhere with the same wording.

88   **"Two aspects of animal life impressed me most during the journeys"**: Peter Kropotkin, *Mutual Aid: A Factor of Evolution* (London: W. Heinemann, 1902; published in facsimile by Dover Books, 2006), vii.

89   **"strove with their enemies and their competitors"**: Thomas Henry Huxley, reprinted in ibid., 272–73.

89   **"the elements of civilized society were broken down"**: Michael J. Bird, *The Town That Died: A Chronicle of the Halifax Disaster* (London: Souvenir Press, 1962), 88.

89   **"The very persistence of the clan organization"**: Kropotkin, *Mutual Aid*, 71.

90   **"For thousands and thousands of years, this organization"**: Ibid., 153.

91   **"And the life of man"**: Thomas Hobbes, *Leviathan* (New York: Penguin Books, 1982), 196.

92   **Shelley E. Taylor and Laura Cousino Klein:** In "You May Always Have Suspected It, but a Study Suggests That Women *Do* Cope with Stress Differently Than Men," http://www.psu.edu/ur/2000/womenstress.html/.

92   **The Diggers [advocated] "working together, and feeding together"**: Gerrard Winstanley, et al. *True Leveller's Standard Advanced: or, The State of Com-*

munity Opened, and Presented to the Sons of Men (London: 1649; http://www
.bilderberg.org/land/diggers.htm#True, and many other sites).

94   **"and for a longer period in several of the American States":** Thomas Paine,
Rights of Man, in Virginia Hodgkinson and Michael W. Foley eds., *The Civil Society Reader* (Medford, MA: Tufts University Press, 2003), 64.

96   **"a will to meaning in contrast to the pleasure principle":** Viktor E. Frankl,
Man's Search for Meaning (1959; repr., Boston: Beacon Press, 2006), 99.

96   **"a dangerous misconception":** Ibid., 105.

From the Blitz and the Bomb to Vietnam

98   **Over the course of the war about sixty thousand British civilians:** Richard
M. Titmuss, *Problems of Social Policy* (London: Longmans, Green, 1950), 224.

99   **"The experts foretold a mass outbreak":** Ibid., 338.

99   **Eighteen "eminent psychiatrists . . . privately warned":** In Ben Shephard, *A War of Nerves* (Cambridge, MA: Harvard University Press, 2001), 175.

99   **"Once a raid has been experienced":** In Tom Harrisson, *Living Through the Blitz* (New York: Schocken Books, 1989), 21.

99   **"The British working class was thought to be particularly susceptible":** In
Mark Connelly, *We Can Take It!: Britain and the Memory of the Second World War* (Harlow, England: Pearson, Longman, 2004), 138.

100   **"The people's role in their own defense":** Ibid., 140.

100   **"On the first night of the Blitz I put out an incendiary bomb":** In Olivia Cockett, *Love and War in London: A Woman's Diary 1939–1942*, ed. Robert W. Malcolmson (Waterloo, ON: Wilfrid Laurier University Press, 2005), 150.

101   **"I feel much more certainty":** Ibid., 151.

101   **"from the time when she literally:"** Quentin Bell, *Virginia Woolf* (Fort Washington, PA: Harvest Books, 1974), 217.

101   **"in particular, been a massive, largely unconscious cover-up":** In Harrisson,
Living Through the Blitz, 13.

101   **"blitz was a terrible experience for millions":** Ibid., 280.

101   **"The courage, humor, and kindliness of ordinary people":** Molly
Panter-Downes, *London War Notes 1939–1945*, ed. William Shawn (New York: Farrar, Straus and Giroux, 1971), 105.

101   **"Once you've been through three nights":** Shephard, *War of Nerves*, 176.

102   **"The tune for today is *Serenade in the Night,* please":** Cockett, *Love and War*, 133.

102   **"the English were discovering each other":** Ibid., 133.

102   **"New tolerances are born between people":** Titmuss, *Problems of Social Policy*, 350.

102   **"just for something to do":** In Harrison, *Living Through the Blitz*, 78–81.

104   **"As a captain in the U.S. Army Air Corps during World War II":** Charles
Fritz, "Disasters and Mental Health: Therapeutic Principles Drawn from Disaster Studies," University of Delaware Disaster Research Center, 1996, 2. This

report is available online at http://www.udel.edu/DRC/preliminary/handel0
.pdf.

104   **"Under those conditions, one might expect to find"**: Ibid., 3–4.

104   **"my access to British family life was greatly enhanced"**: Ibid., 2.

105   **"Under ruthless Nazi control they showed surprising resistance"**: "United
States Strategic Bombing Survey: Summary Report (European War), September 30, 1945" (available at http://www.anesi.com/ussbs02.htm/), 16.

105   **"people living in heavily bombed cities had significantly higher morale
than people in the lightly bombed cities"**: Fritz, "Disasters and Mental
Health," 6.

105   **"neither organic neurologic disease nor psychiatric disorders"**: Ibid., 7.

106   **"Herd Reaction, Panic, Emergence of Leaders, and Recommendations for
Guidance and Control of Masses"**: in E. L. Quarantelli, "The Earliest Interest
in Disasters and the Earliest Social Science of Disasters: A Sociology of Knowledge Approach," (University of Delaware Disaster Research Center, 2005), 24.
This report is unpublished, but is available from the research center.

106   **"From oral histories obtained later from key officials involved"**: Ibid., 30.

106   **"there are mass panics and wild stampedes. People trample one another"**:
Charles Fritz, "Disaster," in *Contemporary Social Problems: An Introduction to the
Sociology of Deviant Behavior and Social Disorganization*, ed. Robert K. Merton
and Robert A. Nisbet (New York: Harcourt, 1961), 672.

107   **"these malleable moments, when we are psychologically unmoored and
physically uprooted"**: Naomi Klein, *The Shock Doctrine: The Rise of Disaster
Capitalism* (New York: Metropolitan Books, 2007), 21.

107   **"profound disorientation, extreme fear and anxiety, and collective regression"**: Ibid., 42. Klein is talking about the effects of the September 11, 2001,
disaster on New Yorkers.

107   **In a public talk:** Sponsored by City Lights Books and held at the First Unitar-
ian Church, San Francisco, September 26, 2007. She can also be seen on *The
Colbert Report,* October 2, 2008, where she opened with a comparison of societies in crisis to a tortured prisoner who will "do whatever you want." "Whole
societies go into shock, they don't know what's going on and they'll do whatever people in authority want them to do. What happens to you when you're
in a state of shock is you regress, you become childlike and you start thinking
Rudy Giuliani is your daddy and Dick Cheney will take care of you," http://
www.colbertnation.com/the-colbert-report-videos/186550/october-02-2008/
naomi-klein/.

107   **"The traditional contrast between 'normal' and 'disaster' almost always
ignores"**: Fritz, "Disasters and Mental Health," 25.

108   **"Thus while the natural or human forces that created or precipitated"**: Ibid.,
68.

108   **"Disasters provide a temporary liberation"**: Ibid., 63.

108   **"An essential feature of disaster is that the threats and dangers"**: Ibid., 55.

109   **"Disaster provides a form of societal shock which disrupts habitual, institutionalized patterns"**: Ibid., 57.

109   **"The prevention and control of panics in time of attack are important tasks of civil defense"**: In Andrew D. Grossman, *Neither Dead nor Red: Civilian Defense and American Political Development During the Early Cold War* (New York: Routledge, 2001), 59.

110   **"the thin veneer"**: Kenneth D. Rose, *One Nation Underground: The Fallout Shelter in American Culture* (New York: New York University Press, 2001), 111.

110   **"Gun Thy Neighbor"**: *Time*, August 18, 1961.

110   **"slowly but surely millions of Americans were coming to the conclusion"**: Walter Karp, "When Bunkers Last in the Doorway Bloomed: The Fallout-Shelter Craze of 1961," *American Heritage*, February–March 1980. Accessible at http://www.americanheritage.com/articles/magazine/ah/1980/2/1980_2_84.shtml/.

111   **"The indirect effects [of] the bombing on the will of the North Vietnamese"**: In a document whose front page reads "TOP SECRET—NOFORN U.S. BOMBING IN VIETNAM" and stamped "DECLASSIFIED 8/26/96." Supplied by the brilliant Vietnam War historian Nick Turse to the author. The second-page title is "The Effects of U.S. Bombing on North Vietnam's Ability to Support Military Operations in South Vietnam and Laos: Retrospect and Prospect," with more assertions about its top-secret status. The passage appears on p. vi11. Fritz is credited as one of four researchers who prepared the report.

Hobbes in Hollywood, or the Few Versus the Many

123   **"I wrote a master's thesis"**: Enrico Quarantelli, in interview with the author, June 2007.

123   **"In fact, most of the disaster funding"**: Ibid.

123   **"If by panic"**: Ibid.

124   **"instead of ruthless competition"**: E. L. Quarantelli, "The Sociology of Panic," 8. Available online from the University of Delaware Disaster Research Center, labeled "to be published in Smelser and Baites, eds., International Encyclopedia of the Social and Behavioral Sciences in 2001."

124   **more than seven hundred studies:** Quarantelli, cited in Lee Clarke, "Panic: Myth or Reality?" in *Contexts* (Fall 2002): 24.

124   **two thousand people in more than nine hundred fires:** Erik Auf der Heide, "Common Misconceptions About Disasters: Panic, the 'Disaster Syndrome,' and Looting," in *The First 72 Hours: A Community Approach to Disaster Preparedness*, ed. Margaret O'Leary (Lincoln, NE: iUniverse Publishing, 2004), 343.

125   **"Bureaucracy depends on routine and schedules and paperwork and etc.":** Quarantelli, in interview with the author, June 2007.

125   **"reinforce our cultural belief in individualism"**: E. L. Quarantelli, "The Study of Disaster Movies: Research Problems, Findings, and Implications" (Newark: University of Delaware Disaster Research Center, 1980), 11.

125   "Disaster movies . . . usually portray the problem": Ibid., 12.

127   "Elites fear disruption": Kathleen Tierney, notes by the author from talk at University of California, Berkeley, 2006.

127   "fear of social disorder": Ibid.

127   "The media emphasis on lawlessness": Kathleen Tierney et al., "Metaphors Matter: Disaster Myths, Media Frames, and Their Consequences in Hurricane Katrina," *Annals of the American Academy of Political and Social Science* (2006). Available at http://ann.sagepub.com/cgi/framedreprint/604/1/57/.

128   "whereas, in the poor immigrant sections": Judith W. Leavitt, "Public Resistance or Cooperation? Historical Experiences with Smallpox," transcript of talk from the conference "The Public as an Asset, Not a Problem: A Summit on Leadership During Bioterrism," Center for Biosecurity, published online at http://www.upmc-biosecurity.org/website/events/2003_public-as-asset/leavitt/leavitt_trans.html/.

128   "There were signs and buttons": Ibid.

128   "The drug companies": Ibid.

128   in 2005, federal officials speculated that a militarily enforced quarantine would be required. See Jennifer Loven, "Military Might Enforce Quarantines in a Flu Epidemic," Associated Press, October 4, 2005, opening, "President Bush, increasingly concerned about a possible avian flu pandemic, revealed today that any part of the country where the virus breaks out could likely be quarantined and that he is considering using the military to enforce it." Also see Jeanne Guillemin, "Terrorism and Dispelling the Myth of a Panic Prone Public," *Journal of Public Health Policy* (2006). "In 1999, the new Johns Hopkins Center for Civilian Biodefense (reinvented later as the Center for Biosecurity at the University of Pittsburgh) took the lead in defining the bioterrorism threat as distinct from either chemical or radiological attacks. In the Center's published scenarios, the unwitting public succumbs to panic when the necessary vaccines or antibiotics prove insufficient; invariably the military is called in to restore order."

128   Indiana National Guard, 2007: The article is no longer on the Web site.

129   "Caron said: to heck with this idea": Lee Clarke, in interview with the author, July 2007.

130   "Disaster myths are not politically neutral": Lee Clarke, introduction to *Terrorism and Disaster, Vol. 11: New Threats, New Ideas* (Stamford, CT: JAI Press, 2003), 5.

131   "It has made me far more interested": Kathleen Tierney, in interview with the author, 2007.

III. CARNIVAL AND REVOLUTION: MEXICO CITY'S EARTHQUAKE

Power from Below

135   Marisol Hernandez: In interview with the author, April 2007.

137   **A maternity ward collapsed. . . . Eight infants:** In Julia Preston, *Opening Mexico: The Making of a Democracy* (New York: Farrar, Straus and Giroux, 2004), 107.

137   **"I want to state that":** Judith Garcia, quoted in Elena Poniatowska, *Nothing, Nobody: The Voices of the Mexico City Earthquake*, trans. Aurora Camacho de Schmidt and Arthur Schmidt (Philadelphia: Temple University Press, 1988), 83.

137   **"ran on the stairway":** Margarita Aguilar, quoted in Poniatowska, *Nothing, Nobody*, 146.

138   **"Looking back, the seamstresses pinpoint":** Phoebe McKinney, "Fighting to Survive: Mexico's 19th of September Union," *Women and Labor* 10, no. 9 (September 1989), and http://multinationalmonitor.org/hyper/issues/1989/09/mckinney.html/.

139   **"It's absurd to suggest":** Victoria Adato, quoted in Preston, *Opening Mexico*, 113.

140   **"The streets were cordoned off":** Alessandro Miranda, in interview with the author, Mexico City, April 2007.

141   **"From many sectors":** Hernandez, in interview with the author, April 2007.

141   **"They began to have sit-ins":** Laura Carlsen, in interview with the author, Mexico City, April 2007.

141   **"When the stories started coming out":** Ibid.

142   **"In many cases":** Ibid.

142   **They were for a time "the moral center":** Carlos Monsiváis, *"No Sin Nosotros": Los Días del Terremoto 1985–2005*, trans. Brian Whitener, for the author (Mexico City: Ediciones Era, 2005), 136.

142   **"At the beginning before we organized":** Hernandez, in interview with the author, April 2007.

142   **"One of the seamstresses told me":** Carlsen, quoted in "Mexico City Seamstresses Remember: Two Decades of Aftershocks from Mexico's 1985 Earthquake," IRC Americas, www.americaspolicy.org, 1985.

142   **"The word 'crisis' is of Greek origin":** Prince, *Catastrophe and Social Change*, 16.

143   **"since during the time that it took":** Miguel de la Madrid, quoted in Dianne E. Davis, "Reverberations: Mexico City's 1985 Earthquake and the Transformation of the Capital," in *Resilient Cities: How Modern Cities Recover from Disaster*, Lawrence J. Vale and Thomas J. Campanella (Oxford and New York: Oxford University Press, 2005), 265.

143   **A skinny young man . . . "participated in that brigade":** Poniatowska, *Nothing, Nobody*, 142.

145   **Michael Edwards:** *Civil Society* (Cambridge, England: Polity, 2004), 86.

145   **"I am clearly convinced":** Gustavo Esteva, in interview with the author, Oaxaca, Mexico, January 2008. He wrote about Tepito's self-government and autonomy in "Tepito: No Thanks, First World," *Reclaiming Politics* (Fall-Winter 1991).

145 **"As far as I can see":** Ibid.

145 **"a society in which citizens participate":** Václav Havel, in a speech at Macalester College, Minneapolis, April 26, 1999, and online at http://www.eng .yabloko.ru/Publ/Archive/Speech/gavel-260499.html.

146 **Barrios like Tepito:** See Harry Cleaver, "The Uses of an Earthquake," which draws extensively on Gustavo Esteva's work in and writings on Tepito. Cleaver's essay can be found online at many Web sites.

146 **"During the months":** Monsiváis, *"No Sin Nosotros,"* 86.

146 **"Not even the power of the state":** Monsiváis, introduction to Poniatowska, *Nothing, Nobody,* xvii.

147 **"norms of participation are different":** Edwards, *Civil Society,* 30.

148 **"The individual, the isolated self was dead":** Pauline Jacobson, "How It Feels to Be a Refugee," *Bulletin,* April 29, 1906.

149 **One such young man:** José Luis Pacho Paredo, in interview with the author, Mexico City, April 2007.

149 **"promote social contact, collective life, and public engagement":** Eric Klinenberg, *Heat Wave* (Chicago: University of Chicago Press, 2003), 91.

150 **"Residents of the most":** Ibid., 127.

Losing the Mandate of Heaven

152 **"Disasters overload political systems":** A. Cooper Drury and Richard Stuart Olson, "Disasters and Political Unrest: An Empirical Investigation," *Journal of Contingencies and Crisis Management* 6 (September 1998): 4.

153 **Russell Dynes:** "The Lisbon Earthquake in 1755: Contested Meanings in the First Modern Disaster" (Newark: University of Delaware Disaster Research Center), 3.

154 **the earthquake that . . . devastated Nicaragua's capital:** See Richard Stuart Olson and Vincent T. Gawronski, "Disasters as Critical Junctures? Managua, Nicaragua 1972 and Mexico City 1985," *International Journal of Mass Emergencies and Disasters* 21, no. 1 (March 2003): 3–35.

155 **"It is such a shock":** Gioconda Belli, in interview with the author, Santa Monica, California, April 2007.

156 **"kleptocracy":** Olson and Gawronski," "Disasters as Critical Junctures," 10.

159 **"The nuclear meltdown":** Mikhail Gorbachev, "Turning Point at Chernobyl," http://economistsview.typepad.com/economistsview/2006/04/gorbachev _chern.html/.

160 **"Insurrections by a 'nature' that had seemed":** Mark Healey, "The Fragility of the Moment: Politics and Class in the Aftermath of the 1944 Argentine Earthquake," *International Labor and Working Class Journal,* no. 62 (Fall 2002): 5.

161 **secretary of commerce Herbert Hoover:** In John M. Barry, *Rising Tide: The Great Mississippi Flood of 1927 and How It Changed America* (New York: Simon and Schuster, 1998).

161 **"The provision of relief":** Healey, "The Fragility of the Moment," 53.

162   **the public rose up chanting,** "Que se vayan todos!": Marina Sitrin, *Horizontalism: Voices of Popular Power in Argentina* (Oakland, CA: AK Press, 2006), 22.

162   **On New Year's Eve of 2001 the American secretary of state:** Benjamin Blackwell, "Micropolitics and the Cooking Pot Revolution in Argentina," on Znet, http://www.zmag.org/znet/viewArticle/11740.

162   **"What began angrily":** Sitrin, *Horizontalism*, 26.

162   **"I also remember the feeling":** Ibid., 27.

163   **Jonathan Schell points out that:** "Political theory as well as common sense suggests that overthrow, an act of destruction, should require violence. It seems equally obvious that the subsequent stage of foundation of the new regime, an act of creation, should be peaceful. However, the historical record shows that the reverse has much more often been the case. The overthrow has often been carried out with little or no bloodshed, while the foundation—and the revolutionary rule that follows it—has been bathed in blood." *The Unconquerable World: Power, Nonviolence and the Will of the People* (New York: Metropolitan Books, 2003), 144–45.

Standing on Top of Golden Hours

167   **"He hath put down the mighty":** Max Harris, *Carnival and Other Christian Festivals: Folk Theology and Folk Performance* (Austin: University of Texas Press, 2003), 119.

167   **"Carnival celebrated temporary liberation":** Mikhail Bakhtin, *Rabelais and His World*, trans. Helene Iswolsky (Bloomington: Indiana University Press, 1984), 10.

169   **"The TAZ is like an uprising":** Hakim Bey, *T.A.Z.: The Temporary Autonomous Zone, Ontological Anarchy, Poetic Terrorism* (Brooklyn, NY: Autonomedia, 2003), 99.

169   **William Wordsworth:** *The Prelude* (New York: Penguin Books, 1995), 226.

171   **"It was the great national thaw":** Mona Ozouf, *Festivals and the French Revolution* (Cambridge, MA: Harvard University Press, 1991), 134.

171   **"Paris is a true paradise":** Gustave Courbet, in a letter to his family, April 30, 1871, "Paris is a true paradise! No police, no nonsense, no exaction of any kind, no arguments! Everything in Paris rolls along like clockwork. In short, it is a beautiful dream. All the government bodies are organized federally and run themselves," in *Letters of Gustave Courbet*, ed. and trans. Petra ten-Doesschate Chu (Chicago: University of Chicago Press, 1992), 416.

171   **"Down the Ramblas":** George Orwell, *Homage to Catalonia* (New York: Harcourt, Brace and Company, 1952), 5.

171   **Eleanor Bakhtadze:** In Mark Kurlansky, *1968: The Year That Rocked the World* (New York: Random House, 2004), 227.

171   **"Paris was wonderful":** Eleanor Bakhtadze, in Mark Kurlansky, *1968: The Year That Rocked the World* (New York: Random House, 2004), 225.

171 **"Everbody forgot who he was":** Josef Koudelka, in "Invasion 68: Prague," an interview with Melissa Harris, *Aperture*, no. 192 (Fall 2008): 22.

172 **"felt life quicken and accelerate":** Ariel Dorfman, *Heading South, Looking North: A Bilingual Journey* (New York: Penguin Books, 2004), 244.

172 **"two days that felt as if":** Gioconda Belli, *The Revolution Under My Skin: A Memoir of Love and War* (New York: Knopf, 2003), 291.

172 **"The whole earth the beauty wore of promise":** Wordsworth, *The Prelude*.

173 **jubilee:** See Peter Linebaugh, "Jubilating; Or, How the Atlantic Working Class Used the Biblical Jubilee Against Capitalism with Some Success," *Radical History Review* 50 (1991).

175 **"When we initiated the work of working with tenants":** Marco Rascón, in interview with the author, April 2007.

175 **"Another thing that existed in 1985":** Ibid.

176 **"Super Barrio":** Marco Rascón, in interview with Ralph Rugoff, *Frieze* magazine, http://www.frieze.com/issue/article/the_masked_avenger/.

176 **"The first time he showed up":** Ibid.

176 **"Cuauhtémoc Cárdenas, with his face of a statue":** Rascón, in interview with the author, April 2007.

178 **"The means are the end":** This is said many places by Subcomandante Marcos, including in an interview by Gabriel García Márquez and Roberto Pombo, "The Punch Card and the Hourglass," *New Left Review* (May–June 2001): "The seizure of power does not justify a revolutionary organization in taking any action that it pleases. We do not believe that the end justifies the means. Ultimately, we believe that the means are the end. We define our goal by the way we choose the means of struggling for it."

179 **"Marcos is gay":** Subcomandante Marcos, in *The Speed of Dreams: Selected Writings 2001–2007* (San Francisco: City Lights Books, 2007).

179 **"The Zapatista movement proved the power":** Laura Carlsen, "An Uprising Against the Inevitable: An Americas Policy Program Special Report," http://americas.irc-online.org/am/3217/.

180 **"Here the people govern and the government obeys":** See Rebecca Solnit, "Revolution of the Snails," February 2008, http://www.TomDispatch.com/post/174881/.

IV. THE CITY TRANSFIGURED: NEW YORK IN GRIEF AND GLORY

Mutual Aid in the Marketplace

185 **"I said, 'The people who were in the towers'":** The reminiscences of Mark DeMarco (November 27, 2001) in the Columbia University Oral History Research Office Collection (hereafter CUOHROC), 19.

185–86 **"They're back"** and **"I just started down":** Michael Noble, in interview with the author, April 2007.

187   **John Abruzzo:** In Mitchell Fink and Lois Mathias, *Never Forget: An Oral History of September 11, 2001* (New York: Regan Books, 2002), 166–67.

187   **"We had to stop several times":** The reminilscences of Zaheer Jaffery (November 14, 2001, December 4, 2002, and June 24, 2005) in CUOHROC, 17 and 19.

187   **"What are you doing?":** One of the firefighters, in Jules and Gédéon Naudet, *9/11*, documentary film, 28 minutes in.

188   **"I remember looking back":** The reminiscences of John Guilfoy (November 13, 2001, and May 10, 2003) in CUOHROC, 17–18.

188   **"with a deep Brooklyn accent"** and **"8:45 a.m. September 11":** Usman Farman, in Jee Kim et al., eds., *Another World Is Possible: Conversations in a Time of Terror,* 2nd ed. (Chicago: Subway and Elevated Press, 2002), 12.

188   **"For a couple of minutes":** Errol Anderson, in Fink and Mathias, *Never Forget,* 119.

189   **"We could not see at all":** Adam Mayblum, quoted at http://www .snopes.com/rumors/mayblum.asp (accessed 2008) and various other sites online.

189   **"They say, 'No'":** The reminiscences of Maria Zambrano (November 14, 2001, and October 28, 2003) in CUOHROC, 23.

189   **"A couple of young kids":** Stanley Trojanowski, in Fink and Mathias, *Never Forget,* 179.

190   **"Something else that I won't forget is":** Joe Blozis, in ibid., 200.

190   **"I have the greatest admiration":** Ralph Blasi, in ibid., 57.

190   **"I can honestly say":** Ada Rosario-Dolch, in ibid., 38.

191   **"One of our harbor boats pulled in":** Peter Moog, in ibid., 80.

191   **A fireman remembers . . . "People were just diving onto the boat":** Mike Magee, ed., *All Available Boats: The Evacuation of Manhattan Island on September 11, 2001* (Bronxville, NY: Spencer Books, 2002), 40.

191   **A waterfront metalworker . . . says, "Everyone did what they needed to do":** Ibid., 54.

192   **"Maybe by now I have a river view":** The reminiscences of Ellen Meyers (November 4, 2001, and March 16, 2003) in CUOHROC, 17.

192   **"get out of here"** and **"It seemed like a steady surge":** The reminiscences of Marcia Goffin (December 10, 2001) in CUOHROC, 12, 13, and 16.

193   **Astra Taylor:** In interview with the author, San Francisco, March 2007.

The Need to Help

195   **"Movement toward the disaster":** Charles Fritz and Harry B. Williams, "The Human Being in Disasters: A Research Perspective," *Annals of the American Academy* (1957) (unpaginated, copy from Hazard House Library, University of Colorado, Boulder).

196   **"Everybody wanted to respond":** The reminiscences of Temma Kaplan (February 13, 2005) in CUOHROC, 7–8.

196   **"By afternoon, Amsterdam Avenue":** Ibid.

197   **"On 9/11 I just needed to reaffirm":** Ibid.

197   **"From the voice of altruists":** Deborah Stone, *The Samaritan's Dilemma: Should Government Help Your Neighbor?* (New York: Nation Books, 2008), 180.

198   **"I left there":** The reminiscences of Ilene Sameth (October 29, 2001, and May 19, 2003) in CUOHROC, 25–26.

198   **"Restaurants, cooks . . . converged in impromptu kitchens":** James Kendra and Tricia Wachtendorf, "Rebel Food, Renegade Supplies" (Newark: University of Delaware Disaster Research Center, 2001), 15.

198   **Edmund J. Song:** Blog, http://blog.muevelonyc.com/2001/09/30/emails -from-911/.

198   **A volunteer up in the middle of the night:** The reminiscences of Daniel I. Smith (October 24, 2001, and September 20, 2004) in CUOHROC, 73–74.

199   **"and at that point, we realized":** The reminiscences of Emira Habiby Browne (August 1, 2002) in ibid., 21.

199   **One of the organizers wrote me, "We in New York":** Marina Sitrin, comments via e-mail regarding the author's manuscript, August 2008.

200   **"Many of its grand old places":** Marshall Berman, "The City Rises: Rebuilding Meaning after 9/11," *Dissent* (Summer 2003).

201   **"It was the first time that I had been":** Jordan Schuster, in interview with the author, San Francisco, February 2007.

202   **"The George Washington statue":** The reminiscences of Elizabeth Grace Burkhart (January 30, 2002, and April 15, 2003) in CUOHROC, 33–34.

202   **"people kept coming by":** The reminiscences of Temma Kaplan (February 13, 2005) in ibid., 11.

203   **Kate Joyce:** E-mail message to the author, April 14, 2006.

203   **Perhaps memory of the 1993 World Trade Center bombing:** See Wayne Barrett and Dan Collins, *Grand Illusion: The Untold Story of Rudy Giuliani and 9/11* (New York: HarperCollins, 2006), 80.

205   **"I began as one guy behind a table":** Tobin James Mueller, in 9/11 journal, no longer posted online.

205   **"Everyone here was rejected":** Ibid.

206   **"No one is turned away":** Tobin James Mueller, in interview with the author, New York, June 2007.

206   **"We grew until Friday night":** Ibid.

206   **"in any given ten-minute period":** The reminiscences of Daniel I. Smith (October 24, 2001, and October 31, 2001) in CUOHROC, 56 and 62.

207   **"I mean, we had security":** Ibid., 80.

207   **"the appearance of these groups":** Tricia Wachtendorf, in "Rebel Food, Renegade Supplies," 8.

208   **"I do think however":** The reminiscences of James Martin (October 15, 2001, and March 24, 2003) in CUOHROC, 15–16.

208   **"So there's that feeling of unity":** Ibid.

209   **"Osama bin Laden has done a lot to get Catholics":** The reminiscences of Stephen Katsouros (November 4, 2001, and March 2, 2003) in CUOHROC, 21.

209   **"From that day, for a month":** Pat Enkyu O'Hara, in interview with the author, New York, 2007.

209   **"The smell didn't go away":** Ibid.

Nine Hundred and Eleven Questions

211   **A Rand Institute analyst . . . "Terrorists want lots of people":** Louise Richardson, *What Terrorists Want: Understanding the Enemy, Containing the Threat* (New York: Random House, 2006), 141.

211   **"Only relatively small numbers of New Yorkers":** Tom Engelhardt, "9/11 in a Movie-Made World," September 7, 2006, http://www.tomdispatch.com/post/118775/9_11_an_explosion_out_of_the_towering_inferno_/.

212   **a former city detective, "If anybody kept a record of which floors":** Barrett and Collins, *Grand Illusion*, 44.

212   **"I know a lot of the firefighters were very upset":** The reminiscences of Ruth Sergel (December 5, 2003) in CUOHROC, 16.

213   **The space was leased from a landlord who afterward became a major campaign donor:** Wayne Barrett on *Democracy Now* broadcast, Pacifica Network, January 3, 2007.

213   **"Giuliani, however, overruled all of this advice":** Barrett and Collins, *Grand Illusion*, 41.

214   **9/11 Commission Report . . . "Some questioned locating it":** National Commission on the Terrorist Attacks upon the United States, *The 9/11 Commission Report* (New York: Norton, 2004), 284.

215   **When journalist Juan Gonzalez:** Barrett and Collins, *Grand Illusion*, 279.

215   **Seven years later, more than ten thousand exposed people:** Editorial, "Ground Zero's Lingering Victims," *New York Times*, September 15, 2008.

215   **"I think that the nation is not going to be able":** Camille Paglia, in Susan Faludi, *The Terror Dream* (New York: Metropolitan Books, 2007), 23.

215   ***National Review* article:** In Faludi, *Terror Dream*, 23.

215   **Feminism had "slid further into irrelevancy":** Cathy Young, in ibid., 21.

215   **"Giuliani's homoerotic death cult":** Anonymous, in off-the-record interview with the author, New York, February 2007.

216   **9/11 Commission . . . "The existing mechanisms":** *9/11 Commission Report*, 348.

216   **"In responding to the attacks":** Richardson, *What Terrorists Want*, 150.

217   **"A painstaking re-creation":** Dan Eggen and William Branigin, "Air Defenses Filtered on 9/11, Panel Finds," *Washington Post*, June 17, 2004, http://www.washingtonpost.com/wp-dyn/articles/A48471-2004Jun17.html/.

218   **"By the standards of speed":** Elaine Scarry, "Citizenship in Emergency: Can

Democracy Protect Us Against Terrorism?," *Boston Review* (October/November 2002), http://www.bostonreview.net/BR27.5/scarry.html/.

218   **"When the plane that hit":** Ibid.

219   **As one British psychiatrist put it, the new diagnosis "was meant to shift":** Christina Hoff Sommers and Sally Satel, *One Nation Under Therapy: How the Helping Culture Is Eroding Self-Reliance* (New York: St. Martin's Press, 2005), 147.

219   **nineteen psychologists wrote . . . "certain therapists":** Ibid., 177.

219   **One of the authors . . . "The public should be very concerned":** Ibid., 179.

219–20 **"It's been very interesting during my lifetime":** Kathleen Tierney, in interview with the author, March 2007.

220   **"Inherent in these traumatic experiences are losses":** Richard G. Tedeschi, Crystal L. Park, and Lawrence G. Calhoun, eds., *Posttraumatic Growth: Positive Changes in the Aftermath of Crisis* (Mahwah, NJ: Lawrence Erlbaum Associates, 1998), 2.

220   **"Often it is just such":** Viktor E. Frankl, *Man's Search for Meaning* (1959; repr. Boston: Beacon Press, 2006), 72.

221   **Nietzsche once commented, "Man, the bravest animal":** In Berman, "The City Rises."

221   **"Disaster provides a form of societal shock":** Charles Fritz, *Disasters and Mental Health: Therapeutic Principles Drawn from Disaster Studies* (University of Delawre: Disaster Research Center Historical and Comparative Disaster Series #10, 1996), 57.

224   **"and actually within an hour":** The reminiscences of Mark Fichtel (December 11, 2001) in CUOHROC, 16.

225   **I met one couple:** They preferred to remain anonymous.

V. NEW ORLEANS: COMMON GROUNDS AND KILLERS

What Difference Would It Make?

231   **"And I'm screaming":** Clara Rita Bartholomew, in interview with the author for Alive in Truth Oral History Project, San Francisco, November 2005.

233–34 **Cory Delaney** and **"got out of their cars":** *City Pages* Oral History Interviews (*City Pages* is a Minneapolis–St. Paul newspaper): http://recordingkatrina.blogspot.com/2005/09/minneapolisst-paul-city-pages-new.html/.

236   **Compass told . . . Oprah Winfrey, "We had little babies in there":** Quoted in Douglas Brinkley, *The Great Deluge: Hurricane Katrina, New Orleans and the Mississippi Gulf Coast* (New York: HarperCollins, 2006), 573.

236   **Nagin reported . . . "hundreds of gang members":** Brian Thevenot and Gordon Russell, "Reports of Anarchy at Superdome Overstated," Newhouse News Service, September 26, 2005.

236   **"in that frickin' Superdome":** Ray Nagin, in Susannah Rosenblatt and James

Rainey, "Katrina Takes a Toll on Truth, News Accuracy," *Los Angeles Times,* September 27, 2005.

237   **"These are some of the forty thousand extra troops":** Governor Kathleen Blanco, quoted in *When the Levees Broke,* DVD, directed by Spike Lee (2006; HBO Documentary Films and Forty Acres and a Mule Filmworks), and in "Military Due to Move into New Orleans," CNN, September 2, 2005, among other sources.

237   **"On the dark streets, rampaging gangs":** CNN Reports, *Katrina: State of Emergency* (Kansas City: Andrews McMeel Publishing, 2005), 75.

237   **"Chaos gripped New Orleans":** Editorial, *New York Times,* September 1, 2005.

237   **The police were captured on national television:** See NBC report, available at http://www.youtube.com/watch?v=cHcajIRcBvA. Curiously, the header on the TV report is "Stealing for Salvation."

238   **"and that really opened up the mall for us":** Peter Berkowitz, "We Went into the Mall and Began 'Looting': A Letter on Race, Class, and Surviving the Hurricane," *Monthly Review* online, http://mrzine.monthlyreview.org/berkowitz090905.html/.

239   **"In some communities":** Enrico Quarantelli, "Looting and Antisocial Behavior in Disasters" (Newark: University of Delaware Disaster Research Center, 1994).

240   **The job of supplying buses was contracted out:** See Tim Shorrock, "Why Didn't the Buses Come? Bush-Linked Florida Company and the Katrina Evacuation Fiasco," *Counterpunch,* January 21/22, 2006, http://www.counterpunch.org/shorrock01212006.html/.

241   **"Reporters, even from some of the big papers":** Jed Horne, *Breach of Faith: Hurricane Katrina and the Near-Death of a Great American City* (New York: Random House, 2007), 107–8.

241   **"Katrina's big lesson is that the crust of civilization":** Timothy Garton Ash, "It Always Lies Below: A Hurricane Produces Anarchy. Decivilization Is Not as Far Away as We Like to Think," *Guardian,* September 8, 2005, http://www.guardian.co.uk/world/2005/sep/08/hurricanekatrina.usa6/.

242   **"a snakepit of anarchy, death, looting":** Maureen Dowd, "United States of Shame," *New York Times,* September 3, 2005.

242   **"Now the captain is saying, 'Okay' ":** In *City Pages* Online Oral Histories.

243   **"Then came the military helicopters":** Ibid.

243   **"And we were left there":** Denise Moore, in transcript from "After the Flood," *This American Life* (Chicago Public Radio), September 9, 2005, http://www.thislife.org/Radio_Episode.aspx?sched=1097/.

244   they **"got together, figured out":** Ibid.

244   **"I've got a report of two hundred bodies":** In Thevenot and Russell, "Reports of Anarchy at Superdome Overstated."

245   **"Troops Begin Combat Operations":** *Army Times,* September 2, 2005.

245   **"characterized their work"**: Jeremy Scahill, "Blackwater Down," *The Nation*, October 10, 2005, http://www.thenation.com/doc/20051010/scahill/.

Murderers

248   **Danny Brumfield was shot in the back:** See "Autopsy: Man Killed by Police After Katrina Was Shot in Back," CNN online, July 18, 2007, http://www.cnn.com/2007/US/07/16/nola.shooting/index.html/.

248   **Susan Bartholomew . . . "My right arm was on the ground lying next to me":** John Burnett for *All Things Considered*, "What Happened on New Orleans' Danziger Bridge?," National Public Radio, http://www.npr.org/templates/story/story.php?storyId=6063982/.

249   **"Pretty quickly, it became clear":** Michael Lewis, "Wading Toward Home," *New York Times Magazine*, October 9, 2005, http://www.nytimes.com/2005/10/09/magazine/09neworleans.html?scp=2&sq=michael%20lewis%20katrina%20uptown%20new%20orleans&st=cse/.

249   **In the commemorative Katrina book . . . there's a photograph:** *Times-Picayune, Katrina: The Ruin and Recovery of New Orleans* (New Orleans: Spotlight Press, 2006), 70; in the CNN book, *CNN Reports, Katrina: State of Emergency* (Kansas City, MO: Andrews Mc Neel, 2005), 37.

250   **"We made it a policy early on":** Aislyn Colgan, in interview with the author, New Orleans, February 2007.

251   **Donnell Herrington** and *When the Levees Broke:* The four-DVD set includes outtakes of this interview, in which Herrington says more about the circumstances of his near murder.

252   **"During the aftermath":** Malik Rahim, in interview with Amy Goodman on *Democracy Now*, October 24, 2005.

255   **"Another cousin of mine":** Donnell Herrington, in videotaped interview with Adam Clay Thompson, New Orleans, September 17, 2008.

260   **"The evacuation of New Orleans":** Mike Davis, "Poor, Black and Left Behind," TomDispatch.com, September. 23, 2004, http://www.tomdispatch.com/post/1849/mike_davis_on_the_political_sidelining_of_blacks/.

260   **"They won't let them walk out":** Shepard Smith, quoted in many places, including in Russ Baker, "The Media's Labor Day Revolution," TomPaine.com, September 6, 2005, http://www.tompaine.com/articles/2005/09/06/the_medias_labor_day_revolution.php/.

261   **"When we left the hotel":** Larry Bradshaw and Lorrie Beth Slonsky, in interview with the author, San Francisco, March 2007.

261   **"The two hundred of us set off":** Bradshaw and Slonsky, in an account spread widely via e-mail and posted at http://www.zmag.org/znet/viewArticle/5345, among other sites.

262   **"Can you imagine during 9/11":** Lennox Yearwood, "March Demands Accountability of Gretna Police," originally published in *Louisiana Weekly*, November 7, 2005, http://www.commondreams.org/headlines05/1107-05.htm/.

262 **"I don't second-guess this decision":** Arthur Lawson, in Chris Kirkham and Paul Purpura, "Bridge Blockade After Katrina Remains Divisive Issue," *Times-Picayune*, September 1, 2007, http://blog.nola.com/times-picayune/2007/09/bridge_blockade_after_katrina.html/.

263 **A muscular state trooper . . . "Doc, we'll be closing down":** Richard E. Deichmann, *Code Blue: A Katrina Physician's Memoir* (Bloomington, IN: Rooftop Publishing, 2007), 118.

263 **The father told Deichmann, "The thing is, they wouldn't":** Ibid., 113.

264 **"The Louisiana Society for the Prevention":** Tom Jawetz, in "ACLU Report Details Horrors Suffered by Orleans Parish Prisoners in Wake of Hurricane Katrina," August 10, 2006, http://www.aclu.org/prison/conditions/26421prs20060810.html/.

264 **The 1973 volcanic eruption on Heimaey:** See United States Geological Survey, "Man Against Volcano: The Eruption on Heimaey, Vestmannaeyjar, Iceland," 2nd ed., 1983.

265 **A Jamaica writing . . . "Cuba is organised":** John Maxwell, "Children of Prometheus: Common Sense," *Jamaica Observer*, September 14, 2008, http://www.jamaicaobserver.com/columns/html/20080913t050000-0500_140147_obs_children_of_prometheus_.asp/.

265 **"The Cubans have consistently built up":** Oxfam America, "2004 Report Cuba: Weathering the Storm, Lessons in Risk Reduction from Cuba," 19. Available online at www.oxfamamerica.org/cuba/.

Love and Lifeboats

271 **"I really felt like I was somebody":** Louis Armstrong, in Thomas Brothers, *Louis Armstrong's New Orleans* (New York: Norton, 2006), 13.

273 **HurricaneHousing.org:** Quotes downloaded by the author in the weeks after Katrina; the site is not accessibly archived.

274 **"was a nice quiet neighborhood":** Keith Bernard Sr., in interview with the author, New Orleans, February 2007.

276 **"in reality looking at ways to not bring":** Pam Dashiell, in interview with the author, New Orleans, June 2007.

279 **"Even if you take some of the most aggressive plans":** Wade Rathke, in interview with the author, New Orleans, September 2008.

Beloved Community

282 **the president said, "I don't think anyone anticipated":** http://news.bbc.co.uk/2/hi/americas/4204754.stm, and elsewhere.

282–83 **"It wasn't Iraq that did George Bush in": Keith Olbermann,** *Truth or Consequences: Special Comments on the Bush Administration's War on American Values* (New York: Random House, 2007), xv.

283 **"Katrina to me was the tipping point":** Matthew Dowd, in Cullen Murphy

and Todd S. Purdum, "An Oral History of the Bush White House," *Vanity Fair*, February 2009.

285   **"This is the most amazing thing":** Cindy Sheehan, in conversation with the author, Crawford, Texas, August 29, 2005.

285   **King wrote . . . "to foster and create":** Widely quoted, including at http:// www.mlksymposium.umich.edu/07theme/ and http://www.religion-online .org/showarticle.asp?title=1603/.

285   **"realizes that noncooperation and boycotts":** Martin Luther King Jr., "Nonviolence and Racial Justice," February 6, 1957, in Clayborne Carson et al., eds., *The Papers of Martin Luther King, Jr., Volume IV: Symbol of the Movement, January 1957–December 1958* (Berkeley: University of California Press, 2000), 120.

288   **"They're stunned":** Linda Jackson, in interview with the author, New Orleans, February 2007.

289   **Brian from Monterey:** In interview with the author, New Orleans, June 2007.

289   **"Right after the hurricane":** Malik Rahim, in interview with the author, Algiers, Louisiana, February 2007.

292   **"After the disaster":** Emily Posner, in interview with the author, New Orleans, February 2007.

293   **"showed blacks that all whites":** Malik Rahim, in interview with the author, New Orleans, June 2007.

294   **"I was only twenty-five":** Aislyn Colgan, in interview with the author, February 2007.

297   **"As the magnitude of the disaster":** Hawker, from the ashevillecommunity .org/hawker/katrina/Web site.

299   **"It's unfortunate it takes disasters":** Felipe Chavez, in interview with the author, New Orleans, June 2007.

301   **"What seems so beautiful":** Emmanuel David, in an e-mail to the author, September 2008.

Epilogue: The Doorway in the Ruins

306   **"Man, the bravest animal":** Marshall Berman, "The City Rises: Rebuilding Meaning After 9/11," *Dissent* (Summer 2003).

306   **"He who has a *why* to live for":** Viktor E. Frankl, *Man's Search for Meaning* (1959; repr., Boston: Beacon Press, 2006), 104.

310   **Army War College, Henry Paulson,** and **Phoenix Police:** See Mike Sunnucks, "Ariz. Police Say They Are Prepared as War College Warns Military Must Prep for Unrest; IMF Warns of Economic Riots," *Phoenix Business Journal*, December 17, 2008.

310   **San Francisco Fire Department . . . "Hundreds of citizen volunteers assisted":** http://www.sfmuseum.net/quake/revvols.html/.

312   **Mayor Nagin:** Radio and television segments transcribed by author, August 2008.

INDEX

Abruzzo, John, 187
ACORN, 279
Adato, Victoria, 139
Aguilar, Margarita, 137–138
Alexander, Marcel, 253, 256, 257–258
Al-Qaeda, 211, 216, 223
Altruism, 87, 96, 97, 197
American Rainbow Response,
  298–299
Anarchists, anarchism, 67–68, 81, 84,
  90 91, 152, 163, 226, 291
Anderson, Errol, 188
Arafat, Yassir, 204
Arctic Dreams (Lopez), 63
Argentina, 160–162
Argentine earthquake, 160–161
Armstrong, Louis, 271
Army Times, 245
Ash, Timothy Garton, 241–242
Asia, 8, 121
Astrodome (Houston), 233
Austin, Mary, 24,

Bakhtadze, Eleanor, 171
Bakhtin, Mikhail, 167
Barrett, Wayne, 213–214
Bartholomew, Clara Rita, 231–233
Bartholomew, Susan, 248

Bastrop Christian Outreach Center,
  297–298
Behan, Maurice, 26
Bell, Eric Temple, 29
Bell, Quentin, 101
Belli, Gioconda, 155–158, 172, 315–316
Beloved community, 197, 208,
  285–286
Berkowitz, Peter, 238
Berman, Marshall, 200, 306
Bernard, Keith (Sr.), 273–274
Bey, Hakim, 169, 202
Biloxi, Mississippi, 117
Black Panthers, 291
Blackouts, 10
Blackwater security forces, 245
Blanco, Governor Kathleen, 236–237,
  245, 252
Blasi, Ralph, 190
Blitz (Luftwaffe bombing of England),
  98–105
Blood donations, 204
Bombing (other than Blitz, above),
  109–111
Bradshaw, Larry, 261–262
Bring New Orleans Back, 276
Brisette, James, 248
Brosnan, Pierce, 121–122

Brothers, Thomas, 271
Brown, Michael, FEMA director, 47
Browne, Emira Habiby, 199
Brumfield, Danny, 248
Buddhism, Buddhists, 87, 115–117,
    209–210
Buffalo Creek flood, West Virginia, 113
Burkhardt, Elizabeth Grace, 202
Bureaucracy, 125
Burning Man (festival), 117, 298
Burns, Thomas A., 25–26
Bush, George W., 222, 223, 282–283

Cain, 2–3
Camp Casey, Texas, 283–284
Canadian Army, 78
Candide (Voltaire), 154
Capitalism, 93, 94–95, 220–221
Cardenas, Cuauhtémoc, 144, 176
Carlsen, Laura, 141, 179–180
Carnival, 165–171, 270–272
Carr, Jane, 46
Carter, Dumas, 242–243
Catastrophe defined, 10, 235, 269
Catastrophe and Social Change (Prince),
    79–81, 86, 95
Catholic Worker, 67–69, 96, 110
Charity, 47, 87
Chavez, Felipe, 299
Chernobyl nuclear disaster, 159
Chess, Caron, 129
Chicago
    Great Fire, 34, 148
    Heat wave of 1995, 149–150, 260
Chile, 172
China, 85, 151–152, 308
China Syndrome, The (film), 126
Chu, Ed, 311
Churchill, Winston, 99, 100
Civil society, 143, 145–150, 163, 165–178,
    220–223, 226–227, 305, 309
Class, 28, 31, 33, 38, 46, 78, 171
Clarke, Lee, 129–130, 310
Climate change, 22, 308, 309

CNN, 238, 249–250, 312
Cockett, Olivia, 100–101, 102
Cold war, 105, 109–111
Coleman, Vincent, 76, 96
Colgan, Aislyn, 250–251, 294–295
Collins, Dan, 213–214
Common Ground (New Orleans
    activist group), 87, 277,
    289–295
Common Ground Clinic, 250–251,
    289–295
Compass, Eddie, 236
Connelly, Mark, 99, 100
Convergence, 195–210
Corrosive community, 113
Crawford, Texas, 283–284
Crow, Scott, 290
Crowd: A Study of the Popular Mind, The
    (Le Bon), 81–83
Cuba, 265–266
Czechoslovakia, 171, 177

Darby, Brandon, 290
Darwin, Charles, 82, 88
Dashiell, Pam, 275–276, 279
David, Emmanuel, 293, 301–302
Davis, Mike, 112, 260
Day, Dorothy, 59–69, 86, 90, 110, 118,
    147, 306
Deep Impact (film), 122, 125
Deichmann, Dr. Richard E., 263
Delaney, Cory, 233–234
DeMarco, Mar, 185
Diggers, 92–93,
Disaster, definition, 10, 235
Disaster studies (sociology),
    105–109
Doheny-Farina, Stephen, 66
Dorfman, Ariel, 171–172
Dowd, Matthew, 283
Dowd, Maureen, 242
Doyle, Mary, 40
Drury, A. Cooper, 152
Dunkirk evacuation, 184

Earthquakes, 151–152
  See also Argentine earthquake;
    Lisbon earthquake; Loma Prieta
    earthquake; Managua earthquake;
    Mexico City earthquake; San
    Francisco earthquake and fire;
    Tangshan earthquake
Earthquake (film), 120–121, 126–127
Edwards, Michael, 145, 146
Elite panic, 21, 36, 37–38, 127, 129–130,
    148, 152–153, 223, 234–235, 259,
    303, 309
Emergency Communities (volunteer
    group), 287, 295–302
Emerson, Edward, 15
Emotion and disaster, 5, 7, 15–16, 26–27,
    29–30, 54–56, 59–60, 65, 154–157,
    192–194, 196–198, 201–203,
    219–220, 221, 225–226, 251,
    288–289, 294
"Energies of Men" (James), 56
Engelhardt, Tom, 211–212, 224–225
Epidemics, 120, 127–129, 304
Erickson, Kai, 112–113
Escape from New York (film), 211
Esteva, Gustavo, 145

Fallout shelters, 109–111
Faludi, Susan, 215
Famine, 150
Farman, Usman, 188
Fear, 98–100, 102, 235–236, 239
  See also Elite panic; Emotion and
    disaster
Federal Emergency Management
    Agency (FEMA), 240, 244, 260,
    268, 280, 302, 310
Fichtel, Mark, 224
Fitchner, Henry, 40
Floyd, Harold, 77, 96
Fox News, 260
Fradkin, Philip, 37
France, 150
Frankl, Viktor, 96, 97, 114, 220, 306

Freedom Summer, 285, 293
French Revolution, 159, 169–171
Fritz, Charles E., 104–109, 111–112,
    114, 115, 166, 195, 279, 309, 315, 331n
Funston, Brigadier General Frederick,
    34–37, 40, 131

Garcia, Judith, 137
Gender, 92, 125–126, 215–216
Germany, 105
Gibson-Graham, J. K., 94–95
Giuliani, Mayor Rudy, 213–214
Glover, Henry, 258
Glube, Joe, 77, 86
Goffin, Marcia, 192
Gonzalez, Juan, 215
Gorbachev, Mikhail, 159
Graeber, David, 19
Great Depression, 67, 69
Greeley, General Adolphus Washington,
    36, 40, 46
Green, Sam, 20
Guilfoy, John, 188

Habitat for Humanity, 288–289
Halifax, Nova Scotia, 3–4, 73–81
  Halifax Explosion of 1917, 73–81, 86,
    87, 91–92
Hansen, Gladys, 322n
Happiness, *see* Joy
Harris, Max, 167
Harrisson, Tom, 101, 103
Harvey, William G., 28
Havel, Václav, 145–146, 177
Healey, Mark, 160, 161
Heat waves, 149–150
Hedges, Chris, 65
Hernandez, Marisol, 135–138, 141–142
Herrington, Donnell, 251–258
Heston, Charleton, 121, 126
Hobbes, Thomas, 91, 93, 242
Holhouser, Anna Amelia, 13–15,
    16–17, 18
Holme, Rasmus, 252

Holy Cross Neighborhood Association, 275–276
Horne, Jed, 241
Hot Eight Brass Band, 271
Human nature, 49, 94, 99–101, 106–108, 119
Hurricane Katrina 1–2, 47, 231–304
HurricaneHousing.org, 2, 273–274
Huxley, Thomas Henry, 89

Ice storm of 1998, 66
Iceland, 264–265
Ingram, Stuart, 37
Institutional Revolutionary Party (PRI), 38.–39

Jackson, Linda, 288
Jacobson, Pauline, 31–33, 148
Jaffery, Zaheer, 187
James, Henry, 51, 55
James, William, 49–57, 60, 65, 90, 216, 236
Janoff-Bulman, Ronnie, 118
Jawetz, Tom, 264
Johnstone, Dwight, 81
Joy, 5–6, 32, 54, 64–65, 103, 104, 170, 172, 271
    See also Carnival
Joyce, Kate, 203
Jubilee, 173

Kanto Earthquake, Japan, 83–84
Kaplan, Temma, 195–196, 202–203
Katrina, see Hurricane Katrina
Katsouros, Father James, 209
King, Edwin, 258
King Jr., Martin Luther, 285–286, 290
King, Robert (Wilkerson), 290
Klein, Laura Cousino, 92
Klein, Naomi, 107, 160, 330n
Klinenberg, Eric, 149–150
Koudelka, Josef, 171
Kropotkin, Peter, 84–90, 95–96, 113, 180

Lafler, Henry Anderson, 43
Landfield, Jerome Barker, 42, 324n
Leavitt, Judith, 127–128
Le Bon, Gustave, 81–83
Lee, Spike, 251–252, 271
Lewis, Michael, 249
Liang, Hugh Kwong, 44–45
Lincoln, Abraham, 307
Lisbon earthquake, 153–154
Living Through the Blitz, 101
Lloyd, Dorothy, 75–76, 91–92
Loma Prieta earthquake, 4–5, 112, 153, 310
London Can Take It (film), 100
London, England, 98–105
London, Jack, 29–30
The Long Loneliness (Day), 61
Looting, looters, see Theft, Thieves
Lopez, Barry, 63
Lower Ninth Ward Neighbor-hood Empowerment Network Association (NENA), 275, 288
Lucha libre, 174–178

MacDonald, Laura, 78
Made with Love Café, 287–288, 299–300
Madison, Ronald and Lance, 248
Madrid, President Miguel de la, 143
Managua earthquake, 154–158
March, Aggie, 75
Mardi Gras, see New Orleans
Martial law, 34, 310, 332n
Martin, Father James, 208–209
Martin, Lillien Jane, 54
Maurin, Peter, 67
Mayblum, Adam, 189
McKinney, Phoebe, 138
Media, 212, 215–216, 235, 236–244, 251–252, 282–283
Mexico, 174–180
Mexico City, 135–149, 174–178
    Coordinadora Única de Damnifica-dos, 140
    Earthquake, 135–149, 174–176

Seamstresses and sweatshops,
135–139, 141–142
Tepito, 145–146, 148
Tlaltelolco, 139–140
Meyers, Ellen, 192
Miller and Lux, San Francisco wholesale
butchers, 27–28
Miranda, Alessandro, 140–141
Mizpah Café, 17, 22, 295
Monsiváis, Carlos, 146–147
Moog, Peter, 191
"Moral Equivalent of War" (James),
52–54, 148–149, 216
Mounier, Emmanuel, 68
Movies, 120–127, 212
Mueller, Tobin James, 205–206
Mussolini, Benito, 99
Mutual aid, 86–90, 180
Mutual Aid: A Factor of Evolution
(Kropotkin), 86–90

Nagin, Mayor Ray, 236, 312
National Guard, 284
In 1906 San Francisco, 37, 39
In New Orleans, 243, 245
National Opinion Research Center
(NORC), 105
NENA (Lower Ninth Ward Neighbor-
hood Empowerment Network
Association), 275, 288
New Orleans, 1, 120, 231–304, 312
Algiers Point, 250–259, 262
Convention Center, 238, 240, 243–244,
261
Coroner, 253
Crescent City Connection, 255,
260–262
Demographics, 269–270
Gretna (suburb of), 261–262
Hospitals, 243, 263–264, 269, 302
Lower Ninth Ward, 2, 268, 273–274,
280, 288, 292, 299–300
Mardi Gras in, 168, 270

Musicians' Village, 288–289
Murders in, 247–264
New Orleans Police Department, 237,
242–244, 248, 274–277
St. Rita's Nursing Home, 233
Superdome, 236, 240, 243
Vigilantes in, 249–259, 289–290
Volunteers in, 273–274, 280–281,
287–304
New Orleans *Times-Picayune,* 249
New York City, 128, 183–216,
224–227
Chelsea Piers, 203–204, 205–207
Firefighters, 184, 187, 188, 189–190,
212–213, 214–215
Pile (Ground Zero), 214
Union Square, 200, 201–203
World Trade Center, 183–192,
211–212, 225–226
New Waveland Café, 297–299
Nicaragua, 154–158, 172
Nietzsche, Friedrich, 221, 306
9/11 (*see also* New York City), 160,
183–227, 262
Evacuation by boat, 184, 191–192
9/11 Commission, 212
Noble, Michael, 185–187
Nova Scotia, *see* Halifax

Oakland, California, 59, 60
Obama, Barack, 65, 160, 283, 307
Obrador, Andrés Manuel López, mayor
of Mexico City, 144
O'Brien, Soledad, 238
O'Hara, Roshi Pat Enkyu, 209
Olbermann, Keith, 282
Olson, Richard Stuart, 152, 157
"On Some Mental Effects of the
Earthquake" (James), 54
Organic Valley cooperative,
298–299
Orwell, George, 171
Osugi, Sakae

Oxfam, 22, 265–266, 208
Ozouf, Mona, 171

Paglia, Camille, 215
Paine, Thomas, 64, 94
Panic, 29–30, 120, 123–124, 130
    See also Elite panic
Panic in the Streets (film), 120
Panter-Downs, Molly, 99
Paris Commune, 159, 171
Partido Revolucionario Institucional
    (PRI), see Institutional
    Revolutionary Party
Paulson, Henry, 310
People's Hurricane Relief Fund, 281
Perón, Juan, 160–161
Pettipas, Gertrude, 73
Phelan, James, 44, 45, 58
Pitt, Brad, 276, 303
Poland, 21
Policy and disaster, 80
Posner, Emily, 292–293
Post-traumatic stress disorder, see
    Trauma
Pragmatism: A New Name for Some Old
    Ways of Thinking (James), 50
Prince, Samuel Henry, 79–80, 86, 95,
    142, 241
Privatization, 8–9, 62–63, 161, 302–303
Project East River, 109

Quarantelli, Enrico, 111, 123–124, 125,
    152, 239

Racism, 33, 44–45, 58, 111–112, 185,
    199–200, 234–243, 245–246,
    247–263, 269, 271
Rahim, Malik, 252, 253, 277, 289–290,
    293, 303–304
Rainbow Gatherings, 295–298, 299
Rascón, Marco, 175–176
Rathke, Wade, 279–280
Red Cross, 25, 293, 294, 302
Reddy, Charles, 27

Religion, 59–62, 66–68, 80–81, 114–117,
    166–167, 188, 208–210, 224, 271, 287,
    288, 291, 297
Revolution, 19, 61, 151, 156–164, 165–166,
    170–173, 178–180
Richardson, Louise, 216
Rights of Man, The (Paine), 64, 94
Rosario-Dolch, Ada, 190
Ruef, Abe, 42, 44, 58
Russian Revolution, 61, 85

Salvation Army, 39
Sameth, Ilene, 197
San Diego, 111
San Francisco, 1906 earthquake in,
    13–17, 23–49, 53–60, 86
    Chinatown, Chinese, 27, 31, 44–45
    Committee of Fifty, 44
    Deaths, 15
    Firefighting, 35, 41–43
    Japanese, 45
    Soup kitchens, street kitchens,
        1906, 14–15, 17, 25, 27, 47, 86, 295,
        324–325n
    Streetcars, 45–46
San Francisco Fire Department,
    310–311
    Neighborhood Emergency Response
        Teams (NERT), 311
San Francisco Is Burning (Smith), 42
Sandinistas, 155–158
Scahill, Jeremy, 245
Scanlon, Joseph, 80
Scarry, Elaine, 218–219
Schell, Jonathan, 163, 334n
Schmitt, H. C., 24–25
Schmitz, Eugene, mayor of San
    Francisco, 36, 58
Schuster, Jordan, 200–202
Sedgewick, Charles B., 30
Settle, Mary Lee, 102
Sheehan, Cindy, 283–284, 290
Shock Doctrine, 107, 160
Siberia, 85–86

Sitrin, Marina, 162
Slonsky, Lorrie Beth, 261–262
Smith, Daniel, 206–207
Smith, Dennis, 42, 322n
Smith, Shepard, 260–261
Social Darwinism, 7, 82, 88–89, 241–242
Somoza, Anastacio, 154–157
Soviet Union, 19, 21, 110
Spanish Civil War, 171
Spreckels, Adolf, 45–46, 58
St. Bernard Parish, Louisiana, 231–232, 287
Stanford University, 51–52
  "The Struggle for Existence in Human Society" (Huxley), 89
Stucky, Stephen, 116
Student Nonviolent Coordinating Committee, 285
Subcomandante Marcos, 178–179
Sullivan, Dennis, San Francisco Fire Department chief, 41
Super Barrio, 174–178
Survivor (television show), 93

Tangshan earthquake, 151
Tassajara Zen Mountain Center, 116–117
Taylor, Astra, 193–194
Taylor, Shelley E., 92
Temporary Autonomous Zones, 169
Texas, 111
Thatcher, Margaret, 18
Theft, thieves, real and imagined, 24, 36, 37–39, 138–139, 140, 236–239, 253–254, 258–259
Thompson, A. C., 253–254
Tierney, Kathleen, 127, 130, 152, 235
Time magazine, 110
Titanic (ship, disaster), 79, 80
Titmuss, R. W., 99
Tolstoy, Leo, 85
Tomdispatch.com, 225
Tonopah, Nevada, 16

Towering Inferno, The (film), 124
Trauma, 8, 118, 219–220
Tsunami (2004), 121
Turner, Victor, 169
Turtle Grove, Nova Scotia, 75
Twain, Mark, 52
Twilight Zone, The, 110

United Flight 93, 217–219
United States Army
  In 1906 San Francisco, 15, 23–24, 34–43
  In 2005 New Orleans, 245
Utopia, 9, 17, 18–21, 51, 52, 108, 114, 135, 207

Vigilantes, 131, 249–259, 289–290
Voltaire, 154

Wachtendorf, Tricia, 207
Washington, D.C., 122
Waveland, Mississippi, 297–298
Weiner, Mark, 300–301
Welcome Home Kitchen, 299
Welcome to New Orleans (film), 252–253
Wells, Billy, 76
West Virginia, 112–113
Wilde, Oscar, 18
Wilkerson, Robert King, 290
Winfrey, Oprah, 236
Winstanley, Gerard, 92
Women of the Storm, 281
Woolf, Virginia, 101
Wordsworth, William, 169–171
Wright, Colonel Ann, 284

Yemen, 93–94,
Young, Cathy, 215

Zambrano, Maria Georgiana Lopez, 189
Zapatistas, 178–180
Zimmerman, Dave, 116